European Data Pr

Law and Practice

Executive Editor

Eduardo Ustaran, CIPP/E
Partner, Hogan Lovells

An IAPP Publication

© 2018 by the International Association of Privacy Professionals (IAPP)

All rights reserved. No part of this publication may be reproduced, stored in a retrieval system or transmitted in any form or by any means, mechanical, photocopying, recording or otherwise, without the prior, written permission of the publisher, International Association of Privacy Professionals, Pease International Tradeport, 75 Rochester Ave., Suite 4, Portsmouth, NH 03801, United States of America.

CIPP, CIPP/US, CIPP/C, CIPP/E, CIPP/G, CIPM and CIPT are registered trademarks of the International Association of Privacy Professionals, Inc. registered in the U.S. CIPP, CIPP/E, CIPM and CIPT are also registered in the EU as Community Trademarks (CTM).

Copy editor and Proofreader: Joni L. McNeal

Indexer: Jeanne R. Busemeyer, Hyde Park Publishing Services

ISBN: 978-0-9983223-5-3

Library of Congress Number: 2017950206

Contents

Chapter 3: Legislative Framework

Katie McMullan

SECTION II: EUROPEAN DATA PROTECTION LAW AND REGULATION

Chapter 4: Data Protection Concepts

Mac Macmillan

Chapter 5: Territorial and Material Scope of the General Data Protection Regulation

Ruth Boardman

Chapter 6: Data Processing Principles

Mariel Filippidis, CIPP/E, CIPM, FIP

Chapter 7: Lawful Processing Criteria

Victoria Hordern, CIPP/E, CIPT

Chapter 8: Information Provision Obligations

Hannah Jackson, CIPP/E

Chapter 9: Data Subjects' Rights

Jyn Schultze-Melling

Chapter 10: Security of Personal Data

Stewart Room, CIPP/E

Chapter 11: Accountability Requirements

Mary Pothos

Chapter 12: International Data Transfers

Eduardo Ustaran, CIPP/E

Chapter 13: Supervision and Enforcement

Stewart Room, CIPP/E

SECTION III: COMPLIANCE WITH EUROPEAN DATA PROTECTION LAW AND REGULATION

Chapter 14: Employment Relationships

Victoria Hordern, CIPP/E, CIPT

Chapter 15: Surveillance Activities

Robert Streeter, CIPP/E, CIPP/US

Chapter 16: Direct Marketing

Wouter Seinen, CIPP/E

Chapter 17: Internet Technology and Communications

Nick Westbrook

Chapter 18: Outsourcing

Eduardo Ustaran, CIPP/E

About the IAPP

The International Association of Privacy Professionals (IAPP) is the largest and most comprehensive global information privacy community and resource, helping practitioners develop and advance their careers and organisations manage and protect their data.

The IAPP is a not-for-profit association founded in 2000 with a mission to define, support and improve the privacy profession globally. We are committed to providing a forum for privacy professionals to share best practices, track trends, advance privacy management issues, standardise the designations for privacy professionals and provide education and guidance on opportunities in the field of information privacy.

The IAPP is responsible for developing and launching the only globally recognised credentialing programs in information privacy: the Certified Information Privacy Professional (CIPP), the Certified Information Privacy Manager (CIPM) and the Certified Information Privacy Technologist (CIPT). The CIPP, CIPM and CIPT are the leading privacy certifications for thousands of professionals around the world who serve the data protection, information auditing, information security, legal compliance and/or risk management needs of their organisations.

In addition, the IAPP offers a full suite of educational and professional development services and holds annual conferences that are recognised internationally as the leading forums for the discussion and debate of issues related to privacy policy and practice.

Acknowledgments

The IAPP is pleased to present *European Data Protection: Law and Practice* in support of our Certified Information Privacy Professional/Europe (CIPP/E) program.

A comprehensive and practical resource such as the *European Data Protection* textbook is not developed without the contributions of and support from a great number of individuals.

Thank you to Paul Jordan, IAPP Managing Director, Europe, for his leadership and insights. To the members of the Training Advisory Board, we are grateful for your ongoing guidance and expertise. This group represents esteemed privacy and data protection professionals from around the globe. Past and present members include:

Sol Bermann, CIPP/US
Andy Bloom, CIPP/E, CIPP/US, CIPM, CIPT, FIP
Orrie Dinstein, CIPP/US
Renee Fehr, CIPP/US, CIPM
Mark Francis, CIPP/US, CIPT, FIP
D. Reed Freeman, CIPP/US
Nick Graham, CIPP/E
Sachin Kothari, CIPP/US
Susan Lyon-Hintze, CIPP/US
Siobhan MacDermott
Judy Macior, CIPP/C, CIPP/G, CIPP/US, CIPT, FIP
Hyder Masum, CIPP/C, CIPP/E, CIPP/US, CIPM
Sabine O'Keeffe, CIPP/C
Aurélie Pols
K. Royal, CIPP/E, CIPP/US, CIPM, FIP
Todd Ruback, CIPP/E, CIPP/US, CIPT
Stephanie Salih, CIPP/G
James Shreve, CIPP/US, CIPT, FIP

Robert Streeter, CIPP/E, CIPP/US
Jessica Tay, CIPP/E, CIPM
Charlotte Tschider, CIPP/E, CIPP/US
Carlos Vela-Treviño, CIPM
Mr. Robert Yonaitis, CIPM, CIPT
Ernst-Oliver Wilhelm, CIPP/E, CIPM, CIPT, FIP

My first project at the IAPP in 2011 was *European Privacy*, the official textbook for the soon-to-be launched CIPP/E program. I had the great privilege of working with Eduardo Ustaran, who served as the executive editor. He led a team of outstanding data protection professionals who contributed to the book, including Michelle Levin, Brian Davidson, CIPP/E, Nuria Pastor, CIPP/E, Antonis Patrikios, CIPP/E, CIPM, FIP, Phil Lee, CIPP/E, CIPM, FIP, Sian Rudgard, CIPP/E, Lilly Taranto, CIPP/E, Victoria Hordern, CIPP/E, CIPT, Hannah Jackson, CIPP/E, and Stewart Room, CIPP/E. Their work provided the foundation upon which this updated version of the CIPP/E textbook, *European Data Protection*, was built.

Eduardo generously agreed to serve as executive editor of the *European Data Protection* text, as well. He assembled a team of privacy and data protection professionals from around the world, and we are so grateful for the knowledge they shared and their commitment to this project.

Many thanks to Rita Heimes, CIPP/US, CIPM, Callie Shroeder, CIPP/C, CIPP/E, CIPP/US, CIPM, Cobun Keegan, CIPP/US, CIPM, Grace Buckler, CIPP/E, CIPP/G, CIPP/US, Robert Streeter, CIPP/E, CIPP/US, Charlotte Tschider, CIPP/E, CIPP/US, Edward du Boulay, CIPP/E, and Sophie du Boulay who reviewed the draft manuscript and provided thoughtful insight and feedback that guided the revision of the text. Thank you to Jeffrey Lambe, CIPP/US, and Rachel Hawes for their meticulous work validating references for this book. I'm grateful to Joni L. McNeal for her keen eye in both copyediting and proofreading the text, and Jeanne Busemeyer who created the book index.

Thank you to the many professionals who contributed to the publication of this book. We appreciate your hard work, expertise and professionalism. We are delighted to present this textbook as both a practical reference on the General Data Protection Regulation and a helpful tool in preparing for your CIPP/E certification.

Marla Berry, CIPT
Training Director,
International Association of Privacy Professionals

Introduction

There is no hyperbole in saying that all eyes in the global privacy and data protection community currently look to Europe. With the passage of the General Data Protection Regulation (GDPR, or 'Regulation'), the European Union has once again put a stake in the ground to mark the most robust privacy and data protection regime in the world. Whilst it comes with the promise of unifying the approaches of the EU's 28 member states, it is difficult to estimate the impact of the GDPR until it actually comes into force and the world sees how it will be enforced.

As the largest privacy organisation in the world, the International Association of Privacy Professionals ('IAPP'), with more than 30,000 members as of this writing, accepts willingly the responsibility of providing robust tools and information to help you navigate what may seem at times like stormy seas. With this new textbook, I'm confident we have provided an unimpeachable resource, something that will allow professionals at every level to adequately prepare and adjust for what the future holds.

With Eduardo Ustaran, CIPP/E, at the helm, this team of data protection experts has compiled a tome that puts the GDPR in context, that brings data protection law and regulation down to the practical level, and goes beyond a simple explanation of the law. While each organisation will find its own way to operationalise compliance, this textbook is a foundation upon which everyone can build.

We hope, too, that this textbook is just the beginning of your journey through what the IAPP has to offer. From the publications on IAPP.org to the education available at our many conferences to the valuable networking and peer-to-peer intelligence-gathering that can be done at our hundreds of KnowledgeNet meetings around the globe, there is so much more available to you as you build your data protection career. We hope you take advantage.

Ultimately, each reader of this textbook will take away something different. Each organisation has its own data protection challenges that are unique to its business plan or mission. I'm happy to say that we've created something here that is both accessible and truly useful.

Good luck to you as you embark upon your data protection work. Let the textbook that follows be a steady and trustworthy guide.

Paul Jordan
Managing Director, Europe,
International Association of Privacy Professionals

SECTION I
Introduction to European Data Protection

CHAPTER 1

Origins and Historical Context
of Data Protection Law

Sian Rudgard, CIPP/E

1.1   Rationale for data protection

During the early 1970s, there was an increase in the use of computers to process information about individuals. Trans-border trade, facilitated by the European Economic Community (EEC), also encouraged a rise in information sharing.

Rapid progress in the field of electronic data processing and the first appearance of mainframe computers allowed public administrations and large enterprises to set up extensive data banks to improve the collecting, processing and sharing of personal information. Added to this was the fact that computers, in combination with the development of telecommunications, were opening up new opportunities for data processing on an international scale.

Although these developments offered considerable advantages in terms of efficiency and productivity, they also gave rise to concerns that these otherwise positive advancements would have an adverse impact on the privacy of individuals and that this would be exacerbated when personal information was transferred across international boundaries.

Within the individual state legal systems in Europe, there were already some rules aimed at protecting the personal information of individuals, such as laws on privacy, tort, secrecy and confidentiality. However, it was recognised that the automated storage of personal information and the rise in cross-border trade called for new standards that allowed individuals to exercise control over their personal information, whilst allowing the free international flow of information necessary to support international trade.

The challenge was to frame these standards in a way that maintains a balance between concerns at a national level for personal freedom and privacy and the ability to support free trade at the EEC level.

1.2   Human rights law

In the European Union, the right to a private life and associated freedoms are considered fundamental human rights. This concept underlies EU data protection laws and is important for practitioners to fully embrace and understand. Functionally, international human rights law is built on agreements between countries to promote and protect human rights at international, regional and domestic levels. This section explores the foundations of data protection in human rights law.

1.2.1 Universal Declaration of Human Rights

A clear starting point for framing standards for the protection of individuals was the Universal Declaration of Human Rights ('Human Rights Declaration'), adopted on 10 December 1948 by the General Assembly of the United Nations.[1] The Human Rights Declaration was born following the atrocities of World War II and acknowledged what have now become universal values and traditions: 'the inherent dignity and the equal and inalienable rights of all members of the human race in the foundation of freedom, justice, and peace in the world'.

The Human Rights Declaration contains specific provisions in connection with the right to a private and family life, and to freedom of expression. The principles enshrined in the Human Rights Declaration have provided the basis for subsequent European data protection laws and standards.

The right to a private life and associated freedoms is contained in Article 12 of the Human Rights Declaration, which states:

> No one shall be subjected to arbitrary interference with his privacy, family, home or correspondence, nor to attacks upon his honour and reputation. Everyone has the right to the protection of the law against such interference or attacks.

Another fundamental aspect in the Human Rights Declaration is the right to freedom of expression as set out in Article 19:

> Everyone has the right to freedom of opinion and expression; this right includes freedom to hold opinions without interference and to seek, receive and impart information and ideas through any media and regardless of frontiers.

The provisions in Article 19 may seem at first to be at odds with the provisions of Article 12, particularly where the exercise of Article 19 might result in the invasion of privacy contrary to Article 12. This apparent conflict is, however, reconciled in

Article 29(2), which states that individual rights are not absolute and that there will be instances where a balance must be struck:

> *In the exercise of his rights and freedoms, everyone shall be subject only to such limitations as are determined by law solely for the purpose of securing due recognition and respect for the rights and freedoms of others and of meeting the just requirements of morality, public order and the general welfare in a democratic society.*

1.2.2 European Convention on Human Rights

In Rome, in 1950, the Council of Europe invited individual states to sign the European Convention on Human Rights (ECHR), an international treaty to protect human rights and fundamental freedoms. Based on the Human Rights Declaration, it entered into force 3 September 1953. The ECHR applies only to member states. All Council of Europe member states are a party to the ECHR, and new members are expected to ratify the ECHR at the earliest opportunity. Parties to the ECHR undertake to provide these rights and freedoms to everyone within their jurisdiction.

The ECHR is a powerful instrument because of the scope of the fundamental rights and freedoms it protects. These include the right to life; prohibition of torture; prohibition of slavery and forced labour; right to liberty and security; right to a fair trial; no punishment without law; respect for private and family life; freedom of thought, conscience and religion; freedom of expression; freedom of assembly and association; right to marry; right to an effective remedy and prohibition of discrimination.[2]

The ECHR is also significant because there is a system of enforcement established in Strasbourg in the form of the European Court of Human Rights, which examines alleged breaches of the ECHR and ensures that states comply with their obligations under the ECHR. Rulings of the European Court of Human Rights are binding on the states concerned and can lead to an amendment of legislation or a change in practice by national governments. At the request of the Committee of Ministers of the Council of Europe, the European Court of Human Rights may also give advisory opinions that concern the interpretation of the ECHR and the protocols.

On 1 November 1998, the court system was restructured into a single full-time Court of Human Rights.[3]

Article 8 of the ECHR echoes Article 12 of the Human Rights Declaration and provides that:

> (1) *Everyone has the right to respect for his private and family life, his home and his correspondence.*

(2)   *There shall be no interference by a public authority with the exercise of this right except such as is in accordance with the law and is necessary in a democratic society in the interests of national security, public safety or the economic well-being of the country, for the prevention of disorder or crime, for the protection of health or morals, or for the protection of the rights and freedoms of others.*[4]

This article therefore protects the rights of individuals for their personal information to remain private, but again, this is not an absolute right and necessity, and proportionality may justify breaching an individual's privacy rights in the public interest.

Whilst Article 8 deals with the right to privacy, Article 10 protects the right of freedom of expression and the right to share information and ideas across national boundaries.

Article 10(1) of the ECHR reads:

Everyone has the right to freedom of expression. This right shall include freedom to hold opinions and to receive and impart information and ideas without interference by public authority and regardless of frontiers.

This right is also qualified so as to protect the privacy of individuals, as set forth in Article 10(2):

The exercise of these freedoms, since it carries with it duties and responsibilities, may be subject to such formalities, conditions, restrictions or penalties as are prescribed by law and are necessary in a democratic society, in the interests of national security, territorial integrity or public safety, for the prevention of disorder or crime, for the protection of health or morals, for the protection of the reputation or the rights of others, for preventing the disclosure of information received in confidence, or for maintaining the authority and impartiality of the judiciary.

Both the Human Rights Declaration and the ECHR inherently recognise a need for balance between the rights of individuals and the justifiable interference with these rights, which is a recurring theme within data protection law.

1.3   Early laws and regulations

From the late 1960s to the 1980s, a number of countries, mostly in Europe, took the lead in implementing legislation aimed at controlling the use of personal information by government agencies and large companies. These included Austria, Denmark, France, Federal Republic of Germany, Luxembourg, Norway and Sweden, with legislation also being planned in several countries during this period. In three European countries—Spain, Portugal and Austria—data protection was also incorporated as a fundamental right in their Constitutions.[5]

In light of this trend, the Council of Europe decided to establish a framework of specific principles and standards to prevent unfair collecting and processing of personal information. This was the result of concern that, in the context of emerging technology, national legislation did not adequately protect the 'right to respect for his private and family life, his home and his correspondence' under Article 8 of the ECHR. This concern led in 1968 to the publication of Recommendation 509 on human rights and modern scientific and technological developments.

In 1973 and 1974, the Council of Europe built on this initial work with Resolutions 73/22 and 74/29, which established principles for the protection of personal data in automated databanks in the private and public sectors, respectively, the objective being to set in motion the development of national legislation based on these resolutions. This was regarded as an urgent requirement because of the already-existing divergence between the laws of the member states in this area. It was becoming increasingly apparent that comprehensive protection of personal information would require further reinforcement of such national rules by means of binding international standards.

Other significant initiatives in the early 1980s came from the Organisation for Economic Co-operation and Development (OECD) and the Council of Europe in the form of the OECD Guidelines on the Protection of Privacy and Transborder Flows of Personal Data[6] and the Council of Europe Convention for the Protection of Individuals with regard to Automatic Processing of Personal Data.[7]

1.3.1 OECD Guidelines

Broadly speaking, the role of the OECD is to promote policies designed to achieve the highest sustainable economic growth and employment and a rising standard of living in both OECD member countries and nonmember countries, whilst maintaining financial stability and thus contributing to the development of the world economy. OECD membership extends beyond Europe and includes a number of major jurisdictions.

In 1980, OECD developed Guidelines on the Protection of Privacy and Transborder Flows of Personal Data ('Guidelines') laying out basic rules that govern trans-border data flows and the protection of personal information and privacy in order to facilitate the harmonisation of data protection law between countries. (See the box outlining the principles in the Guidelines.)

The Guidelines were prepared in close cooperation with the Council of Europe and the European Community and were published on 23 September 1980. They are not legally binding but are intended to be flexible and to serve either as a basis for legislation in countries that have no data protection legislation or as a set of principles that may be built into existing legislation.

Because OECD membership extends beyond Europe, the Guidelines have a far-reaching effect. The emphasis is on cooperation with other countries so that gaps will not arise in the implementation of the Guidelines amongst the OECD member states. The OECD reaffirmed its commitment to the Guidelines in declarations made in 1985 and 1998.

In developing the Guidelines, the OECD made every effort to ensure consistency with the principles being developed on behalf of the Council of Europe, which means there are distinct similarities between the Guidelines and the Council of Europe Convention for the Protection of Individuals with regard to Automatic Processing of Personal Data.

The aim of the Guidelines is to strike a balance between protecting the privacy and the rights and freedoms of individuals without creating any barriers to trade and allowing the uninterrupted flow of personal data across national borders.

The Guidelines do not draw any distinction between the public and private sectors. Importantly, they are neutral with regard to the particular technology used in that they do not make any distinction between personal information gathered electronically or otherwise.

OECD Guidelines on the Protection of Privacy and Transborder Flows of Personal Data

The Guidelines introduce a set of principles that should be followed by data controllers processing personal information:

- *Collection Limitation Principle:* Personal information must be collected fairly and lawfully and, where appropriate, with the knowledge or consent of the individual concerned.

- *Data Quality Principle:* Personal information must be relevant, complete, accurate and up to date.

- *Purpose Specification Principle:* The purpose for which the personal information is to be used must be specified not later than at the time of collection, and any use must be compatible with that purpose.

- *Use Limitation Principle:* Any disclosure of personal information must be consistent with the purposes specified unless the individual has given consent or the data controller has lawful authority to do so.

- *Security Safeguards Principle:* Reasonable security safeguards must be taken against risks, such as loss or unauthorised access, destruction, use, modification or disclosure of personal information.

- *Openness Principle:* There should be a general policy of openness with respect to the uses of personal information, as well as the identity and location of the data controller.

- *Individual Participation Principle:* This sets out what an individual is entitled to receive from a data controller pursuant to a request for his or her personal information. This has become one of the most important aspects of subsequent data protection legislation.

- *Accountability Principle:* A data controller should be accountable for complying with measures that ensure the principles stated above.

The principles included in the Guidelines in connection with trans-border data flows are within the spirit of the aims of the OECD to advance the free flow of information between member countries and to avoid creating unjustified obstacles to the development of economic relations amongst member countries. The Guidelines state that:

- Member countries should take into consideration the implications for other member countries of domestic processing and re-export of personal data.

- Member countries should take all reasonable and appropriate steps to ensure that trans-border flows of personal data, including transit through a member country, are uninterrupted and secure.

- Member countries may engage in trans-border flows of personal data between themselves except where a country does not yet substantially observe the Guidelines or where the re-export of personal data would circumvent its domestic privacy legislation.

- A member state may impose restrictions on the transfer of information to another country of categories of personal data for which its domestic privacy legislation includes specific regulations in view of the nature of those data and for which the other member country provides no equivalent protection.

- Member states should avoid developing laws, policies and practices in the name of the protection of privacy and individual liberties that would create obstacles to trans-border flows of personal data beyond what is required for that protection. This has become one of the most important aspects of subsequent data protection legislation.

The OECD recognised that some processing involves both automated and non-automated systems, and that concentrating exclusively on computers might lead to inconsistency, as well as opportunities for data controllers to circumvent national laws that implement the Guidelines by using non-automatic means to process personal information. The emphasis of their work was to safeguard personal information, the processing of which might 'pose a danger to privacy and individual liberties'.

1.3.2 Convention 108

The Convention for the Protection of Individuals with regard to Automatic Processing of Personal Data ('Convention 108') was adopted by the Council of Europe and opened for signature to the member states of the Council of Europe 28 January 1981. The fact that it was not referred to as the European Convention was to signify that it was open for signature to countries outside Europe.[8]

Convention 108 consolidates and reaffirms the content of the 1973 and 1974 resolutions and was the first legally binding international instrument in the area of data protection. It differs from the Guidelines in that it requires signatories to take the necessary steps in their domestic legislation to apply the principles it lays down with regard to processing personal information.

In Convention 108, the Council of Europe took the view that those holding and using personal information in computerised form have a social responsibility to safeguard such personal information, particularly as at that time, decisions that affect individuals were increasingly based on information stored in computerised data files.

The preamble to Convention 108 states that its aim is to achieve greater unity between its members and to extend the safeguards for everyone's rights and fundamental freedoms—in particular, the right to respect for privacy, taking into account the increasing transfer across frontiers of personal data undergoing automatic processing.[9]

Convention 108 is the first binding international instrument to set standards for the protection of individuals' personal data whilst also seeking to balance those safeguards against the need to maintain the free flow of personal data for the purposes of international trade.

Convention 108 consists of three main parts:

- substantive law provisions in the form of basic principles (Chapter II);

- special rules on trans-border data flows (Chapter III); and

- mechanisms for mutual assistance (Chapter IV) and consultation between the parties (Chapter V).[10]

Chapter II—substantive law provisions

The principles in Chapter II are based on those contained in the 1973 and 1974 Council of Europe resolutions and are similar in many ways to those contained in the Guidelines:

- Personal information undergoing automatic processing shall be:

    ◦ obtained and processed fairly and lawfully;

    ◦ stored for specified and legitimate purposes and not used in a way incompatible with those purposes;

    ◦ adequate, relevant and not excessive in relation to the purposes for which they are stored;

    ◦ accurate and, where necessary, kept up to date; and

    ◦ preserved in a form that permits identification of the individuals for no longer than is required for the purpose for which the information is stored.

- Appropriate security measures must be taken for the protection of personal information stored in automated data files against accidental or unauthorised destruction or accidental loss, as well as against unauthorised access, alteration or dissemination.

- Personal information that reveals racial origin, political opinions or religious or other beliefs, as well as personal data that concerns health or sexual life or criminal convictions (referred to as 'special categories of data'), may not be processed automatically unless domestic law provides appropriate safeguards.

- Individuals must have the right of communication, rectification and erasure of the personal information held.

When implementing Convention 108, signatories can include an exception to the provisions only when this is a 'necessary measure in a democratic society' (e.g., state security or criminal investigation) reflecting the proportionality requirements embodied in Articles 6, 8, 10 and 11 of the ECHR.

Chapter III—trans-border data flows

Article 12 of Convention 108 provides that where transfers of personal information are made between signatories to Convention 108, those countries shall not impose any prohibitions or require any special authorisations for the purpose of the protection of privacy before such transfers can take place. The reason is that such states, by virtue of the fact that they are signatories to Convention 108, have agreed to the data protection provisions referred to in Chapter II and, as a result, they offer a certain minimum level of protection to the personal information transferred.

Derogation from the provisions is permitted only where the exporting country has in place specific rules in its national law for certain categories of personal data or of automated personal data files and the importing country does not provide equivalent protection or where the transfer is to a country that is not a party to Convention 108.

These provisions were further developed in the Additional Protocol to the Convention for the Protection of Individuals with regard to Automatic Processing of Personal Data, regarding supervisory authorities and transborder data flows ('Additional Protocol'), which opened for signature in 2001. The Additional Protocol was designed to address the fact that Convention 108 did not provide any measures for transfers of personal information to countries that were not signatories to Convention 108. The solution to this was the introduction of the concept of an 'adequate', rather than an equivalent, level of protection for personal information transferred to states falling outside the jurisdiction of the exporting party, subject to exceptions where the transfer is made in the legitimate interests of the individual, is in the public interest or where the transfer is based on contractual clauses approved by the supervisory authority.[11]

Chapter IV—mutual assistance

Parties to Convention 108 must designate a supervisory authority to oversee compliance with data protection law and to liaise with supervisory authorities in other jurisdictions for purposes of consultation and mutual assistance regarding implementation. Supervisory authorities are also required to lend assistance to individuals in the exercise of their rights.

These requirements were reinforced further by provisions in the Additional Protocol.

Convention 108 remains the only binding international legal instrument with a worldwide scope of application in the field of data protection that is open to any country, including countries that are not members of the Council of Europe.

1.4   The need for a harmonised European approach

The objective of Convention 108 and the Guidelines was to introduce a harmonised approach to data protection on the basis of international agreement on principles with implementation left to the discretion of the member states. From the earliest days, however, it became apparent that implementation of these principles into national law was resulting in the development of a diverse set of data protection regimes. It was perceived that the lack of a cohesive approach within the member states in adopting these principles could have serious implications for the fundamental rights of individuals, as well as impede free trade enshrined in the Treaty of Rome.

1.4.1 Data Protection Directive

The European Commission had been called upon by the European Parliament as early as 1976 to prepare a proposal for a directive harmonising data protection laws. Growing concerns regarding the diversity of national approaches to data protection legislation within member states led to the Proposal for a Council Directive Concerning the Protection of Individuals in Relation to the Processing of Personal Data.[12]

Directives are a form of legislation binding upon member states, but they 'leave to the national authorities the choice of form and methods' for implementation.

This proposal described the concerns of the European Commission with regard to the fragmented approach emerging and contained a framework directive for data protection. In this proposal, the European Commission commented, 'The diversity of national approaches and the lack of a system of protection at community level are an obstacle to completion of the internal market. If the fundamental rights of data subjects, in particular their right to privacy, are not safeguarded at community level, the cross-border flow of data might be impeded'.[13]

The European Commission used the principles contained in Convention 108 as a benchmark in drawing up the framework directive because the principles constituted a common set of standards for those countries that had ratified Convention 108. The framework directive supplemented these general principles to provide a high level of equivalent protection, and, to achieve this, the proposals were wide in their scope, extending the protections to both automated and non-automated personal data and covering both public and private sectors.

The culmination of the work undertaken by the European Commission was Directive 95/46/EC on the protection of individuals with regard to the processing of personal data and on the free movement of such data ('Data Protection Directive', or 'Directive'). As the title suggests, the aim of the Directive was to further reconcile protecting individuals' fundamental privacy rights with the free flow of data from one member state to another, maintaining consistency with Articles 8 and 10 of the ECHR.

Unfortunately, there have been significant differences in the ways member states have implemented and applied the Directive, or derogations, making it difficult for businesses to take full advantage of the benefits of the internal market. The first report of the European Commission on the Directive, published in 2003, confirmed this problem.[14]

In some cases, the differences resulted from incorrect implementation of the Directive with the result that the law of the particular member state required rectification. If the member state failed to remedy the position, the European Commission had the power to issue infraction proceedings against it. In other cases, the differences resulted from a member state's implementation of the Directive that, although within the margin of manoeuvre allowed, still gave rise to inconsistencies.

One example of inconsistencies arising due to divergence in the national law concerned the requirement for businesses to notify the Data Protection Authorities (DPAs) of their processing details. The national laws of the member states differed considerably as to their requirements in this regard, which resulted in substantial bureaucracy and cost for businesses, particularly for those that also transfer personal information to countries outside the EU.

1.4.2 Charter of Fundamental Rights

The presidents of the European Parliament, the Council and the Commission signed and proclaimed the Charter of Fundamental Rights on behalf of their institutions 7 December 2000 in Nice. Stemming from the EU Treaty, Court of Justice of the European Union (CJEU) case law, the European Union member state's constitutional traditions, and the European Convention on Human Rights, it further consolidates fundamental rights applicable within the EU.

The Charter includes the general principles set out in the ECHR but specifically refers to the protection of personal data. In December 2009, when the Treaty of Lisbon came into force, the Charter was given binding legal effect.

Articles 7 and 10 of the Charter reflect the provisions of the ECHR in Articles 8 and 10, respectively, and Article 8 deals specifically with data protection as follows:

(1)   *Everyone has the right to the protection of personal data concerning him or her;*

(2)   *Such data must be processed fairly for specified purposes and on the basis of the consent of the person concerned or some other legitimate basis laid down by law. Everyone has the right of access to data which has been collected concerning him or her, and the right to have it rectified.*

(3)   *Compliance with these rules shall be subject to control by an independent authority.*[15]

Article 8 therefore enshrines certain core values for the protection of personal data:

- The processing must be fair.

- The processing must be carried out for specified purposes.

- There must be legitimate basis for the processing.

- Individuals must have the right to access and rectify personal data.

- There must be a supervisory authority to oversee compliance.

Any limitation to these rights must be in accordance with Article 52 of the Charter, which mirrors the limitations based on necessity and proportionality contained in the ECHR.

1.5   The Treaty of Lisbon

On 13 December 2007, the Treaty of Lisbon ('Lisbon Treaty') was signed by the EU member states; it became effective 1 December 2009.[16] Its main aim is to strengthen and improve the core structures of the European Union to enable it to function more efficiently.

The Lisbon Treaty amends the EU's two core treaties: the Treaty on European Union and the Treaty Establishing the European Community (renamed the 'Treaty on the Functioning of the European Union', or 'TFEU'). The TFEU echoes Article 8 of the

Charter and provides at Article 16(1) that everyone has the right to the protection of personal data concerning him or her. Article 16(2) TFEU provides that:

> *The European Parliament and the Council, acting in accordance with the ordinary legislative procedure, shall lay down the rules relating to the protection of individuals with regard to the processing of personal data by Union institutions, bodies, offices and agencies, and by the Member States where carrying out activities which fall within the scope of Union law, and the rules relating to the free movement of such data. Compliance with these rules shall be subject to the control of independent authorities.*

This provision ensures that all institutions of the European Union must protect individuals when processing personal data. There is a European data protection supervisor whose role is to regulate compliance with data protection law within the institutions of the European Union, but the reference to 'authorities' implies that the national DPAs may also have jurisdiction in such matters.

Promoting core values, including human dignity, freedom, democracy, equality, the rule of law and the respect for human rights, is one of the main objectives of the Lisbon Treaty. These values are common to all member states, and any European country wishing to become a member of the European Union must respect them. This is a significant development because the treaty establishing the European Union did not mention fundamental rights at all.

The Lisbon Treaty describes justice, freedom and security as being high priorities,[17] and a significant change in this area is the introduction of one common legal framework for all EU activities, comprising one system through which the EU can govern.

1.6 The General Data Protection Regulation

In addition to the lack of harmonisation in the approach to data protection throughout the member states, it became apparent that the Directive, although technology neutral, was not keeping pace with the rapid technological developments and globalisation that have been changing the way in which personal data is collected, accessed and used.

In response to these concerns, the Commission launched a review of the then-current legal framework on data protection in 2009 and, in 2010, set out a strategy to strengthen data protection rules. This resulted in a proposal from the Commission in January 2012 for a comprehensive reform of the Directive in the form of a General Data Protection Regulation (GDPR, or 'Regulation') imposing a single set of rules across the EU.[18] Agreeing on the text of the Regulation was a lengthy process culminating in a negotiation process (known as a 'trilogue') between the European Commission, the

European Parliament and the Council of the EU. The parties compromised, and the Regulation was published in the Official Journal of the European Union and entered into force in May 2016, becoming fully enforceable by DPAs 25 May 2018.[19]

Regulations are binding in their entirety and apply directly to all member states upon entry into force without the need to be transposed into national law. The purpose of having a regulation rather than a directive is to maximise consistency of approach amongst the EU member states. However, the GDPR does allow for member states to enact more specific rules in some situations.[20] This means that there will still be some divergence of approach between member states in the way in which the GDPR is implemented in practice. Examples of instances where member states may make further legislative provisions include:

- where there are already sector specific laws in place, for example, in relation to the processing of employee data;[21]

- archiving purposes in the public interest, scientific or historical research purposes, statistical purposes;[22]

- processing of 'special categories of personal data';[23] and

- processing in compliance with a 'legal obligation'.[24]

These aspects of the Regulation will be explored in more detail in later chapters.

The Regulation acknowledges that, although the objectives and principles of the Directive remain sound, the Directive has resulted in fragmented implementation of data protection across the European Union, legal uncertainty, and a widespread public perception that there are significant risks to the protection of personal data 'in particular with regard to online activity'.[25] The rapid developments in technology and globalisation have resulted in the use of personal data by private companies and public authorities 'on an unprecedented scale'. The Regulation is designed to bring about 'a strong and more coherent data protection framework, backed by strong and coherent enforcement' in order to create the trust that will 'allow the digital economy to develop across the internal market'.[26]

Key changes that have been incorporated into the Regulation include:

- stronger rights for individuals, particularly in the online environment;

- a requirement that data privacy be taken into account when new technologies are being developed ('data protection by design and by default');

- the introduction of the concept of 'accountability' whereby organisations must be able to demonstrate compliance with the GDPR;

- increased powers for supervisory authorities;

- the concept of the 'one-stop shop'; and

- broader applicability of the Regulation to anyone targeting EU consumers.

These issues will be analysed in later chapters in more detail.

1.7   Related Legislation

1.7.1 The Law Enforcement Data Protection Directive

At the same time as proposing the framework for the Regulation, the European Commission also introduced a directive for the 'protection of natural persons with regard to the processing of personal data by competent authorities for the purposes of the prevention, investigation, detection or prosecution of criminal offences or the execution of criminal penalties, and on the free movement of such data' ('Law Enforcement Data Protection Directive', or LEDP Directive),[27] which entered into force 5 May 2016. Member states have until 6 May 2018 to transpose the LEDP Directive into their national law.

The aim of the LEDP Directive is to harmonise the rules in place across the member states to protect citizens' fundamental rights whenever personal data are used by criminal law enforcement authorities, but it does not preclude member states from providing higher safeguards in their national law to protect of the rights of data subjects.

1.7.2 The ePrivacy Directive

The ePrivacy Directive sets out rules relating to processing personal data across 'public communications networks'.[28]

The GDPR makes it clear that it is not intended to impose additional obligations on top of the obligations contained in the ePrivacy Directive and that the ePrivacy Directive therefore needs to be reviewed and amended as appropriate to ensure consistency across the two regimes.[29] At the time of writing, there is a proposed Regulation on Privacy and Electronic Communications undergoing review.

This chapter has looked at the historical context and origins of European data protection law, including an overview of the key parts of the regulatory framework; Chapter 3 ('Legislative Framework') builds on this background by providing a more-detailed analysis of the key laws and regulations in place.

Evolution of Data Protection Law in Europe

1948 General Assembly of the United Nations created **The Universal Declaration of Human Rights,** recognising universal values and traditions—'the inherent dignity and the equal and inalienable rights of all members of the human race' to freedom, justice and peace in the world.

1950 In Rome, the Council of Europe invited individual states to sign on to **the European Convention on Human Rights (ECHR)** to protect human rights and fundamental freedoms. Entered into force in 1953, it only applies to member states, which are expected to provide these rights and freedoms to everyone within their jurisdiction. It empowers the European Court of Human Rights in Strasbourg to enforce the ECHR throughout the member states.

1951 The Treaty Establishing the European Coal and Steel Community (**'Treaty of Paris'**) set up regional institutions for governing coal and steel. Parties to the Treaty were France, West Germany, Italy, Belgium, Luxembourg and the Netherlands.

1957 Treaty Establishing the European Economic Community ('Treaty of Rome').

1965 Treaty Establishing a Single Council and a Single Commission of the European Communities ('Merger Treaty') established the Common Market and created the European Commission, the Council of Ministers, the Court of Justice of the European Union (CJEU) and the European Parliament.

1970 The German State of Hesse introduces the first modern privacy law.

1973 Sweden creates the **Data Act**, the first national privacy law.

1973–74 Resolutions 73/22 and 74/29 are passed, establishing principles for the protection of personal data in automated data banks in the private and public sectors, respectively, to set in motion the development of national legislation based on these resolutions.

1979 General **data protection laws** had been enacted in seven member states (Austria, Denmark, France, Federal Republic of Germany, Luxembourg, Norway and Sweden) with legislation planned in several others. In three European countries—Spain, Portugal and Austria—data protection was also incorporated as a fundamental right in the Constitution.

1980 OECD Guidelines on the Protection of Privacy and Transborder Flows of Personal Data.

1981 Council of Europe Convention for the Protection of Individuals with regard to Automatic Processing of Personal Data ('Convention 108') consolidates and reaffirms the 1973 and 1974 resolutions and is the first legally binding international instrument in the area of data protection. It differs from the OECD Guidelines in that it requires signatories to Convention 108 to take the necessary steps in their domestic legislation to apply the principles it lays down.

1986 Single European Act amended the prior treaties and created an 'internal market' (effective 1992) and led to a single currency and an end to border regulation.

1992 Treaty on European Union ('Maastricht Treaty') established the European Union (EU).

1995 Directive 95/46/EC on the protection of individuals with regard to the processing of personal data and on the free movement of such data ('Data Protection Directive', or 'Directive') further reconciled the protection of the fundamental rights of individuals with the free flow of data from one member state to another.

2000 Directive 2000/31/EC on certain legal aspects of information society services, in particular electronic commerce, in the Internal Market (Directive on electronic commerce) or the E-Commerce Directive.

2000 Charter of Fundamental Rights of the European Union further consolidated fundamental rights applicable within the EU and included the general principles set out in the ECHR but specifically refers to the protection of personal data.

2001 Additional Protocol to the Convention for the Protection of Individuals with regard to Automatic Processing of Personal Data regarding supervisory authorities and transborder data flows was designed to address the fact that Convention 108 did not provide for transfers of personal information to countries that are not signatories to Convention 108. It introduced the concept of an 'adequate' (rather than an equivalent) level of protection for personal information transferred to non-EU states.

2002 Directive 2002/58/EC concerning the processing of personal data and the protection of privacy in the electronic communications sector ('Directive on privacy and electronic communications', or 'ePrivacy Directive') deals with the regulation of a number of important issues, such as confidentiality of information, treatment of traffic data, spam and cookies.

2006 Directive 2006/24/EC on the retention of data generated or processed in connection with the provision of publicly available electronic communications services or of public communications networks and amending Directive 2002/58/EC.

2007 Treaty of Lisbon was designed to strengthen and improve the core structures of the European Union to enable it to function more efficiently. It made the 2000 Charter binding law. The Treaty established the European Data Protection Supervisor.

Council Framework Decision 2008/977/JHA of 27 November 2008 on the protection of personal data processed in the framework of police and judicial cooperation in criminal matters.

2009 Directive 2009/136/EC amending Directive 2002/22/EC on universal service and users' rights relating to electronic communications networks and services, Directive 2002/58/EC concerning the processing of personal data and the protection of privacy in the electronic communications sector, and **Regulation (EC) No 2006/2004 on cooperation between national authorities responsible for the enforcement of consumer protection laws.**

Regulation (EU) 2016/679 of the European Parliament and of the Council of 27 April 2016 on the protection of natural persons with regard to the processing of personal data and on the free movement of such data, and repealing Directive 95/46/EC (GDPR). (Text with EEA relevance.)

Directive (EU) 2016/680 of the European Parliament and of the Council of 27 April 2016 on the protection of natural persons with regard to the processing of personal data by competent authorities for the purposes of the prevention, investigation, detection or prosecution of criminal offences or the execution of criminal penalties, on the free movement of such data, and repealing Council Framework Decision 2008/977/JHA.

Directive (EU) 2016/681 of the European Parliament and of the Council of 27 April 2016 on the use of passenger name record (PNR) data for the prevention, detection, investigation and prosecution of terrorist offences and serious crime.

Endnotes

1 'Universal Declaration of Human Rights', United Nations, accessed June 2017, www.un.org/en/documents/universal-declaration-human-rights/index.shtml.

2 More rights are granted by additional protocols to the Convention; 'Details of Treaty No.005: Convention for the Protection of Human Rights and Fundamental Freedoms', Council of Europe, www.coe.int/en/web/conventions/full-list/-/conventions/treaty/005.

3 'Details of Treaty No. 155: Protocol No. 11 to the Convention for the Protection of Human Rights and Fundamental Freedoms, restructuring the control machinery established thereby', Council of Europe, www.coe.int/en/web/conventions/full-list/-/conventions/treaty/155.

4 'European Convention on Human Rights'. Council of Europe, www.echr.coe.int/Documents/Convention_ENG.pdf.

5 Article 35 of the 1976 Constitution of Portugal; Article 18 of the 1978 Constitution of Spain; Article 1 of the 1978 Austrian Data Protection Act: Fundamental Right of Data Protection.

6 'OECD Guidelines on the Protection of Privacy and Transboder Flows of Personal Data', OECD, accessed June 2017, www.oecd.org/sti/ieconomy/oecdguidelinesontheprotectionofprivacyandtransborderflowsofpersonaldata.htm.

7 'Details of Treaty No. 108: Convention for the Protection of Individuals with regard to Automatic Processing of Personal Data', Council of Europe, www.coe.int/en/web/conventions/full-list/-/conventions/treaty/108.

8 Mauritius, Senegal and Uruguay (non-COE states) have acceded to the treaty, as well.

9 Ibid.

10 'Details of Treaty No. 108: Convention for the Protection of Individuals with regard to Automatic Processing of Personal Data', Council of Europe, www.coe.int/en/web/conventions/full-list/-/conventions/treaty/108.

11 'Details of Treaty No. 181: Additional Protocol to the Convention for the Protection of Individuals with regard to Automatic Processing of Personal Data, regarding supervisory authorities and transborder data flows', Council of Europe, http://conventions.coe.int/Treaty/EN/Treaties/Html/181.htm.

12 COM(90) 314 final—SYN 287, 13.9.1990.

13 First Report on the implementation of the Data Protection Directive (95/46/EC), http://eur-lex.europa.eu/legal-content/EN/ALL/?uri=CELEX%3A52003DC0265.

14 Ibid.

15 Charter of Fundamental Rights of the European Union, 2012/C 326/02, http://eur-lex.europa.eu/legal-content/EN/TXT/?uri=CELEX%3A12012P%2FTXT.

16 Treaty of Lisbon (2007/C 306/01), http://eur-lex.europa.eu/legal-content/EN/TXT/?uri=celex%3A12007L%2FTXT.

17 Data protection falls within the scope of the Director-General for Justice within the European Commission, http://ec.europa.eu/justice/data-protection/.

18 Regulation (EU) 2016/679 of the European Parliament and of the Council of 27 April 2016 on the protection of natural persons with regard to the processing of personal data and on the free movement of such data, and repealing Directive 95/46/EC; 'Commission proposes a comprehensive reform of data protection rules to increase users' control of their data and to cut costs for businesses', European Commission Press Release, 25 January 2012, http://europa.eu/rapid/press-release_IP-12-46_en.htm?locale=en.

19 'Reform of EU data protection rules', http://ec.europa.eu/justice/data-protection/reform/index_en.htm.

20 See in particular Chapter 9, General Data Protection Regulation.

21 General Data Protection Regulation, Article 88.

22 General Data Protection Regulation, Article 89.

23 General Data Protection Regulation, Article 9(4).

24 General Data Protection Regulation, Article 6.

25 General Data Protection Regulation, Recital 9.

26 General Data Protection Regulation, Recitals 6 and 7.

27 Directive (EU) 2016/680.

28 Directive 2002/58/EC concerning the processing of personal data and the protection of privacy in the electronic communications sector (as amended).

29 General Data Protection Regulation, Recital 173 and Article 95.

CHAPTER 2

European Union Institutions

Lilly Taranto, CIPP/E

2.1   Background

As member countries gain experience working within the European Union, ideas on how to enhance the efficiency and democratic legitimacy of the EU and how to improve the coherence of its actions have emerged. As discussed in the previous chapter, the Treaty of Lisbon amended many of the provisions of the Treaty on European Union ('EU Treaty') and the Treaty Establishing the European Community ('Treaty of Rome', or 'EC Treaty') in response to the enlargement of the EU and the consequential need to improve the efficiency and speed of the EU decision-making processes. One of the main aims of the Lisbon Treaty was to reform the structure of the EU institutions and legislative process in order to reduce the bureaucracy of the EU.

Article 13 of the EU Treaty states that:

1. *The Union shall have an institutional framework which shall aim to promote its values; advance its objectives; serve its interests, those of its citizens and those of the member states; and ensure the consistency, effectiveness and continuity of its policies and actions.*

   The Union's institutions shall be:

   - *the European Parliament,*

   - *the European Council,*

   - *the Council,*

   - *the European Commission ('the Commission'),*

   - *the Court of Justice of the European Union,*

   - *the European Central Bank, and*

   - *the Court of Auditors.*

2. *Each institution shall act within the limits of the powers conferred on it in the Treaties and in conformity with the procedures, conditions and objectives set out in them.*[1]

Under the Treaty of Lisbon, the European Council and the European Central Bank were granted institutional status, meaning that they are now able to make binding decisions as opposed to fulfilling a more advisory role.

2.1.1 The Treaty of Lisbon and the protection of privacy

The Lisbon Treaty changed other treaties by promoting the Charter of Fundamental Rights of the European Union ('the Charter') to the same legal status as treaties, therefore making it legally binding on the institutions. The Charter also establishes the applicability of fundamental rights in EU law. The Charter compiles all the civil, political, economic and social rights of European citizens and residents of the EU into one text. Importantly, in the context of this book, the Charter enshrines the following principles:

- *Everyone has the right to respect for his or her private and family life, home and communications.* (Article 7, Respect for private and family life)

- *Everyone has the right to the protection of personal data concerning him or her. Such data must be processed fairly for specified purposes and on the basis of the consent of the person concerned or some other legitimate basis laid down by law. Everyone has the right of access to data which has been collected concerning him or her, and the right to have it rectified. Compliance with these rules shall be subject to control by an independent authority.* (Article 8, Protection of personal data)

- *Every person has the right to have his or her affairs handled impartially, fairly and within a reasonable time by the institutions, bodies, offices and agencies of the Union. [This specifically includes] the right of every person to have access to his or her file, while respecting the legitimate interests of confidentiality and of professional and business secrecy.* (Article 41, Right to good administration)

2.1.2 Role in relation to data protection

The provisions of the Charter do not extend the competencies of the EU and are binding upon the member states only when the national law implements the EU's legislation.[2] Furthermore, Poland and the United Kingdom, who were concerned that the Charter would constrain their ability to legislate or force them to change their positions on issues governed by the Charter, signed a protocol regarding the application of the Charter in their national territories.[3] The protocol states that the Charter shall only apply to Poland or the United Kingdom to the extent that the rights or principles that it contains are recognised in the law or practices of Poland or of the United Kingdom. The Czech Republic has also been given special arrangements regarding its application of the Charter. Poland and the United Kingdom are still bound by the case law of the Court of Justice, although this may change, of course, following the UK's withdrawal from the Union ('Brexit'). Despite such restrictions, in relation to privacy and data protection, the introduction of the Charter is incredibly important given the overriding influence of EU law over national policy and legislation.

2.2   European Parliament

Article 14 of the Treaty of Lisbon defines the European Parliament as follows:

> *The European Parliament shall, jointly with the Council, exercise legislative and budgetary functions. It shall exercise functions of political control and consultation as laid down in the Treaties. It shall elect the President of the Commission.*[4]

2.2.1 Rationale and functions

The European Parliament is the only European institution whose members are directly elected by the citizens of the EU. Under Article 9A of the EU Treaty, the European Parliament has four responsibilities: legislative development, supervisory oversight of the other institutions, democratic representation and development of the budget.

The first responsibility is the European Parliament's role in the legislative process, although the extent of its influence depends on which procedure applies — the ordinary, consultation or consent procedure (see definitions in box). Although the Parliament cannot propose new legislation of its own accord, it may take the initiative and call upon the Commission to submit a proposal to the Council of the European Union. Furthermore, it may also 'invite' the Commission and the Council to consider amending existing policies or developing new ones. The fact that the Parliament is directly elected by citizens of the EU means that it is a persuasive force within the EU, whilst its involvement in the legislative process helps to guarantee the democratic legitimacy of European law.

The Parliament shares its legislative power with the Council of the European Union. Three procedures may apply to the legislative process:

- *The ordinary procedure*: Both the Parliament and the Council must assent to the legislation. Legislation cannot be adopted if it is opposed by either institution. This places the Parliament on an equal footing with the Council in the majority of matters within the EU.

- *The consultation procedure*: The Council must consult the Parliament; however, the Council is not bound by the Parliament's opinion, as under this procedure the Council alone has legislative power.

- *The consent procedure*: For particularly important decisions (e.g., EU enlargement) the Parliament's consent is required.

The Parliament also exercises democratic and political controls over the other EU institutions. This is particularly true with respect to the Commission, because the Parliament enjoys the power to censure the Commission, including the ability to force the entire College of Commissioners to resign. To ensure democratic oversight of the Commission's activities, the Commission must submit regular reports to Parliament for scrutiny.

Finally, the Parliament shares authority with the Council to determine the EU budget; it can therefore influence EU spending, although both institutions must adhere to the annual spending limits laid down in the multiannual financial perspective.

2.2.2 Working in practice

Elections for Members of the European Parliament (MEPs) are held every five years. Every adult EU citizen is entitled to vote and to stand as a candidate.[5] At the time of writing, the Parliament has 751 members, including the president, representing all 28 EU countries. Article 9(15) introducing 9A of the EU Treaty states:

Representation of citizens shall be degressively proportional, with a minimum threshold of six members per member state. No member state shall be allocated more than [96] seats.

The European Council shall adopt by unanimity, on the initiative of the European Parliament and with its consent, a decision establishing the composition of the European Parliament, respecting the principles referred to in the first subparagraph.

Following the Treaty of Lisbon, no member state is allowed more than 96 MEPs. MEPs sit in Europe-wide political groups rather than in national blocs. Between them, the groups represent all views on European integration, from the strongly pro-federalist to the openly 'Eurosceptic'. A group must have a minimum of 25 members, and at least one-quarter of the member states must be represented within the group. Before every vote, the political groups scrutinise the reports drawn up by the parliamentary committees and propose amendments to them. The position adopted by a particular group is arrived at by discussion with the group; however, no member can be forced to vote in a particular way.

The European Parliament's work is divided into two main stages:

- Preparation for the plenary session is carried out by the MEPs in the various parliamentary committees that specialise in particular areas of EU activity. Where the Commission has proposed a 'legislative text', an MEP will be appointed rapporteur, with the responsibility of preparing a report on the proposed text. The report is then debated and amended within the committee before being submitted to Parliament in the plenary session. The political groups also discuss the papers before the plenary session.

- The plenary session is when the Parliament examines, possibly amends and votes on the proposed legislation and the report prepared by the relevant committee. When the text has been revised and adopted in plenary, Parliament adopts its position. This process is repeated one or more times, depending on the type of procedure and whether or not agreement is reached with the Council. Under the Treaty of Lisbon, the Parliament's voting procedure changed from a default requirement for an absolute majority to a simple majority.

2.2.3 Role in relation to data protection

The European Parliament has the greatest impact on data protection and privacy issues through its role in the legislative process of the EU. In relation to data protection, the Treaty of Lisbon enshrines the universal right to the protection of personal data and states that legislation will be adopted under the ordinary legislative procedure.[6] As such, Parliament's influence in the realm of data protection is ensured.

The Parliament has frequently been a vocal advocate of the right to privacy, often taking a more protective stance than other institutions. This clearly emerged during the legislative process for the reform of the European data protection rules, which culminated in the adoption of the General Data Protection Regulation (GDPR, or 'Regulation') and Law Enforcement Data Protection Directive (LEDP Directive).

2.3   European Council

The Treaty of Lisbon gives the European Council institutional status, defining its role in the following terms:

> The European Council shall provide the Union with the necessary impetus for its development and shall define the general political directions and priorities thereof. It shall not exercise legislative functions.[7]

2.3.1 History, rationale and functions

The European Council began life as an informal body in 1974. It did not gain formal status until the Treaty of Maastricht in 1992, which established it as a forum where heads of state or governments could discuss issues affecting the community. Today, the European Council comprises the heads of each of the 28 member states, together with the president of the Commission, and it meets four times a year to define the EU's priorities and set political direction for the EU.

2.3.2 Working in practice

Decisions of the European Council are generally made by consensus; however, the treaties may provide for alternative mechanisms, such as unanimity or qualified majority. Under the Treaty of Lisbon, the European Council is presided over by a president who is elected by qualified majority for a term of two-and-a-half years, renewable once. The president's term can also be ended in the event of an impediment or serious misconduct by vote of a qualified majority of members.

2.4   Council of the European Union

2.4.1 Rationale and functions

The Council of the European Union ('Council of Ministers', or 'the Council')—not to be confused with the European Council—was established by the treaties of the 1950s, which laid the foundations of the EU. The Council is the main decision-making body of the EU, having a central role in both political and legislative decisions. It is the co-legislator with the European Parliament. Together, the Council of the European Union and the European Parliament develop legislation for the EU. Following the adoption of the Treaty of Lisbon, Article 9C of the EU Treaty states that:

> *The Council shall, jointly with the European Parliament, exercise legislative and budgetary functions. It shall carry out policy-making and coordinating functions as laid down in the Treaties.*

The Council's meetings are attended by one minister from each of the 28 member states. Ministers have the power to commit their governments to Council decisions. Thus, the Council is an important mouthpiece for the national interests of the member states. The ministers are accountable to the national parliaments and therefore, in theory at least, are answerable to the citizens of the member states. However, although the Council's website claims that this structure 'ensures the democratic legitimacy of the Council's decisions', the Council has, in the past, been criticised for being undemocratic and lacking transparency.[8] The Treaty of Lisbon goes some way to addressing this criticism in requiring that the 'Union institutions, bodies, offices and agencies shall conduct their work as openly as possible' and, more specifically, that the Council's meetings shall be held in public 'when it deliberates and votes on a draft legislative act'.[9] However, we can conclude from the limitation on this requirement that deliberations concerning non-legislative activities will still be held in secrecy.

The composition of the Council varies, depending on the agenda of the meetings; however, it is a unitary institution and therefore its powers under the treaties remain the same, notwithstanding its fluctuating membership. At the time of writing, there are 10 different Council formations: General Affairs; Foreign Affairs; Economic and Financial Affairs; Justice and Home Affairs; Employment, Social Policy, Health and Consumer Affairs; Competitiveness; Transport, Telecommunications and Energy; Agriculture and Fisheries; Environment; and Education, Youth, Culture and Sport.

2.4.2 Working in practice

As stated earlier, the Council shares its legislative power with the European Parliament (see Section 2.2.1). Legislation and other matters that must be determined by the Council are generally proposed by the Commission before they are examined by the Council and the Parliament in accordance with one of the three procedures (described in the box in Section 2.2). The Council has the power to amend the proposal before it is adopted. The Council is also responsible for concluding international agreements that have been negotiated by the Commission. The acts of the Council can take the form of regulations, directives, decisions, common actions or common positions, recommendations, or opinions; it can also adopt conclusions, declarations or resolutions.

A president presides over the Council. As established in the Lisbon Treaty, the presidency is held by the member states on the basis of equal rotations to be established by the European Council acting by qualified majority. The treaties set the number of votes each member state can cast. The treaties also define cases in which a simple majority, qualified majority or unanimity are required. Calculating a qualified majority depends on the source of the action. When acting on a proposal from the Commission or the High Representative of the Union for Foreign Affairs and Security Policy, a qualified majority requires at least 55 percent of member states (which currently means 16 out of 28), representing at least 65 percent of the total EU population. When not acting on the basis of a proposal from the Commission or from the High Representative, the qualified majority requires 72 percent of the member states (which currently means 21 out of 28) and at least 65 percent of the EU population.

2.5   European Commission

2.5.1 Rationale and functions

As with the Parliament and the Council, the founding treaties laid the foundations of the Commission in the 1950s. However, the single Commission was created later in 1965, when the executive bodies of the European Coal and Steel Community, the European Economic Community, and the European Atomic Energy Community were merged.

The Commission is sometimes described as the executive body of the EU. It is true that the Commission implements the EU's decisions and policies, but this label ignores its many other functions, which are stated in Article 9D of the EU Treaty, introduced by Article 1(18) of the Lisbon Treaty:

The Commission shall promote the general interest of the Union and take appropriate initiatives to that end. It shall ensure the application of the Treaties, and of measures adopted by the institutions pursuant to them. It shall oversee the application of Union law under the control of the Court of Justice of the European Union. It shall execute the budget and manage programmes. It shall exercise coordinating, executive and management functions, as laid down in the Treaties. With the exception of the common foreign and security policy, and other cases provided for in the Treaties, it shall ensure the Union's external representation. It shall initiate the Union's annual and multiannual programming with a view to achieving inter-institutional agreements.

Paragraph 1 of Article 9D illustrates the broad nature of the Commission's responsibilities. However, the second paragraph of the article introduces an additional responsibility: the power to initiate legislation. This is vitally important because, apart from a few circumstances where the Parliament and the Council can propose legislation together, 'Union legislative acts may only be adopted on the basis of a Commission proposal. Other acts shall be adopted on the basis of a Commission proposal where the Treaties so provide'.[10]

The Commission not only acts as the executive body and influences the legislative function but also as a guardian of the treaties by monitoring compliance of the other institutions, member states and 'natural and legal persons'. To fulfil this task, Articles 226 and 228 of the EC Treaty grant the Commission the power to take legal and administrative action, including the power to impose a fine against a member state that has failed to comply with the law, whilst Articles 230 and 232 provide the necessary supervisory powers over the other institutions.

2.5.2 Working in practice

At the time of writing, each of the 28 member states has its own commissioner. However, as the EU expands, this structure may become unworkable. The number of commissioners should be immaterial, as they are supposed to be independent and have no allegiance to the country that nominates them. Member states are expected not to influence the commissioner's decisions or duties. Commissioners are selected 'on the ground of their general competence and European commitment from persons whose independence is beyond doubt'.[11] Furthermore, although each member state nominates its own commissioner, they are not appointed to office without the Parliament's approval.

The Parliament is able to exercise an important function of oversight of the Commission and its activities. This power is extremely important as it introduces an element of democratic accountability, albeit indirectly.

2.5.3 Role in relation to data protection

The Commission has historically been the most active European Union institution in the area of data protection, as it was responsible for the original 1990 'Proposal for a Council Directive Concerning the Protection of Individuals in Relation to the Processing of Personal Data' and for the 2012 reform of data protection rules in the EU, which led to the adoption of the GDPR and LEDP Directive.

The Commission also has the power to adopt 'adequacy findings' by which non-EU member states are regarded as providing an adequate level of data protection in accordance with EU standards.

Through its power to enforce compliance with the Charter, the Commission can also ensure a high level of protection for the individual's rights of privacy and data protection.

2.6 Court of Justice of the European Union

2.6.1 Rationale and functions

Based in Luxembourg, the Court of Justice of the European Communities (as it was originally called) was set up under the Treaty of Paris of 1951 to implement the legal framework of the European Coal and Steel Community. When the European Community was set up under the Treaty of Rome of 1957, the Court of Justice became the community's court. The Court of Justice's powers were again expanded upon the creation of the EU under the Treaty of Maastricht in 1992. The Treaty of Lisbon further extended the jurisdiction of the Court of Justice and renamed it the Court of Justice of the European Union ('the Court').

The Court is the judicial body of the EU that makes decisions on issues of EU law and enforces European decisions either in respect of actions taken by the Commission against a member state or action taken by an individual to enforce his rights under EU law. The Court is frequently confused with the ECHR, which is not linked to the EU institutions and oversees human rights laws across Europe, including in many non-EU countries.

The Court is divided into two parts:

- The Court of Justice (the 'Court of Justice of the European Union', or CJEU)
- The General Court (the renamed 'Court of First Instance', or CFI)

2.6.2 Working in practice

The ECJ is composed of 28 judges, appointed by common accord of the governments of the member states for a term of six years. The judges elect one of their number as president for a term of three years. The ECJ also has eight advocates general. Their role is to assist the ECJ by giving reasoned, nonbinding opinions as to how the ECJ should decide the case.

The ECJ is composed of one judge per member state, and they are appointed by the member states' governments for a term of six years. Every three years, the judges elect a president from amongst their ranks. The judges and advocates general are completely impartial and independent.

The ECJ has jurisdiction to hear:

- Cases brought by the Commission or by a member state against a member state's failure to fulfil treaty obligations.

- Actions brought by member states, an EU institution, or a natural or legal person to review the legality of acts by an EU institution.

- Actions by member states, EU institutions, or a natural or legal person against EU institutions for failure to act.

- Actions begun in national courts from which references are made for a preliminary ruling to the ECJ on issues of interpretation or validity of EU law.

- Opinions on the compatibility of EU international agreements with the treaties.

- Appeals on points of law from the CFI.

2.6.3 Role in relation to data protection

The ECJ has been involved in several cases related to data protection. Some have been related to actions begun in national courts, which were referred to the ECJ for a preliminary ruling on issues of interpretation of EU law.[12]

Other actions have been connected to cases brought by the Commission against a member state for failure to fulfil treaty obligations. One such example is the action the Commission brought against the United Kingdom. On 30 September 2010, the Commission announced that it referred the United Kingdom to the ECJ for not fully implementing EU rules on the confidentiality of electronic communications.

The ECJ's involvement with data protection has been increasing in the past few years. A number of ECJ decisions has been particularly influential in shaping EU data protection law.

In the Google Spain case on the right to be forgotten, the ECJ held that where individuals object and certain circumstances are met, search engines must remove the list of results displayed following a search made on a person's name, links to web pages published by third parties, and results that contain information relating to that person.[13] This case also dealt with the applicability of EU data protection law in respect of controllers that have an establishment in the European Union.

In the Digital Rights Ireland case, the ECJ examined whether or not the Data Retention Directive was valid in light of Articles 7, 8 and 11 of the Charter.[14] In determining the Data Retention Directive's invalidity, the ECJ laid out arguments later relied upon when examining the specific aspects that led to invalidating the Commission's decision regarding Safe Harbor.

In the ANAF case, the ECJ ruled that personal data may not be transferred between public administrative bodies of a member state without individuals being informed of the transfer.[15]

In the Weltimmo case, the ECJ intervened to clarify how data protection law applies in cross-border situations within the European Union.[16] Specifically, the ECJ took the view that even minimal activities in a member state can trigger the application of that member state's data protection law.

In the Schrems ruling of October 2015, the ECJ invalidated the Commission's decision that Safe Harbor was adequate as a framework to legitimise international data transfers to the United States.[17]

2.7 European Court of Human Rights

2.7.1 Rationale and functions

To complete the picture, it is also necessary to refer to the European Court of Human Rights (ECHR).[18] Based in Strasbourg, the ECHR is an international court founded in 1959. Its role is to oversee the Convention, which protects the fundamental rights of people living in contracting states. The ECHR is not an institution of the European Union, and it has no powers of enforcement.

The ECHR applies the Convention and ensures that contracting states respect the rights and guarantees set out in the Convention. The ECHR does this by examining complaints (known as 'applications') lodged by individuals or states. Where it finds that a state has violated one or more of these rights and guarantees, the ECHR delivers a judgment. Judgments are binding, and the countries concerned are obliged to comply with them.

The ECHR's judgments are final, and the contracting states undertake to abide by its decisions in any case to which they are party. The ECHR must give reasons for a judgment, and if the judgment does not in whole or in part represent the unanimous opinion of the ECHR's judges, any judge may deliver a separate opinion.

If the ECHR finds that a decision or measure taken by a legal or other authority of a contracting state conflicts with the obligations arising from the Convention, and if the internal law of the state allows for only partial reparation to be made for the consequences of the decision or measure, the decision of the ECHR must, if necessary, afford just satisfaction to the injured party.

2.7.2 Working in practice

The ECHR consists of a number of judges equal to that of the members of the Council of Europe that have ratified the Convention (at the time of writing, 49, including a registrar and a deputy registrar, one president, two vice presidents and three section presidents). The ECHR's judges sit in their individual capacity and do not represent any state. No two judges may be nationals of the same state. A chamber of seven judges considers each case referred to the ECHR. It draws up its own rules and determines its own procedures. The expenses of the court are borne by the Council of Europe.

The ECHR's jurisdiction extends to all cases concerning the interpretation or application of the Convention. The cases may be referred to the ECHR by the contracting states or the European Commission of Human Rights. The states that may bring a case before the ECHR are (1) a state whose citizen is alleged to be a victim of a violation of the Convention; (2) a state that referred the case to the Commission; and (3) a state against which the complaint has been lodged, provided in each case that the state or states concerned are subject to the compulsory jurisdiction of the ECHR or have consented to the case being heard by the ECHR. Nationals of contracting states may lodge an application with the ECHR when they consider that they have personally and directly been the victim of a violation of the rights and guarantees set out in the Convention or its protocols. The violation must have been committed by one of the states bound by the Convention.

The ECHR does not have the powers to overrule national decisions or to annul national laws. As the ECHR has no power of enforcement, responsibility to supervise execution and ensure that compensation is paid passes to the Council after the ECHR has given judgment.

As stated above, the ECHR's role is to apply the Convention and to ensure that the rights and guarantees set out in the Convention and its protocols are respected. The Convention and its protocols protect the following rights: (1) the right to life; (2) the right to a fair hearing in civil and criminal matters; (3) the right to respect for private and family life; (4) freedom of expression; (5) freedom of thought, conscience and religion; (6) the right to an effective remedy; (7) the right to the peaceful enjoyment of possessions; and (8) the right to vote and to stand for election.[19]

2.7.3 Role in relation to data protection

Article 8 of the Convention protects the right to respect for private and family life but does not specifically address data protection. However, the ECHR has pointed out that the use of modern electronic techniques to process personal data should be kept under control to ensure that the right to privacy set out in Article 8 is safeguarded.[20] As the case law of the ECHR shows, the ECHR has indeed been active in data protection. Some of the cases in this area are summarised below. In three French cases in 2009 (judgments in the cases of Bouchacourt v. France, Gardel v. France, and M.B. v. France), the court reaffirmed the fundamental role of the protection of personal data but held that automated processing of data for police purposes, and more specifically the applicants' inclusion in the national police database of sex offenders, was not contrary to Article 8 of the Convention. In a 2012 case concerning the United Kingdom (MM v. the United Kingdom), the Court held that, although there might be a need for a comprehensive record of data relating to criminal matters, the indiscriminate and open-ended collection of criminal record data is unlikely to comply with Article 8. Compliance would require clear and detailed statutory regulations clarifying the safeguards applicable and governing the use and disposal of such data, particularly bearing in mind the amount and sensitivity of the data.

In the 2007 judgment in Copland v. United Kingdom, the ECHR concluded that monitoring the applicant's email at work was contrary to Article 8 of the Convention as no provision was made for this in the law.

The ECHR has also considered the protection of personal data from the viewpoint of the right of access to such data. As long ago as 1989, the ECHR's judgment in the case of Gaskin v. United Kingdom said that the restriction of the applicant's access to his personal file was contrary to Article 8 of the Convention. Subsequently, in the 2009 case of Haralambie v. Romania, the ECHR concluded that this same article had been violated by the obstacles placed in the applicant's way when he sought access to the secret service file on him drawn up in the days of the Communist rule.[21]

Endnotes

1 Treaty on the European Union, Treaty on the Functioning of the European Union, Treaty establishing the European Atomic Energy Summit, https://curia.europa.eu/jcms/upload/docs/application/pdf/2009-11/en_extrait_cour_2009-11-30_11-32-32_981.pdf.

2 As of the time of this publication, the EU member states included Austria, Belgium, Bulgaria, Croatia, Republic of Cyprus, Czech Republic, Denmark, Estonia, Finland, France, Germany, Greece, Hungary, Ireland, Italy, Latvia, Lithuania, Luxembourg, Malta, Netherlands, Poland, Portugal, Romania, Slovakia, Slovenia, Spain, Sweden and the United Kingdom. The European Economic Area—which allows countries to be members of the EU's single market—also includes Iceland, Liechtenstein and Norway. Switzerland is neither an EU nor an EEA member, although Swiss nationals may have the same rights to live and work in EU member states because Switzerland is part of the single market, as well. See www.gov.uk/eu-eea.

3 Protocol (No. 30) on the application of the Charter of Fundamental Rights of the European Union to Poland and to the United Kingdom.

4 The Lisbon Treaty, Article 14, accessed June 2017, www.lisbon-treaty.org/wcm/the-lisbon-treaty/treaty-on-european-union-and-comments/title-3-provisions-on-the-institutions/89-article-14.html.

5 The minimum age to stand for election is 18 in most member states, the exceptions being Belgium, Bulgaria, Cyprus, the Czech Republic, Estonia, Ireland, Latvia, Lithuania, Poland and Slovakia (21), Romania (23), and Italy and Greece (25), www.europarl.europa.eu/atyourservice/en/displayFtu.html?ftuId=FTU_1.3.4.html.

6 EC Treaty, Article 16B, introduced by Article 2(29) Treaty of Reform.

7 EU Treaty, Article 9B, inserted by Article 1(16) of the Treaty of Lisbon.

8 'Council of the European Union: Overview', European Union, accessed June 2017, https://europa.eu/european-union/about-eu/institutions-bodies/council-eu_en.

9 EC Treaty, Article 16A(1); EU Treaty, Article 9C(8), introduced by Article 1(17) of the Treaty of Lisbon.

10 EU Treaty, Article 9D(2), introduced by Article 1(18) of the Lisbon Treaty.

11 EU Treaty, Article 9D(3).

12 An example of this type of action is that of Mrs Bodil Lindqvist. In this case, the ECJ ruled that Mrs Lindqvist, who identified and included information about fellow church volunteers on her website, was in breach of the Data Protection Directive 95/46/EC. The ECJ held that the creation of a personal website was not a personal activity allowing Mrs Lindqvist to be exempted from the data protection rules. Case C-101/01.

13 Google Spain SL and Google Inc. v. Agencia Española de Protección de Datos (AEPD) and Mario Costeja González [2014] Case C-131/12, 13 May 2014.

14 Digital Rights Ireland Ltd. v. Minister for Communications, Marine and Natural Resources, Minister for Justice, Equality and Law Reform, The Commissioner of the Garda Síochána, Ireland and the Attorney General, and Kärntner Landesregierung, Michael Seitlinger, Christof Tschohl and Others [2014] Joined Cases C-293/12 and C-594/12, 8 April 2014.

15 Smaranda Bara and Others v. Casa Naţională de Asigurări de Sănătate and Others [2015] C-201/14, 1 October 2015.

16 s.r.o. v. Nemzeti Adatvédelmi és Információszabadság Hatóság [2015] Case C-230/14, 1 October 2015.

17 Maximillian Schrems v. Data Protection Commissioner [2015] Case C-362/14, 6 October 2015.

18 European Court of Human Rights, accessed June 2017, www.echr.coe.int.

19 'European Convention on Human Rights', Council of Europe. www.echr.coe.int/Documents/Convention_ENG.pdf.

20 Jean-Paul Costa, former president of the ECHR.

21 Press release issued by the Registrar, 27 October 2009. http://hudoc.echr.coe.int/app/conversion/pdf/?library=ECHR&id=003-2909811-3196312&filename=003-2909811-3196312.pdf.

CHAPTER 3

Legislative Framework

Katie McMullan

3.1 Background

> *Newly developed techniques such as phone-tapping, eavesdropping,*
> *surreptitious observation, the illegitimate use of official statistical and similar*
> *surveys to obtain private information, and subliminal advertising and*
> *propaganda are a threat to the rights and freedoms of individuals and, in*
> *particular, to the right to privacy.*

The passage above, taken from a Council of Europe Recommendation from 1968, provides an interesting perspective on the concerns about potential threats to individual privacy at the time.[1] As noted in Chapter 1, it was recognised that rapid increases in the field of electronic data processing and the appearance of large mainframe computers in both the public and private sectors provided major advantages to organisations in terms of efficiency and commercial productivity, but also that these developments had the potential to undermine individual human rights and privacy.

European data protection law has been around since 1970, when the German state of Hesse introduced a regional law. The first national law was introduced by Sweden in 1973, but it was not until the early 1980s that Europe started to undertake a serious, concerted approach to data protection regulation.

3.2 The Council of Europe Convention

As discussed in Chapter 1, in 1981, the Council of Europe opened for signature the Convention for the Protection of Individuals with regard to Automatic Processing of Personal Data ('Convention 108'). Convention 108 was the first legally binding international instrument in the field of data protection.[2] There were two main reasons for Convention 108. First, the member states' failure to respond to the Council's 1973 and 1974 resolutions, which concerned the protection of privacy in the private and public sectors, respectively.[3] Second was the need for reinforcement of the principles found in those resolutions by means of a binding international instrument.

Between November 1976 and April 1980, several committees of governmental experts on data protection from Austria, Belgium, France, the Federal Republic of Germany, Italy, the Netherlands, Spain, Sweden, Switzerland and the United Kingdom met to determine the general philosophy and details of the draft convention; the final text opened for signature on 28 January 1981. Convention 108 was a defining moment in the development of European data protection law and is noteworthy for three main reasons:

- Like the earlier resolutions, Convention 108 is based on a series of 'principles' that address the main concerns relating to data protection, including the accuracy and security of personal data and the individual right of access to such data—principles that are still found in the EU Data Protection Directive ('Directive'), as implemented by the national laws in member states and also the EU General Data Protection Regulation (GDPR, or 'Regulation').

- Like the earlier resolutions, Convention 108 ensures appropriate protections for individual privacy but also recognises the importance of the free flow of personal data for commerce and the exercise of public functions —a key component of current EU data protection law. Therefore, signatory states 'shall not, for the sole purpose of the protection of privacy, prohibit or subject to special authorisation transborder flows of personal data going to the territory of another Party'.[4]

- Finally, Convention 108, as a legally binding instrument, requires signatory states to implement its principles by enacting national legislation.

The purpose of Convention 108 is to achieve greater unity between the signatory states and to extend the safeguards for individuals' rights and fundamental freedoms; in particular, the right to respect for privacy, taking into account the increasing amount of personal data undergoing automatic processing and flowing across national borders.

Convention 108 comprises 27 articles and has three main parts:

- 'Basic principles of data protection' (Chapter II, Articles 4–11);

- 'Transborder data flows' (Chapter III, Article 12); and

- 'Mutual assistance' provisions (Chapter IV, Articles 13–17).

For more detailed information on Convention 108, see Chapter 1.

3.3   The Data Protection Directive

Recognising that differences in emerging data protection legislation amongst EU member states were impacting the free flow of data, in 1990 the European Commission ('Commission') proposed the creation of a Data Protection Directive ('Directive').

3.3.1 Background

Unfortunately, by the end of the 1980s, some difficulties with Convention 108 had become apparent; only a small number of states had ratified it and their national data protection laws took a fragmented approach to its implementation. This created an impediment to the consistent protection of the privacy rights of individuals, as well as to the concept of free trade enshrined by the Treaty of Rome.

Therefore, in 1990, the Commission formally proposed a Data Protection Directive.[5] This proposal was significant as it marked the starting point of the European Union's leadership in European data protection and the relative downgrading of the importance of Convention 108. Directive 95/46/EC of the European Parliament and of the Council on the protection of individuals with regard to the processing of personal data and on the free movement of such data ('Data Protection Directive,' or 'the Directive') was formally adopted 24 October 1995.

Unlike the Council of Europe, the EU is unable to make stand-alone human rights laws. Instead, it must base its laws on a specific provision under the Treaty of Rome, which sets out the legal powers of the EU. This is why the Directive was set up as a harmonisation measure under the Treaty of Rome's internal market provisions—which require 'the abolition, as between member states, of obstacles to the free movement of goods, persons, services and capital' and because the free movement of such assets cannot take place without the free movement of personal data.

Therefore, it would be fair to view the Directive as a human rights law that protects the principles of the internal single market—recognising that, for the single market to succeed, the free movement of personal data, coupled with consistent provisions to ensure the protection of individual privacy, is required. This can be seen from Article 1 of the Directive, which describes its objectives:

> In accordance with this Directive, Member States shall protect the fundamental rights and freedoms of natural persons, and in particular their right to privacy with respect to the processing of personal data.

> *Member States shall neither restrict nor prohibit the free flow of personal data between Member States for reasons connected with the protection afforded under Paragraph 1.*

3.3.2 Content

The Directive comprises 72 recitals and 34 articles. The recitals first provide the theories and interpretations behind the Directive and its corresponding obligations, and the articles set out the obligations of the member states in implementing the requirements of the Directive. The 34 articles are arranged in seven chapters:

1. General provisions

2. General rules on the lawfulness of the processing of personal data

3. Judicial remedies, liability and sanctions

4. Transfer of personal data to third countries

5. Codes of conduct

6. Supervisory authority and working party on the protection of individuals with regard to the processing of personal data

7. Community implementing measures

From an operational point of view, the Directive sets out general principles and leaves the member states to implement these principles as they see fit—rather than prescribing in detail how member states must transpose them into national law. This gives member states a margin of manoeuvre in their implementation, resulting in differing interpretations and requirements under data protection laws across Europe. An example of this is seen in the notification obligations, as set out in Articles 18–20 of the Directive, and the different interpretations of these articles in each of the respective national data protection laws implemented by the member states.

Again, because the Directive sets out general principles, certain concepts and phrases recur throughout the Directive text. 'Necessity' is one of these key concepts—on the grounds that, for the data processing activity to be lawful, the processing must be 'necessary'. Another prominent concept is that of 'adequacy'—the Directive, subject to certain exceptions, prohibits international data transfers to jurisdictions that do not offer an adequate level of protection.

A major advance of the Directive over Convention 108 is its applicability to manual data. Under Convention 108, only Council of Europe member countries had this option, and few chose to implement it. However, the Directive changed this, making the processing of manual data held in a 'filing system' subject to the same obligations as the processing of personal data by automatic means.

3.3.3 Key principles

As with the earlier Convention 108, it is possible to identify key principles in the Directive that are central requirements to the lawful processing of personal data. In particular, member states must provide that personal data shall be:

- processed fairly and lawfully;

- collected for specified and legitimate purposes and not processed in a manner incompatible with those purposes;

- adequate, relevant and not excessive;

- accurate and, where necessary, kept up to date;

- kept for no longer than is necessary;

- processed in accordance with the rights of the individual;

- protected against accidental, unlawful or unauthorised processing by the use of appropriate technical and organisational measures; and

- transferred to countries outside the European Economic Area only if those countries ensure adequate levels of data protection or under conditions guaranteeing such adequate protection.

The Directive applies to those organisations acting as 'data controllers' that are 'established' in an EU member state, or where there is no such establishment but where the organisation makes use of data processing equipment on the territory of a member state, in which case, the organisation must appoint a representative to act on its behalf in that member state. (See Chapter 5 for further information on the meaning of 'establishment'.)

The Directive builds on the foundations set by the earlier Convention 108 and identifies 'special categories of data'—personal data revealing racial or ethnic origin, political opinions, religious or philosophical beliefs, trade union membership, or details concerning health or sex life—as well as additional requirements for processing of such data. (See Chapter 4 for more information.) Importantly, as a human rights-based law, the Directive contains specific provisions that articulate an individual's rights with regard to personal data. (See Chapter 9 for more comprehensive analysis on the rights of individuals.)

The Directive also mandates the establishment of a national Data Protection Authority (DPA) in each member state, which shall act with 'complete independence in exercising the functions entrusted to them', and the Article 29 Working Party (WP29)—an independent body composed of representatives of the national Data Protection Authorities (DPAs), the European Data Protection Supervisor and the Commission.[6] The WP29's duties are set out in Article 30 of the Directive and require it to examine the operation of the Directive and to provide opinions and advice to the Commission.

3.3.4 Review of the Directive and reform of the EU data protection framework

Since the introduction of the Directive, the main focus of the Commission has been on improving implementation in the member states and on achieving a more consistent application and interpretation of the Directive. However, a number of factors led the Commission to initiate a comprehensive review of data protection rules in the EU. Key factors, including the divergence of national measures and practices implementing the Directive and the resulting impact on businesses and individuals, together with developments in technology since the Directive was drafted.

In 2010, the Commission set out its proposed strategy for the reform, with the primary goals of protecting individuals' data, including in relation to access to data by law enforcement agencies, reducing red tape for businesses and guaranteeing the free circulation of data within the EU.[7] The Commission invited reactions to its ideas and also carried out a separate public consultation.

Two years later in January 2012, the Commission published its proposals for a comprehensive reform of the Directive, which included two legislative proposals: a regulation setting out a general EU framework for data protection (the GDPR) and a Directive on protecting personal data processed for the purposes of prevention, detection, investigation or prosecution of criminal offences and related judicial activities (the 'Law Enforcement Data Protection Directive', or LEDP Directive).

The Commission's press release at the time explained the following by way of background to the reforms:

> 17 years ago less than 1% of Europeans used the internet. Today, vast amounts
> of personal data are transferred and exchanged, across continents and
> around the globe in fractions of seconds. The protection of personal data is
> a fundamental right for all Europeans, but citizens do not always feel in full

control of their personal data. [Our] proposals will help build trust in online services because people will be better informed about their rights and in more control of their information. The reform will accomplish this whilst making life easier and less costly for businesses. A strong, clear and uniform legal framework at EU level will help to unleash the potential of the digital single market and foster economic growth, innovation and job creation.[8]

Key changes in the reform included:

- A single set of rules on data protection, valid across the EU. Certain administrative requirements contained in the Directive, such as the notification requirements for companies, were removed as unduly costly to businesses.

- Increased responsibility and accountability for those processing personal data.

- Enabling organisations to deal with a single national data protection authority (DPA) in the EU country where they have their 'main establishment' in some instances. Similarly, providing individuals with the ability to refer matters to the DPA in their country, even when their data is processed by a company based outside the EU.

- Giving individuals greater control of their data, for example, by requiring that wherever consent is required for data to be processed, it must be 'explicit' rather than assumed.

- Easier access for individuals to their own data and the ability to transfer personal data from one service provider to another more easily (the right to data portability). The stated aim of this proposal was to improve competition amongst services.

- A 'right to be forgotten' to help people better manage data protection risks online. The Commission proposed that individuals should be able to delete their data if there are no legitimate grounds for a business to retain it.

- Ensuring that EU rules apply if personal data is handled abroad by companies that are active in the EU market and offer their services to EU citizens.

- Strengthening of the powers of independent national DPAs so they can better enforce the EU rules at home, including penalties of up to 1 million euros or up to two percent of the global annual turnover of a company.

- General data protection principles and rules for police and judicial cooperation in criminal matters as contained in the LEDP Directive and applicable to both domestic and cross-border transfers of data.

The Commission's proposals were submitted to the European Parliament (the 'Parliament') and EU member states (meeting in the 'Council of Ministers', or 'Council') for their review and discussion. The Parliament proposed numerous amendments to the Commission's draft texts in 2014, and the Council also put forward its own proposals. The three parties then needed to reach agreement on the draft texts before they became law through a negotiation process known as the 'trilogue'. During the trilogue, proposals were thoroughly debated, and after an intensive legislative process of more than four years and following a degree of compromise by all involved, the European Parliament, the Council and the Commission reached agreement on the new data protection rules 15 December 2015.

On 4 May 2016, the official texts of the Regulation and the Directive were published in the Official Journal of the EU in all the official languages, following political agreements from the European Parliament's Committee on Civil Liberties and the Permanent Representatives Committee (Coreper) of the Council, the European Council and the European Parliament. The Regulation officially entered into force 24 May 2016 and will apply from 25 May 2018. The LEDP Directive entered into force 5 May 2016, and member states must transpose it into their national law by 6 May 2018.

3.4   The General Data Protection Regulation

3.4.1 Background

The Regulation is seen by the Commission as an 'essential step to strengthen citizens' fundamental rights in the digital age and facilitate business by simplifying rules for companies in the digital single market'.[9] It is an enormously ambitious, complex and strict law that is set to transform the way in which personal information is collected, shared and used globally. The new regime contains familiar concepts and principles to those in the Directive. However, despite the similarities, the effect of the Regulation will be far greater.

3.4.2 Content

In terms of its structure, the Regulation is much longer than the Directive and comprises 173 recitals and 99 Articles. As with the Directive, the recitals first provide the theories and interpretations behind the Regulation and its corresponding obligations and the articles set out the substantive obligations. Whilst the articles contain the operative law, the related recitals contain crucial detail about how the article should be interpreted, and so the two need to be considered alongside each other in practice.

The 99 articles are arranged in 11 chapters, as follows:

1. General provisions

2. Principles

3. Rights of the data subject

4. Controller and processor

5. Transfers of personal data to third countries or international organisations

6. Independent supervisory authorities

7. Cooperation and consistency

8. Remedies, liability and penalties

9. Provisions relating to specific processing situations

10. Delegated acts and implementing acts

11. Final provisions

The subsequent chapters of this text consider the requirements of the Regulation in more detail. However, by way of a summary, the main changes compared to the current Directive which will affect companies operating in the EU or processing data of individuals in the EU are as follows:

- *Application of the law*: Unlike the Directive, the Regulation will be directly applicable across all member states of the EU without any further intervention from the national parliaments. Like the Directive, the Regulation will apply to businesses that are established in the EU, although a crucial difference is that the new regime is not limited to data controllers—many of the new requirements apply equally to processors, which highlight the new focus on compliance across all roles of the information lifecycle. (See Chapter 4 for a more detailed explanation of the concepts of controllers and processors.)

- In terms of the Regulation's applicability for businesses not established in the EU, the legislators have done away with the references found in the Directive to EU-based processing 'equipment'. Instead, the applicability of the Regulation to organisations not established in the EU will be determined by the location of the data subject. The Regulation will apply wherever the use of personal data by a business relates to the offering of goods or services to individuals in the EU, irrespective of whether a payment is required, or the monitoring of those individuals' behaviour in the EU. Significantly, Recital 24 of the Regulation clarifies that tracking data subjects on the Internet to analyse or predict their personal preferences will trigger the application of the Regulation. This measure represents a massive widening of the application of the rules, as it makes almost every website that drops tracking cookies or app that retrieves usage information subject to the Regulation.[10]

- *Putting individuals in control of their data*: This is a theme that is present throughout the text of the Regulation and is emphasised by the strengthening of 'consent' in relation to the use of data as compared with the Directive. When consent is relied upon as a justification for the use of data, it will need to meet very high standards and overcome certain conditions. In this connection:

  - Consent cannot be bundled within terms and conditions without clearly distinguishing between the uses of personal data and the other matters governed by the terms and conditions.

  - Consent can be withdrawn at any time and in an easy way that should be explained to the individuals before it is obtained.

  - Consent requested in return for goods or services in a 'take-it-or-leave-it' manner may not be regarded as freely given.

  - The requirement for parental consent for the use of personal information of those under 16 years will be at the discretion of individual member states, which will lead to the need for a country-by-country approach to compliance where teenagers' data is involved.

- *New and stronger rights for individuals*: Under the Regulation, individuals are afforded a lot more control over their data through significantly reinforced rights, which include the following:

  - Much more detailed transparency obligations—the Regulation adds to the categories of information that must be provided to individuals at the point of data collection or within a reasonable period otherwise. Clear and plain language must be used, adapted to the individual data subject, so if information is being collected from a child, the language of the notice must be such that a child can understand it.

- New rights of data portability, restriction of processing, the right to be forgotten and in relation to profiling. The right to portability introduces a right for people to receive information they have provided to businesses in a 'structured, commonly used and machine-readable format' when the information was originally obtained from an individual based on their consent or as part of a contract. There will also be a general right to have that data transmitted from one business to another where technically feasible in certain circumstances.

  - The retention of existing rights, such as subject access, rectification, erasure (i.e., the right to be forgotten) and the right to object, from the current Directive. In relation to subject access requests, the right to charge a fee has been removed unless the request is 'manifestly excessive'.

- *A new accountability regime*: Some of the most notable novelties of the Regulation are the various requirements to make businesses more accountable for their data practices. Accountability is about demonstrating compliance and being transparent about such compliance. The new responsibilities include:

  - Implementation of data protection policies and measures to ensure that an organisation's data processing activities comply with the Regulation.

  - Data protection by design and data protection by default.

  - Record-keeping obligations by controllers and processors.

  - Cooperation with supervisory authorities by controllers and processors.

  - Carrying out data protection impact assessments (DPIAs) for operations that present specific risks to individuals due to the nature or scope of the operation.

  - Prior consultation with DPAs in high-risk cases.

  - Mandatory data protection officers (DPOs) for controllers and processors for the public sector and big data processing activities.

- *Data processors' new obligations*: As mentioned above, the Regulation imposes a number of compliance obligations and possible sanctions directly on service providers (i.e., data processors) which signal a significant change to the current rules under the Directive, which only apply to data controllers. One of the most radical changes is the requirement that a processor may not subcontract a service without the consent of the controller. The Directive requires prescriptive terms for contracts with controllers, and most processors will be required to maintain records of their processing activities, implement appropriate security measures, appoint a DPO in certain circumstances, comply with the international data transfer requirements and cooperate with a supervisory authority if requested to do so.

- *International data transfers*: The existing restrictions contained in the Directive that affect international data transfers will continue to exist under the Regulation. Aside from transfers to jurisdictions that are officially recognised by the Commission as adequate, both controllers and processors may only transfer personal data outside the EU if they put in place appropriate safeguards and on the condition that enforceable rights and effective legal remedies for individuals are available. The Regulation has helpfully expanded the range of measures that may be used to legitimise such transfers, which now explicitly include Binding Corporate Rules (BCRs), standard contractual clauses adopted by the Commission, standard contractual clauses adopted by a DPA and approved by the Commission, an approved code of conduct, an approved certification mechanism, and other contractual clauses authorised by a DPA in accordance with the so-called 'consistency mechanism'.

- *Security*: Under the Regulation, both data controllers and data processors are under an obligation to have in place appropriate technical and organisational measures to protect the personal data that they process (currently the obligations in law are only imposed on controllers). The Regulation also introduces a requirement to report data breaches to the relevant DPA within 72 hours of becoming aware of it unless the breach is 'unlikely to result in a risk for the rights and freedoms of natural persons'. If the risk of harm to individuals is high, then individuals must be notified, as well.

- *Enforcement and the risk of noncompliance*: The Regulation affords individuals the right to compensation for breaches for material or immaterial damage. They are also afforded judicial remedies against decisions of a DPA which concern them, to compel a DPA to act on a complaint and against data controllers and processors that breach their rights by failing to comply with the Regulation. These rights can be exercised by consumer bodies on behalf of individuals. There is a significant increase in the potential severity of sanctions, including fines of up to 20 million euros or up to four percent of the total worldwide annual turnover, whichever is higher. These include infringements of the following provisions:

- the basic principles for processing, including conditions for consent;

- the data subjects' rights;

- the conditions for lawful international data transfers;

- specific obligations under national laws, where permitted by the Regulation; and

- orders by DPAs, including suspension of data flows.

3.5   The Law Enforcement Data Protection Directive

The Directive is complemented by other legal instruments, including specific rules for the protection of personal data in police and judicial cooperation in criminal matters ('2008 Framework Decision').[11] The 2008 Framework Decision was reviewed at the same time as the Directive.

Along with the agreement on the Regulation, the Commission, Council and Parliament reached an agreement on a new EU Directive for the police and criminal justice sector, aimed at protecting citizens' fundamental right to data protection whenever personal data is used by criminal law enforcement authorities.[12]

The new rules contained in the LEDP Directive have three main objectives, as follows:

- *Better cooperation between law enforcement authorities*: Under the LEDP Directive, law enforcement authorities in EU member states will be able to exchange information necessary for investigations more efficiently and effectively, improving cooperation in the fight against terrorism and other serious crime in Europe. According to the Commission, the LEDP Directive 'takes account of the specific needs of law enforcement, respects the different legal traditions in member states and is fully in line with the Charter of Fundamental Rights'.[13]

- *Better protection of citizens' data*: The LEDP Directive aims to ensure that individuals' personal data is protected when processed for any law enforcement purpose, including prevention of crime—regardless of whether they are a victim, criminal or witness. Accordingly and similar to the position under the Regulation, all law enforcement processing in the EU must comply with the principles of necessity, proportionality and legality with appropriate safeguards for the individuals. Supervision is ensured by independent national DPAs, and effective judicial remedies must be provided.

- *Clear rules for international data flows*: The LEDP Directive also contains specific rules for the transfer of personal data by law enforcement authorities outside the EU with the aim of ensuring that the level of protection of individuals guaranteed in the EU is not undermined.

3.6 The Privacy and Electronic Communications Directive

Another instrument that complements the Directive is the Privacy and Electronic Communications Directive (the 'ePrivacy Directive'), which contains specific rules for the communications sector. By way of background to the ePrivacy Directive, the EU Parliament and the Council recognised that, with the Internet overturning traditional market structures and the development of the information society with new advanced digital technologies, there was a need to address privacy issues that couldn't have been anticipated a decade ago.

3.6.1 Background

Directive 2002/58/EC of the European Parliament and of the Council of 12 July 2002 concerning the processing of personal data and the protection of privacy in the electronic communications sector (the 'ePrivacy Directive') replaced the 1997 directive to reflect the process of 'convergence'.[14] In it, the EU widened its then-existing telecommunications laws to cover all electronic communications, including telecommunications, faxes, the Internet, email and similar methods of communication.

In explaining the reasons for the new ePrivacy Directive, the authors recognised advances in digital technologies being introduced in public communications networks, 'which give rise to specific requirements concerning the protection of personal data and privacy of the user' and developments in the markets and technologies for electronic communications services. They saw the need for consistent and equal protections regardless of the technologies used. The aim of the ePrivacy Directive is identified in Article 1:

> This Directive harmonises the provisions of the Member States required to ensure an equivalent level of protection of fundamental rights and freedoms, and in particular the right to privacy, with respect to the processing of personal data in the electronic communication sector and to ensure the free movement of such data and of electronic communication equipment and services in the community.

The Directive was originally proposed by the Commission 12 July 2000, but the adoption process took nearly two years. The last approval hurdles were completed 25 June 2002, when the Council approved amendments as voted by the plenary of the European Parliament. The Directive was published in the Official Journal of the EU 31 July 2002 and had to be implemented into national law by the member states no later than 31 October 2003.

The ePrivacy Directive was amended again 24 November 2009 as part of wider reforms to the EU telecommunications sector affecting five different EU directives.[15] The package of reforms was designed to encourage greater industry competition, consumer choice and protections, including a stronger entrenchment of the consumer's right to privacy.

3.6.2 Content

Generally, the ePrivacy Directive applies to 'the processing of personal data in connection with the provision of publicly available electronic communications services in public communications networks' in the EU. If the electronic communications service is not publicly available, the Directive does not apply. This means that communications over a private network, such as a company intranet, generally are not covered—although the principles of the Directive still apply if personal data is processed.

The ePrivacy Directive contains the following key provisions:

- The providers of publicly available electronic communications services are required to take appropriate technical and organisational measures to safeguard the security of their services, working with the network provider on which the service is based, where appropriate, to ensure such security. In addition, the service provider is under a general obligation to inform the subscriber of any particular risk of breach of the network's security.

- Member states are required to ensure the confidentiality of communications and of the traffic data generated by such communications, subject to specific exceptions, including where users of such services give their consent to interception and surveillance or where the interception and surveillance is authorised by law.

- Most forms of digital marketing, including emails, SMS and MMS messaging and faxes, but not person-to-person telephone marketing, require prior (opt-in) consent. However, there is a limited exemption for businesses to send marketing to their existing customers for similar products and services on an opt-out basis. (See Chapter 16 for a more comprehensive analysis of the relevant rules.)

- Processing of traffic and billing data is subject to certain restrictions. For example, users of a publicly available electronic communication service have certain rights with regard to itemised billing, call-line identification, directories, call forwarding and unsolicited calls.

- Location data may be processed only if that data is made anonymous or, alternatively, if processed with the consent of users and for the duration necessary for the provision of a value-added service.

- Subscribers must be informed before being included in any directory.

Relevant measures can be adopted 'to ensure that terminal equipment is constructed in a way that is compatible with the right of users to protect and control the use of their personal data'. However, member states should avoid imposing mandatory technical requirements, 'which could impede the placing of equipment on the market and the free circulation of such equipment in and between Member States'.[16]

3.6.3 Amendments

As already stated, certain provisions of the ePrivacy Directive have been amended and were due to be implemented by member states by the end of May 2011.[17] The most pertinent changes relate to the introduction of mandatory notification for personal data breaches by electronic communications service providers—to both the relevant national authority and the relevant individual in cases where the breach is likely to 'adversely affect the personal data or privacy of a subscriber or individual'.[18]

Other changes include enhanced clarifications on the scope of the amended Directive and enhancements of the right of actions against unsolicited communications. Specifically, Article 13 ('Unsolicited communications') now provides a right for individuals and organisations—including Internet service providers (ISP)—to bring legal proceedings against unlawful communications. The text refers to 'electronic communication service providers' protecting their 'legitimate business interests' in such cases, which would include instances where spammers use their services to distribute unsolicited communications.

However, perhaps the most pertinent and arguably controversial amendment to the ePrivacy Directive concerns the provisions affecting 'cookies'—the small text files sent automatically by many websites to the terminal equipment of the users of those websites. Despite their simplicity, cookies are vitally important for organisations and individuals, enabling organisations to personalise websites based on users' browsing habits and deliver online advertising to individuals based on their preferences—thereby supporting the revenues generated by the online advertising industry and also allowing users to more easily navigate a site's page, quickly retrieve information found in the past, and facilitate online shopping.

Under the amended ePrivacy Directive, Article 5(3) now says that the storing of information (or the gaining of access to information already stored) in the terminal equipment of a subscriber or user is allowed only on the condition that the user concerned has given their consent, having been provided with clear and comprehensive information, in accordance with the Directive. The exceptions to this are where the technical storage or access is:

- for the sole purpose of carrying out the transmission of a communication over an electronic communications network; or

- strictly necessary for the provision of an information society service explicitly requested by the subscriber or user.

Each EU member state had two years to transpose the cookie consent requirements noted above into national legislation, and this has been done by most—but not all—with a degree of variation on a country-by-country basis.

The means by which consent must be obtained is undefined in both the ePrivacy Directive and in the laws of individual member states.[19] Therefore, in suitable contexts (i.e., where the nature of the data processing in question is not particularly intrusive or does not involve the special categories of data), it is entirely possible and indeed appropriate to rely on 'unambiguous consent [which] may be inferred from certain actions ... when the actions lead to an unmistakable conclusion that consent is given' provided that consent meets the standard of being a 'freely given, specific and informed' indication of an individual's wishes.[20] This approach is known as 'implied consent', which has emerged as one of the most common strategies for international businesses seeking to comply with the cookie consent requirements across Europe. The cookie consent requirements are considered in further detail in Chapter 17.

3.6.4 Reform of the ePrivacy Directive

In July 2015, the Commission published a study on the effectiveness of the ePrivacy Directive, which proposed recommendations for its reform in these areas (the 'ePrivacy Study').[21] This was followed by the launch of a public consultation in April 2016. On 10 January 2017, the Commission released a legislative proposal for a new ePrivacy Regulation ('ePrivacy Regulation') to replace the existing ePrivacy Directive.

The high level aim of the draft ePrivacy Regulation is to harmonise the specific privacy framework relating to electronic communications within the EU and to ensure consistency with the General Data Protection Regulation. According to the press release and fact sheet issued by the European Commission alongside its publication of the ePrivacy regulation, the key features of the ePrivacy Regulation are as follows:

- *Wider application:* The Commission proposes extending the application of the current ePrivacy Directive to all providers of electronic communications services (e.g., messaging services on mobile phones, email and voice services, and not just traditional telecoms operators).

- *A single set of rules*: Replacing the ePrivacy Directive with a directly applicable Regulation has the aim of providing all people and businesses in the EU with the same level of protection (and a single set of rules) for electronic communications.

- *Confidentiality of electronic communications*: Under the Commission's proposal, listening to, tapping, intercepting, scanning and storing of, for example, text messages, emails or voice calls, would not be allowed without the consent of the user. There are a number of exceptional circumstances in which interference is permitted (e.g., to safeguard public interest).

- *Consent is required to process communications content and metadata*: Under the proposed rules, content and metadata derived from electronic communications (e.g., time of a call, location, duration, websites visited) will need to be anonymised or deleted if users have not given their consent, unless the data is required for instance for billing purposes.

- *New business opportunities:* Once consent is given for communications data (both content and/or metadata) to be processed, the aim of the ePrivacy Regulation is to enable traditional telecoms operators to have more opportunities to use data and provide additional services. For example, they could produce heat maps that indicate the presence of individuals to help public authorities and transport companies when developing new infrastructure projects.

- *Revised rules on cookies*: The Commission is of the view that the cookie rules contained in the ePrivacy Directive have resulted in an overload of consent requests for internet users and should be streamlined in the ePrivacy Regulation. The new rules proposed in the ePrivacy Regulation seek to allow users to be more in control of their settings, providing an easy way to accept or refuse the tracking of cookies and other identifiers in case of privacy risks. The proposal clarifies that no consent is needed for non-privacy intrusive cookies improving Internet experience (e.g., to remember shopping cart history, for filling in online forms over several pages, or for the login information for the same session). Cookies set by a visited website counting the number of visitors to that website will no longer require consent. The concept of consent is in line with the GDPR.

- *Protection against spam:* The Commission's proposal bans unsolicited electronic communication by any means (e.g., by emails, SMS and, in principle, also by phone calls, if users have not given their consent, although a 'soft opt-in' is retained for marketing of similar products of services where individuals are provided with a right to object). Member states may opt for a domestic legislation that gives consumers the right to object to the reception of voice-to-voice marketing calls, for example, by registering their number on a do-not-call list. Marketing callers will need to display their phone number or use a special prefix that indicates a marketing call.

- *Enforcement:* The enforcement of the confidentiality rules in the Regulation will be the responsibility of national DPAs.[22]

The consequences for noncompliance follow a two-tier approach, as follows:

- Breaches of the rules regarding notice and consent, default privacy settings, publicly available directories and unsolicited communications as contained in the ePrivacy Regulation may be punished with fines of up to 10 million euros or two percent of the total worldwide annual turnover, whichever is higher.

- Breaches of the rules regarding the confidentiality of communications, permitted processing of electronic communications data and the time limits for erasure of data may be punished with fines of up to 20 million euros or four percent of the total worldwide annual turnover, whichever is higher.

The publication of the Commission's draft of the ePrivacy Regulation was the beginning of the formal legislative process, and now the draft is in the hands of the European Parliament and the Council of the EU. Notably, members of the European Parliament's civil liberties committee submitted more than 800 amendments to the proposed Regulation, including a proposal to introduce 'legitimate interests' as a justification for further processing of data.

The ePrivacy Regulation is intended to come into force in May 2018 (alongside the GDPR), though this is generally seen as a very ambitious timescale.

3.7   The Data Retention Directive

Until recently, data retention in the EU was underpinned by a legal framework established by Directive 2006/24/EC of the European Parliament and of the Council of 15 March 2006 on the retention of data generated or processed in connection with the provision of publicly available electronic communications services or of public communications networks (the 'Data Retention Directive').

The Data Retention Directive was designed to align the rules on data retention across the EU member states in order to ensure the availability of traffic and location data for serious crime and antiterrorism purposes. It was introduced in the midst of heightened national security concerns about the threat of international terrorism and faced considerable criticism concerning its scope and whether it was a measured response to the perceived threat. Over the years, a number of constitutional courts in EU member states struck down the local implementing law as unconstitutional. Then, in 2014, the CJEU ruled that the Directive was invalid on the grounds that it was disproportionate in scope and incompatible with the rights to privacy and data protection under the EU Charter of Fundamental Rights.[23] The Data Retention Directive is no longer part of EU law, although member states retain competence to adopt their own national data retention laws under Article 15(1) of the ePrivacy Directive (2002/58/EC) provided that those laws comply with the fundamental rights principles that form part of EU law and the CJEU ruling. Accordingly, a number of EU member states has introduced draft legislative amendments or implemented national data retention laws at an individual country level, such as Belgium, the United Kingdom and Finland.

3.8   Impact on member states

As discussed earlier in this chapter, under each directive, consistent and timely implementation has been one of the greatest challenges in EU privacy protection. Because of differences in constitutional structures, differences in interpretation and other differences, a great deal of latitude has been extended to member states in implementation. The need for harmonisation was recognised in the passing of the Regulation, which is a single law aimed at reducing the fragmentation under the existing EU data privacy rules.

3.8.1 Implementation challenges with EU directives

As discussed in Chapter 1, EU directives by their very nature are not 'directly applicable' to EU member states, which generally means that, in order to become law, they must be implemented by national legislation. Therefore, although EU directives are binding in terms of the final result to be achieved, the form and methods of that implementation are left to the member states themselves. This can be seen from, for example, Article 5 of the Directive, which states that 'Member States shall, within the limits of the provisions of this Chapter, determine more precisely the conditions under which the processing of personal data is lawful'. Member state law therefore often varies in its approach, structure and content, thus resulting in some member states passing one general piece of implementing legislation and other member states enacting several different mechanisms, some of which may be applicable only to certain sectors.[24] The ePrivacy Directive is an example of an EU directive that has been implemented in some member states using different pieces of legislation rather than one single piece of legislation.[25]

This flexibility in approach creates practical challenges, particularly for multinational organisations, which have data processing activities in various member states and therefore must comply with conflicting compliance obligations in areas such as notifications, international data transfers and direct marketing requirements.

3.8.2 Enforcement

Member states' discretion to implement EU legislation is not unlimited and can be the subject of enforcement action. Member states generally have a time limit in which to implement a directive, and the Commission, which is also responsible for ensuring that directives are implemented properly, can take action against a member state if a directive is not implemented on time or if the implementation contravenes European law. For example, in 2010, the Commission announced that it will be taking the UK to the Court of Justice of the European Union (CJEU) over its failure to properly implement some of the provisions in the Data Protection Directive and the ePrivacy Directive.[26]

Also in 2010, the Commission sued six member states (Denmark, France, Germany, Ireland, Luxembourg and the Netherlands) for failing to implement the Data Protection Directive on time. The Commission has since dropped its actions against those member states that implemented the Directive; however, the CJEU later declared that Luxembourg had failed to meet all its obligations to implement the Directive and ordered it to pay the costs of the proceedings.[27]

All EU member states have now implemented the Data Protection Directive and the ePrivacy Directive; however, as indicated in the previous section, current problems still exist at the national level. Moreover, even if a member state failed to implement a directive, some of that directive's provisions could still have 'direct effect'— which means individuals could rely on those provisions to bring actions against the

~~governments in national courts~~. The CJEU has held that certain provisions of the Data Protection Directive have 'direct effect'.[28] Additionally, member states and their courts must interpret their laws in light of the text and purpose of a directive, even if it has not yet been implemented.

3.8.3 The direct effect of the Regulation

Unlike EU directives, EU 'regulations' are, by nature, ~~directly applicable~~ in EU member states and so do not require further implementation into national laws. The new general data protection law is set out in a Regulation, so when it becomes law 25 May 2018, it will apply immediately throughout the EU due to its direct effect. As a consequence, national data protection acts will cease to be relevant for all matters falling within the scope of the Regulation. On paper, at least, having a single law will provide for much-needed consistency, although it is anticipated that it will still be interpreted in accordance with national approaches and idiosyncrasies.

Endnotes

1 Council of Europe Recommendation 509 on human rights and modern scientific and technological developments, 31 January 1968.

2 'Details of Treaty No. 108', Council of Europe, www.coe.int/en/web/conventions/full-list/-/conventions/treaty/108.

3 The Council addressed two resolutions to member states on the protection of privacy: (1) Council of Europe Resolution (73) 22 on the protection of the privacy of individuals vis-à-vis electronic data banks in the private sector, 26 September 1973; and (2) Council of Europe Resolution (74) 29 on the protection of the privacy of individuals vis-à-vis electronic data banks in the public sector, 20 September 1974.

4 The Convention, Article 12(2).

5 Proposal for a Council Directive Concerning the Protection of Individuals in Relation to the Processing of Personal Data, COM (90) 314 final —SYN 287, 13.9.1990.

6 Directive, Article 28; Directive, Article 29.

7 'European Commission sets out strategy to strengthen EU data protection rules', European Commission, 4 November 2010, http://europa.eu/rapid/press-release_IP-10-1462_en.htm?locale=en and 'Data protection reform—frequently asked questions', European Commission, 4 November 2010, http://europa.eu/rapid/press-release_MEMO-10-542_en.htm?locale=fr.

8 'Commission proposes a comprehensive reform of data protection rules to increase users' control of their data and to cut costs for businesses', European Commission, 25 January 2012, http://europa.eu/rapid/press-release_IP-12-46_en.htm?locale=en.

9 'Reform of EU data protection rules', European Commission, accessed July 2017, http://ec.europa.eu/justice/data-protection/reform/index_en.htm.

10 See Section 3.6 and Chapter 16 for additional information on cookies and the ePrivacy Directive, soon to be replaced by the ePrivacy Regulation.

11 Council Framework Decision 2008/977/JHA.

12 Directive (EU) 2016/680 of the European Parliament and of the Council of 27 April 2016 on the protection of natural persons with regard to the processing of personal data by competent authorities for the purposes of the prevention, investigation, detection or prosecution of criminal offences or the execution of criminal penalties, and on the free movement of such data, and repealing Council Framework Decision 2008/977/JHA.

13 http://europa.eu/rapid/press-release_IP-15-6321_en.htm.

14 Directive 97/66/EC of the European Parliament and of the Council of 15 December 1997 concerning the processing of personal data and the protection of privacy in the telecommunications sector.

15 Directive 2002/19/EC of the European Parliament and of the Council of 7 March 2002 on access to and interconnection of electronic communications networks and associated facilities (Access Directive); Directive 2002/20/EC of the European Parliament and of the Council of 7 March 2002 on the authorisation of electronic communications networks and services (Authorisation Directive); Directive 2002/21/EC of the European Parliament and the Council of 7 March 2002 on a common regulatory framework for electronic communications networks and services (Framework Directive); Directive 2002/22/EC (Universal Service Directive); and Directive 2002/58/EC (Directive on privacy and electronic communications).

16 Directive, Article 14.

17 Directive 2009/136/EC of 25 November 2009 amending Directive 2002/22/EC on universal service and users' rights relating to electronic communications networks and services; Directive 2002/58/EC concerning the processing of personal data and the protection of privacy in the electronic communications sector and Regulation (EC) No 2006/2004 on cooperation between national authorities responsible for the enforcement of consumer protection laws.

18 Article 4 of the amended Directive. It should be noted, however, that the requirement to notify the individual shall not apply if the 'provider has demonstrated to the satisfaction of the competent authority that it has implemented appropriate technological protection measures, and that those measures were applied to the data concerned by the security breach. Such technological protection measures shall render the data unintelligible to any person who is not authorised to access it'.

19 However, if the use of cookies results in the collection the legally sensitive information (i.e., the 'special categories of data', such as information relating to an individual's health or sex life, racial or ethnic origin or religious beliefs), then explicit consent may be required under general data protection law.

20 Opinion 15/2011 on the definition of consent adopted (01197/11/EN; WP 187), http://ec.europa.eu/justice/policies/privacy/docs/wpdocs/2011/wp187_en.pdf.

21 'ePrivacy Directive: assessment of transposition, effectiveness and compatibility with proposed Data Protection Regulation' (the 'ePrivacy Study'), published by the European Commission on 10/06/2015.

22 'Commission proposes high level of privacy rules for all electronic communications and updates data protection rules for EU institutions', European Commission, 10 January 2017, http://europa.eu/rapid/press-release_IP-17-16_en.htm and 'Digital Single Market—Stronger privacy rules for electronic communications', European Commission, 10 January 2017, http://europa.eu/rapid/press-release_MEMO-17-17_en.htm.

23 CJEU decision in Digital Rights Ireland Ltd. v. Minister for Communications, Marine and Natural Resources C-293/12 joined with Kärnter Landesregierung C-594/12.

24 For example, the Data Protection Act 1998 in the case of the UK; see, for example, Norway's Act of 18 May 2001 No. 24 on Personal Health Data Filing Systems and the Processing of Personal Health Data (Personal Health Data Filing System Act), which relates to processing of health and medical data and supplements the general Act of 14 April 2000 No. 31 and associated 'Personal Data Regulations'.

25 For example, in the case of Poland, the Directive on Privacy and Electronic Communications was implemented via the Act on the Provision of Services by Way of Electronic Means of 18 July 2002, which entered into force on 10 March 2003, and by the Telecommunication Law of 16 July 2004, which entered into force 2 September 2004.

26 'Digital Agenda: Commission refers UK to Court over privacy and personal data protection', European Commission, 30 September 2010, http://europa.eu/rapid/press-release_IP-10-1215_ en.htm.

27 Commission v. Grand Duchy of Luxembourg [2001] Case C-450/00, 4 October 2001.

28 Rechnungshof v. Österreichischer Rundfunk and Others [2003] Case C-465/00, 20 May 2003, in relation to Articles 6(1)(c) (Member states shall provide that personal data must be adequate, relevant and not excessive in relation to the purposes for which they are collected and/or further processed) and Articles 7(c) and (e) (Member states shall provide that personal data may be processed only if processing is necessary for compliance with a legal obligation to which the controller is subject and processing is necessary for the performance of a task carried out in the public interest or in the exercise of official authority vested in the controller or in a third party to whom the data are disclosed).

SECTION II
European Data Protection
Law and Regulation

CHAPTER 4

Data Protection Concepts

Mac Macmillan

4.1 Introduction

Even though data protection law has existed for decades, it is very telling that some of its more fundamental concepts are still under debate. Developments in the field of technology and changes in the way businesses operate often test the flexibility of the definitions of some of the most fundamental data protection concepts. Despite this, the core data protection concepts established by the 1995 Data Protection Directive ('Directive') remain essentially the same in the General Data Protection Regulation (GDPR, or 'Regulation'), with limited amendments to clarify some of the more frequently canvassed issues.

For example, the use of Internet protocol (IP) addresses and cookies to generate profiles about individuals' online behaviour has produced extensive debate about whether IP addresses and cookies are personal data. This issue has been addressed in the new definition of personal data, which expressly includes online identifiers. Another challenge for the core concepts has been the growth of outsourcing and an increase in the level of autonomy of service providers. Despite the question marks over the boundaries between controllers and processors, legislators have decided to leave those definitions unchanged.

This chapter looks at the Regulation's core data protection concepts of personal data, special categories or sensitive personal data, controller, processor and processing.

4.2 Personal data

The concept of personal data is central to data protection law, and its definition is intentionally broad. This has created some challenges of interpretation as technology has evolved. Notwithstanding this, the four building blocks in the definition of personal data which the Article 29 Working Party (WP29) identified in its Opinion on the concept of personal data in June 2007 ('Opinion 4/2007') remain the same in the

Regulation, so the WP29's Opinion remains relevant for understanding the definition of personal data.[1]

The authorities of the European Union aimed for a wide notion of the concept of personal data so as to include all information concerning an identifiable individual. The definition is, on the whole, far broader than that of many U.S. state data breach laws, for example. On that basis, the concept encompasses considerable amounts of information, even where the link between such information and an identifiable individual is tenuous.

Broadly interpreted; tenuous link btwn person + info still PI

The definition of 'personal data' in the Regulation reads as follows:

Art. 4(1)

> *Personal data means any information relating to an identified or identifiable natural person ('data subject'); an identifiable natural person is one who can be identified, directly or indirectly, in particular by reference to an identifier, such as a name, an identification number, location data, an online identifier or to one or more factors specific to the physical, physiological, genetic, mental, economic, cultural or social identity of that natural person.[2]*

Within Opinion 4/2007, the WP29 set out four 'building blocks' that comprise the meaning of personal data. These are:

- 'any information'.
- 'relating to'
- 'an identified or identifiable'
- 'natural person'.

4.2.1 First building block: 'any information'

Three aspects of the concept 'information' help define when information will be considered personal data. These are its nature, content and format.

4.2.1.1 Nature

objective & subjective

Any type of statements about a person, both objective and subjective, may be considered personal data. For example, employment records held by an employer about an employee may include different types of objective and subjective statements. Examples of an objective statement are '[the employee] has a degree in computer science' or '[the employee] is the head of IT'. Subjective statements are those that express someone's opinions or an assessment. An example of a subjective statement is '[the employee] is a good worker and merits promotion'.

doesn't need to be true

Information does not need to be true to be considered personal data.

4.2.1.2 Content

The content of personal data includes any sort of information and it is not limited to information that refers to a narrow interpretation of the individual's private and family life. The Court of Justice of the European Union (CJEU) has established that the concept of private and family life must be widely interpreted.[3] Therefore, personal data includes information about an individual's private life and information regarding any activity undertaken by the individual. This activity may relate to activities in the professional or public sphere as much as in an individual's private life. An individual's contact information at their place of work will be personal data in the same way as their home address or personal phone number. As Recital 30 explains, information that constitutes an online identifier, such as an IP address, cookie or radio frequency tag, may be used to create a person's profile and identify them, demonstrating the breadth of content considered personal data.

[handwritten margin notes: Broad interpretation of the concept of private & family life; Any info: private, public & professional life; Include online identifier cookie, IP Addres]

4.2.1.3 Format

The concept of personal data includes information available in any form. The Regulation expressly applies to information processed by automated means, but Article 2(1) includes processing by manual means as well if 'for part of a filing system'.[4] For example, it includes information kept on paper in a hospital clinic's history, in a computer memory that records someone's electronic bank records, on a tape kept by a travel agent's customer services department that records telephone calls for training purposes, or images recorded on closed-circuit TV. Recital 15 clarifies that the Regulation is intended to be technology neutral but is vague about when a 'filing system' is covered by manual processing.

[handwritten margin notes: Automated means + Manual means if part of a "filing system"; "filing system" not clearly defined]

4.2.2 Second building block: 'relating to'

To be personal data, information must be about an individual. The relationship between the individual and the information is not always easily established. Sometimes, it will not be obvious whether information relates to an individual or not.

Information that relates to objects, processes or events may constitute personal data under certain circumstances. For example, objects may belong to an individual (e.g., an individual owns a car). Information about the value of the car may be personal data if it is considered an asset of the owner to determine whether the owner has the obligation to pay some taxes. Technical information about the car (e.g., about its mileage or number of breakdowns) may also qualify as personal information if processed by the garage for the purpose of issuing the owner's bill.

[handwritten margin notes: Info must be about an "individual."; Under certain circumstances. info about objects, process, events can be personal data.; e.g. value of car for tax purposes; vehicle specs for bill issuance from mechanic]

In Opinion 4/2007, the WP29 also considered that for personal data to relate to an individual, one of the following three elements must apply: the 'content' element, the 'purpose' element or the 'result' element.[5]

The 'content' element is present when the information is about an individual in the most common sense of the word. For example, the result of a test clearly relates to a student. The existence of the 'purpose' element depends on whether the information is processed to evaluate, consider or analyse the individual in a certain way. The 'result' element exists when the processing of certain information has an impact on the individual's rights and interests.

These elements do not need to apply cumulatively. However, the same piece of information may or may not be personal data based on different elements in relation to different individuals.

4.2.3 Third building block: identified or identifiable

In Opinion 4/2007, the WP29 states that a natural person is 'identifiable' when, although the person has not been identified yet, it is possible to do it. A person may be identified directly by name, but they may also be identified indirectly, for example, by an identification number or IP address. Furthermore, a person can be identifiable because 'information combined with other pieces of information, whether the latter is retained by the data controller or not, will allow the individual to be distinguished from others'.[6] An example given by the WP29 is where web traffic surveillance tools make it possible to identify the behaviour of a machine and, behind the machine, its user. On that basis, 'the individual's personality is pieced together in order to attribute certain decisions to him or her'.[7]

The rise of big data, with low storage costs and super-fast processing that enables the collection and piecing together of information, increases the likelihood of this type of jigsaw identification and means the element of identifiability has become an increasing challenge for data controllers. What is the threshold for the possibility of identification? Guidance on this is set out in Recital 26, which states that:

> To determine whether a natural person is identifiable, account should be taken of all the means reasonably likely to be used, such as singling out, either by the controller or by another person to identify the natural person directly or indirectly. To ascertain whether means are reasonably likely to be used to identify the natural person, account should be taken of all objective factors, such as the costs of and the amount of time required for identification, taking into consideration the available technology at the time of the processing and technological developments.

So, a hypothetical possibility of identification is not sufficient to make information identifiable—there must be a reasonable likelihood. The WP29 has recognised that, when the possibility of singling out an individual 'does not exist or is negligible', the person should not be considered as identifiable, and the information is not personal data.[8]

Some controllers have argued that if they are unlikely ever to identify most of the individuals in a data set, that data set will not comprise personal data, although certain elements may become personal data once they are linked to identifiable individuals. A common scenario is the use of closed-circuit television (CCTV), where identification will only happen in a small percentage of the material collected. However, the WP29 has always taken the view that this information must be treated as personal data since the fundamental purpose of the processing is to single out and identify individuals when required: 'to argue that individuals are not identifiable, where the purpose of the processing is precisely to identify them, would be a sheer contradiction in terms'.[9]

Confirming the wide scope of the notion of identifiability, the CJEU has ruled that dynamic IP addresses are capable of constituting personal data under certain circumstances. In Patrick Breyer v. Bundesrepublik Deutschland, the German Federal Court of Justice referred two questions to the CJEU in a case brought by Patrick Breyer, a member of the Pirate Party. He challenged the collection and use of device dynamic IP addresses to allow data on a website to be transferred to the correct recipient, where a new number is assigned to the device for each connection from websites run by the German federal government. The government justified this practice as prevention of crime, particularly denial-of-service attacks.

But the CJEU took the view that dynamic IP addresses could constitute personal data on the grounds that a person could be 'indirectly identified' if the IP addresses were combined with data held by Internet service providers (ISPs), such as the time of connection and the pages visited on the website. The CJEU decided that, in circumstances where a third party holds information likely to be used to identify the website user when put together with the dynamic IP addresses held by the provider of that website, those IP addresses constitute personal data. In this case, the federal government would naturally go to ISPs as a third party to obtain such further information, and German law provided a mechanism through which this could be done legally in the event of a cyberattack, hence creating the likelihood of various bits of information being combined to identify an individual.

One important point of discussion regards the anonymisation of data. The Regulation does not apply to anonymous information, 'namely information which does not relate to an identified or identifiable natural person or to personal data rendered anonymous in such a manner that the data subject is not or no longer identifiable'.[10]

However, for the reasons explained above, complete anonymisation is difficult, particularly within a single organisation. Pseudonymisation provides a middle ground, but whilst pseudonymisation helps to satisfy data minimisation requirements, it does not remove pseudonymised data from an organisation's obligations under the Regulation. Pseudonymisation is defined as:

> the processing of personal data in such a manner that the personal data can no longer be attributed to a specific data subject without the use of additional information, provided that such additional information is kept separately and is subject to technical and organisational measures to ensure that the personal data are not attributed to an identified or identifiable natural person.[11]

If a business wants to analyse its customer database to look at individual behaviour patterns or to discover the characteristics of a typical customer but is not interested in the actual identify of those individuals, it can pseudonymise the data by replacing the obvious identifiers, such as name and email address, with a simple reference number. Staff working on the project will not know who these individuals are, although the company still has the ability to link these individual records, and therefore the conclusions, back to the individuals concerned. On the face of it, the database is anonymised, but in data protection terms, it is only pseudonymised. It is important to recognise that this means it is still personal data and subject to the Regulation. However, the Regulation promotes pseudonymisation as an important safeguard to achieve data minimisation for privacy and acknowledges that the additional protection it provides may be helpful when determining the compatibility of a new purpose with the original purpose of processing.[12]

Aggregation of data for statistical purposes is likely to result in nonpersonal data. However, care should always be taken when anonymising data in this way as context may allow the identification of individuals if the sample size is not sufficiently large.

4.2.4 Fourth building block: 'natural person'

Since the definition of personal data refers simply to 'natural persons', the protection it affords applies to 'natural persons' universally, regardless of their country of residence, subject, of course, to the provisions of Article 3 on territorial scope. The Regulation does not seek to define the concept of a natural person, leaving it to member state legislation. However, Recital 27 states that the Regulation does not apply to the personal data of deceased persons or organisational data, which may be protected through standard contractual confidentiality clauses, although member states may provide for rules in this area.

4.3   Sensitive personal data

The Regulation identifies certain types of personal data as special categories of personal data meriting specific protections, as the nature of these categories means their processing could create significant risks to individuals' fundamental rights and freedoms. These are 'personal data revealing racial or ethnic origin, political opinions, religious or philosophical beliefs, or trade union membership, and the processing of genetic data, biometric data for the purpose of uniquely identifying a natural person, data concerning health or data concerning a natural person's sex life or sexual orientation'.[13]

Genetic data is defined as 'personal data relating to the inherited or acquired genetic characteristics of a natural person which give unique information about the physiology or the health of that natural person and which result, in particular, from an analysis of a biological sample from the natural person in question'.[14] Additional guidance is also given on the meaning of data that relates to health, a phrase clearly meant to be given a broad interpretation. It means personal data 'related to the physical or mental health of a natural person, including the provision of health care services, which reveal information about his or her health status' and includes 'all data pertaining to the health status of a data subject which reveal information relating to the past, current or future physical or mental health status of the data subject', including:[15]

- information about the natural person collected in the course of the registration for, or the provision of, health care services;

- a number, symbol or particular assigned to a natural person to uniquely identify the natural person for health purposes;

- information derived from the testing or examination of a body part or bodily substance, including from genetic data and biological samples; and

- any information on, for example, a disease, disability, disease risk, medical history, clinical treatment, or the physiological or biomedical state of the data subject independent of its source, for example, from a physician or other health professional, a hospital, a medical device or an in vitro diagnostic test.[16]

The recitals also say that the 'processing of photographs should not systematically be considered processing of special categories of personal data as they are covered by the definition of biometric data only when processed through a specific technical means allowing the unique identification or authentication of a natural person'.[17] However, they do not address the point that photographs may also reveal a person's racial origin, religious beliefs or certain physical disabilities, which may be regarded as information about the individual's health status.

4.4 Controller and processor

The concepts of controller and processor were established by the Directive and remain fundamentally similar under the Regulation. This does not mean they are straightforward or mutually exclusive. In practice, the application of these concepts has become increasingly complex owing to the evolving nature of the business environment, the increased sophistication of outsourcing, and the growing tendency of organisations to centralise IT systems. However, they remain key for determining the allocation of legal obligations arising under the Regulation, which is essential for protecting the rights and freedoms of data subjects.[18]

A data controller is the natural or legal person, public authority, agency or any other body which alone or jointly with others determines the purposes and means of the processing of personal data. In other words, the data controller is the key decision maker with regards to personal data. As a result, most of the responsibilities for compliance with the Regulation fall on the data controller's shoulders. For example, the data controller is responsible for providing information to the data subject, ensuring that processing has a legitimate basis and that the data subject's rights are honoured, carrying out data protection impact assessments in the case of high risk processing, ensuring that there is appropriate security for data, and determining whether notification to data protection authorities (DPAs) or data subjects is necessary in case of a personal data breach.

The processor has some obligations under the Regulation (e.g., ensuring its international data transfers comply with the Regulation, having appropriate security in place, and notifying data controllers if there is a data breach), but it remains very much a subordinate figure, required by contract to process personal data only on documented instructions from the controller, who retains most liability under the Regulation. It is evident from this that determining the status of parties processing personal data is a critical issue, since, in most cases, the data controller will be the first target of the enforcement actions of DPAs.

In practice, the key aspect of a controller is the ability to determine the purposes for which personal data is being collected, stored, used, altered and disclosed. In contrast, a processor is a person, other than an employee of the controller, who processes personal data on behalf of a controller.

4.4.1 Concept of controller

The first and foremost role of a data controller is to determine who shall be responsible for compliance with data protection law and how individuals can exercise their rights.

In other words, a controller has the role of allocating responsibility. Because parties can be a controller in one transaction and a processor in another, determining which party is a controller is crucial to assigning primary data protection responsibility and liability. This will also determine which supervisory authority has responsibility for supervising the data processing activity. The location of the controller may also be relevant in cases where the Regulation gives member states discretion to implement additional legislation.

4.4.2 Definition of controller

'Controller' is defined in the Regulation as:

> the natural or legal person, public authority, agency or other body which, alone or jointly with others,[determines the purposes and means of the processing of personal data] where the purposes and means of such processing are determined by Union or Member State law, the controller or the specific criteria for its nomination may be provided for by Union or Member State law.[19]

Therefore, a data controller is defined according to three building blocks:

- the natural or legal person, public authority, agency or any other body

- which alone or jointly with others

- determines the purposes and means of the processing of personal data.

Again, these building blocks are the same as under the Directive, so there is the benefit of an Opinion from the WP29 to assist in their interpretation.[20]

4.4.3 First building block: 'natural person, legal person or any other body'

A data controller may be a legal or a natural person. Opinion 1/2010 recommends that, despite the broad nature of the definition of who may be a data controller, 'preference should be given to consider the controller to be the company or body as such' rather than an individual appointed by the company or body.[21] This is so that data subjects may exercise their rights before a more reliable entity.

When an individual within an organisation or body (i.e., a legal entity) is appointed by an organisation to ensure compliance with data protection law or to process personal data, this appointment will not turn this person into the data controller because, in carrying out this role, they will act on behalf of the legal entity. This, of course, will not be the case if the individual processes the personal data outside the scope and control of the data controller.

[handwritten margin notes:] preferably the company vs individual

Individual right exercised before more reliable body:

Individual appointed (DPO) not controller if act on behalf of org.

4.4.4 Second building block: 'alone or jointly with others'

Different organisations, bodies or 'natural persons' may be data controllers of the same set of personal data. Opinion 1/2010 identifies that the complexity of the realities of data processing means that 'jointly' may be interpreted both as 'together with' or 'not alone'.[22] Joint processing does not necessarily need to occur at the same time or be equal in proportion.

Different organisations may be controllers of the same set of personal data. This does not mean they will always be joint data controllers. It will depend on how the data is passed between them. For example, if a person books a holiday via a travel agent, and the travel agent forwards that person's details to their chosen airline and hotel, the airline and hotel are holding identical data but separately and for distinct purposes. They will each determine how long they hold that data for and whether they use it to provide the individuals with special offers without involving the other two entities. The airline and hotel are not joint controllers; however, if they agree to set up a shared website with the travel agent, where holiday bookings are entered directly into a shared database, and the parties carry out integrated marketing activities, they are likely to be joint controllers.

Another common situation where joint controllership may arise is within corporate groups. A parent company may provide centralised IT services to its subsidiaries, including centralised databases for employee or customer records. Each subsidiary remains a controller for the data of its employees and customers as the data is held for the purposes of its business. If the parent company conducts its own independent operations on the data, for example, to compare the rates of employee turnover across the group, it may become a joint controller with its subsidiaries.

There are numerous forms of joint control. Intra-group scenarios may be particularly complex because employees often think in terms of the purposes of the corporate group as a whole without focusing on the dividing lines between the legal entities which make up the group, and there is a risk that de facto joint controllerships may evolve over time. The Regulation makes clear that joint controllers must determine their respective responsibilities for compliance with the Regulation in a transparent manner, placing on a statutory footing the WP29's statement that 'the bottom line should be ensuring that even in complex data processing environments … compliance with data protection rules and responsibilities for possible breach of these rules are clearly allocated'.[23] A concrete example of where this might apply is the responsibility to issue fair processing notices to data subjects. Where only one of the joint controllers has a direct relationship with the data subject, it will be logical for that controller to take responsibility for issuing the relevant information on behalf of all the controllers. To further protect individuals, the joint controllers are required to make 'the essence of the arrangement' available to the data subject. The data subject may exercise their rights under the Regulation in respect of and against each of the controllers.[24]

[handwritten margin notes: The essence of the arrangement must be made available to data subjects. Art 26(2)
Individual rights enforceable against each controller regardless of the arrangement Art. 26(3)]

4.4.5 Third building block: 'determination of the purposes and means of the processing of personal data'

In reality, the central aspect of the definition of controller is whether an entity 'determines' the purposes and means of the processing. Indeed, Article 28(10) says that if a processor infringes the Regulation by determining the purposes and means of processing, the processor will be considered to be a controller with respect to that processing. This demonstrates another key aspect of the definition that, whilst legal context may be relevant in identifying the controller, the <u>factual elements</u> or <u>circumstances</u> are likely to be decisive. Why is the processing taking place? Who has initiated it? The contractual designation of the parties' roles is not decisive in determining the actual status of the parties under data protection law if it differs from what is happening in practice.

[handwritten margin notes: Key: determining the purpose & means of processing: processor who does such act will be deemed controller; Art 28(10)
Facts over legal element in determining controller status; factual influence]*

The WP29 favours a pragmatic outlook when trying to work out which party is the controller, keeping in mind that the concept of the data controller is a functional one, intended to allocate responsibilities where the factual influence is. Opinion 1/2010 comments that 'the need to ensure effectiveness requires that a pragmatic approach is taken with a view to ensure predictability with regard to control. In this regard, rules of thumb and practical presumptions are needed to guide and simplify the application of data protection law'.[25]

This heralds a less legalistic and more commercially friendly approach to dealing with what can be complicated networks of data processing arrangements.

4.4.6 Identifying the source of control

Opinion 1/2010 sets out a number of circumstances where a controller can be identified by the source of control:

Control stemming from *explicit legal competence*	Explicit appointment of a controller under national or community law. More typically, the law establishes a task or imposes a duty on someone to collect data.
Control stemming from *implicit competence*	Control stems from common legal provisions or established legal practice (e.g., an employer with employee data). The capacity to determine processing activities can be considered to be naturally attached to the functional role of an organisation.
Control stemming from *factual influence*	Responsibility as controller is attributed on the basis of an assessment of the factual circumstances. Where the matter is not clear, an assessment should consider the degree of actual control exercised by a party, the impression given to individuals and the reasonable expectations of individuals on the basis of this visibility.

Handwritten margin notes:
Explicit legal competence: law imposes duty
Implicit legal competence: employer w/ employee data
Factual influence: degree of control exercised, impression given to individuals, reasonable expectations

4.4.7 Determining purposes and means of processing

The controller determines the purposes and means of processing—that is, the why and how of a processing activity. Consider, for example, a company deciding which cloud service provider to use as a database for storing customer information. The company is the controller, and the cloud service database provider is the processor.

In an assessment, it is crucial to consider whether the level of detail involved in making the determination of 'the purposes and means' of processing meets the threshold for that person to be considered a controller. Opinion 1/2010 follows a pragmatic approach for complex situations, outlining the questions to ask in order to arrive at a reasonable conclusion: Why is the processing happening, and what is the role of those parties involved in the processing? The Opinion allows that 'a processor could operate further to general guidance provided mainly on purposes and not go very deep into the details with regard to means'.[26] In other words, a processor could have some discretion as to how it carries out the processing on behalf of the controller without itself becoming a controller. But this outcome is possible only if the processor can point to another party who is responsible for the overall processing.

In considering the original proposal for the definition of a controller's role under European law, Opinion 1/2010 affirms that 'means' does not refer only to the technical ways of processing personal data but also to the 'how' of processing, which includes questions regarding which data shall be processed, which third parties shall have

Handwritten margin notes:
Processors can have discretion re: non-essential means (i.e. 'how' of processing) w/o becoming a controller, e.g. technical & organizational decisions. General instructions from controller may be ok.

access to this data and when data shall be deleted.[27] For example, does the cloud-based customer database provider use the stored data for any purposes other than to serve the controller? If the relationship ends, what assurances does the controller have that the customer information will be deleted?

Certain technical and organisational decisions can be delegated to a processor. For instance, the processor can advise on what type of software to use. Opinion 1/2010 goes on to say that 'while determining the purpose of the processing would in any case trigger the qualification as controller, determining the means would imply control only when the determination concerns the essential elements of the means'.[28]

The 'essential elements of the means' point to decisions at the crux of the processing. A controller may delegate decisions about the technical and organisational aspects of the processing to the processor provided it reserves the most important determinations of purposes or means to itself. Of course, the controller should still be fully informed about the means used to achieve the data processing purpose, but, more importantly, 'substantial questions which are essential to the core of lawfulness of processing are reserved to the controller'.[29] For instance, a person who decides how long data shall be stored or which other parties have access to the data is acting as a controller.

[handwritten margin note: Essential elements of the means: factors that go to the core of lawfulness of processing; e.g. period of detention; reserved for controllers]

4.4.8 Concept of processor

A processor may be more closely involved in the processing of personal data but does not have the authority to allocate responsibility that a controller has. In some cases, the mechanics of processing (i.e., the means) may be determined entirely by the service provider (e.g., a pension scheme administrator or a cloud provider offering infrastructure as a service), but it remains a processor so long as the overall purposes are still determined by its client.

[handwritten margin note: processor: Not allocating responsibility; process pd o/b/o controller]

4.4.9 Definition of processor

The Regulation defines a processor as 'a natural or legal person, public authority, agency or other body which processes personal data on behalf of the controller'.[30]

There are therefore two building blocks that must be present for a person to be a data processor:

- The person is a separate legal entity with respect to the controller.
- The person processes personal data on behalf of the controller.

[handwritten margin note: Two factors ① Separate legal entity ② Process PP o/b/o controller]

The existence of a data processor depends upon a decision by the controller to delegate all or part of a processing activity to an external organisation or individual.

The role of a processor stems from the organisation's 'concrete activities in a specific context'.[31]

The controller can delegate the determination of the means of processing to a processor, as far as technical or organisational questions are concerned. This division is reflected in the obligations which the Regulation imposes directly on processors: security, recording-keeping, notifying controllers of data breaches and ensuring they comply with the restrictions on international data transfers set out in Chapter V of the Regulation. This recognises that processors frequently have a very wide degree of discretion in how they carry out their duties, but these obligations all relate to the 'how'. Obligations relating to purpose, such as ensuring processing has a lawful ground and respecting data subjects' rights, are only imposed on the data controller.

Further recognition of this comes in Article 28(10). A processor who goes beyond their mandate and decides on the purposes of the processing or the essential means of the processing (e.g., if the pension scheme administrator decided to use details of pension scheme members to market its other financial products to them) shall be considered to be a controller in respect of that processing. This is significant because it immediately increases the scope of the supposed processor's obligations under the Regulation, and hence its potential liability for its activities.

The Regulation requires that the processor processes personal data only on the controller's instructions and that a contract or a binding legal act regulating the relations between the controller and the processor be put in writing. The contract must expressly set out the nature and purpose of any data processing, the type of personal data and the categories of data subjects. It is likely that controllers using non–European Economic Area (EEA) processors will need to explain this requirement because previously many cloud providers have presented themselves as a neutral platform provider with no knowledge of or interest in knowing what is being hosted on their platform. Article 28 sets out further detailed content for the processing contract, which must stipulate that the processor shall:

- process the personal data only on documented instructions from the controller, including with regards to transfers of data outside the EEA;

- ensure that persons authorised to process the personal data have committed themselves to confidentiality or are under an appropriate statutory obligation of confidentiality;

- take all measures pursuant to Article 32 on security of processing;

- respect the conditions for enlisting another processor;

- assist the controller by appropriate technical and organisational measures for the fulfilment of the controller's obligation to respond to requests to exercise data subjects' rights;

  [handwritten: ⑦ Assist controller w/ DS rights re: tech & org measures]

- assist the controller in complying with the obligations in Articles 32–36 (security, data protection impact assessments and breach notification), taking into account the nature of the processing;

  [handwritten: ⑧ Assist controller w/ security, DPIA, & breach notification]

- at the choice of the controller, delete or return all personal data to the controller after the end of the provision of data processing services; and

  [handwritten: ⑨ delete/return PD @ the end of processing services]

- make available to the controller all information necessary to demonstrate compliance with the obligations laid down in Article 28 and allow for and contribute to audits, including inspections, conducted by the controller or another auditor mandated by the controller.

  [handwritten: ⑩ Make info available for compliance audit/inspection & to cooperate w/ audit/inspection]

The fact that the service provider prepares the terms of the contract does not, in itself, imply that it is a controller.

[handwritten: preparing terms ≠ controller]

The complex structures of modern outsourcing may mean that a controller subcontracts processing operations to more than one processor or a data processor subcontracts the processing operations totally or partially to two or more subcontractors ('multilayered subcontracting'). Article 28 regulates this possibility by requiring that:

[handwritten: Art. 28 Subcontracting]

i.   a processor may not engage another processor without prior authorisation of the data controller. This authorisation may be general or specific. If it is general, the processor is required to give the controller an opportunity to object to the addition or replacement of other processors; [32]

  [handwritten: ① Prior authorization required; can be general or specific; if general, must give controller opp. to object]

ii.   the contract between the initial processor and its sub-processors must include the mandatory provisions set out above; [33] and

  [handwritten: ② Cascade down obligations to subcontractors]

iii. the initial processor remains fully liable to the controller for the performance of its sub-processors. [34]

  [handwritten: ③ Initial processor liable for subcontractor performance]

4.4.10 Factors to consider when distinguishing the roles of data controller and data processor

Opinion 1/2010 sets out the following criteria to help determine the roles of the parties:

- Level of prior instruction given by the controller, which determines the degree of independent judgment the processor can exercise.

  [handwritten: Factors to consider ① Level of prior instruction; degree of independent judgment]

- Monitoring by the controller of the execution of the service—closer monitoring by a controller suggests that it is in full and sole control of the processing.

- Visibility/image portrayed by the controller to the individual and expectations of the individual on the basis of this visibility.

- Expertise of the parties—the greater the expertise of the service provider relative to that of its customer, the greater the likelihood that it will be classified as a controller.

4.5 Processing

Processing is defined by the Regulation as follows:

> *any operation or set of operations which is performed on personal data or on sets of personal data, whether or not by automated means, such as collection, recording, organisation, structuring, storage, adaptation or alteration, retrieval, consultation, use, disclosure by transmission, dissemination or otherwise making available, alignment or combination, restriction, erasure or destruction.*[35]

This broad definition makes it difficult to identify uses involving personal data that would not amount to 'processing' as defined by the Regulation. However, Article 2(1) of the Regulation, by defining the scope of its application, establishes limitations to the processing of personal data that will fall within the meaning of the Regulation. According to Article 2, the following conditions must apply for the processing of personal data to be covered by the Regulation: (1) the processing must be wholly or partly carried out by automated means; or (2) where the processing is not by automated means, it must concern personal data that forms part of a filing system or is intended to form part of a filing system. A filing system refers to a structured set of personal data that is accessible according to specific criteria.

4.6 Data subject

It may seem surprising that such a key concept as 'data subject' does not get a definition in its own right, but it does not. Instead, it is defined parenthetically within the definition of personal data, which refers to 'an identified or identifiable natural person' as being a data subject.[36]

Recital 14 makes clear that the protection of the Regulation does not extend to legal entities:

> *The protection afforded by this Regulation should apply to natural persons, whatever their nationality or place of residence, in relation to the processing of their personal data. This Regulation does not cover the processing of personal data which concerns legal persons and in particular undertakings established as legal persons, including the name and the form of the legal person and the contact details of the legal person.*

Deceased persons, as natural persons, may constitute data subjects, but the Regulation itself does not apply to the personal data of deceased persons, although member states may provide for rules in this area.[37]

4.7   Conclusion

Knowing the Regulation's fundamental concepts will help organisations determine whether they are subject to its provisions in any given instance, what role they are playing in a transaction (controller or processor), and where to look for additional guidance on Regulation compliance.

Endnotes

1 Opinion 4/2007 on the concept of personal data (01248/07/EN: WP 136), http://ec.europa.eu/justice/data-protection/article-29/documentation/opinion-recommendation/files/2007/wp136_en.pdf.

2 Article 4(1) of the Regulation (EU) 2016/679 of the European Parliament and of the Council of 27 April 2016 on the protection of natural persons with regard to the processing of personal data and on the free movement of such data, and repealing Directive 95/46/EC (General Data Protection Regulation, or 'Regulation').

3 Judgment of the European Court of Human Rights in the case Amann v. Switzerland of 16.2.2000.

4 General Data Protection Regulation, Article 2.

5 WP 136, Section III, Part 2, page 10.

6 WP 136, Section III, Part 3, page 13.

7 Ibid., page 14.

8 WP 136, Section III, page 15.

9 WP4/2007, Section III, Part 3, page 16.

10 General Data Protection Regulation, Recital 26.

11 General Data Protection Regulation, Article 4(5).

12 General Data Protection Regulation, Article 6(4)(e).

13 General Data Protection Regulation, Article 9(1).

14 General Data Protection Regulation, Recital 34.

15 General Data Protection Regulation, Article 4(15).

16 General Data Protection Regulation, Recital 35.

17 General Data Protection Regulation, Recital 51.

18 General Data Protection Regulation, Recital 79.

19 General Data Protection Regulation, Article 4(7).

20 WP 169, Opinion 1/2010 on the concepts of 'controller' and 'processor'.

21 WP 169, Section III 1(c).

22 WP 169, Section III, 1(d).

23 General Data Protection Regulation, Article 26(1); WP 169 Opinion 1/2010 on the concepts of 'controller' and 'processor'.

24 General Data Protection Regulation, Article 26(3).

25 WP 169, Opinion 1/2010 on the concepts of 'controller' and 'processor'.

26 WP 169, Section III, 1(b).

27 Ibid.

28 Ibid.

29 Ibid.

30 GDPR Article 4(8).

31 WP 169, Section III, 2.

32 General Data Protection Regulation, Article 28(2).

33 Regulation 28(4).

34 Ibid.

35 General Data Protection Regulation, Article 4(2).

36 General Data Protection Regulation, Article 4(1).

37 General Data Protection Regulation, Recital 27.

CHAPTER 5

Territorial and Material Scope of the General Data Protection Regulation

Ruth Boardman

5.1 Introduction *Territorial Scope & Material Scope*

This chapter concerns:

- The territorial scope of the General Data Protection Regulation (GDPR, or 'Regulation')—i.e., the application of the Regulation to organisations established in the EU and its application on an extraterritorial basis and pursuant to public international law.

- Its material scope: The GDPR has a broad scope, but there are types of processing to which it does not apply (e.g., processing for domestic purposes, or processing which is regulated by another EU data protection law, such as Regulation 45/2001, which applies to the processing of personal data by EU institutions).

5.2 Territorial scope

The Regulation applies:

- to EU-established organisations (see Section 5.2.1); and *EU established or offer*
- on a long-arm, extraterritorial basis to organisations which offer to sell goods or *goods/services* services to or who monitor individuals in the EU (see Section 5.2.2). *to or monitor individuals in EU*

5.2.1 Article 3(1): EU 'established' controllers and processors

5.2.1.1 The concept of establishment

Article 3(1) of the Regulation provides that it:

> applies to the processing of personal data in the context of the activities of an establishment of a controller or a processor in the Union, regardless of whether the processing takes place in the Union or not.

The first question is, therefore, whether an organisation has an 'establishment' in the EU within the meaning of Article 3(1).

There is no definition of 'establishment' in the Regulation; however, Recital 22 gives the term a broad meaning:

> *establishment implies the effective and real exercise of activity through stable arrangements. The legal form of such arrangements, whether through a branch or a subsidiary with a legal personality, is not the determining factor in that respect.*

The Article 29 Working Party (WP29) considered territorial scope (albeit in the context of Article 4(1)(a) of the Data Protection Directive) in Opinion WP 179[1] (adopted in 2010 and updated, following Costeja[2] in 2015). The Opinion notes that the concept of 'establishment' reflects earlier Court of Justice of the European Union (CJEU) case law.[3] This results in a broad concept of 'establishment'. The test is whether necessary human and technical resources are available, not just where an entity is incorporated.[4] A single server would not, however, be enough.

'Establishment', as used in the Directive, was considered by the CJEU in Weltimmo v. NAIH.[5] Weltimmo ran a website advertising properties. Weltimmo was incorporated in Slovakia. However, its website targeted the Hungarian market—advertising Hungarian properties and being written in Hungarian. The first month of advertising was free but thereafter was chargeable. Individuals in Hungary complained to the Hungarian data protection authority (DPA) that Weltimmo had not actioned requests to remove their properties from the site, leading to the individuals incurring charges. The Hungarian authority took action against Weltimmo, which argued that Hungarian law did not apply and that instead this should be a matter for the Slovakian DPA.

The CJEU confirmed that establishment is a 'broad' and 'flexible' phrase that should not depend on legal form. An organisation may be established where it exercises 'through stable arrangements in the territory of that member state, a real and effective activity even a minimal one'.[6] The presence of a single representative may be sufficient to satisfy there being an establishment. In that case, Weltimmo was considered to be established in Hungary notwithstanding that it was incorporated in Slovakia. The relevant factors taken into account by the CJEU in coming to the decision were:

- Weltimmo's website was mainly or entirely directed at Hungary—as evidenced by the fact that it concerned properties situated in Hungary and was written in Hungarian.

- Weltimmo had a representative in Hungary, who represented Weltimmo in administrative and judicial proceedings.

- Weltimmo had opened a **bank account in Hungary**, intended for the recovery of its debts.

  — Bank acct in Hungary

- Weltimmo used a **letter box in Hungary** for the management of its everyday business affairs.

  — Letter box in Hungary for day to day mgmt of business

- However, the nationality of the data subject was irrelevant.*

  Nationality of DS irrelevant

5.2.1.2 'In the context of the activities'

The second question to be answered is whether the processing of personal data at issue is carried out 'in the context of the activities' of the establishment. Where this is the case, then the Regulation will apply 'regardless of whether the processing takes place in the Union or not'.

"In the context of the activities" then location of processing irrelevant

In **Google Spain SL v. AEPD**, the CJEU held that the phrase 'in the context of the activities' in the Directive **should not be interpreted restrictively**, given the objective of the Data Protection Directive ('Directive') was to ensure the effective protection of the fundamental rights and freedoms of natural persons and, in particular, their right to privacy.[7]

Google Spain vs. AEPD : Broad interpretn

In that case, which concerned a request from a Spanish citizen requiring Google not display certain information that related to him in response to a search against his name, it was found the activities of Google Spain SL in **promoting and selling** advertising space in Spain on behalf of Google Inc. were sufficient to satisfy Article 4(1)(a) of the Directive. This was the case **notwithstanding** that Google Spain SL was not itself involved with the functionalities of the search engine and, thus, the actual processing of the data. The CJEU held there was **sufficient connection** between the activities of Google Spain SL and the search engine's data processing activities that '… the activities … in [Spain] … are **inextricably linked** since the activities relating to the **advertising** space constitute the **means** of rendering the search engine … **economically profitable** and that engine is, at the same time, the means enabling those activities to be performed'.[8]

Google Spain sells ad g/b/o Google Inc: not involved in actual processing. CJEU: activities in Spain & processing

"inextricably linked" b/c ad makes money for SE. thus enable processing to be performed

Updated Opinion WP 179 of the WP29 considers this 'inextricable link' concept. The WP29 notes that it **should not be stretched too far**: Being part of the same corporate group is not of itself sufficient to establish that there is an 'inextricable link' between entities.

WP29 : endorses "Inextricable link" concept

Conversely, the WP29 also notes that the decision is not just specific to a search context: Any organisation that has EU sales offices, which promote or sell advertising or marketing, or which target individuals in the EU, will fall within the scope of

— Being part of same corp group not sufficient in itself

— Not specific to SE

Article 3(1). They suggest it would also extend to overseas companies with EU offices which market EU services paid for by membership fees or subscriptions.[9]

5.2.1.3 'Or a processor'

[handwritten margin note: WP29: overseas companies w/ EU offices which market EU services paid for by membership fees & subscriptions]

Article 4(1)(a) of the Directive required each member state to apply its law to the processing of personal data carried out in the context of activities of a controller. Article 3(1) of the Regulation applies to the processing of personal data in the context of the activities of an establishment of a controller or a processor in the EU. As mentioned above, the GDPR also applies whether the processing takes place in the EU or not.

[handwritten margin note: Processing by Processor w/ EU establishment regardless of Controller's location & location of processing]

As discussed more fully in Chapter 4, not all the provisions in the GDPR apply to processors. However, the effect of this provision is still very broad and would appear to apply to data processing where the data processor has an EU establishment notwithstanding that the data controller, data subject and data processing are all located/taking place outside the EU. For example, an IT services company headquartered in Germany may enter into global services agreements with international clients to provide employee data processing services. If the global agreement is entered into by the German entity, then all processing carried out pursuant to the contract would seem to be carried out 'in the context of the activities of' the German entity. Say that the German entity entered into an agreement with a U.S. client to process U.S. employee data in the U.S.; then, this would seem to result in this data being subject to EU data security and data transfer rules.

5.2.1.4 'In the context of the activities' is no longer explicitly used to determine which, of several, member state laws should apply

Article 4(1)(a) of the Directive stated that 'where the same controller is established on the territory of several member states, he must take the necessary measures to ensure that each of these establishments complies with the obligations laid down by the national law applicable'. Opinion WP 179 considered that this provision, taken together with the requirement that processing be carried out 'in the context of the activities' of an establishment, could mean that processing by local establishments would be subject to the law of the local establishment or to the law of another establishment, dependent on the facts.

Organisations have sometimes sought to designate one of their EU establishments as the relevant controller and to argue that EU-related processing is only being carried out in the context of the activities of this establishment so that the law of only this member state will be applicable.

This provision does not appear in the GDPR. The GDPR will achieve more harmonisation so this and the consistency mechanism (see Chapter 13) should reduce variation of approach between member states and hence the need for a mechanism to determine which member state law should prevail. However, the GDPR does still allow for significant member state variation—especially but not only in relation to the special processing situations described in Chapter 9 of the Regulation. In relation to freedom of expression, Recital 153 notes that 'where such exemptions or derogations differ from one Member State to another, the law of the Member State to which the controller is subject should apply'.

If a controller is established in more than one member state, presumably the courts and DPAs would still turn to the concept of the 'context of the activities of an establishment of a controller...' to determine which member state's laws apply. The CJEU considered this in the context of e-commerce in the case of VKI v. Amazon.pdf.[10] Amazon's Luxembourg incorporated company i.a. manages the group's .de websites and enters into contracts with consumers, using these websites. These sites are used by Austrian consumers, as well as German consumers. Amazon has no presence in Austria. It does have an entity incorporated in Germany.

Amazon asserted that processing of personal data in connection with the sites was subject to Luxembourg data protection law (rather than German or Austrian law).[11] The CJEU confirmed that the fact that a company has a website which is accessible from a member state (here, Austria) is not sufficient to make it 'established' there. The CJEU also noted that whether processing is carried out 'in the context of the activities of' a particular establishment, is a question which should be determined by the national referring court. In this case, it would be for the Austrian referring court to determine this question—in particular, processing was carried out in the context of the activities of Amazon's Luxembourg or German entities.

5.2.2 Non-EU 'established' organisations (Article 3(2))

Article 3(2) provides that the Regulation:

> 'applies to the processing of personal data of data subjects who are in the Union by a controller or processor not established in the Union, where the processing activities are related to:
>
> (a) the offering of goods or services, irrespective of whether a payment of the data subject is required, to such data subjects in the Union; or
>
> (b) the monitoring of their behaviour as far as their behaviour takes place within the Union'.

It is not clear how 'data subjects who are in the Union' will be interpreted, and it should not be assumed that EU residency is a prerequisite.

5.2.2.1 Targeting EU data subjects

Under Article 3(2)(a), non-EU established organisations will be subject to the Regulation where they process personal data about EU data subjects in connection with the offer of goods or services to EU data subjects. Payment by the data subject is not required.

Recital 23 provides that, in determining whether an organisation is offering goods or services to data subjects who are in the EU, it should be ascertained whether it is 'apparent that the controller or processor envisages offering services to data subjects in one or more Member States in the Union'.[12] It is not clear whether non-EU organisations that offer goods and services to EU businesses, as opposed to individuals, will fall within the scope of Article 3(2)(a).

It follows that an organisation which inadvertently sells to an individual in the EU will not necessarily be subject to the GDPR: the term 'envisages' suggests some degree of intent or awareness, and 'apparent' that there should be external evidence of this intent.

Recital 23 gives examples of actions that will or will not suggest this. The mere accessibility of a website from within the EU is not sufficient to satisfy Article 3(2)(a), nor are mere contact addresses accessible from the EU or the use of the same language as used in the controller's home country. Relevant factors will include:

- the use of an EU language;
- the display of prices in EU currency;
- the ability to place orders in EU languages; and
- reference to EU users or customers.

The CJEU has examined when an activity will be considered 'directed' to an EU member state in a separate context under the Brussels I Regulation governing 'jurisdiction … in civil and commercial matters'.[13] Its comments are likely to aid interpretation of Article 3(2)(a) of the Regulation.

The Brussels I Regulation allows consumers to bring proceedings against sellers in the member state where the consumer is domiciled rather than the member state where the business is based if the business has directed activities to the consumer's member state. According to the CJEU, in considering whether goods or services are targeted to an EU member state, consideration will be given to:

> whether, before the conclusion of any contract with the consumer, it is apparent from those websites and the trader's overall activity that the trader was envisaging doing business with consumers domiciled in one or more Member States, including

the Member State of that consumer's domicile, in the sense that it was minded to conclude a contract with them[14]

In addition to the considerations mentioned above, the CJEU notes that an intention to target EU customers may be shown by (1) 'patent' evidence, such as the payment of money to a search engine to facilitate access by those within a member state or where targeted member states are designated by name; and (2) other factors—possibly in combination with each other—including:

① the 'international nature' of the relevant activity (e.g., tourist activities);

②. mentions of telephone numbers with an international code;

③. use of a top-level domain name other than that of the state in which the trader is established (e.g., a U.S. organisation acquiring .de or .eu);

④. the description of 'itineraries … from Member States to the place where the service is provided'; and

⑤. mentions of an 'international clientele composed of customers domiciled in various Member States'.

This list is not exhaustive and the question should be determined on a case-by-case basis.[15]

5.2.2.2 Monitoring of behaviour

Non-EU organisations who monitor (i.e., profile) EU individuals will also be subject to the Regulation provided the behaviour being monitored occurs within the EU.

According to Recital 24, 'monitoring' specifically includes the tracking of individuals online to create profiles, including where this is used to make decisions particularly concerning them or for analysing or predicting their personal preferences, behaviours and attitudes.[16] E-commerce companies and ad tech networks, amongst others, will be caught by Article 3(2)(b).

Under the Directive, organisations that target EU data subjects but with no EU establishments only had to comply with EU rules if they also made use of 'equipment' in the EU to process personal data. This led national supervisory authorities which were seeking to assert jurisdiction, to develop arguments that the placing of a cookie, or to request users to fill in forms would amount to the use of 'equipment' in the EU within the meaning of Article 4(1)(c) of the Directive. Article 3(2) now makes it easier to demonstrate that EU law applies to non EU established organisations, regardless of the 'equipment' limitation.

5.2.3 Public international law (Article 3(3))

[handwritten margin note: Processing in place where EU applies by virtue of public Intl law; embassies & airplanes]

Article 3(3) states the Regulation will apply where 'the processing of personal data [is] by a controller not established in the Union, but in a place where Member State law applies by virtue of public international law'.

Article 3(3) is intended to cover, for example, embassies and consulates of EU member states or airplanes and ships to which the Regulation applies by virtue of international treaties. In general terms, embassies and consulates are not subject to the law of the state in which they are situated but the law of the state which they represent.[17] It has little practical significance for data controllers in commercial and business contexts and is therefore not examined further in this chapter.

5.3 Material scope of regulation

Certain activities fall entirely outside the Regulation's scope.

5.3.1 Matters outside the scope of EU law (Article 2(2)(a) and Article 2(2)(b))

[handwritten margin note: Processing concerning public security, defense, national security outside of scope of EU law]

Article 2(2)(a) states that the Regulation does not apply to the processing of personal data 'in the course of an activity which falls outside the scope of Union law'.

This covers processing operations that concern public security, defence and national security.

Article 2(2)(b) states the Regulation does not apply to the processing of personal data 'by the Member State when carrying out activities which fall within the scope of Chapter 2 of Title V of the Treaty on the European Union'.

This includes activities in relation to the common foreign and security policy of the EU. Personal data initially collected for commercial purposes but subsequently used for security purposes may fall within these exemptions.[18]

[handwritten note: Processing by member state activity under member treaty ⇒ Common foreign & security policy of the EU]

5.3.2 Household exemption (Article 2(2)(c))

[handwritten margin note: Household Exemption: processing related to purely personal or household activity by natural person;]

Also exempt is data processing by 'a natural person in the course of a purely personal or household activity'. This would include, for example, correspondence and the holding of address books even if they incidentally concern or may concern the private life of other persons provided their use is for personal purposes and not connected to professional or business activities. The Regulation will apply to controllers or processors which provide the means for processing personal data for such personal or household activities.[19]

[handwritten note: controller/processor who provides means for such processing still covered by GDPR]

In an extension from the corresponding exemption in the Directive, Recital 18 of the Regulation notes social networking and online activities used for social and domestic purposes will also be covered by Article 2(2)(c).

This represents a possible widening of CJEU case law on the equivalent exemption in Article 3(2) of the Directive. In Lindqvist, the CJEU considered whether publication by Mrs Lindqvist on her personal website of information relating to individuals she worked with on a voluntary basis in her parish church fell within the household exemption.[20] The CJEU held that Mrs Lindqvist could not rely on Article 3(2) on the basis the exemption was confined to activities 'carried out in the course of a private or family life of individuals, which is clearly not the case when the processing consisted of publication on the Internet so that those data are made accessible to an indefinite number of "people"'.[21]

Such restricted interpretation of the household exemption has been criticised by the WP29 as 'unrealistically narrow in scope', given the changes in technology so that the types of data processing undertaken by private persons now bear little relation to those which were undertaken when the Directive was adopted.[22]

It is not clear to what extent the reference to social networking and online activities in Recital 18 will expand the exemption under the Regulation, particularly as the language of Article 2(3) itself has not changed from the Directive and as the WP29 statement still notes that publication of information to the world at large, by comparison to a narrower group of friends, may be a factor in the applicability of the exemption.[23]

In a different context, in Ryneš, the CJEU also held that the household exemption in Article 3(2) of the Directive should be narrowly construed.[24] The case involved use of a security camera for a private residence that captured images of a public footpath outside the home. In that case, the processing of personal data for the purposes of domestic closed-circuit television (CCTV) was not, in the opinion of the CJEU, 'a purely' personal or household activity in contrast with correspondence and the keeping of an address book.[25]

③ 5.3.3 Prevention, detection and prosecution of criminal penalties (Article 2(2)(d))

Article 2(2)(d) of the Regulation exempts processing of personal data 'by competent authorities for the purposes of the prevention, investigation, detection or prosecution of criminal offences or the execution of criminal penalties, including the safeguarding against and the prevention of threats to public security'.

The legislative gap arising from this exemption is filled by the Law Enforcement Data Protection Directive (LEDP Directive), which will come into force at the same time as the Regulation.

The LEDP Directive relates to personal data processed for the purposes of prevention, detection, investigation or prosecution of criminal offences and related judicial activities not covered by the Regulation. The LEDP Directive applies to entities that are 'competent authorities'. 'Competent authority' is defined as:

(a) any public authority competent for the prevention, investigation, detection or prosecution of criminal offences or the execution of criminal penalties, including the safeguarding against and the prevention of threats to public security; or

(b) any other body or entity entrusted by Member State law to exercise public authority and public powers for the purposes of the prevention, investigation, detection or prosecution of criminal offences or the execution of criminal penalties, including the safeguarding against and the prevention of threats to public security.[26]

This definition would include, for example, the police, prosecution authorities, courts and offender support services.

Where competent authorities process personal data for purposes other than the purposes of the LEDP Directive, the Regulation will apply unless the processing is carried out pursuant to an activity which falls outside the scope of European Union law (e.g., national security).[27] A competent authority can therefore be subject to both the Regulation and the LEDP Directive, including in respect of the same data where it is processed for different purposes.

What happens if a competent authority transfers data to a body which is not covered by the LEDP Directive or if a competent authority transfers the data to another competent authority but for purposes which fall outside the LEDP Directive? In these scenarios, the Regulation applies.[28]

Similarly a processor who processes personal data on behalf of a competent authority within the scope of the LEDP Directive will be bound by the provisions applicable to processors pursuant to the LEDP Directive but will be subject to the Regulation for processing activities outside the scope of the LEDP Directive.[29] It is therefore important that processors can identify when they are processing for a customer who is a competent authority within the meaning of the LEDP Directive in order to ascertain which legislative framework applies.

5.3.4 EU institutions (Article 2(3))

EU institutions, bodies, offices and agencies are not covered by the Regulation. However, Regulation 45/2001/EC on the protection of individuals with regard to the processing of personal data by the community institutions and bodies will continue to apply.

Regulation No 45/2001 is to be updated to ensure consistency with and be applied in the light of the Regulation.[30]

5.3.5 Relationship with ePrivacy Directive

Article 95 of the Regulation states the Regulation: 'shall not impose additional obligations on natural or legal persons in relation to processing in connection with the provision of publicly available electronic communications services in public communication networks in the Union in relation to matters for which they are subject to specific obligations with the same objective set out in Directive 2002/58/EC'.

The Regulation may still influence the interpretation of the ePrivacy Directive. For example, the ePrivacy Directive defines consent by reference to the Data Protection Directive, which will be replaced by reference to the Regulation from 25 May 2018; thus, consent for direct marketing activities under the ePrivacy Directive may have to comply with the more stringent consent requirements under the Regulation (see Chapter 17).[31] Article 95 of the Regulation would not seem to prevent such a result on the basis that the ePrivacy Directive does not address requirements on the validity of and evidence for consent.

Recital 173 states that '[o]nce this Regulation is adopted, Directive 2002/58/EC should be reviewed in particular in order to ensure consistency with this Regulation'. The European Commission ('Commission') aims to achieve full coherence between the ePrivacy Directive and Regulation as there are areas of significant difference and overlap between the two instruments, including in relation to territorial scope, data breach notifications, and liability and sanctions.[32] The Commission commenced a public consultation on the evaluation and review of the ePrivacy Directive in April 2016 and published a proposal for a Regulation to replace the ePrivacy Directive on 10 January 2017.

5.3.6 Relationship with E-Commerce Directive

The Regulation is stated to be 'without prejudice' to the rules in the E-Commerce Directive 2000/31/EC, in particular to those concerning the liability of 'intermediary service providers' and which purport to limit their exposure to pecuniary and criminal liability where they merely host, cache or act as a 'mere conduit'. The relationship with the E-Commerce Directive is not straightforward, as the E-Commerce Directive states that issues that relate to the processing of personal data are excluded from its scope and 'solely governed' by relevant data protection legislation.

ISP users
conduct :
E-Comm Div ;

ISP's own
use of pd :
GDPR

The Regulation and E-Commerce Directive can be read consistently if one assumes that the liability of Internet service providers (ISP) for the actions of users will be determined by the E-Commerce Directive but that other matters, such as obligations to erase or rectify data or obligations on an ISP concerning its own uses of personal data, will be governed by the Regulation. However, the point remains unclear.

5.4   Conclusion

The GDPR has broad territorial and material scope. Many organisations that may not have fallen under the jurisdiction of the Directive will find their processing activities trigger application of the GDPR—to the extent they are offering goods or services to EU data subjects, which are not limited to EU citizens. Although the Regulation attempts to limit its material scope with more clarity than the Directive did, moreover, a great deal of processing activities fall under the GDPR as discussed in the chapters that follow.

Endnotes

1 Article 29 Working Party Opinion 8/2010, http://ec.europa.eu/justice/policies/privacy/docs/wpdocs/2010/wp179_en.pdf.

2 Google Spain SL and Google Inc. v. Agencia Española de Protección de Datos (AEPD) and Mario Costeja González [2014] Case C-131/12, 13 May 2014.

3 Article 29 Working Party Opinion 1/2008, page 10.

4 Advocate General Cruz Villalon, in Opinion C2015:426, Paragraphs 28 and 32–34.

5 Weltimmo s.r.o. v. Nemzeti Adatvédelmi és Információszabadság Hatóság [2015] Case C-230/14, 1 October 2015.

6 Weltimmo s.r.o. v. Nemzeti Adatvédelmi és Információszabadság Hatóság [2015] Case C-230/14, 1 October 2015, page 873.

7 Google Spain SL and Google Inc. v. Agencia Española de Protección de Datos (AEPD) and Mario Costeja González [2014] Case C-131/12, 13 May 2014, Paragraph 53.

8 Google Spain SL and Google Inc. v. Agencia Española de Protección de Datos (AEPD) and Mario Costeja González [2014] Case C-131/12, 13 May 2014, Paragraph 56.

9 Article 29 Working Party, Update of Opinion 8/2010 on applicable law in light of the CJEU judgment in Google Spain, page 5.

10 Verein für Konsumenteninformation v. Amazon EU Sàrl [2016] Case C-191/15, 28 July 2016.

11 The case also looked at applicable law relating to contracts and injunctions, but this is beyond the scope of this Chapter.

12 General Data Protection Regulation, Recital 23.

13 (44/2001/EC).

14 Pammer v. Reederei Karl Schlüter GmbH & Co and Hotel Alpenhof v. Heller [2010] Joined Cases C-585/08 and C-144/09, 7 December 2010, Paragraph 95.

15 Pammer v. Reederei Karl Schlüter GmbH & Co and Hotel Alpenhof v. Heller [2010] Joined Cases C-585/08 and C-144/09, 7 December 2010, Paragraph 93.

16 General Data Protection Regulation, Recital 24.

17 Jay, Rosemary, Data Protection Law and Practice, Fourth Edition (Sweet & Maxwell, 2102), page 201.

18 European Parliament v. Council of the European Union and Commission of the European Communities [2006] Joined Cases C-317/04 and C318/04, 30 May 2006.

19 General Data Protection Regulation, Recital 18.

20 Bodil Lindqvist [2003] Case C-101/01, 6 November 2003.

21 Bodil Lindqvist [2003] Case C-101/01, 6 November 2003, Paragraph 47.

22 Article 29 Data Protection Working Party, 'Statement of the Working Party on current discussions regarding the data protection reform package, Annex 2 Proposals for Amendments regarding exemption for personal or household activities', page 2.

23 Van Alsenoy, Brendan, ICRI Working Paper Series 23/2015, 'The evolving role of the individual under EU data protection law'. In addition, Brendan Van Alsenoy, 'I tweet therefore I am … subject to data protection law', https://www.law.kuleuven.be/citip/blog/i-tweet-therefore-i-am-subject-to-data-protection-law/.

24 František Ryneš v. Úřad pro ochranu osobních údajů [2014] Case C-212/13, 11 December 2014.

25 František Ryneš v. Úřad pro ochranu osobních údajů [2014] Case C-212/13, 11 December 2014, Paragraph 33.

26 Law Enforcement Data Protection Directive, Article 3(7).

27 Law Enforcement Data Protection Directive, Article 9(1).

28 Law Enforcement Data Protection Directive, Recital 34.

29 Law Enforcement Data Protection Directive, Recital 11.

30 General Data Protection Regulation, Recital 17.

31 General Data Protection Regulation, Recital 173.

32 Background to the 'Public Consultation on the evaluation and review of the ePrivacy Directive', page 3.

CHAPTER 6

Data Processing Principles

Mariel Filippidis, CIPP/E, CIPM, FIP

6.1 Introduction

The data processing principles have been derived from and contained in previous international and European data protection instruments.[1] The Convention for the Protection of Individuals with regard to Automatic Processing of Personal Data ('Convention 108') was the first international legally binding document which prescribed the data protection principles. From a European perspective, the Data Protection Directive ('Directive') incorporated the fundamental data protection principles, as well.[2]

Under the General Data Protection Regulation (GDPR, or 'Regulation'), the principles are expressly listed in Article 5, which includes the following:[3]

- Lawfulness, fairness and transparency

- Purpose limitation

- Data minimisation

- Accuracy

- Storage limitation

- Integrity and confidentiality

The Regulation redefines and reinforces the existing fundamental principles contained in the Directive. The Regulation also strengthens them by expressly adding the accountability principle and prescribing the duty of data controllers to demonstrate compliance with the above referred principles.[4]

6.2   Lawfulness, fairness and transparency

Under the Regulation, [[p]ersonal data shall be processed lawfully, fairly and in a transparent manner in relation to the data subject.[5] In other words, personal data must be processed only if a legal ground exists and to the extent the processing is carried out in a fair and transparent manner towards the individuals whose personal data is collected and used.

6.2.1 Lawfulness

Lawfulness means that personal data must only be processed when data controllers have a legal ground for processing the data. Lawfulness, therefore, requires that the data processing be allowed by and be carried out within the limits of the applicable laws. This may include data protection laws and also other applicable rules and codes that deal with areas such as employment, competition, health, tax or any other objectives of general public interest, depending on the particular case.[6]

In a nutshell, for the data processing to be lawful, it must be consistent with all applicable laws in the particular circumstances.

In relation to the applicable data protection laws, under the Regulation, the processing of personal data will be considered lawful only when and to the extent one of the following legal grounds is met:[7]

(a)   *Consent:* the data subject has given consent to the processing of his or her personal data for one or more specific purposes;

(b)   *Contract performance:* processing is necessary for the performance of a contract to which the data subject is party or in order to take steps at the request of the data subject prior to entering into a contract;

(c)   *Legal obligation:* processing is necessary for compliance with a legal obligation to which the controller is subject;

(d)   *Vital interest of individuals:* processing is necessary in order to protect the vital interests of the data subject or of another natural person;

(e)   *Public interest:* processing is necessary for the performance of a task carried out in the public interest or in the exercise of official authority vested in the controller;

(f)   *Legitimate interest:* processing is necessary for the purposes of the legitimate interests pursued by the controller or by a third party, except where such interests are overridden by the interests or fundamental rights and freedoms of the data subject which require protection of personal data, in particular where the data subject is a child. Point (f) of the first

subparagraph shall not apply to processing carried out by public authorities
in the performance of their tasks

To seek harmonisation within the EU, the Regulation prescribes a high level of
protection for the rights and freedoms of individuals, in this case, by prescribing the
above mentioned legal criteria and including certain minimum requirements that must
be met in relation to each of them. Member states, however, still maintain certain rights
to introduce or preserve national instruments, to the extent they are consistent with the
Regulation, to further specify the implementation in certain circumstances.[8] Indeed,
the Regulation expressly grants to member states the right to determine more specific
legal requirements to ensure lawful and fair processing of personal data in specific
processing situations (i.e., employer-employee relationships; allowing member states to
define the age of minors; to protect genetic or biometric data; or for statistical, historical
or scientific purposes).[9]

For a detailed analysis of each of the legitimate processing criteria under the
Regulation, please refer to Chapter 7.

6.2.2 Fairness

In addition to being lawful, the processing of personal data must be fair. The fairness of
the processing is essentially linked to the idea that data subjects must be aware of the
fact that their personal data will be processed, including how the data will be collected,
kept and used, to allow them to make an informed decision about whether they agree
with such processing and to enable them to exercise their data protection rights.

However, in certain cases, processing is automatically permitted by law and so is
deemed fair, regardless of the data subject's knowledge or preferences.

For example, 'Personal data will be obtained fairly by the tax authorities if it is
obtained from an employer who is under a legal duty to provide details of an employee's
pay, whether or not the employee consents to, or is aware of, this'.[10]

In addition, fairness also requires an assessment on how the processing will affect the
data subject. If the processing negatively affects individuals and such detriment is not
justified, the processing will be unfair.

For example, a travel agency may collect and process behavioural data whilst
users browse the travel agency website. The company does so by using cookies or
other tracking technologies to analyse the preferences of a user whilst searching for
plane tickets and hotels. If the system is programmed to make automatic decisions
about pricing for a particular holiday and detects that the same individual has visited
the website several times searching for information about a particular destination,
increasing the price based on that information may be regarded as unfair processing.

In contrast, a different situation may occur, when the processing negatively affects individuals but such detriment is justified. In that case, the processing will be considered fair. For example, personal data may be collected by a police officer from an individual who is driving above the speed limit and has previously received multiple fines for speeding. The processing of personal data is carried out to the detriment of the driver, since the data processing will likely lead to issuing an increased fine for speeding in comparison to a driver who has received their first speeding fine. In this case, however, the data processing may be justified by local rules and, therefore, will be considered fair.

Ensuring fair processing requires data controllers to consider all the circumstances in a case and be transparent by providing sufficient information, as well and implementing proper mechanisms. Such mechanisms allow individuals to make informed decisions and exercise their choices and rights, unless the processing is otherwise justified.

6.2.3 Transparency

Directly linked to fairness, the principle of transparency means that a controller must be open and clear towards data subjects when processing personal data.[11]

Significantly, the Regulation eliminates the Directive's general obligation to also notify data protection authorities (DPAs) of the processing of personal data on the basis that this did not necessarily contribute to protecting personal data. Recital 89 explains that '[s]uch indiscriminate general notification obligations should therefore be abolished, and replaced by effective procedures and mechanisms which focus instead on those types of processing operations which are likely to result in a high risk to the rights and freedoms of natural persons by virtue of their nature, scope, context and purposes'.

The Regulation instead promotes notifying data subjects of how their personal data is processed. How much information will be considered sufficient will depend on the particular circumstances. In this respect, the Regulation prescribes the minimum information data controllers are expected to provide, taking into consideration whether the data is directly obtained from the data subject or from other sources.[12]

A detailed analysis of the information provision requirements is provided in Chapter 8.

The Regulation exempts data controllers from the duty to inform in cases where the data was obtained directly from the data subject and the data subject is already aware of the information. In addition, the Regulation frees data controllers from the obligation to provide information when personal data is collected from other sources in the following cases:[13]

③ • when providing the information will involve a <u>disproportionate effort</u> or can be considered <u>impossible</u>;

④ • to <u>protect</u> the data subject's <u>legitimate interest</u>, in which case, the disclosure is expressly governed by <u>the applicable law</u>; and

⑤ • to preserve the <u>confidentiality</u> of the information, also regulated by the laws to which the data controller is subject.

Transparency also requires that the information be provided in a timely manner. *Transparency = provide info timely* When personal data is obtained directly from the data subject, the relevant information must be available at the time of collection. When personal data has been obtained from other sources, however, the Regulation prescribes different periods within which such information must be provided.[14]

In addition, the Regulation requires that the information be clear, concise and easy to understand and that it be provided in an accessible manner.[15] *clear, concise, easy to udstnd provided in accessible manner*

To provide clear and easily accessible information, controllers must consider the most convenient tools or methods to make this information available to data subjects, taking into consideration the following circumstances: type of data to be processed, ② the manner in which the personal data will be collected, and whether the information is obtained directly from the data subject or from other sources.

Further practical guidance includes:

• When the processing involves personal data of children, the Regulation stresses the need for the communication or information to be drafted in simple and plain language to allow children to understand it.[16] *- children: simple & plain language*

• When the information is obtained, for example, in the context of a medical examination, the medical practitioner must inform the patients using plain language (i.e., no scientific or medical terms that may not be understood by individuals who are not medical practitioners must be included unless they are explained). Such information must be provided before the examination is carried out. *- medical: plain language*

• In the digital environment, privacy notices are broadly used to inform individuals. Using short and ad-hoc privacy notices instead of long legal texts is recommended and considered to be best practice.[17] *- short, ad-hoc privacy notices*

The Regulation promotes the use of visual and standardised icons or symbols as an alternative means to inform individuals in a concise and clear way.[18] *use of visual + standardized icons & symbols*

6.3   Purpose limitation

Purpose limitation means that data controllers must only collect and process personal data to accomplish specified, explicit and legitimate purposes and not process personal data beyond such purposes unless the further processing is considered compatible with the purposes for which the personal data was originally collected.[19]

Data controllers, therefore, must first identify the particular purposes for which the personal data will be processed. Such purposes will become the boundaries within which the personal data must be collected and used by data controllers. Secondary processing could only be lawfully carried out when such processing is considered compatible with the original purpose for which the personal data was gathered.

The use of personal data for statistical purposes, public interest, scientific or historical research purposes will be considered compatible as long as such processing takes place within the limits set out by the Union or member state's law that governs the particular processing.

If, however, the secondary or further data processing does not relate to these purposes, controllers must assess whether the further processing is compatible with the purposes for which the personal data was originally collected.

To help the controller assess whether the secondary use of the data is compatible with the original purposes, the Regulation states: '…the controller, after having met all the requirements of the lawfulness of the original processing, should take into account, inter alia:

- any link between those purposes and the purposes of the intended further processing;

- the context in which the personal data has been collected, in particular the reasonable expectations of data subjects based on their relationship with the controller as to their further use;

- the nature of the personal data;

- the consequences of the intended further processing for data subjects; and

- the existence of appropriate safeguards in both the original and intended further processing operations'.[20]

When all the above conditions are met and the processing is considered compatible, no other legal basis separate from the one that allowed the original collection and use of the personal data will be required. However, when the processing is considered incompatible, a separate legal ground will be required (e.g., the consent of the data subject before starting the processing of data for a new purpose).

The following examples may help clarify when a purpose could be considered compatible or incompatible in relation to practical cases:

- Data controllers may collect and process personal data in order to offer services tied to a fitness mobile application. The specific purpose of the data processing will be to analyse personal data to recommend its user a personalised fitness routine. Further processing of the personal data to identify technical errors of such mobile application will be considered compatible because improving the efficiency of the fitness mobile application is linked to the original purpose. In addition, the fact that the company may wish to improve the technical capabilities of the fitness app could be reasonably expected by the users.

- To assist diabetes patients in dispensing medication, an app is developed and offered to monitor blood sugar concentration levels. The app has the capability to share personal information with a company that sells diabetes medication. The promotion and commercialisation of diabetes medication is not compatible with the original purpose (monitoring blood sugar concentrations to assess when the medication must be taken by patients).[21]

- A health professional collects personal data to be able to assess and treat the medical condition of their patients. Sharing the patient list with an insurance company to allow the insurance company to offer its services (e.g., life or health insurance) will be considered incompatible with the original purpose for which the personal data was collected.

To conclude, controllers must identify the specific purposes for which personal data is collected. When further processing takes place, controllers must then verify whether such processing is compatible with the purpose for which the personal data was original collected. If this is the case, no separate legal basis is required.

When, however, the secondary purpose is incompatible with the original one, the controller will be required to properly inform the data subjects and either (1) obtain separate consent in relation to the new purpose; or (2) satisfy one of the other available legal criteria to justify the processing.

[margin handwritten: Art 6(c)]

6.4   Data minimisation

[margin handwritten: Data minimization: only collect/process PD necessary + relevant + adequate for the purpose; Necessity + Proportionality]

The principle of data minimisation means that data controllers must only collect and process personal data that is relevant, necessary and adequate to accomplish the purposes for which it is processed.[22]

In the words of the European Data Protection Supervisor, '... data minimisation means that a data controller should limit the collection of personal information to what is directly relevant and necessary to accomplish a specified purpose ... data controllers should collect only the personal data they really need'.[23]

The practical implementation of this principle requires applying two concepts: necessity and proportionality to the personal data processing.[24]

6.4.1 Necessity

[margin handwritten: Necessity: must ask, can anon. data achieve the purpose?]

Controllers must assess whether the personal data to be collected is suitable and reasonable to accomplish the specific purposes. It will be considered suitable if the personal data is of a nature necessary to attain the purpose. It would be considered adequate if the nature or amount of personal data is proportionate in relation to the purposes.

Verifying whether the specific purpose can be accomplished by using anonymous data could be a useful starting point in the data minimisation assessment. Controllers must evaluate whether the purpose could be accomplished by processing anonymous data which is stripped of all unique identifiers.[25]

[margin handwritten: Can purpose be achieved after excluding obvious identifiers? e.g. DOB]

In addition, data will be excessive and therefore unnecessary in relation to the purpose if such purpose could be accomplished by excluding certain data fields from the processing (e.g., [not storing] date of birth when a generic age (or age bracket, such as ages 25–35) is sufficient for [the] app to function correctly).[26]

6.4.2 Proportionality

[margin handwritten: Proportionality: amount of PD collected; no "save everything" principle]

In terms of proportionality, controllers should also consider the amount of data to be collected. For example, collecting a large amount of data which is excessive in relation to the purposes that the controller aims to accomplish and without any restrictions will be considered disproportionate. Therefore, a 'save-everything' approach will likely be considered a breach of the data minimisation principle.[27]

[margin handwritten: Adequacy: assess potential adverse impact of the means of processing; consider less intrusive/adverse alternatives]

To assess adequacy, data controllers must take into consideration the potentially adverse impact of the means of processing, as well as verify whether alternative means exist that may lead to less intrusive processing or fewer adverse consequences in relation to the privacy of data subjects.[28]

An example of excessive or disproportionate means may include using biometric data (e.g., fingerprints) to identify individuals where alternative and less intrusive means could be used to accomplish the same purpose (e.g., identity cards).[29]

Implementing the data minimisation principle in practice, in certain cases, may require a relatively simple assessment. In other cases, however, performing a data minimisation exercise may become a challenge for controllers.

In particular, implementing the data minimisation principle will require creative thinking when dealing with big data projects. This challenge is recognised by the DPAs who, in their opinions, stress the applicability and validity of the data protection principles in relation to these projects.[30] In this respect:

> The [Article 29] Working Party acknowledges that the challenges of big data might require innovative thinking on how some of these and other key data protection principles are applied in practice. However, at this stage, it has no reason to believe that the EU data protection principles … are no longer valid and appropriate for the development of big data, subject to further improvements to make them more effective in practice.[31]

Big data = challenge to data minimization

To legally process and successfully use and protect personal data in the digital economy, data protection officers (DPOs), as well as data scientists are expected to work together to find creative ways to implement the data minimisation exercises in relation to big data.

6.5 Accuracy

Controllers must take reasonable measures to ensure the data is accurate and, where necessary, kept up to date.[32] Reasonable measures should be understood as implementing processes to prevent inaccuracies during the data collection process (i.e., verifying the data is accurate, complete and not misleading), as well as during the ongoing data processing in relation to the specific use for which the data is processed. The controller must consider the type of data and the specific purposes to maintain the accuracy of personal data in relation to the purpose.

Reasonable measure PD is accurate & up to date "Prevent inaccuracy during collection & processing

During the collection process, inaccuracy of personal data may occur if controllers do not properly verify the authenticity of the information. Controllers must evaluate how reliable the source from which they collect the information is, as well as taking additional care when a potential inaccuracy may have adverse implications for the individual.

Must verify authenticity of data & reliability of the source.

Additional care if inaccuracy leads to adverse result.

When the data is collected for statistical or historical purposes, the controller only needs to maintain the personal data as originally collected.

If collected for stat/historical purpose, only need to maintain PD as originally collected

Accuracy may also require keeping records of or correcting errors. The UK Information Commissioner's Office (ICO) states that 'it is acceptable to keep records of events that happened in error, provided those records are not misleading about the facts'. It illustrates this with the following example: 'A misdiagnosis of a medical condition continues to be held as part of a patient's medical records even after the diagnosis because it is relevant for the purpose of explaining treatment given to the patient, or to additional health problems'.[33]

To summarise, to comply with the accuracy principle, a controller must implement reasonable measures that may or may not require updating the information, depending on the specific purpose. It also embodies the responsibility to respond to data subject requests to correct records that contain incomplete information or misinformation.

6.6 Storage limitation

Storage limitation means personal data must not be kept for longer than necessary for the purposes for which the personal data is processed. In other words, once the information is no longer needed, personal data must be securely deleted.

Article 5(1)(e) of the Regulation states that personal data must be 'kept in a form which permits identification of data subjects for no longer than is necessary for the purposes for which the personal data are processed; personal data may be stored for longer periods insofar as the personal data will be processed solely for archiving purposes in the public interest, scientific or historical research purposes or statistical purposes …'.

The Regulation clarifies that '…the period for which the personal data are stored is limited to the strict minimum… In order to ensure that the personal data are not kept longer than necessary, time limits should be established by the controller for erasure or for a periodic review …'.[34] The controller, thus, must assess whether the personal data is to be used for one or several purposes and limit the processing to a period during which the personal data is needed to accomplish the specific purpose or purposes.

For instance, processing personal data may be needed in the context of a recruitment process, as well as during the employment relationship. Once the recruitment process ends, controllers must not keep personal data of unsuccessful candidates any longer. Controllers must also review the personal records of the employees when the employee relationship comes to an end, in order to determine whether some of those records need to be retained for legal or other reasons.[35]

A controller must verify whether statutory data retention periods exist in relation to the type of processing (e.g., personal data may need to be kept in order to comply with tax, health and safety, or employment regulations).[36] When the law is silent, internal data retention periods must be set to meet the storage limitation principle.

Periods must be set considering the purpose or purpose for which the data is collected and used, and once the storage periods expire, data must be deleted in the absence of a sound new reason to retain it. However, personal data may be stored for longer periods insofar as the personal data will be processed solely for archiving purposes in the public interest, scientific, historical research or statistical purposes. Otherwise, data controllers may keep personal data for an unlimited period only when the data becomes irreversibly anonymised.

May keep data if irreversibly anonymized

6.7 Integrity and confidentiality

Article 5(1)(f) of the Regulation states that personal data must be 'processed in a manner that ensures appropriate security of the personal data, including protection against unauthorised or unlawful processing and against accidental loss, destruction or damage, using appropriate technical or organisational measures ("integrity and confidentiality")'.[37]

Appropriate security of PD, use of appropriate & organizational measures to ensure integrity & confidentiality.

To protect and preserve personal data throughout its lifecycle, controllers should therefore implement an information security framework as described in detail in Chapter 10.

To protect personal data, the Regulation promotes the use of techniques such as pseudonymisation and encryption of personal data.[38]

pseudonymization / encryption promoted by GDPR

When the processing involves sensitive personal data, additional care should be taken. In this respect, a controller must take into account the potential impact on individuals that a breach of the integrity or confidentially of the personal data may cause to implement measures that sufficiently protect the individual.

Sensitive PP requires more strict security

To preserve the integrity, confidentiality and availability of the data, data controllers must assign sufficient resources to develop and implement an information security policy framework.

Develop/implement info sec policy framework;

Having a cross-functional team, including legal and technical data security experts, is standard practice today to properly define an organisation's information security strategy and policies. Setting aside a dedicated budget to properly implement and maintain the organisational and technical measures is crucial to effectively implement proper processes and tools to comply with the integrity and confidentially principle.

cross-functional team & dedicated budget

6.8 Conclusion

The Regulation is one of the first—and certainly the most globally prominent—data protection laws since Convention 108 to expressly embrace and reinforce the data processing principles. It requires organisations to implement privacy concepts from avoiding data collection and retention altogether, to handling personal data in a transparent and secure manner, whilst ensuring its accuracy and respecting the data subject's rights.

Endnotes

1 See, generally, Chapter 1.

2 Article 6, European Parliament and Council Directive 95/46/EC of 24 October 1995.

3 General Data Protection Regulation, Article 5.

4 The accountability principle appears in obligations placed on controllers in the Directive and was featured in OECD Guidelines as: 'a data controller should be accountable for the complying with the measures that ensure the principles states above'; The accountability principle appears in obligations placed on controllers in the Directive and was featured in OECD Guidelines as: 'a data controller should be accountable for the complying with the measures that ensure the principles states above'; see Chapter 11.

5 General Data Protection Regulation, Article 5.

6 This is illustrated by the Recital 73: 'Restrictions concerning specific principles ... may be imposed by the Union or member states law, as far as necessary and proportionate in a democratic society to safeguard public security, including the protection of human life especially in response to natural or manmade disasters, the prevention, investigation and prosecution of criminal offences...or other important objectives of general public interest of the Union or of a member state... Those restrictions shall be in accordance with the requirements set out in the Chapter and in the European Convention for the Protection of Human Rights and Fundamental Freedoms'.

7 General Data Protection Regulation, Article 6.

8 Refer to Article 6(2) Recital 10 states: '...this Regulation, does not exclude member states law that set out the circumstances for specific processing situations, including determining more precisely the conditions under which the processing of personal data is lawful'.

9 Indeed, this will have to be taken into consideration in relation to points (c) and (e) above referred. Article 6 of the General Data Protection Regulation states: '...member states may maintain or introduce more specific provisions to adapt the application of the rules of this Regulation with regard to processing for compliance with points (c) and (e) of Paragraph 1 by determining more precisely specific requirements for the processing and other measures to ensure lawful and fair processing including for other specific processing situations as provided for in Chapter 4'.; see also Article 85 and following of the Regulation.

10 UK Information Commissioner's Office website, https://ico.org.uk/for-organisations/guide-to-data-protection/principle-1-fair-and-lawful/, accessed June 2017.

11 General Data Protection Regulation, Articles 5, 12 and 13.

12 General Data Protection Regulation, Articles 13 and 14.

13 General Data Protection Regulation, Article 14(5)(a).

14 General Data Protection Regulation, Article 14(3).

15 General Data Protection Regulation, Article 12, Recital 39 ('the principle of transparency requires that any information and communication relating to the processing of those personal data be easily accessible and easy to understand and that clear and plain language be used').

16 General Data Protection Regulation, Recital 58.

17 'Key information shall not be embedded in lengthy legal text, and shall be presented in a clear, user-friendly manner'. See, for example, Draft Code of Conduct on privacy for mobile health applications, https://ec.europa.eu/digital-single-market/en/news/code-conduct-privacy-mhealth-apps-has-been-finalised, 7 June 2016.

18 General Data Protection Regulation, Articles 12(7) and (8) Recital 58 states, 'requires that any information … be concise, easily accessible and easy to understand and that clear and plain language and additionally, where appropriate, visualisation be used'.

19 General Data Protection Regulation, Article 5(b).

20 General Data Protection Regulation, Recital 50.

21 This example was obtained from the Code of Conduct on privacy for mobile health applications published, 7 June 2016. This draft was available at https://ec.europa.eu/digital-single-market/en/news/code-conduct-privacy-mhealth-apps-has-been-finalised when visited 3 July 2016. The draft of the Code was submitted to the Working Party 29 for its consideration and approval at the moment this book was written.

22 General Data Protection Regulation, Article 6(c).

23 Refer to glossary on page https://secure.edps.europa.eu/EDPSWEB/edps/EDPS/Dataprotection/Glossary/pid/74, data minimisation definition, accessed 25 June 2016.

24 WP 211 Opinion 01/2014 on the application of necessity and proportionality concepts and data protection within the law enforcement sector; see also Directive 95/46/EC Article 6 (b) and (c), as well as Regulation EC (No) 45/2001, Article 4(1)(b).

25 Anonymous data is personal information that is completely stripped of all unique identifiers; therefore, pseudonymous data shall not be considered anonymous. For information on techniques to anonymise personal data according to European Law, please refer to WP 216 Opinion 05/2014 on Anonymisation techniques adopted 10 April 2014.

26 Code of Conduct on privacy for mobile health applications, https://ec.europa.eu/digital-single-market/en/news/code-conduct-privacy-mhealth-apps-has-been-finalised, published 7 June 2016. The draft of the Code was submitted to the Working Party 29 for its consideration and approval at the moment this book was written.

27 General Data Protection Regulation, Recital 64 exemplifies this whilst stating, 'A controller should not retain personal data for the sole purpose of being able to react to potential requests'.

28 General Data Protection Regulation, Recital 39 states, 'Personal data should be processed only if the purpose of the processing could not reasonably be fulfilled by other means'.

29 The Spanish data protection authority considered the use of the fingerprint as a means to control the access of student to school disproportionate since that purpose can be achieved in a less intrusive manner in relation to the rights of students. The Agencia Espanola de Proteccion de datos INFORME: 0065/2015, available at www.agpd.es/portalwebAGPD/canaldocumentacion/informes_juridicos/common/pdf_destacados/2015-0065_Control-de-acceso-al-comedor-por-huella-digital.pdf.

30 The Article 29 Working Party, as well as the European Data Protection Supervisor (EDPS), supported this thought. EDPS report dated 11 July 2014, 'Report of workshop on Privacy, Consumers, Competition and Big Data 2 June' ('the laws seem not to cover the incremental "day-by-day drops into the ocean of data" which are assembled to construct user profiles, where even seemingly innocuous data can reveal sensitive information. This process will be accelerated as more and more devices go online, which will in turn intensify the need for privacy by design, high standards of data security and data minimisation').

31 WP 221 'Statement on Statement of the WP29 on the impact of the development of big data on the protection of individuals with regard to the processing of their personal data in the EU', adopted 16 September 2014.

32 Recital 39 clarifies that 'Every reasonable step should be taken to ensure that personal data which are inaccurate are rectified or deleted'.

33 UK Information Commissioner's Office, https://ico.org.uk/for-organisations/guide-to-data-protection/principle-4-accuracy/, accessed June 2017.

34 General Data Protection Regulation, Recital 39.

35 This example is a simplification of two examples included on UK Information Commissioner's Office website, https://ico.org.uk/for-organisations/guide-to-data-protection/principle-5-retention/, accessed June 2017.

36 UK Information Commissioner's Office website, https://ico.org.uk/for-organisations/guide-to-data-protection/principle-5-retention/ ('There are various legal requirements and professional guidelines about keeping certain kinds of records—such as information needed for income tax and audit purposes, or information on aspects of health and safety. If an organisation keeps personal data to comply with a requirement like this, it will not be considered to have kept the information for longer than necessary').

37 General Data Protection Regulation, Recital 30 ('Personal data should be processed in a manner that ensures appropriate security and confidentiality of the personal data, including for preventing unauthorised access to or use of personal data and the equipment used for the processing').

38 General Data Protection Regulation, Article 89(1) and Recital 28.

CHAPTER 7

Lawful Processing Criteria

Victoria Hordern, CIPP/E, CIPT

7.1   Background

The General Data Protection Regulation (GDPR, or 'Regulation') requires controllers to process personal information 'lawfully, fairly and in a transparent manner'. Articles 6 and 9 of the Regulation lay out the criteria that must be met for lawful processing, including consent. Article 7 sets out the conditions that must be demonstrated when relying on consent. Article 8 provides further requirements where consent is relied upon when offering an information society service to a child.

Consent is frequently at the heart of data protection and privacy laws. Giving a data subject the opportunity to choose how and when their personal information is used is a feature of best practice. Nonetheless, the Regulation recognises a number of other lawful bases other than consent, such as fulfilling a contractual obligation, complying with a legal obligation, protecting the data subject's vital interests, and performing a task in the public interest and the legitimate interests of the controller or a third party when balanced against the rights and interests of the data subject.

7.2   Processing personal data

Article 6 outlines the lawful bases for processing personal data. If a data controller is unable to demonstrate one of these bases for processing, it will be unlawful to proceed unless the controller can establish some exception, such as processing personal data for journalism or research where free speech and other public interests may prevail. In the debates and drafts of the Regulation, consent was frequently perceived as the main criterion for legitimate processing. However, the final version of the Regulation treats consent as one of several alternatives for legitimate processing. In this section, each separate lawful basis is discussed.

7.2.1 The data subject has given consent to the processing of his or her personal data for one or more specific purposes

[margin note: Consent]

The first lawful basis for processing personal data is where a data subject gives their consent. Although this appears at face value to be relatively straightforward, consent has a particular meaning under the Regulation. A data subject's consent is defined as 'any freely given, specific, informed and unambiguous indication of the data subject's wishes by which he or she, by a statement or by a clear affirmative action, signifies agreement to the processing of personal data relating to him or her'.[1] A data subject's consent must meet the following conditions:

- Freely given
- Specific
- Informed
- Unambiguous indication of wishes

[margin note: ⑤ by a statement or by a clear affirmative action]

[margin note: burden of demonstration on controller]

The responsibility lies with the controller to demonstrate that the data subject has consented to the processing. Where a declaration of consent is pre-formulated by the controller, which will be the case in most circumstances, the consent should be provided in an intelligible and easily accessible form, using clear and plain language, and with no unfair terms, in line with consumer protection requirements.[2] Freely given consent means that the data subject must have a genuine choice and must be able to refuse or withdraw consent. Offering anything less than a genuine choice is unlikely to result in valid consent. Under the Data Protection Directive ('Directive'), a number of countries required the controller to provide a wholly separate document just dealing with obtaining consent. The reasoning behind this separation was that a data subject is not giving free consent if their consent is bundled with some other issue (e.g., purchasing a service). This position has now been enshrined in the Regulation. Under Article 7, where a data subject's consent is given in the context of a written declaration which also concerns other matters, the request for consent must be presented in a manner clearly distinguishable from the other matters. The importance of this separation is underlined in the same Article, which states that any part of such a declaration that infringes the Regulation is not binding. Additionally, controllers should be cautious about stating that consent is required for data processing as part of performing a contract. In considering whether consent is freely given, the utmost account will be taken of whether the performance of a contract is conditioned on consent to processing personal data when such processing is not necessary for the performance of the contract.

[margin note: "Freely given" = genuine choice + ability to refuse and/or withdraw consent]

[margin note: Request for consent can't be bundled w/ other issues + must be clearly distinguishable]

[margin note: Careful to say consent required for performance of contract]

Recital 43 of the Regulation indicates that consent should not be relied upon where there is a clear imbalance between the data subject and controller, in particular, where the controller is a public authority. Although not expressly stated in the Regulation, EU regulators have identified the **employer-employee relationship as potentially problematic for demonstrating freely given consent.** In the regulator's view, because an employee is in a relationship of subordination, valid consent is possible only if an employee has a real opportunity to withhold their consent without suffering any prejudice.

Equally, the employee must have the **option of withdrawing their consent** in the future if they change their mind. Since the regulators foresee that an employer insisting on relying on consent so that it is not free could cause the employee real harm in their work situation, **there are probably very few circumstances where employers should seek to rely on consent as a lawful basis for processing.** Although certain jurisdictions may admit that this portrayal of employer-employee relations is rather extreme, employers would do well to consider other legitimising criteria for processing employee data before focusing on consent.

Indeed, **due to** the fact that freely given consent involves the **freedom to revoke** consent, controllers should consider whether consent is the most suitable condition for long-term processing arrangements. For instance, it probably would not be appropriate to seek employees' consent for uploading their personal data into a human resources database, since an employee, though consenting initially, may legitimately decide in the future to revoke their consent. Thus, employers could possibly seek to rely on consent plus another legitimate processing condition—**relying on consent in order to encourage** their employees to 'buy into' a system design, whilst also relying on another legitimate processing condition in view of the problems with consent. This approach in itself could, of course, have its own problems, since an employee could well feel disgruntled if they have been led to believe that the processing of their data is governed by their consent, only to discover that the giving or withholding of their consent does not influence their employer's use of her data. Although promising so much at first glance, consent can actually be deceptively tricky to manage.

To be valid, consent must also be '**specific**'. That is, consent must be given specifically for the particular processing operation in question. Therefore, the **controller** should be able to **clearly explain its proposed use of the data** so that the consent given by the data subject is consent to that specific processing. When processing has **multiple purposes,** consent should be given for all of them (with proper notice, as well). Processing for multiple purposes can **cause difficulties,** since it may not always be possible to know in advance precisely what processing will be involved, and therefore, consent given at a particular time will be limited to the specific parameters set down then. Where the processing activity changes, there may be a requirement to seek new consents from all the affected individuals, since the previously given consent does not cover the new processing. This requirement has some degree of flexibility when processing personal data for scientific research purposes. Specifically, the Regulation permits that, where it is not possible to fully identify the purpose of data processing for scientific research purposes, data subjects can legally give their consent to certain areas of scientific research consistent with recognised ethical standards for scientific research.

Furthermore, consent must be 'informed' such that a data subject is given all the necessary details of the processing activity in a language and form they can understand so that they can comprehend how the processing will affect them. The onus is always on the controller to demonstrate that the consent of the data subject has been given on the basis of sufficiently precise information, including all the information necessary for the consent to be properly obtained. For example, placing an 'Accept' button on an online form for a data subject to acknowledge their acceptance may not amount to consent under data protection law, unless the controller can prove that the data subject had a reasonable opportunity to be informed of the significance of this consent. The Regulation indicates that for consent to be informed, the data subject should at least be aware of the identity of the controller and purposes of processing.

To be 'unambiguous', the data subject's statement or clear affirmative act must leave no doubt as to their intention to give consent. If there is uncertainty regarding whether consent has been given, the circumstances are construed against the controller. An active indication of consent with a clear statement or affirmative action is required—if a data subject actively ticks a selection box, the action most likely will be considered unambiguous consent, whereas a pre-ticked box may not. It is important to note that unambiguous consent provides a minimum requirement for all consents relied upon under the Regulation.

Silence or pre-ticked boxes do not constitute consent.[3] But when valid consent is obtained, it may be sufficient to rely on ongoing interactions with the data subject. For example, the Regulation also recognises that a data subject's choice of technical settings for information society services provides sufficient consent, so long as the action is sufficient to clearly indicate in the context the data subject's acceptance of proposed processing. Additionally, it goes without saying that consent must be obtained from the data subject before the controller can begin processing their personal data.

The Regulation does not expressly state that a controller must retain written evidence to demonstrate that it has obtained consent from data subjects. However, controllers are obligated to 'demonstrate that the data subject has given consent to the processing operation', which effectively amounts to an obligation on controllers to keep a record of consents given by particular individual data subjects. This administrative requirement is another reason why relying on consent can be burdensome, particularly if a controller is dealing with multiple data subjects and evolving processing activity.

Consent is not the same as giving a data subject the opportunity to opt out. Consent requires an express indication of wishes, whereas opt-out works on the basis that a lack of action by the data subject indicates a lack of objection. For instance, a pre-ticked box that indicates the controller will use the data subject's personal data in some way offers the data subject the option to opt out of allowing personal data to be used in that way. However, if the data subject does not uncheck the box, this does not amount to consent since the data subject has not actively expressed an indication of their wishes. The data subject has chosen not to exercise their right to opt out but has not consented freely, specifically and unambiguously after being informed about the particular use of their personal data. Although Article 6 does not require 'explicit' consent (as required for Article 9 special categories and Article 49 for international data transfers), it is clear that consent requires some sort of action.

Consent obtained through duress or coercion is also not valid consent. There may also be justifiable concerns over whether certain types of vulnerable people have the capacity to give consent. The Regulation specifically addresses this in respect of children and information society services offered to children in Article 8. Under Article 8, where a controller relies on consent as the legitimate processing criterion and information society services are offered directly to a child, then the processing of personal data is only lawful where the child is at least 16 years old. Where the child is under 16 years old, such processing is only lawful 'if and to the extent that consent is given or authorised by the holder of personal responsibility over the child'.[4] Further complicating this requirement, member states may set a minimum age of consent less than 16 years, so long as the age is not lower than 13. It is likely that there will be a range of minimum ages of consent across the EU. For instance, the UK has already announced that it will set the age as 13 years so that a controller offering information society services can lawfully obtain consent from a 13-year-old for processing their personal data without having to obtain parental consent.[5] Inevitably, not all member states will adhere to the same age requirement, so that there will be different ages across the EU. Where parental consent is required, the controller is required to make reasonable efforts to verify that consent is given or authorised by the parent or guardian. It is important to remember that this minimum age of consent rule is only in the context of (1) information society services offered directly to a child, and (2) where the controller relies solely on consent or perhaps cannot rely on another criterion.

Controllers would be well advised to consider another legitimate criterion to process children's personal data. In particular, data protection authorities (DPAs) will wish to see a proper appreciation of the extra protection that children require where their personal data is processed.

7.2.2 Processing that meets a requirement of necessity

All the remaining criteria under Article 6 require that the processing of personal data be necessary for certain reasons. In the past, the Article 29 Working Party (WP29) has indicated the requirement for necessity is a limiting factor that narrows the circumstances available for relying on these criteria.[6] Essentially, the test for necessity requires a close and substantial connection between the processing and the purposes. So, processing that is merely convenient or in the interest of one of the criteria without being necessary will not meet these standards. It is not sufficient for a controller to simply consider processing necessary for its purposes. 'Necessary' has an objective meaning. A data controller must carefully consider whether a particular processing operation is strictly necessary for the stated purpose.

7.2.3 Processing is necessary for the performance of a contract to which the data subject is party or in order to take steps at the request of the data subject prior to entering into a contract

A controller can rely on this criterion when it needs to process the personal data of a data subject in order to perform a contract to which the data subject is or will be a party. Most obviously, this is relevant when a data subject purchases a product or service from a controller and, through the delivery of that product or service, the controller needs to process the individual's personal data. This condition is interpreted narrowly by regulators so that the processing of personal data must be unavoidable in order to complete the contract.

7.2.4 Processing is necessary for compliance with a legal obligation to which the controller is subject

When relying on this criterion, it is important to remember that it relates to a legal obligation with which the controller is required by law to comply (e.g., tax or social security obligations). It cannot be an obligation under a contract that the controller has entered into.

There has been some debate in the past over whether a legal obligation imposed on the controller by a third country (i.e., outside the EU) can meet the requirements of this criterion. Recital 45 of the Regulation makes it clear that obligations imposed on controllers by third countries do not fall within this criterion. In all cases, this criterion is interpreted narrowly. The Regulation sets out further provisions when seeking to rely on this criterion (see Section 7.2.8).

7.2.5 Processing is necessary in order to protect the vital interests of the data subject or of another natural person

Protecting 'vital interests' refers to circumstances of life or death—in other words, where the processing contemplated is vital to an individual's survival. Consequently, this criterion will be relevant only in rare emergency situations. For instance, if the data subject is unconscious, processing of personal data may be necessary in order to provide urgent medical care. Recital 46 indicates that reliance on this criterion based on the vital interests of a natural person 'should in principle take place only where the processing cannot be manifestly based on another legal basis'.

[handwritten margin: necessary to vital interests; only in urgent medical situations where no other basis available]

7.2.6 Processing is necessary for the performance of a task carried out in the public interest or in the exercise of official authority vested in the controller

The Regulation has removed a third category from this criterion that was part of the Directive: where the exercise of official authority is vested in a third party to whom the data are disclosed. Consequently, the circumstances in which a controller can rely on this criterion are narrower than before. It may not be easy to list circumstances where this condition is relevant, but the Regulation provides further provisions that detail when a controller can rely on it (see Section 7.2.8). Of course, it is quite possible that a controller is required to process personal data in the public interest. National EU or member state legislation will determine what tasks are carried out in the public interest under this criterion.

[handwritten margin: necessary to public interest or exercise of official authority vested in controller]

[handwritten margin: National law determines which tasks are in the "public interest"]

Significantly, when processing personal data under this criterion, the controller should be aware that data subjects have the right to object to the use of their data. Under the Regulation, if a controller receives an objection from a data subject, it is the controller's responsibility to be able to demonstrate that it has compelling legitimate grounds to process the personal data. These grounds must be sufficient to 'override the interests, rights and freedoms of the data subject or for the establishment, exercise or defence of legal claims'.[7]

[handwritten margin: DS has right to object under this criteria; controller must, upon objection, demonstrate compelling interest that overrides DS interests or is for legal claims]

7.2.7 Processing is necessary for the purposes of the legitimate interests pursued by the controller or by a third party, except where such interests are overridden by the interests or fundamental rights and freedoms of the data subject which require protection of personal data, in particular where the data subject is a child

This balance-of-interest test is the criterion upon which the majority of personal data processing usually takes place, except that, under the Regulation, public authorities will no longer be able to rely on the legitimate interest ground. Recital 47 explains that it is for the legislator to provide by law for the legal basis for public authorities to process personal data. Consequently, public authorities cannot rely on the legitimate interest ground.

For entities that are not public authorities, there are a number of factors involved in satisfying the legitimate interest condition:[8]

- The processing must be necessary for the purpose.
- The purpose must be a legitimate interest of the controller or a third party.
- The legitimate interest cannot be overridden by the data subject's interests or fundamental rights and freedoms.

In considering whether the controller or third party's legitimate interests override the data subject's interests, rights and/or freedoms, the controller should take into consideration the reasonable expectations of data subjects based on their relationship with the controller. As Recital 47 explains, such legitimate interests can exist 'where there is a relevant and appropriate relationship between the data subject and the controller in situations such as where the data subject is a client or in the service of the controller'. The key emphasis from the Recitals is to consider the reasonable expectations of the data subject concerning processing of their data in view of the time and context of the data collection. But Recital 47 states that processing personal data strictly necessary for the purpose of preventing fraud constitutes a legitimate interest. Notably, the Recital also includes the example of direct marketing as a possible purpose: 'The processing of personal data for direct marketing purposes may be regarded as carried out for a legitimate interest'. Recital 48 describes another possible purpose: the sharing of personal data within a group of undertakings or institutions affiliated to a central body for internal administrative purposes, such as processing client or employee personal data may be a legitimate interest. Finally, Recital 49 specifically identifies processing personal data strictly necessary and proportionate to ensure network and information security as constituting a legitimate interest.

In relying on the legitimate interest criterion, controllers must carefully consider its interpretation by local data protection regulators and courts since this criterion has historically been understood differently across the EU.

For instance, in the UK, the DPA has indicated that the criterion may be interpreted relatively widely. The UK DPA's current guidance sets out the two tests a controller should follow: first, establishing the legitimacy of the interest pursued and, second, ensuring that the processing is not unwarranted in any particular case through prejudice to the individual concerned. On this second test, the UK DPA states that the processing of personal data may prejudice a particular data subject does not necessarily make the whole processing operation prejudicial to all data subjects. For example, an employer may process data about its employees in relation to job performance, which is necessary in pursuit of the employer's legitimate interests. The employer still needs to ensure that such processing is not impinging on individuals' fundamental rights and freedoms. However, even if there is prejudice that relates to one particular employee due to their unique circumstances, this does not necessarily prejudice the entire processing operation relating to all employees.

Whereas the UK, France and other member states have interpreted this condition broadly, in some member states, the position that concerns the legitimate interest criterion has been much narrower.

Separately in Italy, legitimate interest conditions have historically been specifically set out by the Italian DPA. A controller seeking to rely on the legitimate interest criterion therefore needs to bring its use of data within the scope of the decision set out by that DPA.

Significantly, when processing personal data under this criterion, the controller should be aware that data subjects have the right to object to the use of their data. Under the Regulation, it is then the responsibility of the controller to be able to demonstrate that it has compelling, legitimate grounds to process the personal data that overrides the interests, rights and freedoms of the data subject or for the establishment, exercise or defence of legal claims. When there is a justified objection from the data subject, the controller must cease processing the data.

7.2.8 Legal obligations and the public interest

The Regulation provides more detail than the Directive about reliance on these two criteria: necessary for compliance with a legal obligation and necessary for performance of a task in the public interest. In both instances, Recital 45 indicates that the processing should have a basis in EU or member state law. This is presumably meant to prevent any argument that reliance on non-EU law is valid under these criteria. The Regulation allows member states to set out in detail the requirements of the law—specifications for determining the controller, type of personal data that is subject to the processing, data subjects concerned, entities to which the personal data may be disclosed, purpose limitations, storage period and other measures. EU or member state law can also determine whether the controller must additionally be a public authority or not. These two criteria are also considered to be particularly relevant for any specific processing situations set out in Chapter 9 of the Regulation, which includes processing for freedom of expression and information, processing in the context of employment, and processing for archiving, scientific, historical or statistical purposes. What this means in practice is that the scope for relying on these two criteria will require careful consideration of EU and member state law. It also means that there could be variations, since processing that is considered to be necessary for the performance of a task carried out in the public interest may be permitted under the law of one member state but there may not be an equivalent provision for it under the law of another member state.

7.2.9 Conclusions

There is a shift in the treatment of legitimate processing criteria under the Regulation. Under the Directive, a controller does not have to document which legitimate criterion it is relying on when processing personal data, nor is it required to communicate the criterion to the data subject. This changes under the Regulation, since, as part of the obligation to provide a privacy notice, a controller is required to specify in the privacy notice the legal basis for the processing and when relying on the legitimate interest ground must describe the legitimate interests pursued. Additionally, when relying on the legitimate interest ground, the controller must describe the specific legitimate interests pursued. In other words, a controller must have properly considered which criteria it can rely on before commencing data processing activity because it will be required to notify affected data subjects. Processing activity by a controller without any evidence of proper consideration or muddled or no transparent notification to data subjects and which is subsequently found not to be connected to any legitimising criterion will not impress a DPA that is investigating a controller. Therefore, a prudent controller should take steps such that, if a regulator requires evidence, the controller can point to the criteria it relies on when processing personal data, as well as to its proper notification of data subjects.

7.3 Processing sensitive data

Article 9 is concerned with protecting special categories of data, also known as 'sensitive data'. Specifically, Article 9 prohibits the processing of personal data that reveals 'racial or ethnic origin, political opinions, religious or philosophical beliefs, or trade union membership', in addition to prohibiting the processing of 'genetic data, biometric data for the purpose of uniquely identifying a natural person, data concerning health or data concerning a natural person's sex life or sexual orientation'. Of these categories, the Regulation adds genetic data and biometric data for the purpose of uniquely identifying a natural person to the existing special categories under the Directive.

[handwritten margin note: Sensitive data.]

Interestingly, the Recitals to the Regulation clarify that photographs, presumably of individuals, should not systematically be considered to be processing sensitive data since they are covered by the definition of biometric data only when processed through a specific technical means that allow the unique identification or authentication of an individual. The Regulation permits member states to maintain or introduce further conditions, including limitations for the processing of genetic data, biometric data or data that concerns health. Data on criminal convictions and offences is dealt with under Article 10.

[handwritten margin note: photos = not sensitive; biometric only if processed to allow unique Identification or authentication]

Use of these data categories can, by their nature, pose a threat to privacy. Significantly, some of these categories derive from the Council of Europe Convention for the Protection of Individuals with regard to Automatic Processing of Personal Data ('Convention 108'), where they are identified as special categories of data. In the recitals to the Regulation, it is recognised that personal data that is particularly sensitive in relation to fundamental rights and freedoms merits specific protection since the context could create significant risks.

[handwritten margin note: GDPR allows member states to impose further conditions, including limitation on genetic, biometric & health data]

The choice of categories was substantially influenced by anti-discrimination laws, which may explain why certain categories, such as Social Security numbers and credit card details, were not included even though misuse of such data can lead to serious harm to an individual (e.g., fraud and identity theft). The potential harm to data subjects with respect to these additional categories of data is recognised, however, in the breach notification obligations under the Regulation. Therefore, a controller should not necessarily apply a lower standard of data protection compliance just because a category of data does not technically fit within the definition of sensitive data under the Regulation. Those drafting the Regulation clearly decided that certain categories of personal data require an even higher level of privacy protection and, therefore, imposed stringent rules on controllers processing such data.

Historically, the sensitivity surrounding the use of sensitive data has been such that, in some EU countries, controllers had to obtain approval from the regulator before processing sensitive data. For instance, this has been the case in Denmark, Portugal (with certain exceptions) and Austria. Additionally, in some jurisdictions, such as Belgium and Luxembourg, private sector organisations have been prohibited from processing data on criminal convictions, which can affect the ability for employers to carry out background checks. Similarly, in a more limited context, Article 10 requires that processing of personal data relating to criminal convictions and offences can only be carried out 'under the control of official authority or when the processing is authorised by Union or Member State law providing for appropriate safeguards for the rights and freedoms of data subjects'.

Just because a controller can legitimise the processing of sensitive data by relying on one of the exceptions under Article 9, does not mean that the rest of the Regulation does not apply to this processing. A controller must meet a condition under both Articles 6 and 9 when processing sensitive data.

Due to the greater level of protection accorded to sensitive data, the controller will need to pay particular attention to ensuring that all other aspects of compliance are met. For instance, controllers should ensure proper and full notification to individuals about how their sensitive data will be used in accordance with Articles 12–14.

The general starting point under Article 9 is that processing sensitive data is prohibited. There are then a number of exceptions to that prohibition. The drafters of the Regulation favoured sticking with the approach under the Directive to emphasise that sensitive data requires a high level of protection. The preferred position was to begin with a broad prohibition on the use of sensitive data that is then qualified by narrow exceptions.

7.3.1 The data subject has given explicit consent to the processing of those personal data for one or more specified purposes, except where Union or Member State law provide that the prohibition … may not be lifted by the data subject

The consent required under this first Article 9 exception differs from the consent under Article 6 only in that it must be explicit. In other words, any Article 9 consent must still be unambiguous, freely given, specific and informed, but it must in addition be explicit. The definition of consent requires a statement or clear affirmative action to signify agreement to the proceedings. But clearly the consent under Article 9 must be more than this—requiring it to be explicit indicates that the quality of the consent is more than a statement or clear affirmative action. This would suggest, perhaps, that consent must be given in writing with a handwritten signature. But the WP29, in its opinion on consent under the Directive, allows that explicit consent can be given on paper or in electronic form that uses electronic or digital signatures or by clicking on icons or sending confirmatory emails.[9] Due to the greater protection attached to sensitive data, regulators and courts will likely require a strict level of compliance from controllers who wish to rely on the explicit consent of data subjects to use their sensitive data.

A controller must therefore be careful to ensure that it meets the requirements for consent—that it is unambiguous, specific, informed and freely given. Additionally, the consent given must be explicit and set forth the purposes of the processing.

For instance, it would be prudent for a consent form to specifically refer to the actual data or categories of data that will be processed (which is not strictly required in the notification obligation under Article 13, although it is included in Article 14). Meeting the requirement of explicitness may require that the consent be in writing or be documented in some other permanent record.

It is also important to note that there may be circumstances where a member state's law stipulates that the giving of consent is not enough to avoid the prohibition on processing sensitive data. Where this is the case, the controller will need to look for another supporting criterion.

Guidance from DPAs will likely specify what is required to meet the explicit consent standard. Where writing is required, this may pose difficulties for collecting sensitive data through the Internet, depending on whether local law accepts consent expressed in electronic form as evidence of written consent. Different jurisdictions may hold different positions on this according to DPA guidance and case law. For example, the combined action of ticking a box plus pressing an 'Accept' button is likely to amount to explicit consent on the Internet in the UK. Under German law, however, a consent to the processing of sensitive data is valid only if the consent refers specifically to the sensitive data to be processed, potentially requiring 'just-in-time' consent notices, in addition to a broader privacy statement.[10]

7.3.2 Processing is necessary for the purposes of carrying out the obligations and exercising specific rights of the controller or of the data subject in the field of employment and social security and social protection law in so far as it is authorised by Union or Member State law or a collective agreement pursuant to Member State law providing for appropriate safeguards for the fundamental rights and the interests of the data subject

The second exception from the prohibition applies mainly when the processing of sensitive data is necessary for the controller to comply with a legal obligation under employment, social security or social protection law. Thus, this criterion is relevant when data subjects are candidates, employees and contractors as permitted under local employment law. The controller will also need to comply with the necessity test. The extent of this criterion will depend on local employment law and the interpretation of local rules. Additionally, member states may provide for more specific rules relating to personal data processing in the context of employment (see Chapter 14).

7.3.3 Processing is necessary to protect the vital interests of the data subject or of another natural person where the data subject is physically or legally incapable of giving consent

Similar to the criterion of vital interests under Article 6, this criterion refers to circumstances of life or death. The criterion is essentially identical to the provision in Article 6 except for the fact that, under Article 9, the controller must be able to demonstrate that it is not possible to obtain consent since 'the data subject is physically or legally incapable of giving consent'. There are obvious emergency examples where it will not be possible to obtain consent to the processing of sensitive data (e.g., the data subject is unconscious). However, this qualification indicates that the controller is expected to attempt to seek consent.

7.3.4 Processing is carried out in the course of its legitimate activities with appropriate safeguards by a foundation, association or any other not-for-profit body with a political, philosophical, religious or trade union aim and on condition that the processing relates solely to the members or to former members of the body or to persons who have regular contact with it in connection with its purposes and that the personal data are not disclosed outside that body without the consent of the data subjects

This criterion is designed to cover particular nonprofit institutions, such as churches, other religious establishments or political parties. It relates to the processing of sensitive data about either members or former members of the organisation or those who have regular contact with the organisation. This criterion has particular resonance for member states with active civil society institutions, such as churches that hold sensitive data on their members. It is important to note that these bodies must still process sensitive data in compliance with the other requirements of the Regulation and that in relying on this criterion, this processing must only take place (1) in the course of their legitimate activities, (2) with appropriate safeguards, and (3) in connection with their specific purposes. In addition, they may only disclose sensitive data outside the organisation with the explicit consent of the relevant data subject. Further specific requirements relating to this criterion are set down under local law. Article 91 makes clear that where churches and religious associations or communities apply comprehensive data processing rules relating to the protection of individuals, these rules may continue to apply, provided they are brought into line with the Regulation.

7.3.5 Processing relates to personal data which are manifestly made public by the data subject

This criterion is met when data subjects deliberately disclose sensitive data about themselves (e.g., when individuals provide details about their political opinions or health when giving media interviews). Sharing sensitive information publicly on a social networking platform could also potentially fall within this criterion.

7.3.6 Processing is necessary for the establishment, exercise or defence of legal claims or whenever courts are acting in their judicial capacity

Using sensitive data may also be necessary for a controller to establish, exercise or defend legal claims. Reliance on this criterion requires the controller to establish necessity. That is, there must be a close and substantial connection between the processing and the purposes. One example of an activity that would fall under this criterion is processing medical data by an insurance company in order to determine whether a person's claim for medical insurance is valid. Processing such data would be necessary for the insurance company to consider the claim brought by the claimant under their insurance policy.

The Regulation also includes wording that concerns processing that is necessary whenever courts are acting in a judicial capacity. All such processing would still be subject to the data protection principles set out under Article 5.

7.3.7 Processing is necessary for reasons of substantial public interest, on the basis of Union or Member State law which shall be proportionate to the aim pursued, respect the essence of the right to data protection and provide for suitable and specific measures to safeguard the fundamental rights and the interests of the data subject

This provision reflects a similar provision from the Directive, although the Directive gives member states a greater degree of freedom to establish further exemptions for the processing of sensitive data in the substantial public interest, requiring only that these further exemptions are subject to suitable safeguards. The Regulation tightens up the ability for member states to set down in law what they consider to be in the substantial public interest by adding two additional requirements to such laws: that they (1) are 'proportionate to the aim pursued' and (2) show 'respect for the essence of the right to data protection'.[11] Neither the Directive nor the Regulation defines what is meant by the substantial public interest. Therefore, this is left open for member states to interpret.

Specific exemptions for processing sensitive data in the substantial public interest have already been specified by some member states. For instance, the Italian data protection code states that particular activities carried out by the National Health Services and other public health care bodies are considered to be in the substantial public interest.[12]

In the UK, a statutory instrument has set out further criteria for processing sensitive personal data in the substantial public interest.[13] The statutory instrument permits processing of sensitive data in the substantial public interest, permitting such processing when it is necessary for the purposes of preventing or detecting any unlawful act or to discharge any function designed to protect the public against dishonesty, seriously improper conduct or mismanagement in the administration of any organisation or association.

These existing grounds under member state law can continue to apply under the Regulation but only so long as the laws are proportionate to the aim pursued, respect the essence of the right to data protection and provide for suitable and specific measures to safeguard the fundamental rights and interests of data subjects. Significantly, under the Regulation, member states derogating from the prohibition against processing sensitive personal data by relying on reasons of substantial public interests are not required to notify these derogations to the European Commission ('Commission') as they were under the Directive.

7.3.8 Processing is necessary for the purposes of preventive or occupational medicine, for the assessment of the working capacity of the employee, medical diagnosis, the provision of health or social care or treatment or the management of health or social care systems and services on the basis of Union or Member State law or pursuant to contract with a health professional and subject to conditions and additional safeguards

The prohibition on processing sensitive data does not apply when the processing of sensitive data is, broadly speaking, related to a medical or social care purpose.[14] This exception includes data processing in the context of delivering health care services—preventive or occupational medicine, medical diagnosis, treatment or management of health care systems and services. It also includes processing of data in the context of the provision of social care, as well as treatment and management of social care systems and services. The processing may also be carried out on the basis of either EU or member state law or under a contract with a health professional but not necessarily a health professional who is subject to the 'conditions and additional safeguards' provided in Paragraph 3 of Article 9. Under Paragraph 3, sensitive personal data may be processed by (or under the responsibility of) any person who is subject to an obligation of professional secrecy or another obligation of secrecy under EU or member state law or rules established by national competent bodies.

Whilst it is not the easiest provision to understand, it seems clear that this exception mainly will apply to doctors, nurses and others involved in healthcare professions. Such professions are usually subject to their own legislation, rules and professional guidelines about how to conduct the collection and use of health data and how such data can be used. Of course, this exception does not mean that such data is exempt from the operation of the rest of data protection laws. Controllers should still, for instance, ensure that this sensitive data is held securely and not inappropriately accessed.

Significantly, this provision also specifically includes processing necessary for the assessment of the working capacity of the employee. This would likely encompass drug testing of employees and other assessments that need to take place to ensure an employee is fit to work. Companies involved in processing health data where the data subjects are not employees and the purpose of the processing does not otherwise fall under this exception will often have to rely on explicit consent from the individuals concerned.

7.3.9 Processing is necessary for reasons of public interest in the area of public health, such as protection against serious cross-border threats to health or ensuring high standards of quality and safety of health care and of medicinal products or medical devices, on the basis of Union or Member State law which provides for suitable and specific measures to safeguard the rights and freedoms of the data subject, in particular professional secrecy

Recital 54 recognises that processing of sensitive data may be necessary for reasons of public interest in the area of public health without the consent of data subjects. Public health is interpreted, as defined in EU Regulation No. 1338/2008, as 'all elements related to health, namely health status, including morbidity and disability, the determinants having an effect on that health status, health care needs, resources allocated to health care, the provision of, and universal access to, health care as well as health care expenditure and financing, and the causes of mortality'. Mindful of the concerns individuals may have about their health data being used, the Recital stipulates that such processing of data should not result in personal data being processed for other purposes by third parties, such as employers, insurance or banking companies. Evidently, this is included as a safeguard to protect individuals from being worried that they might be discriminated against.

This criterion is designed to cover processing of health data by those engaged in public health care and the supervision of drugs and medical devices to ensure quality and safety. Recital 53 indicates that this ground relates to data processing necessary to achieve health-related purposes for the benefit of natural persons and society as a whole.

7.3.10 Processing is necessary for archiving purposes in the public interest, scientific or historical research purposes or statistical purposes in accordance with Article 89(1) based on Union or Member State law which shall be proportionate to the aim pursued, respect the essence of the right to data protection and provide for suitable and specific measures to safeguard the fundamental rights and the interests of the data subject

Article 8 of the Directive does not have a close equivalent to this Regulation exception. Under the Directive, processing data for statistical purposes, or historical or scientific research has special status in certain contexts. For instance, the Directive dispenses with the obligation to provide notice to data subjects where personal data was not collected directly from them, as well as provides an exemption from the data subject's right of access. Article 9 of the Regulation now provides a specific criterion for controllers involved in archiving, scientific or historical research, or processing for statistical purposes. In order to rely on this criterion, it is necessary that the processing must have appropriate safeguards in accordance with Article 89(1) and must be necessary for one of these purposes based on EU or member state law, which must be proportionate, respect the essence of the right to data protection and provide for suitable safeguards.

Article 89(1) requires safeguards to be put in place for any processing that falls within this criterion. 'Those safeguards shall ensure that technical and organisational measures are in place in particular in order to ensure respect for the principle of data minimisation'. The measures may also include pseudonymisation. Although the Regulation does not expressly require it, anonymisation reflects best practice where feasible as it removes the possibility of data subject identification. Additionally, Article 89 also allows that EU or member state law may provide further derogations from rights granted to data subjects where those rights are likely to render impossible or seriously impair the achievement of these particular purposes and where such derogations are necessary for the fulfillment of these purposes.

Whilst archivists and historians will be grateful for the regime under Article 89, probably the organisations that will be most impacted will be those involved in scientific research and statistical work. In particular, pharmaceutical companies and academic institutions carrying out scientific research will be keen to explore the parameters of this regime. Recital 159 indicates that the processing of personal data for scientific research purposes should be interpreted in a broad manner, including technological development and demonstration, fundamental research, applied research and privately funded research. Whilst scientific research includes studies conducted in the public interest in the area of public health, it does not preclude studies conducted for private research purposes.

7.4 Data on offences, criminal convictions and offences and security measures

Data on criminal convictions and offences or related security measures understandably requires a greater level of protection. Article 10 of the Regulation requires that such data be processed only 'under the control of an official authority or when the processing is authorised by Union or Member State law providing for appropriate safeguards for the rights and freedoms of data subjects'. It seems unlikely that in this context the official authority is a data protection regulator. A comprehensive register of criminal convictions can only be kept under the control of an official authority. Therefore, a private sector controller will need to examine the rules under EU or local law around processing such data in order to understand the scope for legitimate processing. Significantly, this type of data is not additionally considered to be a category of sensitive personal data under Article 9. However, when processing this type of data, a controller must still comply with all other requirements of the Regulation.

7.5 Processing which does not require identification

Article 11 clarifies that 'if the purposes for which a controller processes personal data do not or do no longer require the identification of a data subject by the controller', the controller is not obliged to maintain, acquire or process additional information in order to identify the data subject for the sole purpose of complying with the Regulation. Consequently, a controller is not required to comply with certain obligations concerning the rights of data subjects except that this assumption is reversed if a data subject provides additional information to the controller enabling their identification.[15] This provision is aimed at the type of situation in which an online organisation receives a request for access from an individual to personal data that the organisation holds, but the organisation does not intend to identify data subjects in the personal data. In such a case, it can be technically difficult for the organisation to determine which personal data relates to the individual.

7.6   Conclusion

The criteria justifying the processing of sensitive data are relatively narrow since the intention of the Regulation is to protect individuals from any potential misuse of their data that impacts their fundamental rights. Whilst the Regulation adds two further data elements—genetic and biometric data—to the original list under the Directive, these limited categorisations may be surprising since, in today's world, the greater risk to people is frequently seen to be misuse of their financial information. Arguably, any information that can have a serious impact on an individual, whether on a person's livelihood, safety or purse, should be handled with a strict level of protection. However, EU law identifies only this specific, limited list of data as requiring special protection and requires that it be processed only under a legitimate criterion defined under Article 9.

Endnotes

1 General Data Protection Regulation, Article 4.

2 General Data Protection Regulation, Recital 42.

3 General Data Protection Regulation, Recital 32.

4 General Data Protection Regulation, Article 8.

5 Titcomb, James, 'Britain opts out of EU law setting social media age of consent at 16', *The Telegraph*, 16 December 2015, www.telegraph.co.uk/technology/internet/12053858/Britain-opts-out-of-EU-law-raising-social-media-age-of-consent-to-16.html.

6 Opinion 01/2014 on the application of necessity and proportionality concepts and data protection within the law enforcement sector (536/14EN: WP 211), 27 February 2014, http://ec.europa.eu/justice/data-protection/article-29/documentation/opinion-recommendation/files/2014/wp211_en.pdf.

7 General Data Protection Regulation, Article 21.

8 General Data Protection Regulation, Recital 47.

9   Opinion 15/2011 on the definition of consent (01197/11/EN: WP 187), 13 July 2011.

10 Federal Data Protection Act (BDSG), https://www.gesetze-im-internet.de/englisch_bdsg/englisch_bdsg.html.

11 General Data Protection, Article 9.

12 Italian Personal Data Protection Code, Privacy.it, www.privacy.it/archivio/privacycode-en.html.

13 The Data Protection (Processing of Sensitive Personal Data) Order 2000, No. 417, www.legislation.gov.uk/uksi/2000/417/made.

14 General Data Protection Regulation, Article 9.

15 General Data Protection Regulation, Article 11.

CHAPTER 8

Information Provision Obligations

Hannah Jackson, CIPP/E

8.1 The transparency principle

The first of the General Data Protection Regulation's (GDPR, or 'Regulation') principles that relate to the processing of personal data is that it must be processed 'lawfully, fairly and in a transparent manner in relation to the data subject'.[1] Transparency, or the requirement to be open and honest about the ways in which personal data is used, therefore remains a key component of the European data protection framework. Ultimately, the Regulation aims to ensure that it is clear to data subjects that their personal data is collected and processed, and that they are aware of their rights, and the risks, rules and safeguards in relation to that processing.[2]

The Regulation specifically addresses the principle of transparency by requiring that controllers provide data subjects with certain information about the processing of their personal data.[3] This information is often referred to as 'fair processing information'. Transparency, however, also plays a key role in a number of the Regulation's other principles.

Under the Data Protection Directive ('Directive'), transparency was expressly linked to the concept of fairness of processing.[4] The Regulation retains this link, explaining that 'The principles of fair and transparent processing require that the data subject be informed of the existence of the processing operation and its purposes'.[5] Failure to either provide fair processing information where required by the Regulation or to process personal data in accordance with the information provided is therefore likely to render the processing unfair, as well as to constitute a breach of a number of the Regulation's specific information provision obligations.

Transparency is similarly vital when 'consent' as a basis for processing is considered. As discussed in Chapter 7, for consent to be valid it must meet certain criteria, including that it is informed.[6]

For consent to be informed, data subjects must be clearly told what they are consenting to. In particular, the Regulation requires that, in order to provide valid consent, the data subject must be aware of at least the identity of the controller and the purposes for which personal data is processed.[7] The information provided to a data subject when their consent is sought will therefore have a direct impact on the validity of their consent. Where the information given is inaccurate or incomplete, or it does not otherwise meet the additional requirements set out below, the consent will be invalid.

The provision of information to data subjects is also likely to have a significant impact on the ability of a controller to rely on the 'legitimate interests' basis for processing under Article 6(1)(f) of the Regulation.

Recital 47 of the Regulation states that:

> [T]he existence of a legitimate interest would need careful assessment including whether a data subject can reasonably expect at the time and in the context of the collection of the personal data that processing for that purpose may take place. The interests and fundamental rights of the data subject could in particular override the interest of the data controller where personal data are processed in circumstances where data subjects do not reasonably expect further processing.

In other words, when a data subject is given clear information about how their personal data will be processed, controllers are more likely to be able to support a legitimate interest claim. Conversely, that claim will be difficult to make if no information is provided.

Whilst there are a number of similarities between the Directive and the Regulation in terms of the treatment of transparency, there are also some differences. The Directive, for example, imposed a requirement that controllers notify their processing to the competent supervisory authority.[8] Data subjects could then consult that notification to learn more about the processing conducted by a particular controller. The Regulation removes this general notification requirement, stating that:

> While that obligation produces administrative and financial burdens, it did not in all cases contribute to improving the protection of personal data. Such indiscriminate general notification obligations should therefore be abolished, and replaced by effective procedures and mechanisms which focus instead on those types of processing operations which are likely to result in a high risk to the rights and freedoms of natural persons by virtue of their nature, scope, context and purposes.[9]

8.1.1 The Regulation and the provision of information to data subjects

The primary obligations that govern the provision of information to data subjects are set out in Articles 13 (covering cases where personal data is collected from the data subject) and 14 (relating to instances where personal data is obtained from a source other than the data subject) of the Regulation.

Subject to some exceptions (as described below), the combined effect of these Articles is that data subjects have the right to receive certain information from controllers, regardless of whether they supplied their personal data directly or it was provided to the controller by a third party.

Whilst the information provision obligations set out in the Regulation arise primarily from Articles 13 and 14, these sections do not cover the full range of information that a controller may have to provide to a data subject. Instead, the Regulation also states that certain additional information must be provided to data subjects when specific types of processing are conducted.

[handwritten margin notes: Art 13 (if obtained from data subjects) Art 14 (obtained from 3rd party) ↓ right to recieve info from controller regardless of source]

8.1.2 Article 13: The obligation to provide information to a data subject where personal data is collected from the data subject

Article 13(1) requires that where personal data that relates to the data subject is collected directly from the data subject, all the following information must be provided to the data subject:

- the identity and the contact details of the controller and, where applicable, of the controller's representative;

- the contact details of the data protection officer (DPO), where one is appointed;

- the purposes and legal basis of the processing;

- where the processing is necessary for the purpose of the controller's legitimate interest or the legitimate interest of a third party (under Article 6(1)(f) of the Regulation), the legitimate interests pursued by the controller or the third party;

- the recipients or categories of recipients of the personal data, if any; and

- whether the controller intends to transfer personal data to a third country or international organisation, and, if so:

  - whether or not an adequacy decision by the European Commission (the 'Commission') exists in relation to the transfer; or

- if the transfer is made on the basis of appropriate safeguards pursuant to Articles 46 or 47 of the Regulation (e.g., under standard data protection clauses adopted by the Commission or Binding Corporate Rules (BCR)), or on the basis of the controller's compelling legitimate interests and own assessment that suitable safeguards are in place for the personal data transferred (under the second sub-paragraph of Article 49(1) of the Regulation), reference to the appropriate or suitable safeguards relied upon by the controller and the means by which to obtain a copy of them or where they have been made available.

In addition to the information above, Article 13(2) requires that a controller 'shall ... provide the data subject with the following further information necessary to ensure fair and transparent processing...'. The additional information required by Article 13(2) is:

- the period for which the personal data will be stored or, if that is not possible, the criteria used to determine that period;

- information about data subjects' rights in relation to their personal data, namely the existence of the rights: (1) to request access to and rectification or erasure of personal data; (2) to request restriction of processing concerning the data subject; (3) to object to processing; and (4) in relation to data portability. When providing this information, controllers should note, however, that these rights do not arise in all circumstances (see Chapter 9 for further information on data subjects' rights);

- where the processing is based on consent (under Article 6(1)(a) of the Regulation) or on explicit consent where special categories of personal data are processed (under Article 9(2)(a)), the existence of the right for the data subject to withdraw that consent at any time without affecting the lawfulness of processing based on the consent before its withdrawal;

- the right to lodge a complaint with a supervisory authority;

- whether the provision of personal data is a statutory or contractual requirement or a requirement necessary to enter into a contract, as well as whether the data subject is obliged to provide the personal data and the possible consequences of not doing so; and

- the existence of automated decision-making, including profiling, referred to in Articles 22(1) and (4) of the Regulation (namely where the profiling produces legal effects or otherwise significantly affects a data subject or involves special categories of personal data). When the controller is engaged in profiling, it also should supply meaningful information about the logic involved, and the significance and envisaged consequences of the processing for the data subject.

It is unclear why the information to be provided to data subjects under Articles 13(1) and 13(2) of the Regulation is set out across two slightly different provisions. Reviewing the Directive, its information provision regime comprised, subject to some limited exceptions:

- a mandatory set of information (including the identity of the controller, for example) to be provided to data subjects in all circumstances; and

- a non-exhaustive list of further information which had to be provided insofar as it was necessary, having regard to the specific circumstances in which the personal data was collected to guarantee fair processing in respect of the data subject.[10]

Art 13(1) vs 13(2): mandatory vs. if necessary; conflicting interpretations

The intention of Article 13(2) of the Regulation may have been to follow the Directive's approach such that the information listed in it need only be provided where necessary to ensure that personal data is processed fairly. This approach is supported by Recital 60 to the Regulation, which states that:

> *The principles of fair and transparent processing require that the data subject be informed of the existence of the processing operation and its purposes. The controller should provide the data subject with any further information necessary to ensure fair and transparent processing taking into account the specific circumstances and context in which the personal data are processed.*

Ambiguity in the drafting, however, means that Article 13(2) can also be interpreted such that the provision of the information listed in it is always necessary to ensure that processing is fair and transparent, and that it should therefore always be provided to data subjects. Guidance on the Regulation[11] from the UK's Information Commissioner's Office (ICO) has not distinguished between the information provision obligations set out in Articles 13(1) and 13(2) and implies that both sets of information should be given to data subjects in all cases.[12] If this approach is followed by other supervisory authorities, there will be no distinction in practice between Articles 13(1) and 13(2) and no opportunity for a controller to balance the nature and types of fair processing information provided with the context of the processing and the expectations of the data subject.

8.1.3 Article 14: The obligation to provide information to a data subject where personal data is not obtained from the data subject

Article 14 addresses situations in which personal data is not obtained directly from the data subject. Under Article 14(1) and Article 14(2), the controller must provide the data subject with the same information required in Article 13(1) and in Article 13(2). Pursuant to Article 14(1) and (2), the controller must also provide the following information:

- the categories of personal data concerned; and

- from which source the personal data originate and, if applicable, whether it came from publicly accessible sources (note that where the origin of the personal data cannot be provided to the data subject because a number of sources have been used, Recital 61 provides that general information should be given).

Under Article 14, as personal data is not obtained directly from the data subject, there is no requirement to inform the data subject whether the provision of personal data is a statutory or contractual requirement or a requirement necessary to enter into a contract, or to explain whether the data subject is obliged to provide the personal data and the possible consequences of not doing so.

As with Article 13, however, there is ambiguity as to whether the information listed in Article 14(2) has to be provided to the data subject in all instances or only where necessary to ensure fair and transparent processing. The ICO does not distinguish in its guidance between the information to be provided under Article 14(1) and the information to be provided under 14(2), the inference being that both sets of information should be provided in all circumstances, unless an exemption applies.[13]

Although Articles 13 and 14 of the Regulation are similar in terms of the fair processing information to be provided to data subjects, practical differences between the obligations include the time at which the required information should be provided and the circumstances in which a controller does not have to provide information about its processing. These divergences are described further below.

8.1.4 Situations in which additional information is required

Regardless of whether personal data is obtained directly from the data subject or from a third party, the Regulation requires that further information is provided or made available to data subjects in certain circumstances.

8.1.4.1 Data subjects' rights

Further information provision obligations are imposed on controllers in the context of the rights granted to data subjects by the Regulation.

Although Articles 13 and 14 of the Regulation impose an obligation on controllers to provide a significant amount of information to data subjects about the processing of their personal data, **Article 15 creates a freestanding right for data subjects to request much of this information from controllers.**[14]

The Regulation also grants data subjects the right to require the controller to **restrict the processing of their personal data in some circumstances.**[15] **Where a data subject exercises this right, the controller must inform the data subject before lifting that restriction.**[16]

Data subjects have further rights under the Regulation to object to the processing of their personal data where that processing is:

- conducted on the basis of the controller's 'legitimate interests' (under Article 6(1)(f) of the Regulation) or is necessary for the performance of a task carried out in the public interest (under Article 6(1)(e)), and this includes the right to object to profiling based on these provisions;[17] or

- for the purpose of direct marketing, including profiling to the extent that it is related to direct marketing.[18]

Controllers must **explicitly bring these rights to the attention of data subjects and present this information clearly and separately from any other information.**[19]

8.1.4.2 International data transfers

In addition to the information to be provided under Article 13 or 14, as appropriate, where personal data is:

- transferred to a third country or international organisation on the basis of:

  - a controller's compelling legitimate interests and own assessment of the circumstances surrounding the transfer (under the second subparagraph of Article 49(1) of the Regulation), data subjects must be **informed of the transfer and of the compelling legitimate interests pursued by the controller;**[20]

  - consent, in which case, data subjects must be informed of the **possible risks of the transfer** due to the absence of either an adequacy decision from the Commission or other 'appropriate safeguards', such as standard data protection clauses adopted by the Commission;[21] or

- transferred pursuant to BCR, data subjects must be provided with information about the general data protection principles contained in the BCR; data subjects' rights in relation to the processing and how to exercise them, including the right to obtain compensation for breaches of the BCR; and the liability arrangements under the BCR.[22]

8.1.4.3 New purposes of processing

Where a controller intends to process personal data for a purpose other than that for which it was originally collected or obtained, the controller must provide data subjects with information about the new purpose, together with 'any relevant further information as referred to in Paragraph 2 [of Article 13 and Article 14, as appropriate]'.[23]

8.1.4.4 Multiple controllers

In situations in which two or more controllers jointly determine the purposes and means of processing, the Regulation requires those controllers to transparently determine their respective responsibilities for complying with the Regulation, in particular, in relation to the obligation to provide information to data subjects under Articles 13 and 14. The 'essence' of this arrangement should be made available to data subjects.[24]

The obligation to 'make this information available' is distinct from the active obligation to 'provide' information under Articles 13 and 14. The extent to which controllers will have to include this detail in fair processing information or provide it only on request from data subjects is therefore unclear.

8.1.4.5 Personal data breaches

In some circumstances, data subjects must be notified of personal data breaches.[25] This obligation is discussed in Chapter 10.

8.1.5 When information should be provided to data subjects

Where personal data is collected from the data subject, the information set out in Articles 13(1) and 13(2) must be provided at the time when the personal data is obtained.[26]

Article 14(3) provides that when personal data is obtained from someone other than the data subject, the fair processing information should be provided:

(a) *within a reasonable period after obtaining the personal data, but at the latest within one month, having regard to the specific circumstances in which the personal data are processed;*

(b) *if the personal data are to be used for communication with the data subject, at the latest at the time of the first communication to that data subject; or*

(c) *if a disclosure to another recipient is envisaged, at the latest when the personal data are first disclosed.*

Where personal data is to be processed for a purpose other than that for which it was collected or obtained, the controller must provide data subjects with the required fair processing information before the new processing begins.[27]

Information about the data subject's right to object to processing must be provided to the data subject at the latest at the time of the first communication with the data subject.[28] Information about the right to withdraw consent must be provided before a data subject gives their consent.[29]

8.1.6 How information should be provided to data subjects

The Regulation states specifically that the information provided to data subjects about the processing of their personal data must be given in a concise, transparent, intelligible and easily accessible form, using clear and plain language. In particular, information intended for children should be in language easy for children to understand.[30]

The Regulation also states that information shall be provided in writing or by other means, including, where appropriate, by 'electronic means'.[31] The Recitals to the Regulation explain that electronic means could include through a website and that this will be particularly relevant where there are a number of parties involved in the processing, and technological complexity makes it difficult for data subjects to understand who is processing their personal data and for what purposes. The Regulation specifically cites online advertising as an example of this type of situation.[32]

Fair processing information may also, where requested by the data subject, be provided orally as long as the identity of the data subject is proven by other means.[33] In all cases, the information provided to data subjects under Articles 13 and 14 must be free of charge.[34]

The Regulation permits 'visualisation' to be used to provide fair processing information to data subjects where appropriate and makes provision for the use of standardised icons to give an easily visible, understandable and meaningful overview of the processing.[35] The Regulation empowers the Commission to adopt delegated acts to determine what information will be presented using these standardised icons and the procedures for providing them and lists the provision of an opinion on the standardised icons as one of the tasks of the European Data Protection Board.[36] The Regulation requires that where the standardised icons are presented electronically, they must be machine readable.[37]

Additional format requirements are imposed by the Regulation where information is provided to data subjects in the context of obtaining their consent. Where consent is given in a written declaration that also concerns other matters, the request for consent must be presented in a manner which is clearly distinguishable from those other matters and also in an intelligible and easily accessible form, using clear and plain language.[38]

In addition to the above, information about the right to object to processing must be explicitly brought to the attention of the data subject and presented clearly and separately from other information.[39] The fact controllers have to bring this information to the attention of data subjects rather than simply 'provide' it (as required under Articles 13 and 14) suggests that additional action is required over and above making fair processing information available on a website, for example.

8.1.7 Areas in which further information provision requirements could be imposed

The Regulation sets out a number of areas in which members states may legislate to provide specific rules for the processing of personal data. These areas include, for example, the processing of employee personal data in an employment context. Where additional rules are introduced by member states in this regard, they must include 'suitable and specific' measures to safeguard data subjects' rights, in particular, in relation to the transparency of processing.[40]

The Regulation also provides the opportunity for associations and other bodies representing categories of controllers to prepare codes of conduct setting out the application of the Regulation, including in relation to transparency and the information to be provided to the public, data subjects and children.[41] There is, therefore, the possibility that additional, more specific transparency obligations may be imposed on particular groups of controllers through these codes of conduct.

8.2   Exemptions to the obligation to provide information to data subjects

The Regulation both creates exemptions from the requirement for controllers to provide fair processing information without the need for member states to adopt new domestic legislation and also allows member states to legislate to create their own exemptions in certain situations.

With regard to the Regulation's 'own' exemptions, namely those which do not require an implementing member state law, where personal data is collected directly from the data subject, the fair processing information required by Articles 13(1) and 13(2) or information about a new purpose of processing when applicable need not be provided if the data subject already has this information.[42]

Similarly, where personal data is obtained from a source other than the data subject, the fair processing information required by Articles 14(1) and 14(2) or information about a new purpose of processing, where applicable, need not be provided:

- if the data subject already has this information;[43]

- if obtaining or disclosing the personal data is expressly laid down by Union or member state law to which the controller is subject and which provides appropriate measures to protect the data subject's legitimate interests;[44]

- where the personal data must remain confidential subject to an obligation of professional secrecy regulated by Union or member state law, including a statutory obligation of secrecy;[45] or

- if the provision of the information proves impossible or would involve a disproportionate effort, in particular, for processing for archiving purposes in the public interest, scientific or historical research purposes or statistical purposes, provided that:

  - the conditions and safeguards referred to in Article 89(1) relating to processing for these purposes of archiving or scientific or historical research are met (these are intended to ensure that technical and organisational measures are in place to guarantee data minimisation, for example); or

  - the provision of fair processing information is likely to render impossible or seriously impair the achievement of the objectives of that processing.

The Regulation continues: 'In such cases, the controller shall take appropriate measures to protect the data subject's rights and freedoms and legitimate interests, including making the information publicly available'.[46] It is unclear whether this requirement applies only to situations in which fair processing information is not provided on the grounds that it would prejudice the purposes of processing or whether it applies in such a case, as well as where processing is conducted for reasons of archiving or scientific or historical research. Given the importance placed on transparency by the Regulation, it would be advisable for controllers to consider that the requirement applied in both instances.

In assessing the meaning and application of the term 'disproportionate effort', consideration should still be given to Recital 40 of the Directive, which is largely replicated in Recital 62 of the Regulation. These recitals cite the number of data subjects, the age of the personal data and any compensatory measures applied (or, in the Regulation's Recital, 'appropriate safeguards adopted') as factors that should be considered in assessing whether the effort required to provide fair processing information would be disproportionate. However, in the absence of a clear definition of 'disproportionate effort', the term is open to interpretation by national supervisory authorities, and these are likely to expect considerable effort to be expended by a controller in meeting its transparency obligations.

Despite the likely high expectations of national supervisory authorities, the exemptions listed above retain the Directive's premise that data protection rules should be practical and not unduly burdensome and that there should be a balance between the obligation to notify data subjects and the cost to the controller of compliance.

Article 14(5) acknowledges that when a controller processes personal data about data subjects obtained from others, the provision of information to data subjects can prove to be impossible or involve a disproportionate effort. This exemption could be considered, for example, where information about a data subject may be widely known (e.g., due to media coverage), such that many organisations may hold information about that person. To notify well-known data subjects, such as politicians, that a controller holds certain widely available information about them becomes nonsensical. This is particularly the case where the privacy of the data subject is not violated by the processing undertaken. However, where the privacy of a data subject could be prejudiced and the controller elects, based on this exemption, to dispense with the provision of fair processing information, the controller should rely upon and record robust grounds for collecting and processing the data (see Chapter 7).

Likewise, Article 14(5)(c) recognises that a controller may be under a legal obligation to process personal data. In such cases, the controller may collect personal data from third parties but should not be required to notify each data subject so long as the legal obligation compelling the processing provides sufficient privacy safeguards and protects the data subject's legitimate interests.

In circumstances in which personal data is collected from third parties but no fair processing information is provided, data subjects are, unless an exemption applies, still entitled to request both information about the processing and access to their personal data from a controller (see Chapter 9).

Managing transparency on this basis is realistic and practical; a controller is required to respond to a request for information about its processing if asked by a data subject but is not always required to proactively provide the extensive information required under Article 14 of the Regulation.

In addition to the exemptions listed above, **Article 23** sets out the circumstances in which **member states may legislate to restrict the Regulation's requirements that personal data is processed in a fair and transparent manner and that fair processing information is provided to data subjects** pursuant to Articles 13 and 14.

when member states can lgislate addtl exemptions re: FPI

Article 23(1) states that:

> *Union or Member State law to which the data controller or processor is subject may restrict by way of a legislative measure the scope of the obligations and rights provided for in Articles 12 to 22 [Articles 13 and 14 contain the primary obligations as regards information provision] and Article 34, as well as Article 5 [which requires, amongst other things, that personal data is processed in a fair and transparent manner] in so far as its provisions correspond to the rights and obligations provided for in Articles 12 to 22, when such a restriction respects the essence of the fundamental rights and freedoms and is a necessary and proportionate measure in a democratic society to safeguard:*
>
> *(a)   national security;*
>
> *(b)   defence;*
>
> *(c)   public security [Recital 73 notes that this includes the protection of human life especially in response to natural or manmade disasters];*
>
> *(d)   the prevention, investigation, detection or prosecution of criminal offences or the execution of criminal penalties, including the safeguarding against and the prevention of threats to public security;*
>
> *(e)   other important objectives of general public interest of the Union or of a Member State, in particular an important economic or financial interest of the Union or of a Member State, including monetary, budgetary and taxation a matters, public health and social security;*
>
> *(f)   the protection of judicial independence and judicial proceedings;*
>
> *(g)   the prevention, investigation, detection and prosecution of breaches of ethics for regulated professions;*
>
> *(h)   a monitoring, inspection or regulatory function connected, even occasionally, to the exercise of official authority in the cases referred to in points (a) to (e) and (g);*
>
> *(i)   the protection of the data subject or the rights and freedoms of others*

> [Recital 73 notes that this includes social protection, public health and humanitarian purposes];

(j) the enforcement of civil law claims.

Article 23 continues that any legislative measure implemented as described above shall contain specific provisions as to the right of data subjects to be informed about the restriction (in this case, of the obligation to provide fair processing information) unless to do so would prejudice the purpose of the restriction.[47]

The Regulation's approach to these exemptions is familiar. Article 13 of the Directive permitted member states to enact similar exemptions for circumstances in which it was necessary to withhold information on a controller's processing activities in order to safeguard interests, such as national security or for the purposes of the prevention of crime.

Significant variation existed in the way in which member states implemented these exemptions, however, and given the scope here for national interpretation and implementation under the Regulation, these differences are likely to remain.

The Regulation also allows member states to provide exemptions and derogations from the obligation to provide fair processing information where processing is carried out for the purposes of journalism or academic artistic or literary expression and those exemptions or derogations are necessary to reconcile the right to the protection of personal data with freedom of expression and information.[48]

8.3   The requirements of the ePrivacy Directive

Directive 2002/58/EC concerning the processing of personal data and the protection of privacy in the electronic communications sector as amended ('ePrivacy Directive') sets out additional information requirements relevant to the use of cookies and similar technologies by the operators of websites, apps and, increasingly, other connected devices.[49]

Article 5(3) of the ePrivacy Directive states that, subject to limited exceptions, storing information, or gaining access to information already stored, in the terminal equipment of a subscriber or a user is allowed only on the condition that the user concerned has given their consent, having been provided with clear and comprehensive information, in accordance with the Directive and now the Regulation.

In the view of the Article 29 Working Party (WP29), Article 5(3) imposes an obligation on the entity placing a cookie or similar technology on a user's device to obtain the prior informed consent of that user.[50] Practically, this means that:

- information about the sending and purposes of the cookie or similar technology must be given to the user; and

- the user, having been provided with such information, must consent, before the cookie or similar technology is placed on their device or the information stored in the device is retrieved.

The method by which a website operator chooses to obtain consent to the use of cookies or similar technologies is likely to have an impact on how this information is provided. The requirement to provide full and transparent disclosure of the use of cookies and similar technologies, however, applies irrespective of the mechanism chosen to obtain consent, and operators adopt a stand-alone cookie use policy to meet this obligation. The requirement for consent to the use of cookies is considered in detail in Chapter 17.

8.4   Fair processing notices

Unlike the Directive, which did not mandate how fair processing information should be provided to data subjects, the Regulation specifically refers to the methods by which individuals should be informed of the processing of their personal data.

As fair processing information may be provided in writing, including where appropriate by electronic means, fair processing notices will remain a convenient method by which controllers can achieve compliance with the Regulation's transparency requirements.

8.4.1 Practical considerations for fair processing notices

The Regulation leaves controllers with some discretion in terms of the manner in which fair processing information is communicated to data subjects. It also gives controllers the opportunity to choose the mechanics through which they meet its transparency requirements: controllers' obligations are to 'provide' information, or to 'explicitly bring it to the attention of,' or 'inform' data subjects.

The requirement to 'provide' fair processing information under Articles 13 and 14, for example, leaves controllers to determine whether they will actively communicate the information required or simply make it readily available to data subjects (e.g., in a website privacy policy). This decision will likely depend upon the circumstances of the processing, and controllers should take the following factors into account when making it:

- The level of information already available to the data subjects, including whether or not they know if their personal data will be collected and what it will be used for.

- Whether there is any element of the collection or processing of personal data that data subjects would find unexpected or objectionable.[51]

- Whether or not the consequences of supplying or not supplying their personal data are clear and what those consequences are (where providing or not providing the information will have a significant effect on the data subject, the requirement to actively communicate information will be greater).[52]

- The nature of the personal data collected and processed (e.g., where the processing relates to special categories of personal data, the duty to communicate information to data subjects will be more acute) and the type of individuals, such as vulnerable individuals, concerned.[53]

- The method by which data is collected. It is good practice to provide fair processing information using the same medium through which the personal data was collected.[54] For example, where personal data is collected over the telephone, fair processing information could be given to data subjects orally with a written version available if required and to evidence the interaction. Conversely, where personal data is collected via a website, it is usual for information to be given to data subjects by way of a written notice on the website.

Whereas Articles 13 and 14 of the Regulation require fair processing information to be 'provided', Article 21(4) requires that information about the right to object to certain types of processing is 'explicitly brought to the attention of data subjects' at the latest at the time at which the controller first communicates with the data subject. This is likely to mean that controllers have to do more than make this information available.

According to regulatory guidance, in whatever form fair processing information is provided to data subjects, controllers should ensure that it is:

- Clear, concise and easy to understand in simple, unambiguous and direct language. It is good practice—and in some cases, a legal requirement—to provide fair processing information in the language that data subjects are most likely to understand.[55] From a practical perspective, following this rule will assist in demonstrating that information has been effectively provided.

- Genuinely informative, meaningful and appropriate and designed to help individuals understand how their personal data is used.

- Accurate and up to date (fair processing information should therefore be regularly reviewed).[56]

- Provided in an appropriate manner to people with particular needs (e.g., where data is collected from children, the data controller should ensure that fair processing information is provided in a way they can understand).[57]

- Not misleading.[58] For example, where individuals do not have a choice regarding the processing of their personal data, such as for certain types of processing in the public sector, it would be misleading to suggest to data subjects that they do. Where options are offered in relation to the use of personal data, they must be genuine and honoured.

- Forward looking but realistic. The ICO takes the view that, where a privacy notice is drafted in sufficiently broad terms, it can allow for evolution of processing.[59] However, to avoid making misleading statements and creating an extremely lengthy privacy notice, a controller should not list numerous possible future uses of personal data where it is unlikely that it will ever be used for such purposes.

- Meets the requirements of the Regulation in terms of content and timing of delivery.

8.4.2 Making the provision of fair processing information effective

In addition to assisting with compliance with the Regulation, the provision of effective fair processing information is likely to have a number of commercial benefits:

- Data subjects are more likely to place trust in organisations that are transparent about the use of personal data. This trust will contribute to customer loyalty and retention.

- Data subjects will be likely to provide more and more valuable personal data to organisations that will use it properly.

- The risk of complaints and disputes arising from the use of personal data will be reduced when the processing undertaken by an organisation is explained to the data subject.

Given the amount of information which has to be communicated to data subjects under the Regulation, the requirement that what is provided is concise and easy to understand, the challenges posed by new technologies and the potential benefits, in addition to legal compliance, of effective information provision, controllers are likely to benefit from being flexible and creative in their communications with data subjects. The Regulation assists here, as although technology neutral, it recognises that fair processing information may be most appropriately provided through a number of means depending upon the circumstances of processing (e.g., in writing, through electronic means, orally or using standardised icons). With this in mind, there is a variety of approaches to the provision of fair processing information that controllers could consider, including:

- using layered fair processing notices;
- providing 'just-in-time' notices;
- adopting privacy dashboards;
- alternative formats and channels of communication for information; and
- taking steps to adapt to the requirements of diverse technologies, including, in particular, the Internet of Things (IoT).

8.4.2.1 Layered fair processing notices

In a layered notice, basic information is provided in a short initial notice and further, more detailed information is available should a data subject wish to know more.

Layered notices are particularly suited to processing in an online context, where click-through links can facilitate movement between layers of fair processing information. Where personal data is collected offline, a layered approach can be adopted by providing a simple way for the data subject to access more detailed information, such as a toll-free telephone number.[60]

The concept of the layered notice was introduced by the Berlin Memorandum of March 2004.[61] Under the Directive, the layered notice received backing from the WP29, which stated that fair processing information did not necessarily need to be provided in a single document, providing that the sum of the layers of information resulted in compliance with the relevant local law.[62]

The WP29 advised that each layer of a layered notice should offer data subjects the information necessary to understand their position and to make decisions and set out detailed recommendations for the content of each of three recommended layers based on the requirements of the Directive.[63]

Since 2004, both technology and the information to be provided to data subjects have moved on. As a result, it would be open to controllers to adopt the WP29's acceptance of a layered approach to information provision and update it to account for a changed legal and technological landscape.

In line with recommendations from the ICO, controllers could provide key information and details of processing which may be unexpected or objectionable immediately and prominently.[64] This initial notice should also contain information as to the identity of the controller and high-level description of the purposes of processing. The ICO suggests that this initial notice could then contain links explaining the processing in more detail or a link to a second full notice which can, in turn, link to additional information about particular topics.[65]

There are a number of benefits to layered notices:

- they recognise that, in most circumstances, data subjects can (and wish to) take in only certain amounts of information about the use of their personal data;

- shorter privacy notices are easier to understand and remember;[66]

- layered notices can be used to account for space or time limitations in a number of situations in which personal data is collected;[67] and

- longer notices tend to attract the complicated legal terms and industry jargon that impair readability.

There is reason to believe that this approach would meet the requirements of the Regulation, providing always that the content and timing of the information provided addressed all the requirements of the Regulation and that the information, which must be 'explicitly brought to the attention' of data subjects, was not buried within secondary layers of the notice.

8.4.2.2 'Just-in-time' notices

The ICO also advocates the use of 'just-in-time' notices, or the provision of information about processing at specific points of data collection.[68] Linked to the concept of a layered notice, this approach sees the data subject provided with information at the point at which it is particularly relevant to them. For example, a data subject could be provided with information about the purposes of processing at the point at which they provide personal data using an online form.

8.4.2.3 Dashboards

The ICO suggests that linking a fair processing notice to a dashboard which allows data subjects to control how their personal data is processed is another method through which controllers could inform and engage with data subjects regarding the processing of their personal data.[69]

8.4.2.4 Alternative formats

The Regulation requires that information shall be provided in writing or by other means, including, where appropriate, by electronic means.[70] It also specifically mentions the use of visualisation and allows for legislation to be enacted to create standardised icons.[71]

Controllers could therefore consider the use of animations, for example, to explain processing to children or use icons in combination with 'just-in-time' or layered notices where restrictions on space make it difficult to clearly provide information.

In all cases outlined in this section, however, controllers should make available a full, 'un-layered' version of their fair processing information in order that interested data subjects can search for and refer to it without the need to 'click through' web pages and easily review it in a different medium (e.g., in hard copy) should they require.[72]

8.4.2.5 Fair processing information and diverse technologies

Some technologies present particular challenges in terms of providing fair processing information to data subjects. For example, how should this information be provided if personal data is collected through the use of closed-circuit television (CCTV), by drones, via wearable technologies or as a result of vehicle use? Similarly, how can a controller provide fair processing information to users of mobile devices, where there are extreme constraints on display space?

The WP29 considered a number of these issues in the context of the Directive. Consider, as an example, where personal data is collected using drones.[73] In relation to the transparency requirements of the Directive, the WP29 recognised the difficulties involved in the provision of fair processing information to individuals, in particular, where drones are used in public spaces. In light of these issues, the WP29 recommended a number of practical steps through which fair processing information could be provided in this setting, including:

- using sign posts and information sheets where drones are operated in a specific area;[74]

- using social media, newspapers, leaflets and posters to inform data subjects where drones are used at events;[75]

- always making fair processing information available on the operator's website to inform data subjects about upcoming and past uses of drones;[76]

- taking steps to ensure that the drone itself is visible, such as using bright colours, flashing lights or buzzers;[77] and

- ensuring that the operator is also clearly visible with signage identifying them as the individual responsible for the drone.[78]

The WP29 also adopted this context-specific approach when it considered developments in the IoT in 2014.[79] Here, challenges arise as a result of the discrete nature of sensors that collect personal data and the fact that personal data that relates to a number of data subjects may be collected at any one time. For these types of devices, the WP29 suggested printing a QR code or a flashcode on items equipped with sensors, enabling data subjects to access fair processing information.[80]

8.5   Conclusion

The provision of information to data subjects is a key element of the Regulation. It is not only a stand-alone requirement but its importance is also clear across the data protection framework, from its impact on fairness to the integral role it plays in the obtaining of consent and the ability for a controller to rely on the legitimate interest basis for processing.

Complying with the Regulation's obligations relating to transparency will, however, present challenges to privacy professionals particularly working with mobile technologies and connected devices where the opportunities to provide information are significantly limited.

Endnotes

1 General Data Protection Regulation, Article 5(1)(a).

2 General Data Protection Regulation, Recital 39.

3 General Data Protection Regulation, Articles 13 and 14.

4 Recital 38 of the Data Protection Directive stated that 'Whereas, if the processing of data is to be fair, the data subject must be in a position to learn of the existence of a processing operation and, where data are collected from him, must be given accurate and full information, bearing in mind the circumstances of the collection'.

5 General Data Protection Regulation, Recital 60.

6 General Data Protection Regulation, Article 4(11).

7 General Data Protection Regulation, Recital 42.

8 Data Protection Directive, Article 18.

9 General Data Protection Regulation, Recital 89.

10 Data Protection Directive, Article 10.

11 'Overview of the General Data Protection Regulation (GDPR)', Information Commissioner's Office, 7 July 2016, https://ico.org.uk/media/for-organisations/data-protection-reform/overview-of-the-gdpr-1-11.pdf.

12 'Overview of the General Data Protection Regulation (GDPR)', Information Commissioner's Office, 7 July 2016, pages 13–16, https://ico.org.uk/media/for-organisations/data-protection-reform/overview-of-the-gdpr-1-11.pdf.

13 'Overview of the General Data Protection Regulation (GDPR)', Information Commissioner's Office, 7 July 2016, pages 12–14, https://ico.org.uk/media/for-organisations/data-protection-reform/overview-of-the-gdpr-1-11.pdf.

14 General Data Protection Regulation, Article 15(1).

15 General Data Protection Regulation, Article 18.

16 General Data Protection Regulation, Article 18(3).

17 General Data Protection Regulation, Article 21(1).

18 General Data Protection Regulation, Article 21(2).

19 General Data Protection Regulation, Article 21(4). Data subjects' rights are discussed in more detail in Chapter 9.

20 General Data Protection Regulation, Recital 113 and second subparagraph of Article 49(1); General Data Protection Regulation, second subparagraph of Article 49(1).

21 General Data Protection Regulation, Article 49(1)(a).

22 General Data Protection Regulation, Article 47(2)(g).

23 General Data Protection Regulation, Articles 13(3) and 14(4).

24 General Data Protection Regulation, Article 26(1) and (2).

25 General Data Protection Regulation, Article 34.

26 General Data Protection Regulation, Article 13(1) and 13(2).

27 General Data Protection Regulation, Articles 13(3) and 14(4).

28 General Data Protection Regulation, Article 21(4).

29 General Data Protection Regulation, Article 7(3).

30 General Data Protection Regulation, Article 12(1) and Recital 58.

31 General Data Protection Regulation, Article 12(1).

32 General Data Protection Regulation, Recital 58.

33 General Data Protection Regulation, Article 12(1).

34 General Data Protection Regulation, Article 12(5).

35 General Data Protection Regulation, Recital 58; General Data Protection Regulation, Article 12(7).

36 General Data Protection Regulation, Article 12(8); General Data Protection Regulation, Article 70(r).

37 General Data Protection Regulation, Article 12(7).

38 General Data Protection Regulation, Article 7(2).

39 General Data Protection Regulation, Article 21(4).

40 General Data Protection Regulation, Article 88(2).

41 General Data Protection Regulation, Article 40(2).

42 General Data Protection Regulation, Article 13(4).

43 General Data Protection Regulation, Article 14(5)(a).

44 General Data Protection Regulation, Article 14(5)(c).

45 General Data Protection Regulation, Article 14(5)(d).

46 General Data Protection Regulation, Article 14(5)(b).

47 General Data Protection Regulation, Article 23(2)(h).

48 General Data Protection Regulation, Article 85(2).

49 The ePrivacy Directive is likely to soon be replaced by the proposed Regulation on Privacy and Electronic Communications ('ePrivacy Regulation'); see 'Proposal for a Regulation on Privacy and Electronic Communications', European Commission, 1 January 2017, https://ec.europa.eu/digital-single-market/en/news/proposal-regulation-privacy-and-electronic-communications.

50 Opinion 2/2010 on Online Behavioural Advertising (00909/10; WP 171), page 13.

51 *Privacy notices, transparency and control: A code of practice on communicating privacy information to individuals,* Information Commissioner's Office, 7 October 2016, page 21, https://ico.org.uk/media/for-organisations/guide-to-data-protection/privacy-notices-transparency-and-control-1-0.pdf.

52 Ibid.

53 Ibid.

54 *Privacy notices, transparency and control: A code of practice on communicating privacy information to individuals,* Information Commissioner's Office, 7 October 2016, page 14, https://ico.org.uk/media/for-organisations/guide-to-data-protection/privacy-notices-transparency-and-control-1-0.pdf.

55 *Privacy notices, transparency and control: A code of practice on communicating privacy information to individuals,* Information Commissioner's Office, 7 October 2016, page 24, https://ico.org.uk/media/for-organisations/guide-to-data-protection/privacy-notices-transparency-and-control-1-0.pdf.

56 *Privacy notices, transparency and control: A code of practice on communicating privacy information to individuals,* Information Commissioner's Office, 7 October 2016, page 25, https://ico.org.uk/media/for-organisations/guide-to-data-protection/privacy-notices-transparency-and-control-1-0.pdf.

57 Opinion 10/2004 on More Harmonised Information Provisions (11987/04/EN; WP 100), page 7.

58 *Privacy notices, transparency and control: A code of practice on communicating privacy information to individuals,* Information Commissioner's Office, 7 October 2016, page 23, https://ico.org.uk/media/for-organisations/guide-to-data-protection/privacy-notices-transparency-and-control-1-0.pdf.

59 *Privacy notices, transparency and control: A code of practice on communicating privacy information to individuals,* Information Commissioner's Office, 7 October 2016, page 8, https://ico.org.uk/media/for-organisations/guide-to-data-protection/privacy-notices-transparency-and-control-1-0.pdf.

60 Opinion 10/2004 on More Harmonised Information Provisions (11987/04/EN; WP 100), page 9.

61 Opinion 10/2004 on More Harmonised Information Provisions (11987/04/EN; WP 100), page 4.

62 Opinion 10/2004 on More Harmonised Information Provisions (11987/04/EN; WP 100), page 8.

63 Opinion 10/2004 on More Harmonised Information Provisions (11987/04/EN; WP 100), page 6; Opinion 10/2004 on More Harmonised Information Provisions (11987/04/EN; WP 100), pages 8–9.

64 *Privacy notices, transparency and control: A code of practice on communicating privacy information to individuals,* Information Commissioner's Office, 7 October 2016, page 16, https://ico.org.uk/media/for-organisations/guide-to-data-protection/privacy-notices-transparency-and-control-1-0.pdf.

65 *Privacy notices, transparency and control: A code of practice on communicating privacy information to individuals,* Information Commissioner's Office, 7 October 2016, page 15, https://ico.org.uk/media/for-organisations/guide-to-data-protection/privacy-notices-transparency-and-control-1-0.pdf.

66 Opinion 10/2004 on More Harmonised Information Provisions (11987/04/EN; WP 100), page 7

67 Opinion 10/2004 on More Harmonised Information Provisions (11987/04/EN; WP 100), page 5

68 *Privacy notices, transparency and control: A code of practice on communicating privacy information to individuals,* Information Commissioner's Office, 7 October 2016, page 17, https://ico.org.uk/media/for-organisations/guide-to-data-protection/privacy-notices-transparency-and-control-1-0.pdf.

69 *Privacy notices, transparency and control: A code of practice on communicating privacy information to individuals,* Information Commissioner's Office, 7 October 2016, page 13, https://ico.org.uk/media/for-organisations/guide-to-data-protection/privacy-notices-transparency-and-control-1-0.pdf.

70 General Data Protection Regulation, Article 12(1).

71 General Data Protection Regulation, Recital 58; General Data Protection Regulation, Article 12(8).

72 *Privacy notices, transparency and control: A code of practice on communicating privacy information to individuals,* Information Commissioner's Office, 7 October 2016, page 16, https://ico.org.uk/media/for-organisations/guide-to-data-protection/privacy-notices-transparency-and-control-1-0.pdf.

73 Opinion 01/2015 on Privacy and Data Protection Issues relating to the Utilisation of Drones, WP 231, adopted 16 June 2015.

74 Opinion 01/2015 on Privacy and Data Protection Issues relating to the Utilisation of Drones, WP 231, adopted 16 June 2015, page 19.

75 Ibid.

76 Ibid.

77 Opinion 01/2015 on Privacy and Data Protection Issues relating to the Utilisation of Drones, WP 231, adopted 16 June 2015, page 20.

78 Ibid.

79 Opinion 8/2014 on the Recent Developments on the Internet of Things, WP 223, adopted 16 September 2014.

80 Opinion 8/2014 on the on Recent Developments on the Internet of Things, WP 223, adopted 16 September 2014, page 18.

CHAPTER 9

Data Subjects' Rights

Jyn Schultze-Melling

9.1 Background

European data protection law has always provided individuals with a range of rights enforceable against organisations processing their data.

Compared to the Data Protection Directive ('Directive'), the General Data Protection Regulation (GDPR, or 'Regulation') is considerably more complex and far-reaching in this respect, as it includes a very extensive set of rights. This is in part because bolstering individuals' rights was one of the main ambitions of the European Commission ('Commission') in proposing the new data protection framework. Data subjects' rights, set forth in Articles 12 to 23 of the Regulation, may not only limit an organisation's ability to lawfully process personal data, but they can also have a significant impact upon an organisation's core business processes and even its business model.

These rights encompass the following:

- *Articles 12–14*: Right of transparent communication and information
- *Article 15*: Right of access
- *Article 16*: Right to rectification
- *Article 17*: Right to erasure ('right to be forgotten')
- *Article 18*: Right to restriction of processing
- *Article 19*: Obligation to notify recipients
- *Article 20*: Right to data portability
- *Article 21*: Right to object
- *Article 22*: Right to not be subject to automated decision-making (to profiling)

9.2   The modalities—to whom, how and when

Art 12(2):
requires
facilitation of
exercise of
rights;
reasonable
efforts to
verify DS ID
required

Article 12(2) of the Regulation requires organisations to facilitate the exercise of data subject rights. Whereas the Directive did not explicitly require organisations to confirm data subjects' identities, the Regulation now requires the controller to use all reasonable efforts to verify the identity of data subjects. Consequently, where the controller has reasonable doubts as to a data subject's identity, the controller may request the provision of additional information necessary to confirm it. That said, the controller is not obliged to collect any additional personal data just to link certain pieces of data it holds to a specific data subject.

Art 12(3):
norm = 1 month
from request
date;
2 addit'l months
for specific/complex
situations.
If decided not
to honour request
must inform DS
re: decision &
how to complain

Another operational aspect refers to the time frame to honour data subjects' requests. Preliminarily, the controller should acknowledge receiving the request and confirm or clarify what is requested. Article 12(3) sets out the relevant time windows for responding: one month, starting with receipt of the request, should be the normal time frame, which can be extended by two further months for cases of specific situations and/or especially complex requests. During the first month, however, the organisation has to decide whether it can act on the users' request at all—if the organisation decides not to proceed, it must inform the data subjects about this and even advise them as to any opportunities to lodge complaints with regulators.

In terms of form, the Regulation aims to establish and rely on technology-based processes—electronically received requests should be answered electronically, unless the data subject wants something else. Whilst this seems like a straight-forward requirement, companies should not underestimate the potential security implications of honouring rights through technological means alone. As email encryption is still not a thoroughly widespread mean of providing secure communication for sensitive information, companies will be challenged to adopt ways to deliver this information electronically in a safe and accountable way.

9.3   The general necessity of transparent communication

Transparency =
DS must
be given
info to
understand
nature of
processing &
exercise rights
info must be
concise,
transparent,
intelligible ..etc.

As discussed in the previous chapter, transparency is fundamental to any data protection system, as individuals' right to privacy cannot be assured if they are not properly informed about the data controllers' activities. In essence, the rights established by the Regulation require that data subjects have all the information they need in order to understand the nature of the processing and to exercise their further statutory rights. Consequently, Article 12(1) requires that any information communicated by the organisation be provided in a 'concise, transparent, intelligible and easily accessible form, using clear and plain language'.

9.4 Right to information (about personal data collection and processing)

Under Article 13 of the Regulation, data subjects have the right to be provided with certain pieces of information that describe their relationship with the controller. This includes the controller's identity and contact details, the reasons or purposes for processing their personal data, the legal basis for doing so, recipients of that data (especially if those reside in third countries), and other relevant information necessary to ensure the fair and transparent processing of the data. Additionally, the controller must identify the source of data if collected or obtained from a third party, in order to effectively enable the data subject to pursue their rights (Article 14).

For a detailed explanation of this right, as set out in Articles 13 and 14 of the Regulation, see Chapter 8.

9.5 Right of access

The Regulation's right of access set out in Article 15 is in a sense the active counterpart to the more passive right of information in Articles 13 and 14. Any data subject that requests to know must be told about the personal data the organisation holds about them and, more specifically, why and how it does so. In comparison to the Directive, the Regulation expands considerably the mandatory categories of information that a company must provide.

The Regulation prescribes that the data subject has the right to obtain from the controller confirmation as to whether or not personal data that concerns him or her is being processed. Where that is the case, in addition to providing access to the personal data, the data subject is entitled to receive the following information:

- the purposes of the processing;
- the categories of personal data concerned;
- the recipients or categories of recipient to whom the personal data have been or will be disclosed, in particular, recipients in third countries or international organisations;
- where possible, the envisaged period for which the personal data will be stored or, if not possible, the criteria used to determine that period;

[Handwritten margin notes: Art 15: DS can request & get data org holds about them, why & how. In addition to access, DS has right to learn whether their info is being processed; if so, see the list. purpose. categories of PD. recipients. esp. third countries. storage period]

- the existence of the right to request from the controller rectification or erasure of personal data or restriction of processing of personal data concerning the data subject or to object to such processing;

[margin note: right to rectification & erasure, restriction & objection]

- the right to lodge a complaint with a supervisory authority;

[margin note: - complaint]

- where the personal data are not collected from the data subject, any available information as to their source; and

[margin note: - Source]

- the existence of automated decision-making, including profiling, referred to in Article 22(1) and (4) and, at least in those cases, meaningful information about the logic involved, as well as the significance and the envisaged consequences of such processing for the data subject.

[margin note: - automated decision making]

In practice, these types of requests are likely to pose a substantial administrative burden on organisations, so they should consider upfront what types of processes need to be in place to assist with this task.

9.6   Right to rectification

The scope of this right under the Regulation is largely unchanged from the Directive. In a nutshell, data subjects have the right to rectification of inaccurate personal data, and controllers must ensure that inaccurate or incomplete data is erased, amended or rectified. This right can generate a considerable amount of effort operationally. Rectifying wrong entries in databases is usually not a singular, isolated issue for organisations. Data is often interlinked and processed that way, so any changes to any piece of data might have wider consequences.

9.7   Right to erasure ('right to be forgotten')

The so-called right to be forgotten (RTBF) is probably one of the most actively scrutinised aspects of the original proposal by the Commission.[1]

Article 17(1) establishes that data subjects obtain the right to have their personal data erased if:

- the data is no longer needed for its original purpose and no new lawful purpose exists;

- the lawful basis for the processing is the data subject's consent, the data subject withdraws that consent, and no other lawful ground exists;

- the data subject exercises the right to object, and the controller has no overriding grounds for continuing the processing;

- the data has been processed unlawfully; or

- erasure is necessary for compliance with EU law or the national law of the relevant member state.

In addition, Article 17(2) of the Regulation requires that, where the controller has made any personal data public (e.g., in a telephone directory or in a social network) and the data subject exercises the right to erasure, the controller must take reasonable steps (including applying technological solutions but taking costs into account) to inform third parties which are processing this published personal data as controllers that the data subject has exercised this right. Given how prominent the right to be forgotten was during the legislative process, it seems reasonable to assume that regulators will emphasise the importance of honouring this right in full.

Exemptions to the right of erasure are listed in Article 17(3), which allows organisations to decline data subjects' requests to the extent that processing is necessary:

- for exercising the right of freedom of expression and information;

- for compliance with a legal obligation which requires processing by Union or member state law to which the controller is subject or for the performance of a task carried out in the public interest, like public health, archiving and scientific, historical research or statistical purposes; or

- for the establishment of, exercise of or defence against legal claims.

The Regulation also entitles data subjects to request information about the identities of recipients to whom the personal data has been disclosed. Consequently, Article 19 requires that where a controller has disclosed personal data to particular third parties, and the data subject has subsequently exercised their right of rectification, erasure or blocking, the controller must notify those third parties of the data subject's exercise of those rights. The controller is exempt from this obligation only if it is impossible to comply with it or would require disproportionate effort, which must be proven by the controller. As Recital 66 mentions, this extension of the right of erasure is meant to strengthen the right to be forgotten specifically in the online environment, where personal data is notoriously difficult to control once it has been shared and distributed—so online service providers will probably find dealing with this obligation especially difficult.

In terms of operational impact, this means that organisations, in addition to implementing systems and procedures for giving effect to the new rights that the Regulation grants to data subjects, are also required to implement systems and procedures for reliably notifying affected third parties about the exercise of those rights. For organisations that disclose personal data to a large number of third parties, these provisions may be particularly burdensome.

9.8 Right to restriction of processing

The Directive did not directly address the right to restrict processing on certain grounds. However, it did provide for a right to request the 'blocking' of data (Article 12(b)–(c)). Under some member states' laws, this meant that the controller could keep the data, but it would have to refrain from using it during the period for which that right applied. In a way, this describes a temporary freezing of data assets without actually making them go away for good.

Article 18 of the Regulation establishes something similar. Data subjects have the right to restrict the processing of their personal data if:

- the accuracy of the data is contested (and only for as long as it takes to verify that accuracy);

- the processing is unlawful, and the data subject requests restriction (as opposed to exercising the right to erasure);

- the controller no longer needs the data for their original purpose, but the data is still required by the controller to establish, exercise or defend legal rights; or

- verification of overriding grounds is pending in the context of an erasure request.

From an operational point of view, organisations face a broad range of circumstances under which data subjects can require that the processing of their personal data is restricted under the Regulation. How this will be done technologically remains to be seen. Recital 67 at least provides some guidance by suggesting that compliance with this right could be achieved by 'temporarily moving the selected data to another processing system, making the selected personal data unavailable to users, or temporarily removing it from a website'.

9.9   Right to data portability

Data portability is an entirely new term in European data protection law.[2] Article 20 of the Regulation states that data subjects have the right to receive their own personal data, which they have provided to a controller, in a structured, commonly used and machine-readable format. They also have the right to transmit the data to another controller without hindrance from the controller. Technically, the controller must either hand the data over to the data subject in a usable fashion, or—at their request (Article 20(2))—transfer the data directly to the recipient of the data subject's choice, where technically feasible.

For some organisations, this new right to transfer personal data between controllers creates a significant additional burden, requiring substantial investment in new systems and processes. On top of that, many issues with this particular provision still need further guidance by the regulatory community in order to allow companies to set up their processes. In particular, it remains to be seen what is meant by a 'structured, commonly used and machine-readable' format for modern information services or how the threshold of 'hindrance' and 'technical feasibility' is determined in the context of direct controller-to-controller transfers.

On the other hand, for some organisations, this new right might turn out to be a business opportunity. Recital 68 explicitly states that this provision is intended to encourage data controllers to develop interoperable formats that enable data portability. Companies may be able to attract customers from competitors more easily as in the past, when users may have been reluctant to set up a new account.

9.10 Right to object

In accordance with Article 21(1), whenever a controller justifies the data processing on the basis of its legitimate interests, data subjects can object to such processing. As a consequence, the controller is no longer allowed to process the data subject's personal data unless it can demonstrate compelling, legitimate grounds for the processing. These grounds must be sufficiently compelling to override the interests, rights and freedoms of the data subject, such as to establish, exercise or defend against legal claims.

Under Article 14 of the Directive, data subjects already had the right to object to the processing of personal data for the purpose of direct marketing. Under the Regulation, this now explicitly includes profiling. In addition, the data subject must be explicitly, clearly and separately notified of the right to object   at the latest, at the time of the first communication.

Under Article 21(6), which states that personal data is processed for scientific and historical research purposes or statistical purposes, the right to object exists only as far as the processing is not considered necessary for the performance of a task carried out for reasons of public interest.

9.11 Right to not be subject to automated decision-making

The right not to be evaluated on the basis of automated processing is closely connected with the aforementioned right to object. It is important to take into consideration, though, that Article 22 has a narrow application. The right not to be subject to automated decision-making applies only if such a decision is based solely on automated processing and produces legal effects concerning the data subject or similarly significantly affects them. Because of their ambiguity, however, these terms will need further explanation and probably some solid guidance from the regulators. There is no common understanding of what 'solely automated process' means, and are there no sound rules as to what kind of decisions have significant effects on individuals.

Yet, if a decision-making process falls within these parameters, the underlying processing of personal data is allowed if it is authorised by law, necessary for the preparation and execution of a contract, or done with the data subject's explicit consent, provided that the controller has put sufficient safeguards in place. Such safeguards might include the right to obtain human intervention on the part of the controller or another equally effective opportunity to express the data subject's point of view to contest the decision.

9.12 Restrictions of data subjects' rights

In spite of the Regulation's prescriptive nature, controllers should prepare for further Union or member state law in regard to possible restrictions to the scope of the obligations and rights provided for in Articles 12 to 22. Member states may weigh in on the principles of Article 5, insofar as its provisions correspond to the rights and obligations provided for in Articles 12 to 22. In particular, member states may promote restrictions that, whilst respecting data subjects' fundamental rights and freedoms, are necessary to safeguard interests of national security, defence or public security. Only time will reveal member states' willingness to exploit these caveats.

9.13 Conclusion

Controllers that fundamentally understand and embrace data subject's rights, as articulated in the Regulation, will adopt them into their practices via privacy by design and default, and reflect them in their consumer interactions. Given the potential impact of these rights on a controller's business model, privacy professionals will need to find ways to draw attention and understanding to these rights amongst leadership and throughout the organisation.

Endnotes

1 'Factsheet on the "Right to be Forgotten" ruling'(C-131/12), European Commission, http://ec.europa.eu/justice/data-protection/files/factsheets/factsheet_data_protection_en.pdf.

2 'Guidelines on the right to data portability' (16/EN: WP 242), 13 December 2016, http://ec.europa.eu/newsroom/document.cfm?doc_id=43822.

CHAPTER 10

Security of Personal Data

Stewart Room, CIPP/E

10.1 Background

In a purely legislative sense, it may be hard to argue that certain principles of European data protection rank more importantly than others, yet when a broader view is taken, it is patently clear that a hierarchy of importance has emerged.

For instance, the recent focus of citizen activists on transfers of personal data to the United States has propelled increased awareness, so now ordinary people, not just privacy professionals, are aware of Safe Harbor and the EU-U.S. Privacy Shield Framework. It's no wonder that international transfers are now heading up the agenda for many controllers, processors and regulators.

The topic of personal data security must be seen in this way. If the data protection principles are the celebrities of the data protection world, security is always on the A-list, a true VIP. There are multiple reasons for this.

Firstly, a state of security is often a prerequisite to achieving compliance with the other data protection principles. For example, insecurity can cause the unlawful flow of personal data across international boundaries; it can lead to the alteration of personal data and the embedding of inaccuracies; it can cause data proliferation; and, of course, it can cause distress to the individuals who are the victims of security breaches and more substantive harms, such as identify theft and pecuniary loss and damage.

In other words, as well as being a very serious 'compliance' failure in its own right, absence of security can cause wholesale, serious noncompliance and illegality across, for example, the entire General Data Protection Regulation (GDPR, or 'Regulation') legislative framework. The idea that the security principle is intermingled with and forms part of all the other data protection principles is now well understood. Security isn't a stand-alone risk but part of the fabric of every risk that controllers and processors should be tracking and recording in their risk registers.

Further, serious cases of insecurity are guaranteed press and media attention, with international attention for the very worst cases. The relentless torrent of high profile 'bad news stories' about security breaches affecting personal data, shows no sign of abating. It is likely that the GDPR personal data breach notification regime will amplify the newsworthiness of insecurity to such an extent that we may look back on the past torrent of bad news stories as if it was a mere trickle.

Finally, cases that involve poor security controls show very different features of scale and harm when compared to other breaches of the data protection principles. The Safe Harbor case certainly had security-level scale in the sense that it was argued that an entire country, the United States, was non-adequate for EU data protection purposes, but there was very little sense of tangible harm to the public.[1] People have not turned their back on using U.S. businesses. Cases of data inaccuracy can certainly cause tangible harm, such as where an inaccurate credit score leads to a person being offered a more expensive financial product, or, worse still, locked out of the financial services market, but they don't seem to scale beyond individual cases into large classes or groups of cases.

Indeed, insecurity has both scale and harm. Within the relentless torrent of bad news stories, there are many cases where tens of millions of people have been affected by breaches. In 2016, hackers compromised one billion user accounts at a U.S. online company. In addition to volume, fraud and identify theft are tangible harms that can be easily suffered if the right combinations of data are in play, whilst mental anxiety, anguish and distress are always foreseeable when personal data are lost or stolen (see Recital 75). These features of scale and harm manifest very obviously as ripe pickings for possible compensation claims in civil litigation, with group litigation obviously on the rise.

The close relationship between personal data security and cybersecurity has already been noted, but the 'halo' effect of cybersecurity shouldn't be underestimated. Undoubtedly, cybersecurity has added additional 'sheen' to personal data security's own star quality. This is because the topic of cybersecurity occupies a level of importance that the wider world of data protection has yet to reach, regardless of the awareness-raising effect of the GDPR. Cybersecurity is a topic for presidents and prime ministers. Whilst personal data security and cybersecurity aren't always synonymous, often they are, which helps to put this principle of data protection in a completely different category compared to all the others.

Speaking of synonymous, another special feature of this area of the law is the clear tension between some notions of security and the right to privacy. Privacy and data protection laws introduce security questions, such as national security and law enforcement. The idea that the security principle may be overcome for the benefit of these wider interests is a special feature of this area of data protection law, which will continue to accord the security principle the highest priority.

If, for the reasons just outlined, the topic of security sits in its own special category of importance, in an operational sense, there are other factors that support this claim. One of these is the fact that a considerable body of security best practices has developed through national and international professional, industry and business standards. These standards help to answer one of the most puzzling questions of data protection law, namely, what does the GDPR really mean when it says (in Article 32) that controllers and processors must implement appropriate technical and organisational measures for security?

In new areas within the GDPR, such as 'data protection by design and by default', the mechanics and details of compliance remain much of a mystery for most practitioners. Given the expansive nature of the resources for security that are available, practitioners must look beyond the confines of the legislative text, regulatory guidance and regulatory enforcement cases to understand in a very detailed sense what is required of them.

In an operational sense, personal data security is perhaps the only area of data protection law where the meaning of 'appropriate technical and organisational measures' is capable of full definition. It is an area of astounding clarity, not confusion. Thus, practitioners must raise their heads and widen their vision, and look beyond the narrow confines of the wording of the GDPR and the positions of the regulators and the courts if they are to properly understand the deliverables that they must help their organisations to achieve for security. Data protection officers (DPOs), data protection lawyers and other practitioners who restrict themselves to the strict textual context of data protection law and the immediate regulatory landscape risk missing most of the important considerations with all the attendant consequences, which includes exposure to regulatory enforcement proceedings and litigation. This is an area of science and professional expertise, like medicine and engineering, that data protection law has merely adopted rather than invented.

The presence of this clarity should make it much easier for the regulators and the courts to decide whether a controller or processor has failed in its security obligations, compared to other areas of the law where confusion and uncertainties render the requirements of the law much more ambiguous. Combining this with the personal data breach notification scheme, one future of the GDPR could be the creation of a financial penalties and compensation claim production line for cases of insecurity.

10.2 The security principle and the risk-based approach

Article 5(1)(f) of the GDPR establishes the security principle, communicating that personal data shall be 'processed in a manner that ensures appropriate security of the personal data, including protection against unauthorised or unlawful processing and against accidental loss, destruction or damage, using appropriate technical or organisational measures ("integrity and confidentiality")'. Article 32 expands upon Article 5(1)(f) to set out what the security principle actually requires, namely the taking of appropriate technical and organisational measures to ensure a level of security that is appropriate to the level of prevailing security risk.

Article 5(1) is focused on the processing of personal data, not on who performs the processing activities. In contrast, Article 32 is directed both at the controller and the processor.

Controllers and processors both have to be able to prove that they are applying appropriate security. The accountability principle in Article 5(2), in conjunction with Article 24, places obligations on the controller to be able to 'demonstrate' (i.e., prove) that it is operating in a compliant fashion. Article 28(3)(h) imposes a similar proof requirement on processors. As an added check on the processor, Article 28 requires the controller to cascade down compliance obligations to the processor through the use of contracts or other legal acts.

Of course, in order to deliver on these objectives, controllers and processors need to understand the full extent of their data processing operations, which is the effect of Article 30. Article 30(1) requires controllers to maintain records of the processing activities under their responsibility, which shall include 'a general description of the technical and organisational security measures referred to in Article 32(1)'. Article 30(2) places similar obligations on processors.

Article 32, which sets out the underpinning principles of security, is supported by personal data breach notification requirements at Articles 33 and 34. These requirements are amplified further by the data protection by design and by default requirements in Article 25 and the data protection impact assessment and prior consultation requirements in Article 35.

10.2.1 Article 32—security of processing

Article 32 establishes the obligation to keep personal data secure, and it applies to both the controller and the processor.

The duty of security should reasonably include the continuum of applicable risks, from accidents and negligence at one end of the continuum to deliberate and malevolent actions at the other. Thus, controllers and processors are required to implement controls to protect against complex technological threats, such as malware and denial-of-service attacks, and other criminal threats, as well as to guard against negligent employees.

These controls are called 'appropriate technical and organisational measures' and in this phrase that we find significant nuance. The use of the word 'appropriate' tells us that the law does not require absolute security. In other words, a controller or processor can suffer a security breach without being in violation of the law. This has massive implications for regulatory enforcement actions, because regulators cannot assume legal failure from operational failure. Also, this naturally points the way to possible defensive strategies in the event of enforcement action.

Article 32 requires a risk-based approach to the assessment of what are or are not appropriate controls. In other words, controllers and processors are required to carry out risk assessment when making decisions about controls. The requirement for risk assessments is reinforced by Articles 25 and 35, which, when properly construed, must extend to questions of security.

These risk assessments must reflect on the nature of the data that is to be processed and reasonably foreseeable threats that will exploit business process and technical system vulnerabilities. Presumably, higher probability or higher impact threats will mean organisations need to employ tighter and more sophisticated controls, especially when processing sensitive data. Conversely, less sensitive personal data may require fewer or less sophisticated controls.

The risk assessment also includes a 'state-of-the-art' test and a requirement to consider cost. The state-of-the-art test reflects some of the points made earlier, that security is an area of professional expertise with a long history of developments. The test has the effect of requiring controllers and processors to consider industry best practices, not just industry average practices. An appropriate description of the state-of-the-art test is to say that it requires controllers and processors to reflect upon the consensus of professional opinion for security with the result that, if a body of reasonably informed security professionals considers that a particular control is appropriate in particular circumstances, then the consensus should be considered by the controller/processor in making a decision on whether to apply it in its environment.

An illustration of the primacy of the consensus of professional opinion concerns encryption. Many years before the adoption of the GDPR, we reached the stage whereby the encryption of laptop computers and similar devices that contain personal data was considered to be a de facto mandatory regulatory requirement in most, if not all, jurisdictions, despite the Data Protection Directive ('Directive') being silent on the matter. The catalyst, of course, was the consensus of professional opinion: Controllers and processors were adopting encryption, not because of an express legal requirement to do so, but because in a security sense, it was the right thing to do. The consensus of professional opinion about encryption became part of the regulatory framework as the regulators went about the creation of regulatory guidance and the enforcement of the law. As they considered the wider world to understand the options for security, they discovered best practices and then reflected their findings on the regulatory scheme. The use of encryption did not stem from the mind-set of the lawmakers or the regulators. Now, Article 32(1)(a) identifies encryption, along with pseudonymisation, as a control that must be considered by controllers and processors during the design of their security systems. The integration of encryption as an express control in GDPR reflects an increasing awareness to industry-acceptable security measures.

The consensus of professional opinion is also reflected in the requirements in Article 32(1)(b), (c) and (d). The idea of maintaining 'confidentiality, integrity, availability and resilience' is lifted directly from the infosecurity industry. These are generally regarded as the cornerstones of operational success, which every security professional learns about at the beginning of their careers.

The final reinforcement of the point is found in Article 32(3), which talks about the role that can be played by codes of conduct and certification mechanisms in proving compliance with the security principle.

Of course, not all organisations can afford full-scale security control implementation. The GDPR, unfortunately, leaves open many ambiguities. It might mean that, if a control is exorbitantly expensive to implement, then it does not have to be implemented despite the threats to the data and their sensitivity—but, of course, this construction merely has the effect of displacing the ambiguity to the meaning of 'exorbitant'. Controls should operationalise a process for determining and documenting management decisions for control cost and remediation activities. This approach has the benefit of recognising the superiority of management decision-making in the sense that it should not be the role of the law to replace good management decisions with different decisions made by less-informed regulators or courts.

Of course, a controller or processor that rules out a particular control on account of cost alone will not be treated favourably in the event of enforcement if the consequence is to deny security in circumstances that amount to a rejection of the consensus of professional opinion and/or its own ability to make the financial investment in the control.

10.2.2 Article 32(4)—confidentiality, employees and other workers

Article 32(4) is concerned with the activities of employees and other workers who act under the authority of the controller or processor. The thrust of the requirements within Article 32(4) has traditionally been regarded as confidentiality issues in European data protection law (see Article 16 of the Directive), but whilst Article 32 itself does not make this distinction, when it is read in conjunction with Article 5(1)(f), which is summarised as 'integrity and confidentiality', and Article 28(3)(b), which says that persons working under processors must work under a duty of confidentiality, it is highly likely that, in practice, the logical reasoning that has applied to date will continue to apply when the GDPR comes into effect.

As such, it seems that all people who have access to personal data through their work for controllers and processors are working under circumstances that are tantamount to creating a duty of confidence. The essence of Article 32(4) is that these people must act within the boundaries of their instructions. They should not subvert the controller's position.

So, for example, they must not misuse personal data to their own advantage or to another's advantage, as would occur through unauthorised disclosure to third parties or by the making of unauthorised copies.

In security terms, the risks posed by employees and other workers is often referred to as 'the insider threat'. Controllers and processors alike should have robust policies that alert employees to their responsibilities in handling personal data, provide them with role-based and regular training, and make clear the consequences for violating policy dictates.

10.2.3 Article 28—relationships between controllers and processors

Article 28 contains specific provisions for the controller-processor relationship and the supply chain. It is concerned with the entirety of the relationship between the controller and the processor and all the data protection principles, not just security.

The intention of Article 28(1) is to flow down the security principle and the security requirements into the processor's organisation and through the supply chain to sub-processors.

In order to do this, Article 28 uses the device of limiting the controller's use of processors to those who can provide 'sufficient guarantees' about the implementation of appropriate technical and organisations measures for compliance with the Regulation and for the protection of the rights of data subjects.

This idea of 'sufficient guarantees' encompasses much more than the creation of contracts but the use of contracts is a key control mechanism. Instead, what it is really focused on is getting proof of the processor's competence. To make any sense and to be truly effective, the idea of sufficient guarantees must encompass assurance mechanisms. When looked at in this way, there must be appropriate checking and vetting of the processor by the supplier via a third-party assessment or certification validation, both before a contract is created and afterwards.

The nature of the steps that are required for assurance must necessarily reflect the consensus of professional opinion, of course, for the reasons discussed earlier. In appropriate circumstances, the processes of assurance must include processes of audit, which are made clear in Article 28(3)(h). If the controller is unable to establish proof of the processor's competence, it has to walk away; otherwise, it will be in automatic breach of Article 28. All this has to work in a commercial context.

The defining feature of the controller-processor relationship is that the processor can only act on the instructions of the controller and as can be seen from Article 28(10), if the processor steps outside the boundaries of its instructions, it risks being defined as a controller, with all the attendant obligations. None of this is new to European data protection law from the previous Directive to the GDPR. However, what is new to legislation is the duty to provide assistance to the controller with achieving compliance and reduction of risk, which includes assisting the controller with the handling of the personal data breach notification requirements (Article 28(3)(f)). Giving this more practical application, it is clear that there will need to be close working operations between the controller and the processor in order to ensure effective incident detection and response.

Arguably, Article 28 poses many challenges for the established order of things, particularly where there is an imbalance between the controller and processor in the market. Where the processor is a technology giant, perhaps there is a risk that it may use its more powerful position in a way that the GDPR says triggers controllership under Article 28(10). Thus, for the processor industry, there are very good incentives to behave flexibly during contract formation and procurement.

10.3 Notification and communication of personal data breaches

Articles 33 and 34 impose requirements on controllers to notify personal data breaches to the data protection authorities (DPAs) and, in certain circumstances, to communicate with the people impacted.

Breach notification is effectively a transparency mechanism that shines the spotlight on operational failure. The purported benefits of transparency include mitigation of loss and damage (in the sense that people affected by failure of data handling can take steps to protect their own interests). Transparency around failure also help controllers, regulators and society understand the causes of failure, enabling the development of appropriate responses to minimise the risk of future events and their impact. Additionally, notification provides regulators with the necessary information they need to perform their supervisory functions.

By bringing operational control failure to the attention of regulators and the public, regulators and the public are provided with the evidence that enables them to apply adverse scrutiny, such as regulatory enforcement proceedings and compensation claims. In the UK, where breach disclosure requirements exist mainly in the regulatory policies of the Information Commissioner and the public sector, the reporting of incidents has led directly to enforcement action against the reporting entity in hundreds of cases. In many cases, however, a breach has been investigated, the reporting entity found to have engaged in appropriate security, and no further action is taken.

The GDPR is not the first occasion of breach disclosure rules being embedded into European data protection legislation, but it is the first time that it has been done on a large scale. In 2009, the Citizens Rights Directive amended the ePrivacy Directive 2002 to create a breach disclosure regime for the providers of publicly available electronic communications services.[2]

10.3.1 Meaning of 'personal data breach'

Article 4(12) provides the definition of 'personal data breach' as 'a breach of security leading to the accidental or unlawful destruction, loss, alteration, unauthorised disclosure of, or access to, personal data transmitted, stored or otherwise processed'.

This language can be compared with the language of the security principle (or the 'integrity and confidentiality' principle) in Article 5(1)(f). The two ideas do not map perfectly. For example, Article 5(1)(f) does not refer to alteration. The impact of the tension between the language of these articles is something that might be revealed in subsequent enforcement activity.

It's also worth noting that the language of Article 4(12) means that a personal data breach needs to consist of an actual breach of security that actually leads to one of the negative outcomes described. In other words, risks of security breaches are not caught by the definition. This can be contrasted with the security principle itself, which also seeks to prevent risks.

10.3.2 Article 33—notifying the regulator

Article 33 sets out the requirement for notification of personal data breaches to the data protection regulators and for the keeping of registers of breaches and remedial actions.

The trigger to the notification requirement is the detection of a personal data breach event, in the sense that the obligation to notify the regulator arises after the controller has become aware of a breach. If a controller is not aware of a breach, then the notification requirement cannot be triggered. This literal interpretation can cause a distorted outcome, in the sense that some controllers might conclude that, in order to avoid breach disclosure, they should avoid putting in place measures to detect breaches.

That kind of thinking would be an extreme folly. In a purely operational sense, breach detection measures are necessary in all organisations. In a legal sense, it must surely be an implicit, basic requirement of the security principle in Article 5(1)(f)—and the breach disclosure rule itself—that controllers have to put in place breach detection measures. If that is correct, then a failure to put such measures in place would constitute a breach of the security principle, exposing the controller to legal risk.

Once a suspected breach is detected, the controller needs to determine whether it meets the definition of personal data breach and, if so, whether it is of a kind that is likely to cause a risk to the rights and freedoms of individuals. This has to be done very quickly, because the controller has to notify without undue delay, which is subject to a 72-hour limit. Plainly, for detection, classification and notification to take place within such a short space of time, the controller will need to have put in place an incident response strategy. Examples of an incident response strategy include an incident response plan, incident response playbook, creation of an incident response team and an operational incident detection team, such as a security operations center (SOC).

Controllers could easily get lost in their deliberations about whether the breach is or is not likely to result in a risk to the rights and freedoms of individuals, but the language used in Section 33 seems to set a very low bar to notification. This is because the concept of risk is not subject to a severity threshold and because the concept of rights and freedoms is exceptionally broad. For example, if personal data are unlawfully disclosed to a third party, there cannot be any question about this causing a risk to rights and freedoms, because the right to protection of personal data has been infringed. In most situations, the fact that a personal data breach has occurred will be determinative of the question of whether there is a risk to rights and freedoms.

As regard the mechanics of breach disclosure, Section 33(3) sets out the core parameters, whilst Section 33(4) sets out the position for when the controller is unable to provide all the required information at the point of notification. The DPAs can be expected to issue detailed guidance on how breach disclosure should operate in practice, which will be bound to cover form and content issues.

Section 33(5) contains a very interesting provision about the keeping of records of breaches. Every time a personal data breach occurs, the controller will be expected to make an entry in its records, which should be essentially equivalent to a notification to the regulator. These records are not subject to a long stop date, so, in theory, they should be held in perpetuity. Part of the utility of the records keeping obligation is to enable retrospective examination by the regulator of the controller's decision-making around breach response and breach disclosure. In other words, controllers must maintain full records of every personal data breach that they decide does not fall within the requirements for disclosure, as well as records of every one that does. It can be anticipated that the regulators will ask for disclosure of these records whenever they undertake regulatory investigations of controllers following a suspected security breach.

Finally, Section 33(2) caters for the processor's position. Processors have to notify personal data breaches to the controller without undue delay. This must include the same implied obligation for incident detection measures. (See Article 28(3)(f).)

10.3.3 Article 34—communicating the breach to the data subject

Article 34 requires controllers to inform data subjects of personal data breaches if those breaches are likely to present high risks to the rights and freedoms of individuals. Hence, there is a severity threshold within Article 34, which distinguishes it from Article 33. For example, a breach of names and personal business email addresses to a third party might present a risk and trigger notification to a DPA, but not a high risk, as many people openly share their business email account.

Article 33(3) sets out exceptions to this rule. The first exception is where measures have been taken to render personal data unintelligible, for instance, by use of encryption. This is sometimes called an 'encryption safe harbor' because application of a security control releases a controller from notification obligations. In other words, the use of encryption technologies has a de-regulatory effect. The second exception operates where the controller has taken steps to prevent the high risks from materialising, which is another justification for good-quality incident response strategies. If you have a plan for quickly responding to and mitigating a breach, you are much less likely to have to notify data subjects following a breach.

The third exception is where breach disclosure would involve disproportionate effort, which is most likely to arise where the controller is unable to identify all the individuals impacted by the breach. In such a case, there still has to be some form of broad public announcement, perhaps through a press release or a statement on a website.

By virtue of Article 34(4), regulators can order controllers to engage in these communications. The most obvious route to such an order will be the giving of breach disclosure to the regulators under Article 33. Of course, regulators follow the news like everyone else, and they are likely to exercise their Article 34 powers after hearing about serious incidents. It's also likely that they will order communications after they consider some of the personal data breach records maintained under Article 33(5) if they discover cases were wrongly kept secret.

So, what will constitute a high risk to the rights and freedoms of individuals? Whilst we can expect regulatory guidance and enforcement activity to provide assistance at some point, we can find assistance in the Recitals. Recital 75 gives examples of potential 'physical, material or non-material damage', whilst Recital 76 identifies the need for a risk assessment, whereby risks are evaluated on the basis of objective assessment referencing the 'nature, scope, context and purposes of the processing'.

In total context, it would seem that 'high' can be determined in two different contexts: either through impact to a large number of data subjects or via a particularly large amount of damage to certain individuals.

10.4 Delivering on security

Organisations with GDPR programmes already underway will be familiar with the principles of good programme design that underpin the success of any regulatory large-scale business transformation exercise. Successful programmes are united and guided by a board-endorsed vision, which organisational directors integrate into business operations through strategy and necessary organisational structures, ensuring technical and organisational controls are employed. These structures include programme design and management, governance structures, policy frameworks, technical controls, frameworks, etcetera. Members of the programme steering function will be drawn from key executives and the main functional areas of the business, and they will work together to ensure a holistic, multidisciplinary approach.

When organisations operate in this way, they will connect their security professionals with data protection and legal professionals. This will help them to reach an informed and balanced view of the nature of the technical and organisational measures that need to be put in place to deliver on the security principle and the breach disclosure requirements. The security professional will present their professional views and recommendations on what needs to be done to deliver operational security, which will form part of the risk-assessment process that the organisation has put in place for accountability and privacy by design purposes.

A strong security programme should not only be a consideration for data protection regulatory compliance, but it should also be part of a standard organisational management process to protect financial, operational, reputational and legal interests. Therefore, the data protection professional needs to make sure that they are properly connected to security experts within the organisation.

In broad terms, security experts will advise organisations on situational awareness, including the threat landscape, overall security maturity and controls used to manage security with regard to the risks facing the organisation, its physical and technical environment, its people and its data. This will enable effective dialogue to understand an organisation's potential security exposure, which will, in turn, enable decisions that consider capabilities, resources and priorities with respect to protecting personal information. There should be independent reviews and testing of the organisation's capabilities and necessary scenario planning to enable incident preparedness and incident response.

The discussion below is illustrative of the kind of issues that controllers and processors will address during the development of their positions for compliance with the security principle and for risk reduction.

10.4.1 The threat vectors, causes of failure and risk assessments

As already indicated, the causes of security failure are multiple, ranging from accidents (unintentional) to deliberate (intentional) actions, but in broad terms, controllers and processors should address the following factors when designing their responses:

- Performing threat and vulnerability assessments and security maturity assessments
- The management of security
- Human factors
- The physical environment
- The cyber and technology environment
- The policy, controls and business processes framework
- Incident detection and response

Of course, in order for the organisation to be able to perform comprehensive risk assessments, it needs to identify and understand the full information lifecycle (see Article 30). The controller should go through a data mapping and inventory exercise so as to be able to pinpoint all points of data capture and data entry and should be able to plot the flow of the data through the organisation until the point of redundancy is reached, when the data is finally deleted or destroyed.

Yet, this poses considerable challenges for many organisations who struggle to identify all their data, whether in a granular sense or at a much higher level. Indeed, even the task of full data classification is something that has been overlooked by many, especially as the sensitivity of data, and even whether it is 'personal' or not can depend on context and what other data it is associated with.

The problem is compounded by the growth of cloud computing and bring your own device (BYOD) strategies, where organisations can easily lose control over their data in a meaningful sense. Moreover, the growth of outsourcing has concentrated the skills and expertise in the hands of professional data processors, with the result that many organisations' internal expertise is eroded year on year. Thus, a very large proportion of organisations are ill-equipped to meet in full the compliance obligations within Articles 32–34, 25, 30 and 35, etcetera.

10.4.2 Assistance with understanding what is appropriate

So, what can data protection professionals do to put their organisations in the best position possible? Where should they look to understand the meaning of 'appropriate technical and organisational measures'? As well as consulting with their internal security professionals about the nature of the security threats and risks and the nature of the response strategy, they can seek to familarise themselves with some of the key pieces of readily available learning. Fruitful areas for review include:

- Related pieces of the legislative framework that contain security provisions, such as the EU Cybersecurity Directive, the ePrivacy Directive, the Cybercrime Directive and the Payment Services Directive No. 2.[3]

- The output of institutions, such as the Article 29 Working Party (WP29), the European Data Protection Supervisor and the European Union Agency for Network and Information Security.

- The output of security centres of excellence, such as the National Cyber Security Centre in the UK

- Policy frameworks of national governments, such as national cybersecurity plans.

- Regulatory policy statements and other guidance issued by the national data protection regulators and by sector regulators.

- Decisions in regulatory enforcement actions brought by the national data protection regulators and related regulators.

- Decisions of courts and tribunals in related areas.

- National and international standards for best practice, such as the ISO 27000 series, the Payment Card Industry Data Security Standard, CBEST and the NIST framework.

- Threat assessment reports and subject matter white papers published by IT security companies and security consultants.

- The output of relevant professional associations and affinity groups. There are many operating in the space, such as the Cloud Security Alliance and the Information Security Forum.

This list is not exhaustive, but it should give the data protection professional a fairly good impression of the range of available resources in determining an appropriate level of security.

10.4.3 Effective management

The requirement for appropriate organisational measures for security clearly envisages a need for appropriate management structures. Likewise, this is recognised as key within the consensus of professional opinion for operational security. If all the learning and commentary in this area were drawn together and distilled down to basics, the core proposition would be that an organisation that does not have an engaged management team will suffer otherwise avoidable flaws and an increased risk of failure.

An engaged management team will display certain key attributes. For example, security will be treated as a board-level issue; the board will foster a culture of risk awareness and respect for personal data; a 'multidisciplinary team' will have been constituted for the management of risk, consisting of senior management from areas such as IT, security, legal, compliance, HR, finance, audit, company secretariat and so on; sufficient resources will have been allocated; and the organisation will take seriously departures from policy and other relevant incidents. Of course, the management team will need to engage in planning exercises, such as simulations and role play.

Another way of looking at this issue is to consider the consequences of a serious security breach. Such an incident can attract adverse third-party scrutiny—from the press and media, from regulators, from contracting partners, from litigants, from customers and so on. The question for the data protection professional to focus on is this: Will a true head of business be able to speak clearly and truthfully about management's commitment to security and its understanding of the organisation's security measures?

Distilling this down even further, an engaged management will know who is responsible for what, when and why. An engaged management will create clear management structures.

10.4.4 Culture within the organisation and workers as the 'insider threat'

An organisation with full management buy-in will shape the organisation as a whole towards a culture of risk awareness and respect for personal data as part of the drive for good security. Appropriate organisational measures require a programme to embed and enforce the right cultural profile and behaviours in the workforce. Central to the achievement of the right culture is the selection of competent, trustworthy and reliable workers. Key components of a good culture for security include:

- *Understanding the people risks:* For employees, the journey along the path towards the right culture begins long before they are recruited. The beginning of the process is identifying the security risks within the job and how they will be addressed. The risks within an IT department role are different from the risks presented by a customer-facing role in a shop. A desk-bound job has different risks from those of the mobile worker or the home worker. The process of risk assessment at this micro level will set the path of risk mitigation from that point onwards.

- *The recruitment process:* The recruitment process is designed to get the right person for the job. The way that information about candidates is collected and processed conveys the value that the organisation places on security and confidentiality. This value is reflected in the content and placing of the job advertisement, the interview and assessment process, and the taking of references and any pre-employment vetting or background checks. Some organisations may opt to conduct background checks consistent with applicable laws.

- *The offer letter and the contract of employment:* These stages of the recruitment process provide the final pre-engagement opportunity to embed the organisation's culture. These are incredibly important documents, and they should contain the correct wording, explaining what the organisation expects and how its expectations will be achieved.

- *Acceptance of job offer:* Assuming that there will be a delay between the acceptance of the job offer and the commencement of employment, the organisation has a great opportunity to introduce the new recruit to its policy framework. Where appropriate, core policy documents should be provided, and the recruit should be asked to affirm that they have read and understood them.

- *Induction day:* Many organisations have a new-employee induction programme designed to familiarise new hires with aspects of the business. The induction process provides an unmissable opportunity to further embed the organisation's framework for confidentiality and security, such as providing training on role-specific data protection obligations.

- *Continuous and role-based training:* Policy education doesn't end with induction day. Organisations must provide continuous and role-based training that keeps employees abreast of policy, security threats and their role in mitigating them.

Also, of course, there must be adequate processes to deal with failure, including disciplinary measures that may encompass dismissal for a worker who rejects the organisation's culture in a serious way.

This last point also draws attention to the need to consider cultural issues at the end of the employment lifecycle, whether for dismissal, retirement, redundancy or other cause. At the end of employment, physical assets need to be returned (e.g., laptops, phones and paper files), the worker's personal equipment must be cleansed of the organisational data, access rights and privileges need to be terminated, and sufficient post-termination restrictions to guarantee ongoing security and confidentiality need to be activated, where appropriate. Ensuring that these issues are understood at the beginning of the employment relationship and that workers receive regular reminders throughout their employment via policy and associated training will help achieve the necessary continuity of behavioural ideals.

10.4.5 The policy framework, controls and processes—the security paperwork

The importance of the security paperwork cannot be overstated. This is the repository of all the organisation's rules for security, and it is the natural reference point for anyone who wants to understand the organisation's position.

Data protection professionals should consider the impression that an inadequate or nonexistent policy, controls and processes framework will make on a regulator because, of course, the adequacy of the paperwork is one of the first things that regulators consider during the course of investigations and enforcement proceedings.

Data protection professionals should also consider the dynamics of litigation; in most jurisdictions, a process of disclosure or discovery will take place in litigation, which focuses on documentation. So, if the process of disclosure reveals inadequate paperwork (both policies and record-keeping), this can also create a bad impression. Next, data protection professionals should consider contracting processes between businesses; it is now very common for organisations to be asked to produce security paperwork during contractual due diligence.

It is in the context of regulatory investigations and proceedings for security breaches and data loss that inadequate paperwork can cause the most immediate damage to controllers' interests, because these inadequacies can give regulators sufficient grounds for findings of noncompliance. There are a number of dynamics worth considering.

It is highly significant that the enforcement and supervision of data protection law can operate on an anticipatory basis. Regulators can take action if there is a risk that a law will be breached in the future. If an organisation is incapable of putting its paperwork in order, how can it be trusted to keep personal data secure in an operational sense? Indeed, a regulator will be supported in such a view by the theories and philosophies that underscore best practice, auditing models and the consensus of professional opinion in this area; these say that one of the first steps to achieving operational security is the creation of sound paperwork. Legal compliance flows from the paperwork into the daily operations, provided that the paperwork is properly embedded through training, monitoring and the use of other tools.

In recent years, a preference for policy-based regulation has emerged. During their investigations, regulators have two options: They can examine the organisation's paperwork, or they can examine the organisation's operations. The problem with operations-based regulation is that it is much more time consuming and expensive than policy-based regulation, as well as being much more disruptive to the organisation's daily activities. Basically, models of operations-based regulation require regulators to insert their people into the controller's premises, with no certainty of results. Policy-based regulation has completely different dynamics. It is cheaper, quicker and more efficient than operations-based regulation. It can be performed at the regulator's desk, with the probability of more certain results, because the adequacy of paperwork is almost a box-ticking exercise.

It should be no surprise, then, that the GDPR has put paperwork right at the top of the legal and regulatory agenda. Concepts such as data protection by design, data protection impact assessments and the accountability principle presuppose the creation and distribution, as appropriate, of records.

The creation of strong record-keeping practices can be a very time-consuming task. However, there is an expectation that organisations will adopt a 'layered' approach to the creation of paperwork, which is a prominent concept within the theories and philosophies in this area. The layered approach says that, at the top layer, there is a high-level document that contains the controller's policy statements. The next layer is a more detailed document that sets out the controls that will be implemented to achieve the policy statements. The third layer is the most detailed and contains the operating processes and procedures, which explain how the policy statements will be achieved in practice on the ground.

The table provides an example of how a policy statement will be reflected in controls and operating processes and procedures to help achieve secure data transit.

Example of the layered approach within security policy frameworks		
Top layer	*Policy statements* This layer will contain high-level statements of principle that explain the controller's position on confidentiality and security. This will address the headline issues, such as management structures, engagement of workers and contractors, use of IT and communications systems, the physical environment, and so on	*Secure data transit* 1. This company will ensure the security of personal data in transit.
Middle layer (more detail)	*Controls* The controls expand upon the policy statements to show how the controller will achieve them. Individual policy statements can have many different controls.	*Secure data transit—encryption* 1. All laptop computers will be protected by full hard drive encryption. 2. All USB memory sticks will be protected by encryption. 3. Only company computers can be used for company business.

Lower layer (more detail)	Operating procedures	Secure data transit—encryption of laptops
	The operating procedures show the actual steps and processes that are to be followed in order to deliver the controls into operations. Individual controls can have many different operating procedures.	1. To ensure that encrypted laptop computers are used within the business, the following procedures will apply: 2. Only the IT department may make an order for a new laptop. All orders must be approved by the director of IT. 3. Upon delivery of a new laptop, the IT department will make a record of the machine number and enter it in the asset register. 4. Following registration of the laptop, the IT department will install encryption software and fully test it. 5. After testing, the date when the laptop was encrypted will be entered in the register, together with the name of the IT department member who installed the software. 6. The director of IT will then authorise the release of the laptop to the staff member. The date when the laptop was released and the staff member's name shall be entered in the register. 7. The laptop shall be tested at six-month intervals by the IT department to verify that the encryption software is operating normally. The dates of testing and the name of the IT department member responsible for the testing shall be entered in the register.

10.4.6 The technology stack

Of course, because the main focus of data protection law is electronic information, organisations need to ensure that their technology stacks are robust and fit for this purpose. Beyond encryption, there are many other de facto mandatory security-enhancing technologies in the market, such as antivirus, antispam, firewalls, identity and access management, incident detection, data loss prevention, two-factor authentication and IP log management.

A key focus of security technologies is the filtering of electronic communications and the monitoring of use of IT and communication systems. The use of these technologies in the workplace often involves complex privacy and employment law issues (see

Chapter 14). In some jurisdictions, such as Germany, there are legal requirements to engage with works councils before such technologies are deployed. For an overview of some of the privacy law issues involved in workplace monitoring, see cases such as Halford v. United Kingdom and Copland v. United Kingdom.[4]

Of course, the ability of the technology stack to withstand cyberattacks and misuse needs to be fully tested. Penetration testing by so-called 'ethical hackers' is regularly performed by leading organisations, and the UK Information Commissioner's Office (ICO) has specifically mentioned lack of pen-testing in recent enforcement actions.[5] Testing of coding security is another angle.

10.4.7 The physical environment

The security of the physical environment is another important factor for practitioners to consider. Sophisticated entry control systems, closed-circuit television (CCTV), lock-and-key and clean-desk policies are as much a part of the picture as business continuity and disaster recovery and subject to the same restrictions as other monitoring controls.

10.4.8 Processors, suppliers and vendor risk management

On paper, at least, the GDPR's requirements for the engagement of data processors are straightforward. Controllers must (1) choose reliable processors; (2) maintain quality control and compliance throughout the duration of the arrangements; and (3) frame the relationship in a contract (or other legally binding act, such as a deed) that contains the necessary provisions that require the processor to implement and maintain appropriate security measures, to act only on the controller's instructions, to cooperate with the controller on compliance, including breach disclosure, and to cascade these requirements through the supply chain.

Translating the law's requirements into practical action points throws up many unresolved issues, such as the extent to which the controller can rely upon the processor to attest and monitor its own reliability, or to what extent the controller needs to evaluate third parties before and after contracting, including conducting audits.

The nature of the contractual provisions that need to be introduced into the contracting framework is often much more complex and challenging than the wording of Article 28 suggests. One area of unexpected challenge concerns negotiating contracts between two parties of unequal bargaining power or from EU and non-EU jurisdictions.

Specific technologies may also complicate the contracting process. Situations that involve cloud computing may be particularly tricky due to the difficulties of knowing the precise nature of data processing operations at any given moment in time (see Chapter 17).

So, what can the controller do to 'shield' itself from the accusation that it has not complied with Article 28?

One might start by drawing up a checklist of issues to consider at the pre-contractual due diligence stage, which can provide evidence that the necessary steps were taken. For example, these steps may include:

- Verifying that the processor is cognisant of the core requirements of data protection.

- Researching whether the processor has suffered any recent or high-profile breaches of confidentiality or security.

- Clarifying whether the processor is currently or has been under investigation for any breaches of data protection law.

- Identifying the processor's other clients.

- Clarifying whether the processor is accredited under ISO 27001, CBEST, PCI DSS or under any comparable regime for informational security.

- Reviewing the processor's policy framework for security and data protection.

- Carrying out site visits and inspections.

- Carrying out audits.

- Identifying the processor's places of establishment.

- Understanding the processor's supply chain and subcontracting.

Certainly, all that and more would be part of a risk assessment to understand the threats and challenges posed by outsourcing (see Chapter 18).

It's also important to identify the range of alternative service providers in the market. Where there is inequality in the bargaining position or where the processor refuses to operate other than on its terms, having evidence that there was no better alternative available in the market can support the controller's decisions in the sense that it can help the controller counter the argument that it should have placed its business elsewhere.

Part of the contracting should also include a suitable framework for ongoing assurance. These measures can range from the performance of on-site audits, inspections and testing to the provision of periodic assessments of ongoing compliance.

Creating a contractual framework that goes beyond the mere wording of Article 28 to specify more granular requirements, such as specific minimum security measures; the need to adhere to a security plan; the need to undergo regular systems testing; the need to undertake threat, vulnerability and maturity assessments; permitted and non-permitted locations for processing; permitted and non-permitted subcontracting; a plan for what happens to the data at the close of the business engagement; and indemnities against regulatory sanctions and penalties, along with any other costs associated with a breach, such as a notification or services provided to victims.

10.5 Incident response

The need to put in place appropriate technical and organisational measures for incident detection and response is clearly an implicit requirement within the security principle and the breach disclosure rules. The analysis below builds upon key industry learning in this area.

10.5.1 The scope of an incident response plan

Incident response resides on a very long continuum, from detection through to immediate post-detection activities and then into the long term. Controllers and processors need to define with precision the parts of the incident response continuum that are being addressed by their plan.

10.5.2 Core requirements of a good incident response plan

The core requirements of a good incident response plan include:

- Formal understanding and approval by senior leadership.
- A governance model connected both to the anticipatory aspects of incident response and the response aspects of incident response.
- Principles for decision-making. The incident response team and everyone involved with the performance of incident response functions must know how, when and why decisions can be made and for what purpose.
- A list of who will be involved and what their roles will be.
- Predictive, forward-looking outcome analysis.
- Compulsory reporting up of 'unusual' events.
- A multidisciplinary/multi-jurisdictional expert view at the point of detection, potentially including forensics and law enforcement.
- Performances exercises, such as 'table-top' incidents.
- Performance metrics—what is a successful response?

- Templates of public messaging and communications.

- Benchmarking against peers in the marketplace.

- An updated schedule to make sure the plan is in accordance with prevailing legal and regulatory environment.

10.5.3 Decisions about incident response functions

Organisations will need to take decisions on the nature of the incident response functions to be performed by the incident response team. The achievement of capability requires the organisation to be clear on its ambitions for capability (which is also a scope question) and to measure its current capabilities. Illustrative considerations are set out below.

- *Ambitions versus capabilities*. Does the organisation want a command and control model, or something else? Is the incident response team actually an active team of people, is it a framework/governance/leadership structure, or is it both?

- *Gap analysis*. An organisation must understand the gap between the objectives of the incident response plan and the capabilities of the incident response team.

- *Discovery*. An organisation should perform a discovery exercise to understand what else is being done that is relevant to incident response, to see what is reusable and what is a hindrance, and to avoid conflicts and confusion.

- *Reviewing previous events*. An organisation should understand past successes and failures to get deep views of the processes, including for learning the lessons.

10.5.4 Moving incident response forward

In order to move incident response forward, the organisation will need to ensure that it has incident detection capabilities and appropriately monitors and documents these capabilities. Of course, the threat and vulnerability assessments and maturity assessments that are performed for general security purposes will guide the organisation in the right direction, but, as well as installing necessary incident detection technologies, such as intrusion detection, the organisation needs to understand whether it is already compromised. One of the great problems with cybersecurity is that criminals and hackers are both patient and good at hiding their tracks. It is very common for cyberattacks to lie unnoticed on a network, even for many years. Therefore, compromise testing needs to be performed using advanced forensics techniques.

Even good programmes with good controls get hacked. There is no need for panic should an intrusion be detected. It's better to know, analyse and respond than to be in the dark.

Another critical building block for success is a **taxonomy and classification scheme**, so that everyone knows the sensitivity and personal nature of the data compromised in a breach. Misclassification, false positives and the like are very serious problems to solve. If an organisation misclassifies an incident, it may reach the wrong conclusion on treatment and breach disclosure. It's important to know as quickly as possible when an incident rises to the level of a breach by legal definition.

A good incident response plan that is well rehearsed will contain a playbook or procedures for handling incident categories most likely to occur. The triage and remedial steps that need to be taken should be identified in advance of an incident, which will help to minimise the risk of damage to the organisation.

10.5.5 Handling the fall out

The incident response plan will also address the wider aftermath of an incident, including dealing with third parties (e.g., law enforcement, insurers, etcetera), through to handling breach disclosure. If a personal data breach is suffered, the disclosure to the regulator can trigger regulatory investigations. If disclosure is given to people affected, the organisation will have to be ready for the inbound queries and complaints.

In these circumstances, the organisation will be on the cusp of contentious legal business, such as regulatory enforcement action or litigation. Therefore, organisations need to develop a 'litigation posture', which should be reflected in the incident response plan or playbook. For example, the playbook will explain the roles to be played by internal and external legal advisors and the role of legal professional privilege.

Further, there should be a communications plan, detailing who is available to speak with the media and which types of information will be explained publicly.

10.6 Conclusion

Whilst security has always been a pillar of any good privacy programmes, the GDPR introduces significant new regulatory risk. It will be vitally important for the privacy and security programmes in any organisation to be in lock-step and constant communication.

Whilst the security team is likely to handle technical implementation, it is privacy's role to advise the security team on regulatory obligations, handle the response capabilities and ensure that security incidents don't rise to the level of breaches if at all possible.

Incorporating principles, like data minimisation, and having a good plan for data retention is likely to reduce the impact of any security incident. You can't lose, after all, what you don't have.

Endnotes

1 Maximillian Schrems v. Data Protection Commissioner and Digital Rights Ireland Ltd., [2015] Case C-362/14, 6 October 2015.

2 Directive 2009/136/EC of the European Parliament and of the Council of 25 November 2009 amending Directive 2002/22/EC on universal service and users' rights relating to electronic communications networks and services; Directive 2002/58/EC concerning the processing of personal data and the protection of privacy in the electronic communications sector and Regulation (EC) No. 2006/2004 on cooperation between national authorities responsible for the enforcement of consumer protection laws.

3 Directive (EU) 2016/1148 of the European Parliament and of the Council of 6 July 2016 concerning measures for a high common level of security of network and information systems across the Union; Directive 2013/40/EU of the European Parliament and of the Council of 12 August 2013 on attacks against information systems and replacing Council Framework Decision 2005/222/JHA; Directive (EU) 2015/2366 of the European Parliament and of the Council of 25 November 2015 on payment services in the internal market, amending Directives 2002/65/EC, 2009/110/EC and 2013/36/EU and Regulation (EU) No 1093/2010, and repealing Directive 2007/64/EC.

4 Halford v. United Kingdom [1997] ECHR 32, 25 June 1997; Copland v. United Kingdom [2007] 45 EHRR 37, 3 April 2007.

5 Boomerang Video Ltd., Information Commissioner's Office, 27 June 2017, https://ico.org.uk/action-weve-taken/enforcement/boomerang-video-ltd/.

CHAPTER 11

Accountability Requirements

Mary Pothos

11.1 Introduction and background

The General Data Protection Regulation (GDPR, or 'Regulation') has formally embedded the requirement of accountability into the data protection legislative framework. It describes and extends the overall accountability of organisations that process personal data.

It is important to understand what, in practice, 'accountability' means. It can mean different things in different contexts. But, for present purposes, it is probably best described as the different obligations with which an organisation must comply in order to show and evidence their compliance with the data protection framework.

Accountability, however, is not an entirely new concept in the area of data protection. Accountability was first outlined in 1980 in the influential text of the OECD Guidelines on the Protection of Privacy and Transborder Flows of Personal Data ('Guidelines').[1]

It also featured in the original Data Protection Directive ('Directive'). Although the Directive did not explicitly refer to 'accountability', it nevertheless addressed issues that support the accountability principle. Those issues include, for example, a requirement for organisations to register with or notify their national data protection authorities (DPAs) of their intended processing activities.

It is also important to understand why accountability has become relevant in today's data protection environment. Over the last 20 years, there has been much discussion and debate about how organisations can become better at embedding data protection within their businesses and operations. The Regulation is intended to achieve that outcome.

Regulators and legislators alike seek an approach that is more than merely a 'tick-box' exercise. They are looking to companies to show that they have developed and embedded a culture of data protection within their corporate DNA. Simply implementing policies and procedures, or completing and submitting registration forms, will no longer be sufficient to establish those essential data protection credentials. As will be seen below, the approach to be taken will have to be more considered than that.

Once the Regulation becomes operational, DPAs will likely be focusing in greater detail on how companies manage the accountability principle. Indeed, some regulators may take a more proactive approach to accountability. For example, the French data protection authority, the CNIL—widely considered influential given that its president, Isabelle Falque-Pierrotin, is chairman of the Article 29 Working Party (WP29)—published a standard setting out a number of specific requirements for 'Privacy Governance Procedures' ('the Standard').[2]

The Standard is divided into 25 separate requirements. They outline various steps that the CNIL considers necessary to take as part of an effective data protection governance programme. Such steps include developing internal and external privacy policies, the appointment and status of a company's data protection officer (DPO), data protection audits, and the handling of data subject access requests and data breaches.

Companies that can demonstrate they comply with the new Standard are able to obtain a 'privacy seal' from the CNIL.

The Standard provides some helpful assistance for companies in relation to what they might want to consider and include as part of their preparation for creating an accountability programme in line with the new Regulation.

What follows is a discussion, based on available guidance, as to the practical implications of the new accountability regime and an explanation of some of the key steps that ought to be considered to ensure compliance with that regime.

11.2 Responsibility of the controller

The 'accountability' requirement is first introduced in Article 5 of the Regulation. In particular, Article 5(1) lists the familiar six principles relating to the processing of personal data:

- Lawfulness, fairness and transparency

- Purpose limitation

- Data minimisation

- Accuracy

- Storage limitation

- Integrity and confidentiality

These principles have long covered the different obligations imposed on the data controller for the proper handling and processing of personal data.

Article 5(2), however, is a new addition for the GDPR. It specifically provides not only that the data controller is responsible for complying with the six principles outlined in Article 5(1), but also, crucially, that the data controller must be able to demonstrate its compliance with the six principles.

Article 24(1) further codifies the accountability obligation and requires data controllers to 'implement appropriate technical and organisational measures to ensure and be able to demonstrate that data processing is performed in accordance with the Regulation; and review and update those measures where necessary'. Those measures should take into account the nature, scope, context and purposes of the processing and the risks to the rights and freedoms of the individuals. If the relevant processing results in a higher level of risk to the rights of the individual, the data controller will need to adopt greater measures to protect against that risk.

Recital 75 helpfully provides some examples of high-risk processing in the context of this requirement. Those examples include processing which gives rise to: (1) discrimination; (2) identity theft, fraud or financial loss; (3) damage to reputation; (4) loss of confidentiality of personal data protected by professional secrecy; (5) unauthorised reversal of pseudonymisation; (6) any other significant economic or social disadvantage; (7) processing which might deprive an individual of their rights and freedoms or prevent them from exercising control over their personal data; or (8) processing special categories of personal data, the personal data of children or personal data related to criminal convictions.

Article 24(2) introduces the requirement that the data controller should implement 'appropriate data protection policies'. But as stated earlier, simply implementing policies will not be sufficient to establish compliance. So, with the above in mind, what must the data controller do in order to achieve compliance with this requirement?

There are three key areas to consider, namely: (1) internal policies; (2) internal allocation of responsibilities; and (3) training.

11.2.1 Internal policies

At the core of compliance for the data controller is an internal data protection policy, which outlines the basic contours of the measures to take in the processing and handling of personal data. However, the policy should not simply repeat the six principles in Article 5(1). There are a number of broader key matters that the policy should address. Set out below is a list of some of those matters:

11.2.1.1 Scope

- The policy should include a brief statement that explains both to whom the internal policy applies and the type of processing activities it covers.

11.2.1.2 Policy statement

- This should set out the company's commitment to or position that concerns the personal data it processes.

- It should also include a description of the purposes for which it collects and processes personal data and should specify the types of legitimate business purposes for which personal data is collected and processed.

- It may also be helpful to reiterate the principles for processing personal data (as stated in Article 5(1)), as these are the applicable fundamental principles and should be addressed within an internal policy.

11.2.1.3 Employee responsibilities

- The policy should address the different areas for which employees are directly responsible when processing personal data. For example, a description should be provided of what each employee role is permitted to do in relation to the collection of personal data.

- The limitations around the use of the collected personal data should be specified.

- Additionally, the steps that must be followed in order to ensure that personal data is maintained accurately should be set out.

- Employees should be fully aware of their security obligations and should be required to take all reasonable steps to prevent unauthorised access or loss.

- The 'security obligations', as contained in the internal data protection policy, are usually addressed more fully in a separate company 'information security policy'. The two policies should, of course, be appropriately and properly cross-referenced. An information security policy typically addresses the more detailed technical standards that apply to the physical and digital security of all data a company holds. Some companies base these policies on industry standards, such as ISO 27001/2. Whilst it is best practice, there is no requirement to do so.

- Another key responsibility relates to the transfer of personal data. Transfer of personal data is prohibited unless specific legitimate grounds can be established. The internal policy should outline what are the relevant grounds. It should also specify the steps employees should take before transferring any personal data. This is particularly important when the personal data may be sent by the company outside of the European Economic Area (EEA).

- Destruction or deletion of personal data should also be addressed. Again, some companies deal with this issue separately within a stand-alone policy dedicated to this particular issue. There is no requirement to do so. But, if this issue is dealt with separately in a series of more detailed policies, there should be appropriate cross-referencing between the different policy documents. In any event, there should be sufficient detail contained within this part of the internal policy statement to enable employees to understand what steps they must take regarding the way in which they are permitted to handle personal data.

11.2.1.4 Management responsibilities

- This part of the policy should specify clearly the senior management roles across the business that are responsible for assessing the business risk arising as a result of processing personal data.

- This section of the policy should also record that those senior managers must work with the business to develop procedures and controls to identify and address risks appropriately. This, for example, could include the appointment of a DPO to whom responsibility for data protection is specifically allocated (see further discussion of the DPO below).

- The GDPR contains a wide range of requirements that dictate the allocation of management responsibilities. Responsibility should clearly be allocated to individual organisation roles for everything from determining risk-based technical, physical and administrative safeguards for protecting personal data, including safeguards for equipment, facilities and locations where personal data is stored, to establishing procedures and requirements for transferring personal data to countries other than the country in which it was collected and for transferring personal data to third parties, such as service providers who process personal data on behalf of or for the company.

11.2.1.5 Reporting incidents

- Employees should be expressly required to report immediately all incidents that involve the suspected or actual loss, theft, unauthorised disclosure or inappropriate use of personal data. It should be clearly identified to which business areas a report should be made (e.g., local IT help desk or compliance team).

- Where a company's third-party service provider (i.e., one who processes or has access to company-related personal data) notifies the company of such an incident, then the steps to be taken by employees should also be clarified in the policy.

- With the inclusion in the Regulation of a new data breach reporting obligation, the time taken to make a report is all important. Significant data breaches must be declared to the relevant DPA within 72 hours.

- Many companies will by now have established incident response plans and put incident response teams in place. For those companies now putting such teams in place, they should be made up of representatives from relevant functions and/ or business areas, and this should also be referenced in the policy. There should be a description in the policy of who will be responsible for the investigation of the incident and who will determine the company's obligations under the applicable regulatory and/or legal framework. Incident response plans must be stress tested regularly.

11.2.1.6 Policy compliance

- The policy should make clear that noncompliance and/or failure to comply with applicable data protection laws could mean that an employee may subject the company and the individuals involved to civil and criminal penalties. This could, of course, severely damage the company's reputation. So, the policy should make clear that a failure to comply with the policy may result in disciplinary action. Each company, however, should ensure that any sanctions for breach are in accordance with local employment and commercial laws. Subject to those laws, sanctions for breach may include termination of employment (a contract of service) or contracts for services. Indemnity and/ or liquidated damages provisions could also be included within third-party contracts for services.

11.2.2 Internal allocation of responsibilities

The data controller must be able to demonstrate and provide information to DPAs about the various data protection management resources. The controller must also take primary responsibility for the internal data protection framework to ensure internal compliance.

Internal allocation of responsibilities should facilitate supervision by DPAs, allow data subjects to exercise their rights, and enable policies, procedures and processes to be updated on a regular basis. So, how should this allocation be made?

By way of example, in allocating responsibility, a company/data controller may look to create a privacy management team or council with responsibility for overseeing compliance within the data protection framework. The privacy team or council would comprise representatives from either business function areas or business key stakeholders.

Alternatively or simultaneously, an individual could be appointed to hold primary responsibility for the data protection framework. (See below for further analysis regarding the requirement to appoint a DPO.)

11.2.3 Training

The data controller should create a series of internal training programmes designed to address and inform employees of the legal data protection obligations and the policy requirements. Training modules could also include related policies, such as information security and retention/deletion procedures (as discussed above).

It is important that the training programme not be offered inflexibly or rigidly—one size will not fit all. Data controllers should tailor their training programmes both in terms of frequency and format having regard to their business and operations and the roles and responsibilities of different employees.

Finally, as part of demonstrating accountability, the controller should document and monitor the roll out and completion rates of the training programme.

Companies should also be creating and delivering regular messages and updates to remind employees of their privacy obligations. Procedures should be created for employees to seek clarification of their obligations and responsibilities with regard to processing personal data.

In practical terms, companies could consider, for example, creating a central set of frequently asked questions (FAQs) for the internal intranet with links to all the relevant policies and resources for further study.

11.3 Data protection by design and by default

Data protection by design and by default ('privacy by design and default') are additional new requirements under the Regulation which can be described as the different 'technical and organisational measures' that a data controller is required to implement as part of its overall approach to protecting the rights and freedoms of individuals with respect to the processing of their personal data.[3] This includes the integration of any necessary safeguards into processing activities.

11.3.1 Privacy by design

Former Information and Privacy Commissioner of Ontario, Ann Cavoukian, took a leading role in developing the privacy by design concept, establishing seven foundational principles of privacy by design. In turn, the principles advocate the approach of embedding data protection into the design specifications of new systems and technologies.[4]

In Europe, some DPAs also advocated the privacy by design principles before its inclusion in the Regulation.

In the UK, for example, the Information Commissioner's Office (ICO) supported companies taking a privacy-by-design approach to new projects. Strategically, this was designed to promote privacy and data protection compliance from the outset of the development of new products, services or technologies, which, in turn, helped reduce privacy risks. The ICO also recognises that this approach assists companies to comply with their obligations under the legislation.[5]

But privacy by design does not apply only to the planning and execution stages of new developments. Logically, it should also address the ongoing operation and management of such developments to enable companies to deal effectively with the entire lifecycle of any personal data the company processes.

In order for companies at the product design stage to fulfil their obligations under Article 25, those responsible for design and development should create products with a built-in ability to manage and fulfil and/or which enable data controllers to manage and fulfil all data protection obligations under the Regulation.

In practice, this will impact a number of areas within a company, such as the IT department, which must take data protection into account for the whole lifecycle of the system or process they are developing.

11.3.2 Privacy by default

The Regulation also introduces a specific 'privacy by default' obligation. This requires companies to implement appropriate technical and organisational measures to ensure that, by default, only personal data necessary for each specific purpose of the processing are processed.

This requirement means that companies should take steps not only to limit or minimise the amount of personal data they collect but also to exercise greater controls over the extent of their processing.

Additionally, the period of storage means that, 'by default', companies should only process personal data to the extent necessary for their intended and stated purposes. They should not store that data for longer than is necessary for those purposes. Personal data must, by default, be kept only for the amount of time necessary to provide the product or service.

Whilst the original Directive contains requirements in relation to ensuring that excessive personal data is not processed and is retained only for as long as is necessary, the Regulation contains an explicit obligation to implement appropriate technical and organisational measures designed to deliver this requirement. In practice, this could mean that the strictest privacy settings apply automatically once a customer acquires a new product or service. As outlined above, the concept of privacy by design has existed for some time, and some companies may already have incorporated the concept in their current operations. Now that the concept has been given specific recognition in the Regulation, a failure to comply is likely to result in enforcement action by DPAs.

11.3.3 How can companies comply?

It is clear that the principles of privacy by design and privacy by default will both have to become an integral part of the technological development of any new product, service or system so that privacy is a key consideration from the outset.

But, unhelpfully, the Regulation does not specify the technical steps companies should take to comply with those obligations.

It is possible that, in the future, a data controller will be able to demonstrate compliance with those obligations by becoming certified under certification mechanism approved by the newly created European Data Protection Board. Article 25 provides that an approved certification mechanism—created pursuant to Article 42 of the Regulation—may be used as an element to demonstrate compliance. As of this writing, however, these certification mechanisms remain only theoretical.

At the least, when implementing appropriate technical and organisational measures, as expected by Article 25, data controllers must take account of additional factors, including 'the state of the art, the cost of implementation and the nature, scope, context and purposes of processing as well as the risks of varying likelihood and severity for rights and freedoms of natural persons'.

The type of technical measures that could be taken include: (1) minimising the amount of personal data being processed; (2) pseudonymisation; and (3) allowing individuals greater control over their personal data and visibility over what it is being processed. Other measures include applying appropriate security standards to the personal data held.

To ensure compliance with Article 25, companies should carefully review and assess their data processing systems as well as their operations generally to determine whether:

- personal data is appropriately mapped, classified, labelled, stored and accessible in order to allow it to be searched and collated easily in the event of a request by a data subject either to supply personal data or to rectify or delete personal data;

- systems are set up for automated deletion of personal data (e.g., to determine whether the system implements technical measures to ensure that personal data is flagged for deletion after a particular period);

- paper-based forms and applications or other data collection forms are drafted appropriately to ensure that excessive personal data is not collected;

- personal data can be pseudonymised, where possible;

- personal data can be singled out, so as to allow for the deletion of the personal data of individuals who have objected to receiving direct marketing messages; and

- personal data is structured in a commonly used, machine-readable and interoperable format to allow the company to satisfy the requirements of data portability.

11.4 Documentation and cooperation with regulators

Under the Directive, one of the requirements for a company setting up offices and operations in Europe was to notify or register with the relevant national DPAs their intention to process personal data within their jurisdiction.

That exercise was particularly cumbersome for multinational companies, which tend to have offices in many different European jurisdictions. It meant that such companies had to assess—and, until the Regulation becomes effective, will continue to have to assess—what the local requirements were for notification or registration in each jurisdiction in which they operated.

But, that exercise was—and, for the time being will remain—particularly important because, in some European jurisdictions, failure to notify or register with the DPA before commencing data processing activities could constitute a criminal offence.

Some DPAs also maintain the information in a publicly accessible register, which listed each data controller and the details of their data processing operations.

One of the advantages of the Regulation is that this notification and registration requirement will be abolished. Data controllers will no longer be required to notify their data processing activities. Instead, data controllers will have to keep detailed records of their processing operations. In essence, the type of information that will be required is similar to that which is required to be notified under the current regime. The difference under the Regulation is that the records that a company will be required to keep will not need to be filed with their DPA. Instead, the records will have to be in writing, which includes in electronic form, and will need to be made available to a DPA upon a DPA's request.

Notably, Article 31 contains the general requirement for all companies (both controllers and processors) and where applicable, their representatives, to cooperate, on request, with the DPA in the performance of its tasks.

11.4.1 What data processing records must be kept by a company?

Article 30 of the Regulation outlines the records that must be kept by both data controllers and data processors.

Data controllers are required to maintain a record of the following information:

• the controller's name and contact details and, where applicable, the name and contact details of any joint controller, representative and DPOs;

• the purposes of the processing;

• a description of the categories of data subjects and of the categories of personal data;

• the categories of recipients to whom the personal data have been or will be disclosed including recipients in third countries or international organisations;

• where applicable, transfers of personal data to third countries, including the identification of the transferee third country and, where applicable, the documentation of appropriate safeguards;

- where possible, the retention periods for erasure/deletion of the different categories of personal data; and

- where possible, a general description of the technical and organisational security measures.

Data processors are required to maintain a record of the following information:

- the name and contact details of the processor or processors and, where applicable, the name and contact details of representatives and DPOs;

- the name and contact details of each data controller for whom the processor acts and, where applicable, the name and contact details of representatives and DPOs;

- the categories of processing carried out on behalf of each controller;

- where applicable, details of the transfers of personal data to third countries, including the identification of the transferee third country and, where applicable, the documentation of appropriate safeguards; and

- where possible, a general description of the processor's technical and organisational security measures.

11.4.2 Do the record-keeping requirements apply to all companies?

There is an exemption to the above record-keeping requirements for companies that employ fewer than 250 people. This exemption does not apply, however, if the processing by a company, no matter the number of employees: (1) is likely to result in a risk to the rights and freedoms of data subjects; (2) is frequent and not occasional; or (3) involves special categories of data,[6] including biometric and genetic data, health data or data related to a person's sex life or sexual orientation. Additionally, the exemption does not apply to data related to criminal convictions and offences.

In light of the above limitations, it is more likely than not that the exemption will rarely be used, as most processing of personal data will be caught by one or more of the above.

Questions that have yet to be answered include: (1) how detailed should the description be of the full processing of personal data carried out by a data controller; and (2) will the documentation obligation require companies to conduct regular audits of data processing to record, maintain and keep up to date what is being processed?

As things stand under the existing registration/notification system, DPAs have different expectations. Some require high-level information only, whilst others request more detailed information of each data processing activity. It is difficult to determine, at this stage, either the approach that DPAs will take to this obligation or, indeed, whether DPAs will take a consistent approach to this obligation.

11.5 Data protection impact assessment

Data protection impact assessments (DPIAs), or privacy impact assessments (PIAs), as they are also known, can be used by companies to identify and address any data protection issues that may arise when developing new products and services or undertaking any new activities that involve the processing of personal data. In some instances, the Regulation requires them, particularly when a processing activity may present a 'high risk' to the rights and freedoms of a data subject.

Simply put, a DPIA is the process by which companies can systematically assess and identify the privacy and data protection impacts of any products they offer and services they provide. It enables them to identify the impact and take the appropriate actions to prevent or, at the very least, minimise the risk of those impacts.

The concept of DPIAs has been discussed and promoted in privacy circles and by DPAs for a number of years. And, many companies today already embed and carry out DPIAs as part of their existing project management and risk management methodologies and policies.

In the UK, for example, the ICO has supported the use by companies of DPIAs as a 'best practice' tool and has issued guidance on how companies should conduct DPIAs.[7]

Other European jurisdictions have also adopted the DPIA concept. For example, the German Federal Office for Information Security, the Bundesamt für Sicherheit in der Informationstechnik (BSI), published a paper on data security and data protection for radio-frequency identification (RFID) applications. The accompanying paper, 'Technical Guidelines RFID as Templates for the PIA Framework', describes how to use RFID in compliance with data protection requirements and the European Commission's DPIA framework.[8]

The Regulation, however, will make it mandatory for companies to undertake a DPIA for any new project that is likely to create 'high risks', or, in any case, before proceeding with 'risky' personal data processing activities.

Specifically, Article 35 of the Regulation requires that a DPIA will need to be carried out by data controllers or processors acting on their behalf, 'where a type of processing in particular using new technologies, and taking into account the nature, scope, context and purposes of the processing, is likely to result in a high risk to the rights and freedoms of natural persons'.

It is possible that a single assessment may address a set of similar processing operations that present similar high risks.

11.5.1 What is the process for complying with the DPIA requirement?

A company should adapt its product development and governance procedures to ask itself the following questions to determine whether a DPIA is necessary and how it should be carried out.

11.5.1.1 Is the processing likely to be 'high risk'?

To answer this question, one must turn to Article 35(3), which gives examples of 'risky' types of processing activities for which a DPIA would be required. Activities which are considered to be risky include: (1) systematic and extensive profiling that produces legal effects or significantly affects individuals; (2) processing activities that use 'special categories of personal data' on a large scale; and (3) the systematic monitoring of a publicly accessible area on a large scale (e.g., closed-circuit television (CCTV), other video surveillance in public areas and potentially the use of drones).[9]

It should be noted that when the WP29 published their 2016 action plan for the implementation of the Regulation, one of their priorities was to develop guidelines, tools and procedures to allow the new legal framework to be effective.

The action plan includes proposals for the issuance of guidance on the notion of 'high risk'. It is anticipated that, when that guidance is published, it might expand the above current list of risky types of processing.

11.5.1.2 What if the processing is high risk and therefore an assessment is required?

When an assessment is required, the company should first seek the advice of its DPO, if one is appointed, when carrying out a DPIA (see Article 35(2)).

Under Article 35(7) of the Regulation, the DPIA must contain and document at least the following:

- a systematic description of the envisaged processing operations and the purposes of the processing, including any legitimate interests pursued by the controller;
- an assessment of the necessity and proportionality of the processing operations in relation to the purposes;
- an assessment of the risks to the rights and freedoms of individuals; and

- the measures adopted to address the risks, including safeguards, security measures and mechanisms to ensure the protection of personal data.

The methods for conducting DPIAs vary widely from organisation to organisation, with some using paper forms, others emailing documents to appropriate stakeholders, and still others employing 'automation' technology that can assign tasks alert stakeholders that information is needed.

Where appropriate, it may also be necessary to seek the views of affected individuals or their representatives on the intended processing (Article 35(9)). That decision should be taken on a case-by-case basis.

11.5.1.3 What if the processing is still high risk?

Where, having carried out a DPIA, the DPIA reveals that processing, in fact, poses a high risk, if there are no sufficient measures capable of mitigating the risk, the controller will be required to consult their DPA before commencing processing.[10] But, it should be borne in mind that, if a consultation with the relevant DPA is required, it may as well take time for the DPA to consider whether the company's processing activities are compatible with the requirements under the Regulation.

The periods that have been outlined in the Regulation allow DPAs up to eight weeks to consider a referral by a data controller. There is an option to extend this period by an additional six weeks and inherent power to suspend the timetable if the DPA is waiting to receive information from the data controller.

The DPIA is one example of such documentation required by the DPA. It is intended for a DPIA to show not only that an organisation has considered the risks associated with its particular personal data practices but also that it has taken reasonable steps to control or mitigate them.

11.6 Data protection officer

The appointment of a data protection officer (DPO) is formally recognised in the Regulation, although not every company must appoint one.[11] The circumstances where data controllers and processors must designate a DPO are:

- where processing is carried out by a public authority;

- if the core activities of the controller or processor consist of regular and systematic monitoring of individuals on a large scale; or

- if the core activities consist of processing special categories of personal data on a large scale.

The WP29 issued interpretive guidance in December 2016 in which it defined 'core activities' as 'key operations necessary to achieve the controller's or processor's goals'. This does not mean that the organisation must be in the business of data analytics, however, but rather that data processing is 'an inextricable part of the controller's or processor's activity'.

The WP29 defined 'large scale' with particular reference to the number of data subjects rather than the organisation's size. This means an organisation with few employees may nonetheless engage in 'large-scale' processing if it serves a large customer base, whilst a company serving a small clientele is unlikely to meet the 'large-scale' definition.

In particular, the WP29 identified the following 'large-scale' factors:

- The number of data subjects concerned—either as a specific number or as a proportion of the relevant population

- The volume of data and/or the range of different data items being processed

- The duration or permanence of the data processing activity

- The geographical extent of the processing activity

The term 'regular and systematic monitoring of data subjects' includes all forms of Internet-based tracking and profiling, but is 'not restricted to the online environment and online tracking'. The WP29 interprets 'regular' as meaning one or more of the following:

- Ongoing or occurring at particular intervals for a particular period

- Recurring or repeated at fixed times

- Constantly or periodically taking place

It interprets 'systematic' as meaning one or more of the following:

- Occurring according to a system

- Pre-arranged, organised or methodical

- Taking place as part of a general plan for data collection

- Carried out as part of a strategy

The Regulation also provides that a DPO must be appointed if required by member state law. Germany, for example, requires a DPO to be appointed by companies that have either at least nine people employed in the automated processing of personal data or at least 20 people who are engaged in non-automated data processing.

In France, on the other hand, whilst there is no legal requirement to appoint a DPO, known as a Correspondant Informatique et Libertés (CIL), there are potential advantages if a company appoints a DPO. That company is then exempt from making prior declarations to the Commission Nationale de l'Informatique et des Libertés.

It is, of course, entirely possible if not probable that in the future, more member states might make the appointment of a DPO a requirement under national laws.

So, although DPOs will be mandatory in the public sector, private sector commercial organisations will need to assess themselves against the above key criteria (e.g., monitoring on a large scale) to decide whether to appoint a DPO.

11.6.1 Group-wide appointment

A group of undertakings may appoint a single DPO. However, this is subject to the condition that the DPO must be 'easily accessible' to each undertaking.

Companies should consider that there may be challenges in doing this if, for example, the group-wide DPO does not speak the local language or if they are not sufficiently familiar with the way in which the rules operate in that jurisdiction, taking into account the potential for many member state derogations, which will be established once the Regulation becomes operational. This, then, may have an impact on the DPO's ability to demonstrate their expertise and fulfil their role.

11.6.2 What is the role of the DPO?

Under the Regulation, companies must ensure that DPOs are involved 'properly and in a timely manner' on all issues which relate to the protection of personal data.[12] DPOs will have to have support and access to proper resources to fulfil their job functions and to maintain their technical skills and knowledge.

They must be able to operate independently. They should not be dismissed or penalised for performing their tasks properly. And, they can have other roles, provided that any additional or other roles do not give rise to a conflict of interest.

There is no limitation on the length of tenure for a DPO. But that does not prevent companies from appointing a DPO for a fixed term. Nor does it prevent companies from terminating the role upon notice (e.g., the ability to dismiss a DPO for performance and/or conduct issues, subject, of course, to local labour laws).

DPOs must have a direct reporting line 'to the highest management level' of the company. They must also have access to the company's data processing operations. The DPO should also have sufficient technical knowledge and expertise. But, the Regulation does not specify the qualifications or credentials that DPOs must or should have.

DPOs should be appointed on the basis of their experience and abilities in the field of privacy. They will require credentials, such as knowledge of data protection law and practices and the ability to:[13]

- inform and advise the company and the employees of their obligations under the Regulation;

- monitor compliance with the Regulation and with company policies in relation to the protection of personal data, including managing internal data protection activities, training staff and conducting internal audits;

- provide advice, where requested, concerning the DPIA and monitor its performance;

- cooperate with the supervisory authority; and

- act as the point of contact for the supervisory authority on issues relating to processing and with regard to any other matter.

In addition, the DPO is required to have due regard to the risks associated with processing operations, taking into account the nature, scope, context and purposes of processing.

The Regulation also allows the DPO function to be performed by either an employee of the company or by a third-party service provider. This is helpful because, initially, a potential key issue may be a lack of experienced people to fill such roles.

11.7 Other accountability measures—Binding Corporate Rules

Another measure that may support a company's accountability framework is Binding Corporate Rules (BCRs).

BCRs are sometimes referred to as the 'gold standard' of global data protection. They can best be described as a privacy framework or code implemented by companies. Initially, the European Commission ('Commission') created them to facilitate cross-border transfers of personal data, and they have now been articulated clearly in Article 47 of the Regulation to allow cross-border data transfer.

Whilst BCRs allow personal data to move freely between the various entities of a corporate group worldwide, they do so by ensuring that the same high level of protection of personal data is complied with by all members of the group by means of a single set of binding and enforceable rules.

Arguably, BCRs achieve 'gold standard' status because, in using them, companies are required to demonstrate their privacy compliance framework upon application to their lead DPA. In turn, if the lead DPA approves an application, it will also monitor ongoing compliance by the applicant.

The privacy compliance framework, amongst other things, must show that a policy is in place, employees are aware of it and have been trained appropriately, a person who is responsible for compliance has been appointed, audits are undertaken, a system for handling complaints has been set up, and the organisation is being transparent about the transfer of data.

Put shortly, BCRs compel organisations to demonstrate their compliance with all aspects of applicable data protection legislation. Logically, BCRs should, therefore, also be available as part of the toolkit for demonstrating an organisation's accountability.

In practice, obtaining BCRs has proven to be a laborious undertaking, which may indicate the thoroughness DPAs expect in accountability programmes in general. See Chapter 12 for more information on BCRs.

11.8 Conclusion

For companies to achieve and demonstrate accountability, they must first achieve a culture of data protection within their organisation. That is achieved by incorporating and implementing a number of key requirements. Those requirements include, amongst other things, developing appropriate privacy policies and embedding good privacy standards and practices expressly within the corporate operations and, ultimately, the corporate culture. A number of concepts has been outlined in this chapter, which can help to achieve this. For instance, as part of the process of developing new products and services, consideration should always be given to ensuring the privacy and protection of personal data during development phases. This must become part of a company's overall approach so that the company can build towards a clear picture of its data processing activities and understand whether they are risky or not, how to protect and minimise against those risks, and whether each employee understands that they have a role to play in delivering the privacy framework for their organisation.

Endnotes

1 Guidelines in the form of a Recommendation by the Council of the OECD were adopted and became applicable on 23 September 1980, www.oecd.org/sti/ieconomy/oecdguidelinesontheprotectionofprivacyandtransborderflowsofpersonaldata.htm.

2 'Deliberation No. 2014-500 of 11 December 2014 on the Adoption of a Standard for the Deliverance of Privacy Seals on Privacy Governance Procedures', https://www.cnil.fr/sites/default/files/typo/document/CNIL_Privacy_Seal-Governance-EN.pdf.

3 Article 25(1) and Recital 78, Regulation (EU) 2016/679 of the European Parliament and of the Council 27 April 2016 (Regulation); note that this obligation of privacy by design and default does not apply to data processors.

4 'Privacy by Design', Information and Privacy Commissioner of Ontario, accessed June 2017, https://www.ipc.on.ca/privacy/protecting-personal-information/privacy-by-design/.

5 'Privacy by design', Information Commissioner's Office, accessed June 2017, https://ico.org.uk/for-organisations/guide-to-data-protection/privacy-by-design/.

6 This is also referred to and known as 'sensitive personal data'. Under the Data Protection Directive, the definition of special categories of data includes elements such as racial/ethnic origins, political opinions, religious/philosophical beliefs, trade union membership, and health or sex life.

7 For details of the ICO Privacy Impact Code of Practice, see 'Conducting privacy impact assessments code of practice', Information Commissioner's Office, https://ico.org.uk/media/for-organisations/documents/1595/pia-code-of-practice.pdf.

8 'Technical Guidelines RFID as Templates for the PIA-Framework', Federal Office for Information Security (BSI), https://www.bsi.bund.de/SharedDocs/Downloads/EN/BSI/Publications/TechGuidelines/TG03126/TG_RFID_Templates_for_PIA_Framework_pdf.pdf?__blob=publicationFile; 'Privacy and Data Protection Impact Assessments Framework for RFID Applications', 12 January 2011, http://cordis.europa.eu/fp7/ict/enet/documents/rfid-pia-framework-final.pdf.

9 Special categories defined in Articles 9(1) and 10 of the General Data Protection Regulation.

10 General Data Protection Regulation, Article 36(1).

11 General Data Protection Regulation, Article 37.

12 General Data Protection Regulation, Article 38.

13 General Data Protection Regulation, Article 39.

CHAPTER 12

International Data Transfers

Eduardo Ustaran, CIPP/E

12.1 Introduction: limitations affecting international data transfers

One stated objective of the General Data Protection Regulation (GDPR, or 'Regulation') is to allow the free flow of personal data between member states based on agreed-upon principles of personal data protection. At the same time, however, the Regulation recognises that transfers of personal data to third countries require special consideration. This chapter considers the way in which European data protection law specifically regulates international transfers of personal data.

12.1.1 Legislative background

As the Data Protection Directive ('Directive') did 20 years earlier, the Regulation establishes a challenging restriction in the context of today's increasingly interconnected and digitally borderless world: Transfers of personal data to any country outside the European Economic Area (EEA) may only take place subject to the conditions of Chapter 5 of the Regulation, namely:

- the third country ensures an adequate level of protection for the personal data as determined by the European Commission ('Commission');

- in the absence of that adequate level of protection, the controller or processor wishing to transfer the data provides appropriate safeguards on condition that enforceable data subject rights and effective legal remedies for data subjects are available; or

- in the absence of an adequate level of protection or of appropriate safeguards, a transfer or a set of transfers of personal data fits within one of the derogations for specific situations covered by the Regulation.

The same restriction applies to transfers of personal data to what the Regulation defines as an 'international organisation', in other words, an organisation and its subordinate bodies governed by public international law or any other body that is set up by or on the basis of an agreement between two or more countries.

The Recitals of the Regulation do not clearly explain the reason behind this radical approach. Recital 101 recognises that cross-border flows of personal data are necessary for the expansion of international trade but also states that the level of protection of natural persons ensured in the EU by the Regulation should not be undermined.

To understand the basis for this approach, it is necessary to bear in mind that the European institutions responsible for drafting and adopting the Regulation have tried to preserve the effect of the new regime by preventing any attempts to weaken the protection afforded to individuals. In practice, this creates a situation that effectively imposes EU data protection standards in jurisdictions outside Europe.

12.1.2 Practical implications

Bearing in mind the high standards of privacy protection imposed by the Regulation, it is difficult to see how countries without the same strict legislative approach to this issue can meet adequacy requirements for data transfer. As a result, this element of the Regulation will continue to be seen as a serious barrier to international commerce.

In practical terms, for some large multinational organisations, this issue has meant the adoption of EU data protection practices across their operations irrespective of where the data processing activities actually take place.

12.2 Scope of data transfers

The Regulation does not define the concept of transfer. However, transfer is not the same as mere transit; it is the processing in the third country that completes the 'transfer'. Therefore, the fact that personal data may be routed through a third country on the way from a EEA country does not bring such transfer within the scope of the restriction of the Regulation unless some substantive processing operation is conducted on the personal data in the third country.

In practice, there are two common situations that have been a source of concern in the past but are not subject to the conditions dealing with data exports:

- Technical routing of packet-switch technology, such as Internet email and web pages, which may involve random transfers of personal data between computer servers located anywhere in the world.

- Electronic access to personal data by travellers who happen to be physically located for a short period of time in a place that does not afford an adequate level of protection (e.g., a person who logs on to a computer system based in the EU to access data from a foreign airport).

In addition, following the European Court of Justice decision in the Swedish case against Bodil Lindqvist (C-101/01) in November 2003, in which an individual in a member state merely loads personal information onto a website that is hosted in that state or another member state so that the information can be accessed by anyone who connects to the Internet does not constitute a transfer of data to a third country.[1]

However, where there is an international exchange of information about individuals with the intention of automatically processing that personal information after it has been exchanged, that should be regarded as a transfer for the purposes of the Regulation, even if the original exchange does not qualify as processing of personal data. An example of this would be where information is provided by someone in the EU over the telephone to someone in a third country who then enters the information on a computer.

12.3 Meaning of an 'adequate level of protection'

Article 45(1) of the Regulation states that:

> A transfer of personal data to a third country or an international organisation may take place where the Commission has decided that the third country, a territory or one or more specified sectors within that third country, or the international organisation in question ensures an adequate level of protection.

When assessing the adequacy of the level of protection, the Commission must, in particular, take account of the following elements:

> (a) the rule of law, respect for human rights and fundamental freedoms, relevant legislation, both general and sectoral, including concerning public security, defence, national security and criminal law and the access of public authorities to personal data, as well as the implementation of such legislation, data protection rules, professional rules and security measures, including rules for the onward transfer of personal data to another third country or international organisation which are complied with in that country or international organisation or case-law, as well as effective and enforceable data subject rights and effective administrative and judicial redress for the data subjects whose personal data is being transferred;

(b) the existence and effective functioning of one or more independent supervisory authorities in the third country or to which an international organisation is subject, with responsibility for ensuring and enforcing compliance with the data protection rules, including adequate enforcement powers, for assisting and advising the data subjects in exercising their rights and for cooperation with the supervisory authorities of the EU member states; and

(c) the international commitments the third country or international organisation concerned has entered into, or other obligations arising from legally binding conventions or instruments, as well as from its participation in multilateral or regional systems, in particular, in relation to the protection of personal data.

12.4 Procedure to designate countries with adequate protection

The Commission, after assessing the adequacy of the level of protection, may decide, by means of implementing act, that a third country, a territory or one or more specified sectors within a third country, or an international organisation ensures an adequate level of protection within the meaning given by the law, as described above.

The Commission's implementing act must provide for a mechanism for a periodic review, at least every four years, which must take into account all relevant developments in the third country or international organisation. The implementing act must specify its territorial and sectoral application and, where applicable, identify the supervisory authority or authorities with responsibility for ensuring and enforcing compliance with the data protection rules.

In addition, the Commission must, on an ongoing basis, monitor developments in third countries and international organisations that could affect the functioning of any adequacy decisions adopted, including those that were adopted under the original Directive. As a result, where available information reveals that a third country, a territory or one or more specified sectors within a third country, or an international organisation, no longer ensures an adequate level of protection, the Commission is entitled and required to repeal, amend or suspend the decision as appropriate.

For completeness, the Regulation confirms that any adequacy decisions adopted by the Commission on the basis of the Directive will remain in force until amended, replaced or repealed by another Commission decision. Under the Directive, the

Commission recognised Andorra, Argentina, Canada, Faroe Islands, Guernsey, the Isle of Man, Israel, Jersey, New Zealand, Switzerland and Uruguay as providing adequate protection.

12.5 The situation in the United States

12.5.1 The original Safe Harbor

Considering the large volume of data transfers carried out between the EU and the United States, the U.S. Department of Commerce and the Commission originally developed the Safe Harbor mechanism as a self-regulatory framework that would allow organisations to satisfy the requirements of EU data protection law in respect of transatlantic data transfers. On 26 July 2000, following extensive negotiations, the Commission issued a decision stating that the Safe Harbor Privacy Principles provided adequate protection for personal data transferred from the EU.[2] This decision enabled EU personal data to be transferred to U.S.-based companies that agreed to abide by the Safe Harbor Privacy Principles.

However, since its adoption, the Safe Harbor Framework was fraught with challenges. Although the data protection requirements set out in the Safe Harbor Privacy Principles were meant to match the adequacy standards of the Directive, its self-certification nature and the non-European style of its provisions attracted much criticism over the years. Perceived weaknesses included that participants did not perform required annual compliance checks and the lack of active enforcement by the Federal Trade Commission (FTC) compared to other domestic cases. These factors led some EU data protection authorities (DPAs) to question the validity of the Safe Harbor Framework as an adequacy mechanism.

12.5.2 The Snowden effect

The disclosures by Edward Snowden in June 2013 about the mass surveillance operations carried out by the U.S. National Security Agency (NSA) had a very visible knock-on effect on the way in which the EU regulates international transfers of personal data.[3] In light of the existing criticisms of the Safe Harbor Framework and amid allegations that companies that participated in the scheme might have been involved in U.S. surveillance activities, calls for the revocation of the Safe Harbor Framework from activists and some of the DPAs led the European Parliament to adopt a resolution seeking its immediate suspension.

The Commission rejected doing so because of concerns that suspending the Safe Harbor Framework would adversely affect EU business interests and the transatlantic economy. However, it agreed that there were a number of weaknesses in the Safe Harbor Framework and had no choice but to reopen the dialogue with the U.S. government to find a way of strengthening the framework and restoring its credibility.

renegotiation

The Commission announced this renegotiation 27 November 2013 through two communications to the European Parliament and the Council of the European Union, entitled 'On the functioning of the Safe Harbor from the Perspective of EU citizens and Companies Established in the EU' and 'Rebuilding Trust in EU-U.S. Data Flows'.[4] In these communications, the Commission stressed that the EU and U.S. were strategic partners and that transatlantic data flows were critical to commerce, law enforcement and national security on both sides of the Atlantic. However, it also recognised that the Snowden revelations had damaged the EU's trust in this partnership and that this trust needed to be rebuilt.

12.5.3 Towards 'Safe Harbor II'

Safe Harbor II

The Commission began discussions with U.S. authorities aimed at updating the Safe Harbor Framework in January 2014. The original aim was to identify remedies by the summer of 2014 and implement them as soon as possible afterwards.

The Commission had provided 13 specific recommendations aimed at addressing Safe Harbor's weaknesses and ensuring that the framework remained an effective mechanism for facilitating commercial transatlantic data flows. These recommendations focused on four broad priorities, namely: transparency, redress, enforcement and access to data by U.S. authorities. In June 2014, then–Commissioner for Justice Viviane Reding provided an update on the negotiations, reporting that the Department of Commerce (DOC) had agreed to 12 of the Commission's 13 recommendations. However, the sticking point was the final recommendation that the national security exception was only to be applied when strictly necessary and proportionate.

Schrems

At the same time, the validity of Safe Harbor was questioned by Austrian law student Maximillian Schrems, who lodged a complaint with the Irish Data Protection Commissioner requesting the termination of any transfers of personal data by Facebook Ireland to the United States. Mr Schrems claimed that Facebook Ireland—the data controller for Facebook's European users' data—could no longer rely on the Safe Harbor Framework to legitimise the transfers of his data to the U.S. because of the wide access that U.S. intelligence agencies had to such data as revealed by Snowden.

The complaint was then escalated to the Irish High Court, which in turn referred the matter for decision by the Court of Justice of the European Union (CJEU), the highest judicial authority on the interpretation of EU law. On 6 October 2015, the CJEU issued its judgment and declared the Safe Harbor adequacy decision invalid.[5] This ruling increased the pressure on the Commission to agree to a more robust alternative mechanism for transfers of data from the EU to the U.S.

12.5.4 The Privacy Shield is born

On 29 February 2016, and after more than two years of negotiations with the DOC, the Commission released its much-awaited draft decision on the adequacy of the new EU-U.S. Privacy Shield Framework, accompanied by information on how the framework will work in practice.[6] The Privacy Shield Framework's documentation is significantly more detailed than that associated with its predecessor[imposing more specific and exacting measures on organisations wishing to join the framework.]

Privacy shield

Crucially, the Privacy Shield Framework also includes [additional checks and balances designed to make sure that the privacy rights of EU individuals can be exercised when their data is being processed in the United States] as well as various official letters from U.S. government officials providing [assurances] regarding the legal limitations affecting access to personal data by U.S. government agencies.

Following the Commission's original announcement concerning the Privacy Shield, the Article 29 Working Party (WP29) issued a preliminary statement 3 February 2016, before the relevant documentation had been publicly disclosed, welcoming the conclusion of the negotiations between the EU and the U.S. on the introduction of the Privacy Shield.[7] But on 13 April 2016, the WP29 published an Opinion setting out their detailed analysis of the framework.[8] In this Opinion, the WP29 set out its concerns on the commercial aspects of the Privacy Shield and the ability for U.S. public authorities to access data transferred under the Privacy Shield.

In particular, the WP29 considered that the Privacy Shield did not include certain key data protection principles from EU law. The WP29 also expressed concern about the protection for onward data transfers and that the redress mechanism for individuals could prove too complex. Finally, the WP29 noted that the documentation did not exclude massive and indiscriminate collection of personal data originating from the EU by U.S. intelligence agencies and that the new ombudsperson was not sufficiently independent or powerful. The Opinion concluded by urging the Commission to resolve these concerns and improve the Privacy Shield.

WP29: didnt include some key data protection principles; redress mechanism too complicated; didn't address bulk access / collection by US intelligence

12.5.5 The operation of the Privacy Shield

Following further negotiations to address WP29's concerns, on 12 July 2016, the Commission finally issued its adequacy decision concerning the Privacy Shield

Adequacy decision re: Privacy shield

Framework for the transfer of personal data from the EU to the U.S.[9] The Privacy Shield formally entered into operation 1 August 2016, and U.S. businesses subject to the jurisdiction of the FTC or Department of Transportation (DOT) can join the Privacy Shield by filing an online registration with the DOC. This covers most U.S. for-profit businesses but excludes a number of banks, financial services companies, telecoms and other businesses that are not subject to the jurisdiction of those regulatory agencies.

The seven principles with which Privacy Shield companies must comply are similar to the principles under Safe Harbor. However, each of them was strengthened in important ways, especially the principle of recourse, enforcement and liability.

The seven principles are:

1. Notice

2. Choice

3. Accountability for onward transfer

4. Security

5. Data integrity and purpose limitation

6. Access

7. Recourse, enforcement and liability

The Privacy Shield requires companies that self-certify compliance with the Privacy Shield principles to take certain steps to demonstrate that they can comply, including:

- Conduct an internal compliance assessment to determine the company's ability to comply with the principles with respect to information that will be covered by the certification. To the extent there are any gaps in its ability to comply, the company should adopt internal controls, policies and procedures to come into compliance.

- Register with a third-party arbitration provider to handle any complaints from EU individuals about the handling of their information that the company is unable to fully resolve, and pay any registration fees.

- Adopt a Privacy Shield notice that contains 13 specified details about the company's privacy practices, and publish the notice online.

From the public statements made by a number of privacy activists—including Max Schrems himself—it is very likely that the Privacy Shield will be put to the test in the CJEU. Ongoing concerns about government surveillance have been cited as the main reasons for a potential legal challenge. If so, it will take several years before the CJEU makes a final decision. However, it is important to note that the negotiations between the Commission and the DOC were specifically aimed at addressing the issues that affected Safe Harbor, so it is by no means certain that the CJEU would rule against the Privacy Shield unless the U.S. government changed its commitments under the framework.

12.6 Providing adequate safeguards

In reality and given the reduced number of countries that qualify as 'adequate', in the majority of cases, controllers or processors wishing to transfer personal data internationally will need to deploy a mechanism that provides appropriate safeguards for the data. The Regulation addresses this situation by listing several possible mechanisms that may be suitable for these purposes, namely:

- A legally binding and enforceable instrument between public authorities or bodies.
- Binding Corporate Rules (BCRs) in accordance with Article 47.
- Standard data protection clauses adopted by the Commission.
- Standard data protection clauses adopted by a supervisory authority and approved by the Commission.
- An approved code of conduct pursuant to Article 40 together with binding and enforceable commitments of the controller or processor in the third country to apply the appropriate safeguards, including as regards to data subjects' rights.
- An approved certification mechanism pursuant to Article 42, together with binding and enforceable commitments of the controller or processor in the third country to apply the appropriate safeguards, including as regards to data subjects' rights.
- Contractual clauses between the controller or processor and the controller, processor or the recipient of the personal data in the third country or international organisation, or provisions to be inserted into administrative arrangements between public authorities or bodies, that are specifically approved for that purpose by the competent data protection supervisory authority.

This menu of options represents an improvement compared to the Directive as it provides greater choice and flexibility for both exporters and importers of personal data.

12.6.1 The contractual route

Traditionally, the most frequently used mechanism to legitimise international data transfers to countries that are not deemed to provide an adequate level of protection has been the so-called 'standard contractual clauses' or 'model clauses'. Under the Directive, this was a contract pre-approved by the Commission and establishing certain obligations applicable to both exporters and importers aimed at safeguarding the personal data in accordance with EU standards.

In this regard, on 15 June 2001, the Commission adopted a Decision setting out standard contractual clauses ensuring adequate safeguards for personal data transferred by controllers in the EU to controllers in 'non-adequate' jurisdictions.[10] This Decision obliged member states to recognise that companies or organisations using these standard clauses in contracts concerning personal data transfers to countries outside the EEA were offering adequate protection to the data.

Similarly, on 27 December 2001, the Commission adopted a second Decision setting out standard contractual clauses for the transfer of personal data to processors established in non-EEA countries that were not recognised as offering an adequate level of data protection.[11]

In 2003, the Commission stated in its 'First report on the implementation of the Data Protection Directive' that it intended to adopt further Decisions so that economic operators would have a wider choice of standard contractual clauses.[12] Accordingly, the Commission issued a new Decision 27 December 2004 amending its Decision of June 2001 and adding a second version to the sets of standard contractual clauses that could be used to legitimise international transfers between controllers.[13] This second version was based on an alternative draft pioneered by the International Chamber of Commerce (ICC).

The inflexible nature of the original 2001 controller to processor clauses led to a further proposal by the ICC and, on 5 February 2010, the Commission notified its Decision updating and replacing the original controller to processor standard clauses with a new set of model clauses.[14] Since 2010, EEA-based controllers wishing to rely on standard contractual clauses to legitimise international data transfers to processors outside the EEA have had to use the updated controller to process clauses for new processing operations.

These sets of standard contractual clauses, namely:

- the 2001 controller to controller clauses;

- the 2004 alternative controller to controller clauses; and

- the 2010 controller to processor clauses

will remain valid until they are replaced or amended by new versions which match the more prescriptive framework under the Regulation.[15]

Whilst the Commission-approved model contracts will indeed continue to be a suitable mechanism to legitimise international data transfers, the ability of DPAs to either adopt standard contractual clauses themselves or to authorise transfers based on ad-hoc contracts presented to them by the parties is likely to play an important role in the development of the contractual route for transfers.

Some technology companies, such as Microsoft, Amazon Web Services and Google, have already pioneered the idea of obtaining the approval of the DPAs for their own versions of data transfer agreements. The advantage of this approach is that companies may enjoy greater flexibility in the way they contractually commit to the protection of personal data, allowing them to adopt more realistic contractual obligations they are less likely to breach.

12.6.2 Codes of conduct and certification mechanisms

One of the novelties of the Regulation in the area of international data transfers is the express addition of codes of conduct and certification mechanisms as adequacy mechanisms. Both these mechanisms are yet to be tested so it remains to be seen whether they provide a practical and effective solution to legitimise international data transfers.

12.7 Data transfers within a multinational corporate group—Binding Corporate Rules

The most significant development in the area of international data transfers under the Regulation is the inclusion of Binding Corporate Rules (BCR) as a mechanism available to both controllers and processors to legitimise such transfers within their corporate groups. In 2003, the EU DPAs developed the concept of BCR to allow multinational corporations and groups of companies to make intraorganisational transfers of personal data across borders in compliance with EU data protection law. Its express inclusion in the Regulation confirms both the commitment by the EU policy makers to it and the increasingly important role that intra-group global privacy programmes have in ensuring compliance with EU data protection law.

12.7.1 BCR concept

Data exports within a multinational corporate group are subject to the same rules as exports outside the group. However, using contractual arrangements is hardly a cost-effective way of legitimising international transfers for data-reliant organisations operating on a worldwide basis. For many global companies, using personal data is all about sharing information beyond national borders and jurisdictional differences. Therefore, a flexible, tailor-made solution that does away with the impracticalities of having to enter into innumerable contracts amongst subsidiaries is likely to be the only practical option.

Over the years, the EU DPAs have acknowledged the role of BCR as a mechanism to legitimise data exports within a corporate group. In essence, BCRs are a global set of rules based on European privacy standards, which multinational organisations draw up and follow voluntarily and national regulators approve in accordance with their own legislations.

The idea of using BCR to create adequate safeguards for the purposes of the Directive was originally devised by the WP29 in its Working Document WP 74. Since then, the EU DPAs have increased their level of cooperation to streamline the BCR approval process. This cooperation led to the adoption of a 'mutual recognition' process, which was effectively incorporated into the Regulation.

12.7.2 BCR requirements

According to the Regulation, DPAs must approve a set of BCR following the so-called 'consistency mechanism' (see Chapter 13) provided that it is legally binding and expressly confers enforceable rights on data subjects.

A full and valid set of BCR must specifically include the following elements:

- (a) the structure and contact details of the corporate group and of each of its members;
- (b) the data transfers or set of transfers, including the categories of personal data, the type of processing and its purposes, the type of data subjects affected, and the identification of the third country or countries in question;
- (c) their legally binding nature, both internally and externally;
- (d) the application of the general data protection principles, in particular, purpose limitation, data minimisation, limited storage periods, data quality, data protection by design and by default, legal basis for processing, processing of special categories of personal data, measures to ensure data

security, and the requirements in respect of onward transfers to bodies not bound by the BCR;

(e) the rights of data subjects in regard to processing and the means to exercise those rights, including the right not to be subject to decisions based solely on automated processing, including profiling, the right to lodge a complaint with the competent supervisory authority and before the competent courts, and to obtain redress and, where appropriate, compensation for a breach of the BCR;

(f) the acceptance by the controller or processor established on the territory of a member state of liability for any breaches of the BCR by any member concerned not established in the Union;

(g) how the information on the BCR is provided to the data subjects;

(h) the tasks of any data protection officer (DPO) or any other person or entity in charge of the monitoring compliance with the BCR;

(i) the complaint procedures;

(j) the mechanisms for ensuring the verification of compliance with the BCR;

(k) the mechanisms for reporting and recording changes to the rules and reporting those changes to the supervisory authority;

(l) the cooperation mechanism with the supervisory authority to ensure compliance;

(m) the mechanisms for reporting to the competent supervisory authority any legal requirements to which a member of the corporate group is subject in a third country which is likely to have a substantial adverse effect on the guarantees provided by the BCR; and

(n) the appropriate data protection training to personnel having permanent or regular access to personal data.

12.8 Relying on derogations

In the absence of an adequate level of protection or of appropriate safeguards, a transfer or a set of transfers of personal data may still take place if it fits within one of the derogations for specific situations covered by the Regulation.

12.8.1 Consent

Data exports can lawfully be made with the explicit consent of the individual. Consent must still be specific and informed. This means that the individual must be informed of the possible risks of such transfers due to the absence of an adequacy decision and appropriate safeguards.

12.8.2 Contract performance

The Regulation allows data transfers in cases where specific types of contracts are in place or being contemplated. In the case of a contract between the exporter and the individual to whom the data relates, a transfer may be carried out if such transfer is necessary for performance of the contract or is a necessary part of pre-contractual measures taken by the exporter at the request of the individual.

In the case of a contract between the exporter and someone other than the individual, the transfer will be lawful if the contract is entered into at the individual's request or in their interests, and the transfer is necessary for the performance or conclusion of the contract.

The contracts covered by these provisions are not restricted to the supply of goods or services, and may apply in the case of employment contracts. However, whether a transfer is necessary for the performance of a contract will depend on the nature of the goods or services provided under the contract rather than the way in which the exporter's operations are organised. In other words, a transfer is not necessary if the only reason for it is the fact that the exporter has chosen to structure its operations in a way that involves transferring data overseas.

Therefore, if a customer books a holiday abroad through an EEA-based travel agent, the travel agent must transfer the booking details to the foreign hotel in order to fulfil the contract with the customer. However, if for pure efficiency or cost-cutting reasons that travel agent decides to place its customer database in a computer based outside the EEA, it cannot be said that the transfer of personal data to the computer located overseas is necessary for the performance of the contract with the customer.

12.8.3 Substantial public interest

Transfers can be carried out where necessary for reasons of substantial public interest. This case is most likely to apply in situations where the transfer is necessary for reasons of crime prevention and detection, national security and tax collection.

12.8.4 Legal claims

Transfers can be made where they are necessary for establishing, exercising or defending legal claims.

12.8.5 Vital interests

Exports of personal data can lawfully be carried out where necessary to protect the vital interests of the data subject or other persons. In practice, this relates to matters of life and death, such as the transfer of medical records of an individual who has become seriously ill or been involved in a serious accident abroad.

12.8.6 Public registers

Exports of personal data can also be made from information available on a public register provided that the person to whom the information is transferred complies with any restrictions on access to or use of the information in the register. This allows transfers of extracts from a public register of directors, shareholders or professional practitioners, for example, but would not allow transfers of the complete register. In addition, if there are conditions of use imposed by the body or organisation responsible for compiling the register, they must be honoured by the importer and any further recipients.

12.8.7 Not repetitive transfers

Finally, and as a last resort, a transfer may take place if the transfer is not repetitive, concerns only a limited number of data subjects, is necessary for the purposes of compelling legitimate interests pursued by the controller which are not overridden by the interests or rights and freedoms of the data subject, and the controller has assessed all the circumstances surrounding the data transfer and has on the basis of that assessment provided suitable safeguards with regard to the protection of personal data.

In these situations, the controller must inform the supervisory authority and the data subject of the transfer. The individual must also be informed of the compelling legitimate interests pursued by the controller.

12.9 The future of the restrictions on international data transfers

Overcoming the restrictions on international data transfers is one of the most difficult compliance challenges faced by global organisations operating in the EU. As described above, finding and implementing the right mechanism to ensure an adequate level of protection in every case is likely to be onerous and time consuming. However, even in the face of technological developments, greater globalisation and surveillance threats, the appetite of the EU institutions for a softer approach in the foreseeable future is likely to be low.

Accordingly, and to ensure compliance, organisations are strongly advised to develop a viable global data protection compliance programme in line with the adequacy criteria devised by the Commission and commit to abiding by it through either a contractual mechanism or a set of BCRs.

Endnotes

1 Bodil Lindqvist [2003] Case C-101/01, 6 November 2003.

2 Commission Decision pursuant to Directive 95/46/EC of the European Parliament and of the Council on the adequacy of the protection provided by the Safe Harbor Privacy Principles and related frequently asked questions issued by the U.S. Department of Commerce, 26 July 2000, http://eur-lex.europa.eu/legal-content/en/ALL/?uri=CELEX:32000D0520.

3 'Edward Snowden comes forward as source of NSA leaks', The Washington Post, 9 June 2013, https://www.washingtonpost.com/politics/intelligence-leaders-push-back-on-leakers-media/2013/06/09/fff80160-d122-11e2-a73e-826d299ff459_story.html.

4 Communication from the Commission to the European Parliament and the Council on the functioning of the Safe Harbor from the Perspective of EU citizens and companies established in the EU, COM(2013) 0847 final, http://eur-lex.europa.eu/legal-content/EN/TXT/?uri=CELEX%3A52013DC0847; Communication from the Commission to the European Parliament and the Council rebuilding the trust in EU-U.S. data flows, COM(2013) 846 final, http://eur-lex.europa.eu/resource.html?uri=cellar:4d874331-784a-11e3-b889-01aa75ed71a1.0001.01/DOC_1&format=PDF.

5 Maximillian Schrems v. Data Protection Commissioner [2015] Case C-362/14, 6 October 2015.

6 'Restoring trust in transatlantic data flows through strong safeguards: European Commission presents EU-U.S. Privacy Shield', European Commission—Press Release, 29 February 2016, http://europa.eu/rapid/press-release_IP-16-433_en.htm.

7 Statement of the Article 29 Working Party on the Consequences of the Schrems Judgment, 3 February 2016, http://ec.europa.eu/justice/data-protection/article-29/press-material/press-release/art29_press_material/2016/20160203_statement_consequences_schrems_judgement_en.pdf.

8 Opinion 01/2016 on the EU-U.S. Privacy Shield draft adequacy decision, (16/EN: WP 238), http://ec.europa.eu/justice/data-protection/article-29/documentation/opinion-recommendation/files/2016/wp238_en.pdf.

9 Commission Implementing Decision (EU) 2016/1250 pursuant to Directive 95/46/EC of the European Parliament and of the Council on the adequacy of the protection provided by the EU-U.S. Privacy Shield, 12 July 2016, http://eur-lex.europa.eu/legal-content/EN/TXT/?uri=OJ%3AJOL_2016_207_R_0001.

10 Commission Decision on standard contractual clauses for the transfer of personal data to third countries, under Directive 95/46/EC, 15 June 2001, http://eur-lex.europa.eu/legal-content/en/TXT/?uri=CELEX:32001D0497.

11 Commission Decision on standard contractual clauses for the transfer of personal data to processors established in third countries, under Directive 95/46/EC, 27 December 2001, http://eur-lex.europa.eu/legal-content/EN/TXT/?uri=CELEX%3A32002D0016.

12 Report from the Commission: First report on the implementation of the Data Protection Directive (95/46/EC), 15 May 2003, http://eur-lex.europa.eu/LexUriServ/LexUriServ.do?uri=COM:2003:0265:FIN:EN:PDF.

13 Commission Decision amending Decision 2001/497/EC as regards to the introduction of an alternative set of standard contractual clauses for the transfer of personal data to third countries, 27 December 2004, http://eur-lex.europa.eu/legal-content/EN/TXT/?uri=CELEX%3A32004D0915.

14 Commission Decision on standard contractual clauses for the transfer of personal data to processors established in third countries under Directive 95/46/EC of the European Parliament and of the Council, 5 February 2010, http://eur-lex.europa.eu/legal-content/EN/TXT/?uri=celex%3A32010D0087.

15 'Model Contracts for the transfer of personal data to third countries', European Commission, accessed June 2017, http://ec.europa.eu/justice/data-protection/international-transfers/transfer/index_en.htm.

Supervision and Enforcement

Stewart Room, CIPP/E

13.1 Introduction

If the fundamental purpose of regulatory law is to shape or influence the behaviour of individuals and organisations, it follows then that, to be effective, a regulatory system must have the ability to hold these individuals and organisations accountable. Any regulation is only as good as the means by which it is supervised and enforced. Certainly, powers of supervision and enforcement should not lie only in the hands of regulators. Models of optimum regulatory efficiency also vest power in the courts, the markets, in self-regulatory schemes and, of course, the citizens.

The General Data Protection Regulation (GDPR, or 'Regulation') incorporates all these tools. The table at the end of this chapter identifies some of the key components of supervision and enforcement with their corresponding articles.

Throughout this chapter, the national supervisory authorities, those member state bodies charged with overseeing data protection law, will be referred to as the 'regulators' and the data protection authorities as 'DPAs', which will be addressed extensively in Section 13.4. Data subjects will be referred to as 'citizens' and 'individuals'.

13.2 Self-regulation

Arguably one of the most effective tools of supervision and enforcement is self-regulation due to the fact that controllers and processors directly control application of appropriate processes, procedures and measures to protect data. From a first principles basis, regulatory laws should require the regulated entity to supervise itself and enforce the need for appropriate measures to achieve the required policy objectives.

The GDPR advances this idea in a number of ways, including through the introduction of the concept of accountability (see Article 5(2)), which places a positive obligation on the controller to be able to demonstrate compliance with the data protection principles, through the introduction of requirements for data protection officers (DPOs) (see Articles 37 to 39), and through a heightened focus on codes of conduct and certification schemes for data protection seals and marks (see Articles 40 to 43). Likewise, controllers have regulatory functions over their processors, and processors must regulate their sub-processors (see Article 28).

13.2.1 Accountability—delivering demonstrable compliance through risk management

Chapter 4 of the Regulation expands the Article 5(2) accountability requirement of demonstrable compliance, which provides a comprehensive framework for effective risk management. The intent of Chapter 4 is that controllers will identify their risks, then set their positions to address them, which they shall supervise and enforce through their business-as-usual activities. In combination, the requirements in Chapter 4 look very much like forms of self-regulation.

Chapter 11 deals with accountability extensively, but a few components to note in the context of self-regulation include:

- The focus on demonstrable proof of compliance should cause the controller to look critically at its data processing activities through performance testing and similar exercises and make it adjust and refine its activities as need requires in order to achieve good data protection. In other words, as part of their business-as-usual activities, controllers should carry out tasks similar to some of those that DPAs are empowered to carry out by Article 58.

- Controllers' relationships with processors are governed by Article 28, which creates relationships of supervision and enforcement. The principal tools advanced by Article 28 include pre-contractual due diligence, contract formation and post-contractual requirements for demonstrable compliance, including audits, inspections, the delivery-up of necessary information and breach notification pursuant to Article 33. Article 28(4) requires processors to cascade these requirements down to their sub-processors, creating similar relationships of supervision and enforcement.

- Articles 33 and 34 require notification of personal data breaches to the DPAs in all cases and to individuals affected in serious cases. The most obvious self-regulatory role of breach notification is that it acts as a deterrent against bad practice for the obvious reason that, once regulators and citizens are equipped with knowledge of breaches, they can take action against the controller. The idea that deterrence is a key tool of supervision and enforcement is clear from the wording of Articles 83 and 84, which require the imposition of 'effective, proportionate and dissuasive' administrative penalties (fines) in appropriate cases. The breach notification rules also play the same role as the other concepts discussed here: Once seized with knowledge of a breach, the controller can take steps to remediate its environment.

- Article 35 requires controllers to perform data protection impact assessments (DPIAs), where processing 'is likely to result in a high risk to the rights and freedoms' of individuals. The supervisory and enforcement role of DPIAs is perhaps more immediately obvious than the other examples due to the explicit references to 'the supervisory authority' in Article 35(4–6) and the requirement for prior consultations with the DPAs, which need to take place when a DPIA 'indicates that the processing would result in a high risk [to the rights and freedoms of individuals] in the absence of measures taken by the controller to mitigate the risk', which is set out in Article 36.

DPIAs

13.2.2 Data protection officers

The function of the data protection officer (DPO) is nothing new to data protection and is also discussed extensively in Chapter 11. Many organisations employ them to lead on data protection matters, and now the status of the DPO has been formalised by the Regulation, which mandates their appointment for the first time.

Notably for this discussion, the set of requirements outlined in the GDPR for the role puts the DPO in a clear supervisory and enforcement position in the organisations where they are employed or engaged. As they are focussed only on compliance rather than the broader set of considerations that controllers and processors have to weigh up as they decide how to tackle the Regulation (including whether to run the risk of technical noncompliance in order to focus scarce skills and resources on areas where substantive harms might be suffered) and are immune from dismissal, the DPO looks more like a quasi-DPA rather than an ordinary employee, and, taking account of their duty of cooperation with the DPA, they are effectively an extension of the regulator. It seems likely that, if their organisations come under pressure from the DPAs, individuals or privacy activists for compliance issues, DPOs will take a challenging role within the organisation.

13.2.3 Codes of conduct, certificates, seals and marks

Chapter 4 Articles 40–43 create a framework for self-regulation by way of codes of conduct and data protection certification mechanisms, such as seals and marks.

Article 40 encourages representative bodies for controllers and processors, like industry associations, to create codes of conduct on any aspect of data protection compliance, and a key feature of them is that the controllers and processors that undertake to apply them should be monitored for compliance (see Articles 40(4) and 41(1)). Any representative body can submit draft codes to their DPA for approval (see Article 40(5)) on any compliance issue, although Article 40(2) provides a non-exhaustive list of areas where codes might be helpful.

The adoption of codes is subject to the use of the consistency mechanism in Article 63, where a draft code will impact at least two EU member states, which is discussed in more depth later.

The characteristics and tasks of the monitoring body are set out in Article 41. They have to prove their independence and their expertise and avoid conflicts. They must have procedures for effective monitoring of compliance and for dealing with complaints, and they should take appropriate action against any infringements. Of course, the DPAs do not abandon their supervisory and enforcement roles by approving codes. They retain their jurisdiction over the subject matter covered by codes and the controllers and processors that have undertaken to follow them. In serious cases, controllers and processors can be fined by the DPAs for breaching the requirements of a code (see Article 839(4)(c)). The DPAs also have the power to revoke the monitoring body's accreditation (see Article 41(5)).

For some indication as to how this might work in practice once the GDPR is in force, one might look to the Network Advertising Initiative (NAI) Code of Conduct in the United States, whereby the NAI first enforces its code within its membership, then refers the matter to the U.S. Federal Trade Commission (FTC) should a member continue to be out of compliance.

The certification rules for seals and marks in Articles 42 and 43 work in much the same way as the rules for codes of conduct. They are issued by certification bodies that are accredited either by the DPAs or the national accreditation bodies in the member states (see Article 43(1)). In order to be accredited, certification bodies need to satisfy the DPAs of their independence and expertise and avoid conflicts of interest; they must have procedures for issuing, reviewing and revoking seals and marks; and they must have procedures for handling complaints (see Article 43(2)). Controllers and processors can be fined for breaching the rules of the certification (see Article 83(4)(b)), whilst certification bodies can have their accreditations revoked by the DPAs (see Article 43(7).)

Again, the consistency mechanism applies in appropriate cases.

13.3 Regulation by the citizen

If controllers and processors provide the first line of defence against bad data protection, the citizen provides the second line. Moreover, as a collective body, there are roughly 500 million EU citizens, counting pre-Brexit UK, which constitutes massive supervisory and enforcement firepower.

In recent times, the 'citizen regulator' has driven much of the non-legislative agenda for data protection reform in Europe. In 2014, landmark litigation about 'the right to be forgotten', for example, brought by a Spanish citizen, turned on its head thinking about the concepts of controllership under the Data Protection Directive ('Directive') 1995.[1] In 2015, an Austrian citizen was successful in litigation against the Safe Harbor Decision.[2] Civil Society Organisations (CSOs) have also demonstrated the power that citizens can wield in litigation: In another piece of landmark litigation, the Data Retention Directive 2006 was declared invalid.[3] For many organisations, their primary risk of adverse scrutiny will come from citizens as litigators rather than from the DPAs.

13.3.1 Regulating the controller through the use of data subject rights

As discussed in other chapters, the Regulation creates many rights for individuals, which they can use to protect themselves from bad practice and unfair actions of controllers and to supervise and enforce compliance. These are the right of transparency (Articles 13 and 14), the right of access to data (Article 15), the right to rectification (Article 16), the right to erasure (Article 17), the right to restriction of processing (Article 18), the right to data portability (Article 20) and the right to object (Articles 21 and 22). Individuals also have a right to be informed of serious personal data breaches (Article 34). If individuals are dissatisfied with their ability to exercise these rights, they can pursue both administrative and judicial remedies.

Of course, the Regulation does not require that individuals must use and pursue their data subject rights against controllers before they can pursue complaints and remedies before the DPAs or the courts. If so minded, an individual can go down either of these paths without having first taken their concerns to the controller, although, in practice, it is hard to think of situations where individuals will benefit from not raising their complaints with controllers before going to the DPAs or courts. Leaving that aside, there will be many situations where the rights in Sections 13–22 and 34 do not provide the individual with a direct and obvious route to the controller.

For example, the integrity and confidentiality principle in Article 5(1)(f) (and see also Article 32) is not the focus of any of the rights in Articles 13–22 so the individual cannot use them preemptively to understand whether their personal data is at risk of a security breach. All that the law gives them is a right to be told that a breach has occurred and then only in serious cases, which leaves the individual without any direct recourse to the controller to prevent their personal data being exposed to a security breach. In order to prevent their personal data being put at risk in this way, the individual has no choice but to take their complaint to the DPA or the court, if the controller fails to deal with things on a voluntary basis.

13.3.2 Remedies for breach of obligations

If individuals have complaints about noncompliance, they can take them to the DPAs or to the courts, regardless of whether they have used the data subject rights or made prior complaints to the controller. The operative elements of the Regulation are Articles 77 and 79.

Taken together, it can be seen that the Regulation operates so as to give individuals choices about the route to pursue. If they feel that their rights have been breached, they can pursue litigation in accordance with their national laws, complain to their regulator, or, indeed, they can pursue both remedies at the same time. Both avenues are available against controllers and processors.

In reality, making a complaint to regulators would be the logical, preferred choice for most individuals. Litigation is expensive, time-consuming business and, in some countries, like the UK, the losing party can be ordered to pay the winning party's costs. Turning to the DPAs for remedies is essentially the low-risk option.

It's worth noting the forum provisions in these articles. Article 77(1) gives the individual the right to pursue complaints before the DPA for their place of residence, before the DPA for their place of work, or before the DPA for the place where the infringement took place, if different. Article 79(2) contains similar provisions. Whatever the place of establishment of the controller or processor or the individual's place of work, the individual always has the right to pursue their remedies before their home DPA or court.

13.3.3 Representative actions

In many countries, there is access to justice barriers that stand in the way of individuals, usually due to lack of financial and legal resources for individual litigation. One way of balancing this power is to pursue representative actions, sometimes called group litigation or class actions, whereby groups of individuals are represented as a collective before the courts, thereby spreading the financial risks, leveraging collective case information and likely securing more experienced legal representation.

The Regulation introduces new representative action rights, in Article 80.

Under Article 80(1), individuals can elect to be represented by not-for-profit organisations that are commonly known as CSOs and sometimes as 'privacy advocates' or, indeed, 'pressure groups'. These representative actions can be on behalf of a single individual or a group of individuals. Moreover, it is open to member states to give these organisations representative powers that stand independent of any mandates from individuals.

Europe has already seen examples of representative bodies bringing together groups of individuals on a consensual basis for group litigation. In the UK, the Vidal-Hall litigation is the most prominent example.[4] The Europe v. Facebook group, which established a class action against Facebook in Austria, is another prominent example.[5]

13.3.4 Liability and compensation claims

Article 82 creates the right for citizens to pursue compensation claims against controllers and processors if they suffer damage as a result of an act of noncompliance. Controllers and processors have the possible defence of not being responsible for the event that gives rise to damage. Where multiple parties are at fault, any individual controller or processor that is responsible for any part of the damage suffered can be held liable for all the damage, in which case, the compensating party can seek indemnities from the others.

The meaning of 'damage' has given rise to some problems in the past. For example, in the UK, it was long the case that damage meant financial loss, but that position was reversed by the decision of the Court of Appeal in the Vidal-Hall case, which held that damage also means distress and other nonpecuniary harms. In contrast, the DPAs have always been sure that 'damages' includes distress.[6] The Regulation resolves any remaining ambiguities. The phrase 'material or non-material damage' points very clearly to the idea that damage includes distress. Recital 146 also makes it clear that the concept of damage should be interpreted broadly. Moreover, if data protection law is considered in the same context as human rights law, where the law has always recognised the right to compensation for distress, the position should be unambiguous: Damage must include distress for the law to make any sense.

This has very significant implications for controllers and processors if a compensation culture around the Regulation develops, which is a distinct possibility due to the very size of the class of people who will have compensation rights.

13.3.5 Regulating the regulators

If an individual puts a complaint before a DPA, but it is not dealt with, or if they hear nothing within three months, they are entitled to take action against the DPA before the courts to force the issue. This is set out in Article 78.

The Safe Harbor litigation, known as the Schrems case, commenced with litigation against the Irish Data Protection Commissioner in judicial review proceedings with the argument being that the Commissioner had fettered his powers by refusing to undertake an investigation into the lawfulness of transfers of personal data to the United States. The position of the Commissioner was that any questions of lawfulness had been conclusively determined by the Safe Harbor adequacy decision by the EU Commission ('Commission') itself. Those proceedings would now be conducted under Article 78.

Article 78(1) is concerned with the situation where a person (an individual or a legal entity) is unhappy with a DPA's decision that affects them. The primary purpose of this provision is to enable appeals against corrective action taken under Article 58 and sanctions under Article 83. It seems possible that Article 78(1) could also be used by an individual who is concerned that a DPA has failed to take the right kind of corrective action or has been too lenient in sanctioning.

13.4 Administrative supervision and enforcement

Regardless of the regulatory functions and powers of controllers and processors, individuals, CSOs and monitoring and certification bodies or their relative strengths and weaknesses, when people talk about supervision and enforcement, most think immediately of the national supervisory authorities in the EU member states, sometimes called the data protection authorities (DPAs), such as the Commission Nationale de l'Informatique et des Libertés (CNIL) in France, Information Commissioner's Office in the UK (ICO) and Agencia Española de Protección de Datos (AEPD) in Spain. The DPAs are the only bodies that are equipped with administrative supervisory and enforcement powers.

13.4.1 Independent national regulators

The Regulation's provisions on administrative supervision are found in Chapter 6. The starting point is that the member states are required to designate independent public authorities to monitor the implementation of the Regulation, which shall act with complete independence in performing their tasks and exercising their powers.[7] The provisions about independence are found in Articles 51 and 52.

An essential feature of an independent regulator is sufficient skills and resource. If a regulator is beholden on a third party, including a government, for skills and resource, its independence will be challenged. This is reflected in Article 52(4).

The importance of the regulators' independence has played out in high-level litigation. For example, in the case of Commission v. Germany the European Court of Justice found that Germany had failed to transpose Article 28(1) of the Directive properly because it made the regulators in the Länder 'subject to State scrutiny'. Similar litigation was brought against Austria.[9]

Articles 53 and 54 provide rules for how DPAs shall be established in the member states. As there are already DPAs in each member state, these articles are likely to be of academic interest only.

13.4.2 Embedding the regulators in national lawmaking

Article 36(4) contains a structural control—a consultation requirement—that effectively embeds the national regulator in the law-making processes of the member states.

Consultation requirement; DPAs taking legislative vole (Art 36).

This is a very clever and powerful provision in that it gives the regulators influence over legislative agendas. In other words, it helps to embed data protection in the DNA of member states' laws at the beginning of the legislative and rule-making process.

The obligation of consultation in Article 36(4) is bolstered by provisions in Articles 57(1) and 58(3), which task and empower the DPAs to provide advice and guidance to their parliaments and governments on data protection matters.

13.4.3 Regulators' tasks

The tasks of the DPAs are contained in Article 57, and they amount to a very long list. In addition to monitoring and enforcing the Regulation and providing advice to their national parliaments and governments, they have to:

- promote awareness and understanding of data protection, including risks, safeguards and rights (see Article 57(1)(b) and (d));

- handle complaints and carry out investigations (see Article 57(1)(f) and (h));

- support the consistent application of the Regulation internationally, which includes working within the consistency mechanism, providing mutual assistance and supporting the European Data Protection Board (EDPB) (see Article 57(1)(e)–(h)); and

- monitor the development of information and communications technologies and commercial practices (see Article 57(1)(i)).

Article 57 also lists a number of discrete tasks that arise from other articles.

13.4.3.1 Receiving and dealing with complaints

Effective regulation needs to respond to problems discovered by the citizen, not just to deliver good outcomes for personal data, but also to maintain trust and confidence in the regulatory system. The heightened importance of this requirement flows from the fact that, despite all the other tools of regulation, regulators have relatively little insight into the actual operations of particular controllers at any given time. It is the citizen who has the most day-to-day contact with the data controller, and therefore, they are in an excellent position to bring data protection contraventions to the attention of the regulator. Moreover, the citizen needs an official champion, which is the regulator.

Article 57(1)(f) addresses these issues by giving the DPAs the duties to receive and hear complaints. Article 57(2) is aimed at streamlining the complaints process through the use of standardised complaints forms.

13.4.3.2 Data protection impact assessments

Article 35(4) requires the DPAs to publish lists of situations where data protection impact assessments (DPIA) should be carried out, whilst Article 35(5) also allows them to publish lists of situations where DPIAs are not required. Article 36(1) requires controllers to consult with their DPAs whenever a DPIA 'indicates that the processing would result in a high risk [to the rights and freedoms of individuals] in the absence of measures taken by the controller to mitigate the risk'.

Article 57(1)(k) reflects the requirements of Article 35(4), whilst Article 57(1)(l) requires the DPAs to give advice on processing activities that are referred to them by controllers pursuant to the requirement in Article 36(1) after the performance of DPIAs. (See more on DPIAs in Chapter 11.)

13.4.3.3 Codes of conduct, certifications, seals and marks

The DPA's role in the area of codes of conduct is discussed above. In addition to encouraging their development, Article 40(5) requires the DPAs to 'provide an opinion on whether the draft code, amendment or extension complies with [the Regulation] and shall approve that draft code, amendment or extension if it finds that it provides sufficient appropriate safeguards'. Article 57(1)(m) reflects these requirements.

In Article 42(5), the DPAs are also required to approve criteria for the issuing of certifications, seals and marks by certification bodies, whilst Article 42(5) enables the DPAs to withdraw certifications when the requirements of them are no longer met. Article 57(1)(n) and (o) reflect these requirements.

See also Article 57(1)(p) and (q) for further provisions about the DPA's roles in the code of conduct and certification system.

13.4.3.4 Contractual clauses and BCRs for international transfers

European data protection law provides a number of avenues for controllers and processors to follow if they want to export personal data from the EU to a third country. Current options include using the white list of countries with adequacy decisions, the Privacy Shield arrangement for transfers to the United States, Binding Corporate Rules (BCRs) and the standard contractual clauses approved by the Commission. Additionally, Article 46(3) enables controllers and processors to obtain authorisations from their DPAs for the use of their own contractual models, whilst public authorities can seek approvals for administrative arrangements between themselves. On a case-by-case basis, the DPAs will review requests for authorisations, subject to the use of the consistency mechanism. Article 57(1)(r) reflects these provisions.

The BCR process is set out in Article 47 and is reflected by Article 57(1)(s). See Chapter 12 for extensive discussion of international data transfers.

13.4.3.5 Records of infringements and action taken

Article 57(1)(u) requires the DPAs to keep records of any infringements of the Regulation, as well as records of any actions taken under Article 58(2). The keeping of these records is already a standard practice across the member states, and, indeed, they provide a primary source material for the regulators when devising their national and collective work programmes. Moreover, in some jurisdictions, such as the UK, the DPAs consider the regulatory track record of organisations when taking decisions on discrete issues. In other words, the worse the track record, the greater the possibility of adverse results for the controller or processor.

13.4.3.6 Charging costs

Article 57(3) makes it clear that DPAs cannot charge data subjects or DPOs for their services. However, Article 57(4) does give the ability to charge back administration costs on manifestly unfounded or excessive requests.

13.4.3.7 Activity reports

Another tenet of good regulation is that it shall be conducted transparently. Thus, DPAs should be required to make regular public statements about their activities. This promotes confidence in the regulatory system, as well as provides society generally with critical insight into trends and developments within regulation. Transparency by way of delivering an annual report also enables society to form value judgments on whether the regulators are meeting their objectives and serving the public

Article 59 addresses these issues.

13.4.4 Regulators' powers

The powers of the DPAs are contained in Article 58, of which there are three types, namely investigatory powers, corrective powers, and authorisation and advisory powers.

13.4.4.1 Investigatory powers

The investigatory powers, outlined in Article 58(1), are intended to give the DPAs access to all necessary evidence, materials and facilities to enable them to deliver on their tasks, together with a mechanism to actually start investigations, namely the power to notify controllers and processors of alleged breaches of the Regulation.

These investigatory powers are very comprehensive, and they leave controllers and processors with nowhere to hide bad practices. Also, they render the trajectory of regulatory investigations somewhat predictable. For example, as far as documentary evidence is concerned, it seems obvious that the DPAs will seek disclosure of all the accountability documentation that exists inside the organisation under investigation, such as their policy frameworks built under Article 24, their privacy-by-design frameworks pursuant to Article 25, their processor contracts under Article 28, their records of data processing activities compiled under Article 30, their breach logs maintained under Article 33, and their risk assessments undertaken for the purposes of Articles 24 and 35. Indeed, it would seem that, aside from documents that are privileged (legal professional privilege and privilege from self-incrimination), the DPAs will be able to obtain access to any relevant documentation held by the organisation under investigation, which would extend to third-party papers and reports, such as external audit reports.

Arguably the greatest innovation within Article 58(1) is the ability for the DPAs to carry out operational reviews, such as audits and the inspection of premises and processing equipment. This means that the DPAs have two lines of attack, if they are determined to pursue a controller or processor, namely the data protection written system and the data protection business operations. The Regulation certainly increases the vulnerability of controllers and processors to regulatory investigations.

13.4.4.2 Corrective powers

The corrective powers, outlined in Article 58(2), cover the full spectrum of options, from enabling the DPAs to warn controllers and processors about dubious data processing activities through to enabling them to put a stop to business activities. Many commentators in the data protection field see the risk of financial penalties as the major regulatory risk, but being ordered to stop data processing could be a much more dramatic outcome, particular for data-centric businesses.

13.4.4.3 Authorisation and advisory powers

The authorisation and advisory powers set out in Article 58(3) map to the DPAs' duties in the areas of codes of conduct, certifications, marks and seals and international transfers of personal data, discussed above.

13.4.5 Litigation by the regulators

Article 58(5) envisages that the DPAs will need to take legal proceedings against controllers and processors from time to time. Having effective litigation powers is fundamental to the successful operation of the investigation and corrective powers: If the DPAs cannot force compliance through the courts, they will be toothless.

13.4.6 Protecting controllers and processors from precipitous regulatory action

The Safe Harbor litigation demonstrates that regulators can get things wrong, and, as we saw in relation to the analysis of Article 78(1), above, natural and legal persons who are affected by decisions of the DPAs can take legal proceedings to protect their positions. Article 78(1) is supported by Article 58(4), which is a safeguards provision against regulatory action.

13.4.7 Professional secrecy

Article 54(2) imposes obligations of professional secrecy on the DPAs and their staff in respect of confidential information to which they have access.

13.5 Competence and international cooperation

In an area of legal harmonisation, which the Regulation is seeking to achieve in the EU for data protection, where there are multinational actors and cross-border processing, the question of who has legal competence to engage in supervisory and enforcement activities is a critical issue. How does the law decide which regulator should be responsible for the regulatory work if there are competing options? The Regulation resolves this question through its rules on competence, cooperation and consistency.

13.5.1 Competence—regulating controllers and processors established in the DPA's member state

The starting point, within Article 55, is that each DPA shall be competent to act in the territory of its own member state. As regards the controllers and processors whom they are competent to regulate, this turns on the question of establishment: The DPA can regulate the controllers and processors established in their territory. This is the easy part. It becomes more complex when the controller or processor is established in multiple territories or where there is cross-border processing, in which case, the 'lead authority' has competence.

13.5.2 Competence—regulating cross-border processing

Where a controller or processor is established in multiple territories, the question of regulatory competence turns on the location of the 'main establishment'. The concept of main establishment is defined in Article 4(16) and focuses on where the decision-making for the processing of personal information is done. Usually, that is at the controller's or processor's 'central administration', but if another location has the power to implement decisions over how data is processed, the main establishment moves there.

Under Article 56(1), a lead authority will be required to regulate situations of cross-border processing. Cross-border processing is not restricted to multinationals; however, as Article 56(1) makes clear through its reference to main or single establishments, an entity established in only one member state can engage in cross-border processing, for example, by targeting goods and services to people in other countries.

Article 56(1) is reinforced by Article 56(6), which designates the lead authority as the 'sole interlocuator' of that cross-border processing.

Article 56(2) permits non-lead authorities to take action in cross-border situations where the complaint relates only to their territory or if it substantially affects individuals only in their territory. In cases of this nature, the DPA that is asserting competence needs to notify the lead authority, which may or may not then trigger a battle of competence, as indicated by Article 56(3). If the lead authority rejects the assertion of competence by the other DPA and decides to take up the matter itself, the procedure in Article 60 must be followed. If the lead authority accepts the other DPA's assertion of competence, the other DPA can then proceed, subject to following the rules in Articles 61 and 62 about mutual assistance and joint operations.

Disputes and challenges about competences in multinational and cross-border situations are most likely to arise following a complaint by an individual to one of the DPAs. As discussed earlier, Article 77(1) gives individuals a choice about where to make their complaints: They can choose to complain to the DPA in the member state of their habitual residence, to the DPA of the member state for their place of work if different, or to the DPA for the place where the alleged infringement took place if different. If the complaint is made to a non-lead authority, the procedure in Article 56 will have to be triggered, which, in turn, with trigger the procedure in Article 60.

13.5.3 The lead authority—achieving cooperation and resolving disputes

To recap, the lead authority rules relate only to cross-border processing. If no cross-border processing takes place, the lead authority rules do not apply. Where they do, the cooperation procedure in Article 60 applies. The cooperation procedure encompasses the mutual assistance and joint operations rules in Articles 61 and 62 and will usually start with either a request for mutual assistance or joint operations, but as was discussed above, it might commence with a non-lead DPA asserting competence.

The essence of the cooperation procedure is the supply of a draft decision by the lead authority to other concerned DPAs, which may trigger comments, a 'reasoned objection' from another DPA, or simply agreement to the draft decision (see Article 60(3) and (4)). If a reasoned objection is made, the lead authority has a choice: It can accept the objection or reject it (see Article 60(4) and (5)). If it accepts the objection, then it must issue a revised draft decision (see Article 60(5)). The other DPAs can accept the revised decision or make another reasoned objection. If they make another reasoned objection, there will be another draft decision, and the process will carry on until the impasse is broken (this can be done by a referral to the EDPB). If reasoned objections are received but rejected, the lead authority must follow the consistency mechanism (which is discussed in more depth later) (see Article 60(4)). If no objections are made (whether at the first draft decision stage or later), the lead authority and the other DPA are deemed to be in agreement, and the draft decision is then binding (see Article 60(6)). Article 60 contains a timetabled procedure for all these key events.

If the draft decision is deemed accepted, the lead authority shall adopt it and notify the controller or processor at its main establishment or single establishment, the other DPAs that are concerned in the matter, and the EDPB (see Article 60(7)). If the complaint that triggered the decision process came from an individual via a non-lead authority, that authority should notify the complainant of the outcome. The burden then shifts to the controller or processor that is the subject of the decision to deliver compliance, which includes reporting back to the lead authority on how that is achieved (see Article 60(10)).

Article 60(9) makes provision for situations where the lead authority and other DPAs agree to accept or dismiss parts of a complaint. In those situations, separate draft decisions are required.

13.5.4 Mutual assistance and joint operations

Articles 61 and 62 are concerned with mutual assistance and joint operations between the DPAs. The essence of the mutual assistance rule is contained in Article 61(1), which mandates cooperation and exchange of information.

Article 61(1) requires the DPAs to put in place appropriate measures to provide assistance without undue delay, which is subject to a one-month-long stop. These requests must be supported by necessary information to enable the receiving DPA to understand the nature and purpose of the request. The receiving DPA must then comply, save for very limited exceptions in Article 61(4), which are concerned with competence to provide assistance and the need to avoid illegality. However, if the receiving DPA does not provide assistance within one month, the requesting DPA can adopt a provisional measure, which, in turn, triggers the urgency procedure (which is discussed later).

The joint operations rules in Article 62 are designed to ensure that all concerned DPAs are properly represented in supervisory and enforcement work. Where controllers and processors are established in multiple territories or where processing activities substantially affect a significant number of individuals in multiple territories, all the concerned DPAs have a right to participate in the joint operation. The obligation rests on the competent authority to issue invitations to participate to all the other DPAs.

13.5.5 The consistency mechanism and the European Data Protection Board

The EDPB is at the heart of the consistency mechanism. Established by Article 68, it is the successor to the Article 29 Working Party (WP29). It consists of a chairperson, the heads of the DPAs and the European Data Protection Supervisor, and the Commission is entitled to send a delegate to its meetings. The EDPB is subject to a requirement to act independently (see Article 69) and a very long list of tasks (see Article 70).

13.5.5.1 Opinions of the EDPB

Article 64 requires the EDPB to issue opinions on the lists of circumstances when DPIAs are required on the adoption of proposed codes of conduct that affect multiple member states, the criteria for accreditation of code monitoring bodies and certification bodies, contractual clauses approved by the DPAs, and BCR authorisations (see Article 64(1)). It will be remembered from the discussion earlier that these opinions will be provided after the DPAs have done their initial work (the rules on DPIA lists, etcetera, require the DPAs to send their decisions to the EDPB for opinions).

Additionally, any DPA, EDPB chairperson or the Commission can request opinions on matters of general application or producing effects in multiple member states (see Article 64(2)). The production of these opinions is subject to a timetabled process (see Article 64(3)).

13.5.5.2 Dispute resolution by the EDPB

A key part of the consistency mechanism is the dispute resolution procedure, which is contained in Article 65. This is triggered whenever a lead authority rejects reasoned objections to a draft decision concerning cross-border processing (see the discussion above about Article 60 and the lead authority), whenever there is a dispute between the DPAs about who is competent to regulate the main establishment, or a DPA fails to refer its decisions on DPIA lists, codes of conduct and international transfer mechanisms to the EDPB. The outcome of the dispute resolution procedure is the adoption of a binding decision. Again, there is a timetabled process for the adoption of the EDPB's binding decisions (see Article 65(2)).

Where the dispute resolution procedure relates to a draft decision concerning a complaint connected to cross-border processing, the lead authority or the other DPA which received the complaint, as the case may be, is required to adopt its final decision on the basis of the binding decision, again subject to timetabled process (see Article 65(1)).

13.5.5.3 The urgency procedure

There will sometimes be exceptional circumstances which demand that a DPA should take urgent action to protect the rights and freedoms of individuals. If the case of urgency is great enough, there may not be sufficient time available to pursue the cooperation procedure in Article 60, or the consistency mechanism. In these circumstances, Article 66 allows DPAs to immediately adopt provisional measures that are intended to produce legal effects in their territories. These provisional measures are subject to a three-month lifespan, and whenever they are adopted, they have to be referred by the DPA with reasons to the other DPAs that have a concern in the matter, the EDPB and the Commission.

At the end of the three-month period, the provisional measures will lapse unless the DPA considers that final measures need to be urgently adopted, in which case, it can request an urgent opinion or an urgent binding decision from the EDPB, which directs the process to Articles 64 or 65.

13.6 Sanctions and penalties

Arguably the most impressive innovation of the Regulation is the administrative fines regime, which is contained in Article 83. Depending on the nature of the contravention and the status of the entity that is being pursued, fines may be imposed up to a set financial cap (up to 10 million euros, in some cases, or 20 million in others), or up to a percentage of worldwide annual turnover (2 percent or 4 percent). The table below shows how this works.

Article 88(4)	Article 88(5)
Fines up to 10 million euros for non-undertakings (not engaged in economic activity, e.g., public authorities)	Fines up to 20 million euros for non-undertakings
Fines up to the higher of 10 million euros or 2 percent of total worldwide annual turnover in preceding year for undertakings (e.g., companies)	Fines up to the higher of 20 million euros or 4 percent of total worldwide annual turnover in preceding year for undertakings
Articles 8, 11, 25–39, 42 and 43 (controller and processor infringements) Articles 42 and 43 (certification body infringements) Article 41(4) (monitoring body infringements)	Articles 5, 6, 7, 9, 12–22, 44–49 and 58(1) and (2)
Covers issues such as children consent, data protection by design and by default, engagement of processors by controllers, records of processing, cooperation with regulators, security, breach notification, DPIAs, DPOs, codes of conduct and certifications.	Covers issues such as the data protection principles, lawfulness of processing, consent, processing of special category data, the data subject rights, international transfers, failure to comply with the DPAs' investigatory and corrective powers.

13.6.1 Factors to be considered before fines can be imposed

All fines have to be 'effective, proportionate and dissuasive', and they can be imposed in conjunction with the exercise of the DPAs' investigatory and corrective powers in Article 58, meaning that serious breaches of the Regulation can be met with multiple responses. However, if the controller or processor breaches various requirements of the Regulation, the total amount of the fine cannot exceed the amount that is specified for the most serious breach, which means that each breach will need a particular quantum assigned to it (see Article 83(3)).

Before a fine can be imposed or the quantum decided upon, the DPAs need to have regard to the factors listed in Article 83(2), which are worth detailing here:

2. *Administrative fines shall, depending on the circumstances of each individual case, be imposed in addition to or instead of measures referred to in points (a) to (h) and (j) of Article 58(2). When deciding whether to impose an administrative fine and deciding on the amount of the administrative fine in each individual case due regard shall be given to the following:*

(a) *the nature, gravity and duration of the infringement taking into account the nature scope or purpose of the processing concerned, as well as the number of data subjects affected and the level of damage suffered by them;*

(b) *the intentional or negligent character of the infringement;*

(c) *any action taken by the controller or processor to mitigate the damage suffered by data subjects;*

(d) *the degree of responsibility of the controller or processor taking into account technical and organisational measures implemented by them pursuant to Articles 25 and 32;*

(e) *any relevant previous infringements by the controller or processor;*

(f) *the degree of cooperation with the supervisory authority, in order to remedy the infringement and mitigate the possible adverse effects of the infringement;*

(g) *the categories of personal data affected by the infringement;*

(h) *the manner in which the infringement became known to the supervisory authority, in particular whether, and if so, to what extent, the controller or processor notified the infringement;*

(i) *where measures referred to in Article 58(2) have previously been ordered against the controller or processor concerned with regard to the same subject matter, compliance with those measures;*

(j) *adherence to approved codes of conduct pursuant to Article 40 or approved certification mechanisms pursuant to Article 42; and*

(k) *any other aggravating or mitigating factor applicable to the circumstances of the case, such as financial benefits gained or losses avoided directly or indirectly from the infringement.*

13.6.2 The maximum fines for undertakings and non-undertakings

Article 83(4) allows the DPAs to impose fines of up to 10 million euros or 2 percent of worldwide annual turnover in the financial year preceding the fine, whichever is the higher. Article 83(5) raises these thresholds to 20 million euros and 4 percent. So, to understand a controller or processor's maximum liability, it needs to be established whether they are an undertaking or not. This is a relatively simple problem to solve: An undertaking has been defined by European law as an entity engaged in commercial activity, which means companies. Therefore, it should follow that public authorities are not undertakings and nor are unincorporated associations.

Article 83(8) adds ambiguity however, as it says that the member states may lay down rules on whether and to what extent fines may be imposed on public authorities and bodies established in their territories, which suggests that public authorities can be taken out of the fining regime.

13.6.3 The maximum fines for undertakings

Are companies exposed to fines at 2 or 4 percent of their worldwide annual turnover, or are they exposed to fines based on the group worldwide annual turnover, assuming that they are part of a group?

Articles 83(4) and (5) talks about 'an undertaking', which means a single entity. They do not talk about groups of undertakings. However, the BCR regime in Article 47 talks about groups of undertakings, which is a defined term in Article 4.

Taking these points together, it should follow that a company that is a member of a group of companies can only be fined up to the maximum percentage of its individual turnover rather than a percentage of the group's turnover (assuming that the percentage threshold is higher than the 10 million or 20 million number).

13.7 The Law Enforcement Data Protection Directive

The Regulation is accompanied by the Law Enforcement Data Protection Directive 2016/680 (LEDP Directive), which covers the activities of the law enforcement community in the public sector. It contains a mirror supervision and enforcement regime, except for the absence of the lead authority concept (and the related cooperation and consistency mechanisms) and financial penalties.

13.8 Regulation supervision and enforcement—key provisions

Article(s)	Subject	Impact
12(4)	Information about right of complaint—after exercise of rights	If controllers do not take action in response to the exercise of individuals' rights, they shall inform those individuals that they can lodge complaints with the regulators and seek judicial remedies.
13(2)(d) and 14(2)(e)	Information about right of complaint—general transparency	As part of the rules about transparency, controllers must inform individuals that they can lodge complaints with the regulators.
15(1)(f)	Information about right of complaint—in response to subject access	When replying to subject access requests, controllers must inform individuals that they can lodge complaints with the regulators.
27(4)	Cooperation with regulators and individuals—by representatives	Representatives shall be mandated to deal with individuals and the regulators about compliance issues.
28	Processors—supervision by controllers	Controllers are required to ensure compliance by their processors, through selection mechanisms, provision of instructions, contractual mechanisms and inspections.
30(4)	Records keeping—processing activities	Controllers, processors and their representatives shall make their records of data processing activities available to the regulators on request.
31	Cooperation—with regulators	Controllers, processors and their representatives shall cooperate with the regulators on request.
33(1) and 34(1)	Breach notification	Controllers shall inform regulators of personal data breaches and shall inform individuals if there are high risks to their rights and freedoms.
33(5)	Records keeping—breach documentation	Controllers should document personal data breaches to enable the regulators to verify compliance with the breach notification rules.

35(4, 5 and 6)	DPIAs—lists	The regulators may publish lists of situations where DPIAs do or do not need to be performed, subject to following the consistency mechanism when goods or services are offered to multiple member states, where there is monitoring of individuals' behaviours in several member states, or where there could be a substantial effect on free movement of personal data.
36(1) and 5	Consultation with regulators—after DPIAs and before processing in the public interest	Controllers shall consult with the regulators where DPIAs indicate that processing would result in high risks to individuals' rights and freedoms in the absence of risk mitigation measures. Member states may also require controllers to consult with regulators when processing tasks performed in the public interest.
36(4)	Consultation with regulators—proposed legislation	Members states shall consult with the regulators during the preparation of proposed legislation that relates to the processing of personal data.
37(1) and 39(1)	DPOs—appointment and tasks	DPOs must be appointed by public authorities (except courts when performing judicial activities); where the core activities of controllers or processors involve regular, systematic, large-scale monitoring of individuals; or where the processing involves special category personal data or criminal data; and their tasks shall include monitoring compliance and cooperating with the regulators.
40(1) and (7) and 41(1)	Self-regulation—codes of conduct and accreditation	The drawing up of codes of conduct for compliance by bodies representing controllers and processors shall be encouraged, and the regulators may accredit bodies to monitor compliance with them, subject to the consistency mechanism.
42(1) and 43(1) and (3)	Self-regulation—certifications, seals, marks and certification bodies	The establishment of certification mechanisms, seals and marks shall be encouraged, and the regulators and the national accreditation bodies may accredit certification bodies to issue certifications, subject to the consistency mechanism.
46(3)	Transfers—authorisations	Regulators may approve transfers on the basis of appropriate safeguards, subject to the consistency mechanism.
47(1)	Transfers—BCR	Regulators may approve transfers by way of BCRs, subject to the consistency mechanism.

50	Cooperation—international cooperation	The Commission and the regulators shall take steps to develop international cooperation and mutual assistance mechanisms with third countries for effective enforcement.
51	Regulators—independent public authorities	Member states shall provide for regulators, which shall be independent public authorities.
52	Regulators—independence and resources	Regulators shall act with complete independence and shall be properly skilled and resourced.
53	Regulators—members	Member states shall provide transparent procedures for appointing people to be regulators, who shall have the necessary skills and experience.
54	Regulators—law and rules	The rules governing the establishment and appointment of the regulators shall be contained within member state law.
55	Regulators—territorial competence	The regulators shall be competent to perform the tasks and exercise the powers of the Regulation in their territories, except for processing by the courts in their judicial capacity.
56	Regulators—lead authorities and cooperation	For the purposes of cross-border processing, multinational controllers and processors shall be supervised by the regulator in the country of their main establishment, which shall be the lead authority, although each regulator can handle complaints about processing related to establishments in their territories, provided that the complaints only concern or substantially concern individuals in their territory and provided they notify the lead authority, which shall follow the cooperation procedure in Article 60.
57	Regulators—tasks	The regulators' wide range of tasks include monitoring and enforcing the Regulation; promoting awareness and understanding of processing risks, rules, safeguards and rights; handling complaints; monitoring developments in technological and commercial practices; promoting the schemes of self-regulation (codes, seals, etcetera); providing authorisations and approvals for transfer mechanisms (contracts, BCR); and they shall provide their services to individuals and DPOs free of charge.
58	Regulators—powers	The regulators have wide ranging powers, including the ability to order the provision of information and the right to conduct audits and to access premises, data and equipment; the ability to issue warnings, reprimands and enforcement orders, and the power to impose fines and to bring legal proceedings; and powers to provide advice and authorisations.
59	Regulators activity reports	The regulators shall publish annual reports on their activities, which shall be placed before member states' parliaments and governments and before the Commission and the EDPB.

60	Cooperation—lead authority and other regulators	Cooperation between the lead authority and the other regulators is based around information sharing, mutual assistance, a timetabled decision process that gives the wider community of regulators the opportunity to make relevant and reasoned objections to the lead authority's draft decision with escalation to the EDPB, and an urgency procedure.
61	Cooperation—mutual assistance	Cooperation between regulators is achieved through requests for assistance, which followed a timetabled process, but if these requests are not complied, the urgency procedure will be triggered.
62	Cooperation—joint operations	In appropriate cases, the regulators must engage in joint investigations and enforcement operations, and in cases against multinationals, the regulators of any member state where there are establishments or substantial effects on individuals have rights to be involved.
63	Consistency mechanism	The consistent application of the Regulation is achieved through the cooperation procedures and the consistency mechanism.
64	Consistency—EDPB opinions	As part of the consistency mechanism, the EDPB will issue opinions on DPIA lists, codes of conduct, accreditations, contractual clauses, BCRs and matters of general application, such as refusals of requests for mutual assistance and joint operations, which is subject to a timetabled process.
65	Consistency—dispute resolution	Pursuant to a timetabled process, the EDPB can issue binding decisions on objections to lead authority decisions, on disputes about which regulator should be the lead authority, and where there has been a failure to request the EDPB's opinion under Article 64 or the opinion is not followed.
66	Consistency—urgency procedure	In exceptional cases where there is an urgent need to protection individuals' rights and freedoms, a regulator can bypass the cooperation procedures and consistency mechanism to adopt provisional measures in its country, after which it should notify other regulators who have an interest in the matter, the Commission and the EDPB, and it can apply to the EDPB for an urgent opinion or decision where it feels that final measures are needed, whilst any regulator can apply for an urgent opinion or decision where it feels that another regulator has failed to take appropriate action in a case of urgency.
67	Consistency—exchange of information	The Commission has the power to adopt legal measures to specify the arrangements for the exchange of electronic information between the regulators.
68	EDPB—composition	The EDPB will be made up of the heads of the national regulators and the European Data Protection Supervisor with meetings being attended by a representative of the Commission.

69	EDPB—independence	The EDPB will act independently, taking instructions from nobody.
70	EDPB—tasks	The EDPB's role is to ensure the consistent application of the Regulation and, in addition to supporting cooperation between the regulators and applying the consistency mechanism, it shall publish advice, guidance, recommendations and best practices.
77	Remedies—complaints	Individuals have the right to lodge complaints with the regulator for their place of residence, place of work or place of alleged infringement, and the regulator shall inform them of progress, the outcome and the possibility of a judicial remedy.
78	Remedies—against regulators	Individuals and legal entities have a right to an effective judicial remedy against legally binding decisions of the regulators that concern them, and proceedings shall be brought in the courts where the regulator is established.
79	Remedies—against controllers and processors	Individuals have the right to effective judicial remedies against controllers or processors for infringements of their rights due to noncompliance and, except where the controller or processor is a public authority, they can choose to sue either in their home courts or in the courts where the controllers or processors are established if different.
80	Remedies—representation of individuals	Individuals can mandate not-for-profits (CSOs) to lodge and pursue complaints and legal proceedings on their behalf and to receive any compensation that is awarded, and member states may allow these representative proceedings without individuals' mandates.
81	Remedies—suspension of proceedings	If a court has information about similar proceedings in another member states, it shall contact the other court for confirmation, which may lead to suspension of proceedings, the declining of jurisdiction or the consolidation of proceedings.
82	Remedies—compensation	Individuals are entitled to compensation from controllers or processors for material or non-material damage suffered as a result of an infringement of the Regulation, unless the defendant can prove they were not responsible for the event that gave rise to the damage.
83	Remedies—penalties and fines	Regulators can impose fines, in addition to taking other action, which should be effective, proportionate and dissuasive, up to 2 percent and 4 percent annual worldwide turnover depending on the case, but before doing so, they should take account of the nature, gravity and duration of the infringement and other prescribed factors.
84	Remedies—other penalties	Member states shall put in place rules for other penalties, which should be effective, proportionate and dissuasive.

13.9 Conclusion

As should now be clear, the Regulation introduces significant new powers for regulatory authorities in the EU, including the ability to issue sanctions that should prove intimidating for most organisations. Whilst enforcement actions instigated by DPAs have been relatively rare in most member states, with the exception of the UK's ICO, many believe the enhanced powers granted by the GDPR will embolden DPAs into increased action.

However, there remains the question of resources granted to the DPAs by their respective members states. Many DPAs have asked for increased staffing and funding as the GDPR approaches. It remains to be seen just how active they will be.

Endnotes

1 Google Spain SL and Google Inc. v. Agencia Española de Protección de Datos (AEPD) and Mario Costeja González, C-131/12, 13 May 2014.

2 Maximillian Schrems v. Data Protection Commissioner, C-362/14, 6 October 2015.

3 Digital Rights Ireland, Seitlinger and Others, C-293/12, C-594/12, 8 April 2014.

4 Vidal-Hall v. Google Inc. [2015] EWCA Civ 311, 27 March 2015.

5 Europe v. Facebook, accessed June 2017, http://europe-v-facebook.org/EN/en.html.

6 Declaration of the Article 29 Working Party on Enforcement, WP 101, November 2004, when it was argued that 'it should be borne in mind that "damage" in the sense of the data protection directive includes not only physical damage and financial loss, but also any psychological or moral harm caused (known as "distress" under UK law)'.

7 'Data Protection Authorities', IAPP, accessed June 2017, https://iapp.org/resources/dpa/.

8 European Commission v. Federal Republic of Germany [2010] C-518/07, 9 March 2010.

9 European Commission v. Republic of Austria [2012] C-614/10, 16 October 2012.

Compliance with European Data Protection Law and Regulation

CHAPTER 14

Employment Relationships

Victoria Hordern, CIPP/E, CIPT

14.1 Employee data

Employers collect and use personal data about employees—potential, present and past—for various purposes, including recruitment, benefits, salary, personnel files, sickness records, monitoring and appraisals, personnel reports and severance. Employers may have to collect employee data in order to comply with obligations under employment law, as well as to protect employees.

In dealing with employees' personal data, employers should always consider any obligations under member state employment law that apply to the situation. For example, there may be a requirement to consult with the various national works councils (see below for more on works councils). Consultation is often required in those jurisdictions where employee rights law is strong and in situations where the collection of data significantly impacts an employee's privacy.

Because local employment law varies considerably across the EU, the mix of data protection and employment law can make compliance complicated. Furthermore, certain EU countries, such as Finland, have specific laws that deal with employee data or, like Germany, may have specific workplace privacy laws that surround surveillance. Indeed, Article 88 of the General Data Protection Regulation (GDPR, or 'Regulation') recognises that member states may provide for more specific rules around processing employees' personal data. These rules must include suitable and specific measures to safeguard the data subject's human dignity, legitimate interests and fundamental rights, with particular regard to the transparency of processing (a concept covered extensively in Chapter 8), the transfer of personal data within a group of undertakings, or a group of enterprises engaged in a joint economic activity and monitoring systems at the workplace. Where a member state does implement national law, it is required to notify the European Commission ('Commission') of such laws.

Employers should ensure that employee data is processed in accordance with all aspects of the Regulation, including giving employees the right to access their personal data.

14.2 Legal basis for processing employee personal data

Employers will usually rely on the following grounds to process employees' personal data:

- The employee has given consent (although relying on consent has considerable disadvantages, as discussed below).

- Processing is necessary to fulfil the employment contract between the employer and employee.

- Processing is necessary for compliance with a legal obligation to which the employer is subject.

- Processing is necessary for the employer's legitimate interests.

Typically, the employment contract between employer and employee includes a provision stating that the employee agrees the employer can use their personal data.

Frequently, the employment contract does not spell out what this means but instead directs the employee to the employee handbook or a data privacy notification that explains in more detail how personal data collected about employees will be used by the employer.

14.2.1 Consent

Although obtaining the consent of the employee appears to be an easy solution for processing employee data, in reality, it is best avoided. True consent as required under EU data protection law is notoriously difficult to achieve because, to be valid, consent must be a freely given, specific, informed and unambiguous indication of the employee's wishes signifying agreement.

The data protection authorities (DPAs) have stipulated that reliance on consent should be confined to those circumstances where a worker has a genuine free choice and is able to withdraw their consent without suffering any detriment. When consent is not free, it is not valid. The concern of the DPAs is that employees do not have genuine freedom due to the unequal balance of power in an employer-employee relationship. Recital 43 of the Regulation specifically states that consent should not provide a valid legal ground for processing of personal data in a specific case where there is a clear imbalance between the data subject and controller. Employees may feel pressured into providing consent to the use of their data because they may fear that to refuse would have a prejudicial effect on their employment. Therefore, employers are ill advised to rely solely on consent other than in cases where a subsequent withdrawal of consent would not be problematic for the lawfulness of the processing activity or detrimental to the employee's employment.

It is also important to recognise that the processing of employee data may be unlawful or unfair under local law even if the employee has consented. An employee may have consented to the collection of particular personal data, for example, even when local law stipulates that consent cannot be given for this type of processing. Alternatively, the consent given may involve the collection of data that is disproportionate to the purpose the employer is pursuing. In other words, even if consent is obtained, the employer must still comply with all other aspects of data protection law.

Consent should effectively be a measure of last resort to which an employer turns only when absolutely necessary. Having said this, certain EU countries require consent. This can mean that employers must obtain written employee consent, often resulting in lengthy notices setting out in some detail how the employer seeks to use the employee's data.

14.2.2 Processing necessary to fulfil an employment contract

Certain processing of employee personal data by the employer is necessary in order to fulfil the employment contract. For example, to pay the employee, the employer must process the employee's name and bank details. Or, by virtue of using the employer's communication system, certain information about the employee will be captured and processed by the employer.

14.2.3 Processing necessary for a legal obligation

Specific laws are likely to place specific obligations on employers that may require the processing of employee data, but the Regulation is clear that these must be EU or member state law. For example, the employer is usually required to provide details on salaries to the local tax authorities.

14.2.4 Legitimate interests

In many cases, an employer will be able to rely on the legitimate interest ground to process personal data about employees. For example, when an employer carries out a structural systems change to migrate employee data from an old payroll system to a new one, this is likely to be processing on the basis of legitimate interest. However, public authorities are not able to rely on the legitimate interest ground at all, even for processing employee data.

14.3 Processing sensitive employee data

Where sensitive personal data on employees—racial or ethnic origin, political opinions, religious or philosophical beliefs, trade union membership, genetic data, biometric data or data concerning health or sex life, all of which can be interpreted broadly—is collected and processed, the employer must ensure that it complies with one of the exceptions specified in Article 9 of the Regulation. The first of those exceptions is relying on the explicit consent of the individual, but again, this option should be an employer's last resort, not the first, because of the difficulties inherent in obtaining the valid consent of an employee in an employer-employee relationship. Additionally, in some member states, it is not possible to lift the prohibition on processing sensitive personal data even if an employer obtains consent from employees.

Article 9(2) of the Regulation recognises that processing sensitive personal data is necessary for the controller to carry out obligations and exercise specific rights under employment, social security and social protection law where authorised by EU or member state law or a collective agreement. In a number of jurisdictions, the extent to which sensitive employee data can be processed depends on the accompanying employment or labour law. For example, the Labour Code in Poland sets out the data that an employer is entitled to ask for from an employee or job candidate. In Portugal, the employer must seek the authorisation of the DPA to process sensitive data on employees. Alternatively, the local DPA may issue specific authorisations relating to the processing of employee data. The Italian DPA has issued a number of authorisations relating to the processing of sensitive data without the employee's consent. This includes where the processing is necessary 'to fulfil specific tasks or duties that are set out in laws, regulations or EU legislation in connection with management of the employer-employee relationship, as also related to occupational and/or population hygiene and safety, social security and assistance'.[1]

It may also be necessary for the employer to process employee sensitive personal data in order to establish, exercise or defend legal claims, such as in the context of an employee's claim for unfair dismissal by a former employer. Employers must carefully examine the grounds available under local law, including any relevant employment rules that apply.

14.4 Providing notice

Regardless of the lawful grounds used to process employee data, it is still necessary to provide an appropriate notice to employees informing them about the use of their data, for what purposes, whom they should contact with queries, and what their rights are in relation to the data. Employers can choose to do this through an employee handbook or through a specific notification document provided to all new employees and available elsewhere on request, such as on the company's intranet. The notification must be kept up to date, and employees should be notified when any new purpose is added. In particular, under the Regulation, the notice must provide the required level of detail so that employees can understand the purposes for the processing, the legal basis, what the legitimate interests are, when that ground is relied upon, the recipients of their data, where the data will be transferred to and for how long their employer will retain their data.

14.5 Storage of personnel records

Employers start collecting details about employees from the moment an individual applies for a position. Records that relate to employees cover a broad range of activities, from recruitment, sick leave, medical insurance and salary to appraisals, performance evaluations and severance. These records contain personal data that should not be retained for longer than is necessary under data protection rules. Generally speaking, whilst an individual is a current employee, the employer has a legitimate reason to retain that employee's data. However, once the employee has left that job, such reasons are likely to diminish.

Different local laws require employers to retain employee data. These include obligations under company law, employment law, and health and safety law. The latter may include records that the employer is required to keep relating to health and safety checks on individuals who operate machinery. The employer may also be required to keep the employee's personal data to the extent necessary to comply with labour, tax and social security legislation, or with any other regulations that require the retention of employees' personal data.

Once someone's employment ends, however, the employer should generally change the internal access to the former employee's records. There is unlikely to be a day-to-day requirement for the human resources (HR) department to access records of former employees. In such circumstances, the data on former employees that must be retained should be securely archived.

14.6 Workplace monitoring and data loss prevention

An employee does not lose their right to privacy in the workplace. European law recognises that an employee's private sphere in the workplace is protected. However, this right to privacy is balanced against the legitimate rights of an employer to operate its business and protect the company or organisation from any rogue actions of employees.

14.6.1 Background checks

Background checks on potential and existing employees are increasingly common. One of the reasons for this increase is the recognition that data breaches can be the work of unscrupulous employees. The weak link in the chain is often human rather than technical. Additionally, outsourcing or service companies can be asked by their customers to carry out background checks on those persons who will work on customer projects. Background checks can operate on a range of levels, from checking a person's status on social networking websites to verifying their educational background to checks on past criminal activity. An employer must be careful not to compile blacklists as part of its background checking procedure or to identify individuals who it will not employ.

Blacklists are considered to be a significant intrusion into a person's privacy and are generally illegal. Occasionally, a jurisdiction has a law that specifically deals with background checks, as in Finland with the 2002 Act on Background Checks, which defines who can conduct a check and requires the prior written consent of the individual who is the subject of the check. Otherwise, the rules to be followed when carrying out background checks will stem from data protection and employment law, which can vary between member states.

14.6.2 Data loss prevention

Data loss prevention (DLP) technologies have become increasingly popular with employers over recent years. Businesses use DLP tools in order to protect their IT infrastructure and confidential business information from external and internal threats. DLP tools inevitably involve processing employee and other third-party personal data since they operate on networks and systems used by employees, such as the email exchange server, which can contain personal information even if employees are not allowed to use it for personal activities. Use of a DLP tool is a form of employee monitoring even though the overriding intention of the tool is to focus on preventing loss of the organisation's data.

14.6.3 Employee monitoring

Personal data about employees that is generated in the workplace should still be used by the employer in accordance with data protection rules. An employer must also comply with relevant local employment laws and any specific rules that relate to the privacy of electronic communications. An employer may decide to monitor its employees for a number of different reasons, including employee use of employer equipment or suspected unauthorised activity.

If an employer wishes to carry out workplace monitoring, it should ensure compliance in particular with the following data protection principles:

- *Necessity:* An employer must be able to demonstrate that the monitoring is really necessary.

- *Legitimacy:* An employer must have lawful grounds for collecting and using the personal data and, if appropriate, sensitive personal data, and the processing must be fair.

- *Proportionality:* Any monitoring that takes place must be proportionate to the issue that the employer is dealing with.

- *Transparency:* An employer must clearly inform employees of the monitoring that will be carried out.

Any personal data about employees collected through monitoring activity must be held securely and accessed only by those within the company who have a legitimate reason to view it, such as those deciding whether the employee has breached company policy or the law. Such data should be deleted when there is no longer a need to hold onto it. Of course, there may be a business need to retain it. One example where a company might have a need to retain data would be in the case of an employee who is dismissed due to information obtained through monitoring, and the former employee then challenges the dismissal.

14.6.4 Necessity

The employer must be confident that the monitoring activity envisaged is really necessary for the purpose before going ahead. In other words, the employer should consider other less-intrusive methods of supervision before commencing with the monitoring. Under the Regulation, an employer must carry out a data protection impact assessment (DPIA) or privacy impact assessment (PIA) when the monitoring is likely to result in a high risk to the rights and freedoms of individuals. Carrying out a DPIA helps to determine whether the planned monitoring is really required and proportionate (see Section 14.6.6 for further discussion on proportionality). A DPIA is required if the monitoring amounts to a systematic and extensive evaluation of personal aspects of individuals that is based on automated processing and on which decisions are based that produce legal effects or similarly significantly affect the individuals.

A DPIA is a process that considers the privacy risks to individuals of any proposed data processing activity. It is a transparent, consultative process that should be started at the beginning of an initiative to process personal data. A DPIA would be appropriate, for example, if the company is deciding to use DLP software with which to monitor employee activity. Carrying out a DPIA enables organisations to identify the privacy risks at an early stage and consider what needs to be done to mitigate the risk. (See Chapter 11 for more information on carrying out a DPIA.)

14.6.5 Legitimacy

The monitoring that an employer wishes to carry out must be legitimate—that is, there must be a lawful basis for the monitoring. An employer could wish to monitor Internet use to ensure that employees are not using the Internet to download pornography or to disclose confidential information about the employer to outsiders. Alternatively, monitoring could be intended to ensure worker safety. From a data protection perspective, this will often mean relying on the legitimate interest balancing test. The employer has a legitimate interest in protecting its business from significant threats, like preventing confidential information from being sent to a competitor. Therefore, an employer will need to carry out the balancing test required by the legitimate interest ground. In contrast to the ground of legitimate interest, the Article 29 Working Party (WP29) has indicated that the use of employee consent to legitimise the monitoring of emails is very limited. The same principle—that the use of consent is very limited—extends to all types of monitoring.

Monitoring that involves the collection of sensitive data is likely to be problematic. However, Article 9 permits processing of sensitive data where necessary for the purposes of carrying out the obligations and exercising specific rights of the employer according to employment, social security and social protection law, insofar as the processing is authorised by EU or member state law or a collective agreement providing for adequate safeguards. The employer will therefore need guidance on EU and local law when it foresees that monitoring is likely to involve the processing of data relating to such things as ethnicity, race, religion, political opinions and sexual life. In certain instances, there may not be sufficient grounds to process employee sensitive data through monitoring activity.

Employers should also consult local employment law. It will not always be legitimate to monitor individuals, and, in some EU countries, the rules are strict concerning what type of monitoring is considered legitimate.

Furthermore, it may be necessary to consider collective agreements or to consult works councils (more on these below), which can be necessary in countries like

Germany for companies with as few as five employees, to see what protections are in place regarding use of employee data. As just one example, in Austria, employment law restricts an employer from implementing a monitoring system that interferes with human dignity without first entering into an agreement with the works council. An agreement between an employer and a works council, which may simply have to be consulted on any significant change in the employee experience, may set out specifically what type of monitoring is permitted. Any other monitoring by the employer may be unlawful.

Any monitoring of employees is considered to be intrusive, but there are degrees of intrusiveness. The WP29, for example, has indicated that screening of emails to detect viruses and filter unsolicited commercial emails is justified as part of ensuring appropriate security measures. Certain jurisdictions permit the monitoring of Internet time or the regularity of telephone calls made to non-work numbers but do not permit the recording of the content of websites visited or phone conversations. Additionally, exploring other mechanisms to prevent employees from misusing employer equipment is encouraged before monitoring is implemented. Employers can block access to certain websites visited by employees as a way of discouraging employees from spending time on such websites. The WP29, in particular, has emphasised that prevention is more important than detection.

It is also necessary to consider the implications under human rights law, including decisions by the Court of Justice of the European Union (CJEU) on the Charter of Fundamental Rights and the European Court of Human Rights (ECHR) on the European Convention on Human Rights.

14.6.6 Proportionality

When an employer wishes to carry out monitoring, it must consider whether the proposed monitoring is proportionate to the employer's concern. The wholesale monitoring of all employee emails to ensure that employees are not passing on confidential information about the employer would be disproportionate. However, wholesale automated monitoring of emails is likely proportionate to ensure the security of the employer's IT systems where such monitoring is carried out using technical means that detect weaknesses in the system.

Monitoring activity must therefore be devised to be a reasoned and realistic response to a potential or known threat. The need for proportionality is linked to the principle under the Regulation of data minimisation—that personal data must be adequate, relevant and limited to what is necessary in relation to the purposes for which they are processed. Therefore, monitoring emails should, where possible, be limited to the traffic data generated by emails, such as who sent the email and at what time rather than monitoring the contents of the message. Technical means can be used to assess the size and number of emails. Actually opening emails to read the contents is usually disproportionate.

Collective bargaining agreements are useful markers for employers considering the proportionality of monitoring activity. If a collective agreement acknowledges that the employer should be entitled to carry out certain monitoring activity in certain circumstances, then the balance of interest concerning proportionality is likely to have been struck.

14.6.7 Transparency

As required by the notice requirement under the Regulation, employers must provide employees with sufficient information about the monitoring activity (see Chapter 8 for more on required notice and transparency). This transparency is important not only to meet the notice requirement but also to set employees' expectations about how their time at work will be monitored. Setting expectations is central to ensuring that monitoring is lawful. If employees have been notified in advance of the standards expected in the workplace concerning their use of employer equipment and that this use will be monitored, then employees have less scope to argue in the future that they were unaware that their activity was contrary to the standards and was being monitored. In the past, the requirement to inform employees in advance about monitoring has been crucial to how courts see this issue. If an employer fails to notify employees that their activity will be monitored, that employer could lose an action against a rogue employee whose behaviour was caught only through monitoring.

If employees have not been told that their behaviour will be monitored in the workplace, they have a greater expectation of privacy. Informing employees of how they will be monitored can reduce that expectation. But it is not possible for an employer to argue that a lack of privacy in the workplace is acceptable just because the employer has warned employees that they have no workplace privacy. A court or DPA would not recognise such a comprehensive warning as legitimate since the law recognises that workers enjoy a certain degree of privacy in the workplace that cannot be completely eradicated.

Therefore, employers should introduce an acceptable use policy (AUP) that is brought to the attention of all new and existing employees and sets out in detail the expected standard of use for employer communications equipment (e.g., telephone, Internet, email) and which indicates that employee use may be monitored. The AUP should also specify how much private use of employer equipment is permitted.

Generally, the private communications of employees should not be opened or monitored. Employers could be tempted to circumvent this rule by stating in the AUP that no private use of employer equipment is permitted. However, courts, as well as certain DPAs, have stated that employees have a right to limited private use of employer equipment. An alternative way of dealing with the use of email could be for the employer to stipulate that the company email account is for company business only, but employees may use personal email accounts on company equipment for limited personal use.

Employers could also remind employees of the expectation concerning their use of company equipment and of the employer's right to monitor their use through pop-up boxes triggered when, for example, an employee logs on to a company computer.

Of course, there may be circumstances where an employer considers covert monitoring necessary since informing a particular individual that they are being specifically monitored is a tip-off that the person is suspected of wrongful activity. If an employer has reasonable grounds to suspect an employee of theft, it may be appropriate to engage in undercover surveillance. In some EU jurisdictions, this type of covert surveillance is permitted only in very narrow circumstances and, in certain jurisdictions, not permitted at all. Instead, the police should be involved. The WP29 has stated that no covert email monitoring is allowed by employers except in cases permitted by local law. Such monitoring is likely to be where specific criminal activity by the employee has been identified.

14.6.8 Information to be provided by employers

The WP29 has provided guidance concerning what information employers should provide employees:

- Company email/Internet policy, which should describe in detail the extent to which employees may use communication facilities owned by the company for personal/private communications (e.g., any limitations on time and duration of use).

- Reasons and purposes for which surveillance, if any, is being carried out. Where the employer has allowed the use of the company's communication facilities for express private purposes, such private communications may, under very limited circumstances, be subject to surveillance—for example, to ensure the security of the information system (virus checking or ransomware prevention).

- The details of surveillance measures taken: Who? What? How? When?

- Details of any enforcement procedures that outline how and when workers will be notified of breaches of internal policies and be given the opportunity to respond to any such claims against them.

Specific guidance in relation to monitoring email:

- Whether a worker is entitled to have an email account for purely personal use, whether use of webmail accounts is permitted at work and whether the employer recommends the use, by workers, of a private webmail account for the purpose of accessing email for purely personal use.

- The arrangements in place to access the contents of a worker's email—for example, when the worker is unexpectedly absent—and the specific purposes for such access.

- The storage period for any backup copies of messages.

- Information that concerns when emails are definitively deleted from the server.

- The involvement of workers' representatives in formulating the policy.

Specific guidance in relation to monitoring Internet use:

- Clear delineation of conditions on which private use of the Internet is permitted, as well as specifying material that cannot be viewed or copied. These conditions and limitations have to be explained to the workers.

- Information about the systems implemented both to prevent access to certain sites and to detect misuse. The extent of such monitoring should be specified—for instance, whether such monitoring may relate to individuals or particular sections of the company, or whether the content of the sites visited is viewed or recorded by the employer in particular circumstances. Furthermore, the policy should specify what use, if any, will be made of any data collected in relation to who visited what sites.

- Information about the involvement of the employer's representatives, both in the implementation of this policy and in the investigation of alleged breaches.

Where the employer detects any misuse of the employer equipment by an employee, the employer should notify the employee immediately of such misuse unless there is an important reason to justify the surveillance without notifying the individual.

Employers may also need to provide information to works councils, depending on any requirement of local law or collective agreement. In certain cases, works councils only need to be consulted about monitoring arrangements. However, some collective agreements require the employer to obtain the consent of the works council before commencing the particular monitoring. Local laws will vary. As an example of a local variance, under the Belgian Collective Bargaining Agreement (13 December 1983), before the introduction of new technology that will significantly impact working conditions, an employer must provide information to employee representatives about the nature of the new technology, the factors that justify its introduction and the consequences.

14.6.9 Rights of the accused employee

Employers should exercise caution when dealing with a potential misuse of the Internet by an employee. In view of the ease with which websites can be visited unwittingly through unclear hypertext links or miskeying, employers should not jump to conclusions about the employee's intention without first presenting the facts to the individual and providing the individual with an opportunity to explain their behaviour. The employer may also be required in some cases to involve the employee's representative or works council.

14.6.10 Unlawful monitoring by the employer

Usually it is harder to justify monitoring that involves the collection of sensitive personal data. Furthermore, monitoring that is particularly intrusive is usually unlawful. In certain jurisdictions, covert surveillance is deemed to be unlawful unless the employer has obtained prior permission from the DPA or an exception applies. Or it may be unlawful for employers to access the private communications of employees if such emails are marked as private, even if they are received through a work-related email account.

Failure to comply with the rules can lead to serious consequences for the employer, including fines and/or potential criminal offences.

14.7 Works councils

When dealing with employee data, it is vital that employers not view data protection as an isolated area of compliance. They should consider their obligations under employment law and collective agreements with trade unions and any works councils. Works councils are bodies that represent employees and have certain rights under local law that affect the use of employee data by employers. Works councils can have a role in deciding whether employees' personal data can be processed because they typically have an obligation to safeguard employee rights, which include data protection and privacy rights. Generally, works councils are more active in certain jurisdictions, such as France, Germany and Italy. The UK, by contrast, does not have works councils, and UK trade unions do not usually have any influence on how employers use employee data. These differences reflect the evolution of the different working cultures across the EU.

But in certain situations, works councils wield considerable power. Under the German Works Council Act, for example, a works council may object to the use of employee monitoring devices.

Usually employers have to engage with works councils in one or more of the following three ways:

- *Notifying the works council:* Local law may require the employer to notify works councils about changes to the working environment that will affect employee working conditions.

- *Consulting with the works council:* Local law may require the employer to consult with the works council about proposed data processing activity. The works council may have the right to issue an opinion about the activity, although the employer may not be bound by the opinion.

- *Seeking the approval of the works council:* Local law may give the works council the right to approve or reject certain decisions of the employer. This is also known as a right to codetermination. Where the works council rejects a decision, the employer's only option may be to challenge this in the local courts.

Certain jurisdictions have a strong tradition of works council involvement in decision-making that concerns the use of employee data, and employers should carefully note any obligation to engage with works councils. Where processing activity that involves employee data also involves interacting with the DPA, a DPA may not approve the processing unless and until the works council has been involved.

Therefore, an employer should factor in time required to engage with the works council in any processing operation that requires their involvement. A failure to involve the works council can mean in certain countries that the data processing is unlawful, the works council may have the right to seek an injunction, and the employer may be subject to financial penalties.

14.8 Whistle-blowing schemes

If illegal or improper activity is taking place within a company, often it is the employees of a company who will first observe it and who could help to stop it by reporting it to individuals with more authority. In setting up procedures to make it possible for an employee to report such activity, a company will want to be sure that appropriate privacy safeguards are put in place.

14.8.1 Sarbanes-Oxley

Whistle-blowing schemes that permit employees to expose any unlawful or improper activity taking place within the workplace have been around for a while. They have gained particular prominence since the passing of the U.S. Sarbanes-Oxley Act (SOX) in 2002.[2] This has implications under EU data protection law since U.S. companies with EU subsidiaries or affiliates are bound by SOX, and so the effect of SOX filters down to the operations of EU companies. Frequently, an EU company is required to comply with two compliance regimes that can, to some extent, conflict—one relating to SOX, where a company is required to facilitate the ability of employees to make allegations about wrongdoing, and another relating to EU data protection laws, which limit the use of personal data in these circumstances due to the potential prejudice to individuals.

SOX was passed following a number of high-profile corporate and accounting scandals involving global companies. The aim of SOX is to ensure that company and accounting decision-making is more responsible and accountable. Companies regulated by SOX must establish a way for the company to confidentially receive and deal with complaints about actual or potential fraud from misappropriation of assets and/or material misstatements in financial reporting. Such complaints typically come from employees and other insiders in a position to witness a breakdown in internal controls.

Most SOX-regulated companies comply with this requirement by: (1) implementing a company policy that reinforces a strong adherence to internal controls; (2) encouraging those with knowledge of actual or potential fraud to report such instances, and (3) reiterating the confidential nature of the reporting and protection for the whistle-blower. To properly manage such complaints and avoid a reporting process that might inhibit whistle-blowers, many companies employ an independent third-party whistle-blowing or ethics hotline provider available to all employees to report their complaints. The whistle-blowing mechanism—be it a telephone line and/or email address—allows employees to make allegations about other personnel in the company.

Certain EU jurisdictions (e.g., Spain and Portugal) are particularly sensitive about enabling employees to make anonymous reports. The concern is that the subject of an allegation has no right of reply to the person making the allegation. Additionally, people could abuse the anonymity function by making malicious reports.

14.8.2 Issues for compliance

An employer seeking to comply with the EU data protection rules whilst operating a whistle-blowing scheme needs to consider the following:

- A DPIA for the envisaged whistle-blowing scheme to assess the impact on the protection of personal data.

- Liaison with works councils as required under local employment law or according to a collective agreement.

- Processing contracts with any processors who are based outside the EU (i.e., in the United States), where such contracts will need to comply with the requirements under the Regulation concerning appointing processors, as well as the requirements for legitimising international data transfers.

- Mechanism for transferring personal data in reports outside the EU to a non-EU-based company for further processing—typically, this would be on the basis of either standard contractual clauses or Binding Corporate Rules (BCRs).

- Whether consent from employees is required and, if so, in what form.

- Whether compliance in a particular jurisdiction is complicated due to the policy of the DPA (e.g., Portugal).

- Developing a whistle-blowing policy and process that is transparent to employees informing them of the scope of the scheme and how their personal data will be used in relation to the scheme.

- Ensuring individual employee's rights under data protection law are protected appropriately under the scheme.

14.8.3 A whistle-blowing policy

The WP29 has issued an opinion on whistle-blowing.[3] This was preceded by guidelines from the French DPA, which was one of the first DPAs to consider the lawfulness of whistle-blowing schemes under EU data protection law. Taking into account the guidance provided by the French DPA and the WP29, a company's whistle-blowing policy should cover the following specific elements:

- *Individuals reporting*: Consider limiting the persons entitled to report alleged improprieties or misconduct through a whistle-blowing scheme to those who are in a position to know about the potential conduct of the incriminated persons (i.e., whilst all the company employees may be entitled to make a report, not everyone will be entitled to report on everyone else).

- *Individuals incriminated:* Consider limiting the individuals who may be incriminated to those who are known or are likely to be known because they work in the same section or department by the persons reporting them.

- *Confidentiality versus anonymity:* Whilst the identity of the whistle-blower should remain confidential, and this should be made clear in the company's policy materials, it should also be emphasised that such reports are a serious matter. Anonymous reporting should not be encouraged, and examples of frivolous reports should be included for illustration. Consider pointing out in the policy that providing the whistle-blower's identity is likely to result in a more accurate and thorough investigation.

- *Scope of reports:* Consider limiting the scope of reportable matters to those who realistically affect the organisation's corporate governance. Reports of bullying and harassment should arguably be dealt with through HR channels rather than through a whistle-blowing scheme.

- *Management of reports:* Irrespective of whether reports are collected and processed internally or by a service provider, they should be subject to an objective, confidential and unbiased investigation. Consider establishing a specific mechanism to manage reports in a consistent manner.

- *Data retention:* Consider (1) establishing a strict data retention period following the completion of any investigation of the facts reported (e.g., two months); and (2) deleting immediately any reports found to be entirely unsubstantiated.

- *Information provision:* The company's policy should be clear about the way in which the whistle-blowing scheme is operated as set out in the whistle-blowing policy. Consider placing within the company's corporate code either a link to the whistle-blowing policy itself or a link to a version of the whistle-blowing policy drafted from the point of view of a potential user of the scheme. All notices must meet the requirements under the Regulation for transparency.

- *Rights of incriminated persons:* Consider setting out specific circumstances under which the data protection rights (i.e., information provision, access, rectification, erasure and restriction) of incriminated individuals may be limited (e.g., where notifying a person who has been incriminated is likely to jeopardise the ability of the company to investigate any allegations).

- *Security of reports:* Consider adopting a specific information security policy dealing with reports collected via the whistle-blowing scheme.

- *Transfers outside the EEA:* Where reports originating from the EU are processed outside the European Economic Area (EEA), the data must be processed in accordance with EU data protection standards. Accordingly, the whistle-blowing policy should state the mechanism used to legitimise any international transfers of data.

14.9 Bring your own device

Many employers permit their employees to use their own personal devices (e.g., smartphones/tablets) for communications in the workplace. An employee may choose to integrate their work email onto their personal device so that they use one device for both personal and work communications.

Bring your own device (BYOD) poses certain data protection compliance issues since the employer remains responsible as a controller for any personal data processed on the employee's device for work-related purposes using the work email settings. But the device also contains information about the employee's personal life that an employer would not usually have a lawful reason to access. Yet, the employer has good reason to seek strong protection over the device given that it holds data that relates to the employee's working life. Additionally, in the hands of the employee outside the workplace, a mobile device is vulnerable to being lost or misused.

Companies introducing BYOD into the workplace should:

- Establish a BYOD policy that explains to employees how they can use BYOD and what their responsibilities are.

- Be clear about where the data processed via the device is stored and what measures must be taken to keep the data secure.

- Ensure the transfer of data from the personal device to the company's servers is secure to avoid any interceptions as far as possible.

- Consider how to manage personal data held on the device once the employee leaves the company or the device is stolen or lost. Mobile device management software can be used to locate devices and remove data on demand.

Endnotes

1 Authorisation 1/2004 (document 1037032) Concerning Processing of Sensitive Data in the Employment Context, 30 June 2004 [1115278], www.garanteprivacy.it/web/guest/home/docweb/-/docweb-display/export/1115278.

2 Authorisation 1/2004 (document 1037032) Concerning Processing of Sensitive Data in the Employment Context, 30 June 2004 [1115278], www.garanteprivacy.it/web/guest/home/docweb/-/docweb-display/export/1115278.

3 Opinion 1/2006 on the application of EU data protection rules to internal whistleblowing schemes in the fields of accounting, internal accounting controls, auditing matters, fight against bribery, banking and financial crime (00195/06/EN; WP 117), http://ec.europa.eu/justice/policies/privacy/docs/wpdocs/2006/wp117_en.pdf.

Surveillance Activities

Robert Streeter, CIPP/E, CIPP/US

15.1 Introduction

Surveillance is getting easier. The equipment used for monitoring is getting cheaper and more sophisticated, software allows more complex analytics, and the technology used by individuals produces more and more data that can be captured by that equipment and analysed. Surveillance is of significant public concern, whether by government or law enforcement, by an employer, or by a company gathering data on its customers. The debate between the need to carry out surveillance, especially in relation to national security and commercial interests, and an individual's right to privacy is ongoing: What the right balance should be is a very difficult question to answer.

Technology evolution continues to reduce the technological and economic barriers to surveillance and facilitates the collection, exchange, retention and processing of personal data. This includes the ability to combine information collected from various sources, create huge databases and search those databases for information about individuals. At the same time, the Internet, technology convergence and the proliferation of mobile devices mean that more information about individuals is generated and is available for surveillance. Once this information is collected, there is a natural tendency by organisations, whether public or private, to process, combine and use that data for their respective legitimate purposes, such as national security, the prevention and detection of crime, or the personalisation of consumer services.

Surveillance law is complex. Surveillance by law enforcement and other state bodies is legislated for by member states, subject to limits imposed by national constitutions and EU charters. Employee monitoring may be similarly regulated by member states.

This chapter discusses the regulation of surveillance activities under EU instruments and introduces the issues around four key types of data used for surveillance purposes: communications data, video surveillance, biometric data and location data.

15.2 Technology

The purpose of new technologies is to make our lives safer, easier or more pleasant. However, our use of these technologies generates a wealth of data about us and, in some cases, about the people with whom we interact. For instance, each time we call someone on the phone, send a text message or electronic mail, or surf the web, we generate detailed information about the type, time, duration, destination and content of each communication.

Closed-circuit television (CCTV, an acronym still used despite much video surveillance now residing on TCP/IP networks) cameras record our actions to help protect our security at home, at work and in public spaces. Our biometric data may be used for identification, authentication and verification, as well as for law enforcement purposes. Payment cards keep track of every purchase we make with the card, along with where and when the purchase was made. Our mobile phones generate accurate information about our location and moves. The fitness monitors we wear provide detailed health information. In the longer term, such technologies can lead to the networked interconnection of everyday objects, known as the Internet of Things (IoT).

It follows that nowadays surveillance activities are undertaken on a daily basis, by both public and private sector entities and for a host of lawful purposes. Examples include employee monitoring (see Chapter 14, which is devoted to this topic); social networks analysis and mapping; data mining and profiling; aerial surveillance; satellite imaging; telecommunications surveillance for purposes as wide ranging as law enforcement, improvement of commercial services and online behavioural advertising (OBA); monitoring of people's movements through mobile telecommunications location data, CCTV cameras or geolocation technologies, such as the global positioning system (GPS); and biometric surveillance for purposes as wide ranging as preventing crime and identifying candidates sitting an exam.

The volume and level of granularity of the personal information that may be subject to surveillance, combined with the relevant ease of its collection and processing, opens a significant scope for abuse. As a result, there can be a conflict between surveillance and privacy. In many countries, this potential conflict manifests itself in the context of the debate on whether our societies are becoming 'surveillance societies'. The purpose of privacy and data protection law and regulatory practice in this regard is to regulate, limit and condition surveillance activities to ensure that, where surveillance activities result in invasion of privacy, this invasion is necessary, lawful, fair and proportionate, although achieving the correct balance is difficult.

15.3 Regulating surveillance

Surveillance involves the observation of an individual or a group of individuals. This may be covert or carried out openly and conducted in real time or by access to stored material. It may be carried out by:

- public and state agencies for national security or law enforcement purposes, conducted in a manner to respect individual rights enshrined the Charter of Fundamental Rights ('Charter'),[1] specifically the rights to a private and family life (Article 7) and protection of personal data (Article 8); or

- private entities for their purposes, subject to European Union and member state legislation governing confidentiality, privacy, data protection and other civil rights, such as those provided for under employment law.

Surveillance may need to be conducted in a manner that overrides data subject rights. This need is recognised by the General Data Protection Regulation (GDPR, or 'Regulation') in Article 23 'Restrictions', which permits European Union or member state law to restrict the rights granted in Chapter 3 'Rights of the data subject', where such a restriction 'respects the essence of the fundamental rights and freedoms and is a necessary and proportionate measure in a democratic society', as set out in the Charter and in the European Convention for the Protection of Human Rights and Fundamental Freedoms (Recital 73). These restrictions are to act as safeguards to protect states, society and other individuals. National and public security, the prevention and detection of crime, and the protection of the data subject and the rights and freedoms of others are included in the allowable reasons for the restrictions to be applied.

The particular requirements of law enforcement are recognised in the Law Enforcement Data Protection Directive (LEDP Directive) for the 'protection of natural persons with regard to the processing of personal data by competent authorities for the purposes of the prevention, investigation, detection or prosecution of criminal offences or the execution of criminal penalties, and on the movement of such data'.[2] In Recital 66, the LEDP Directive recognises that, although the processing of personal data must be lawful, fair and transparent, this should not prevent law enforcement authorities from carrying out activities such as covert investigations or video surveillance. These activities can be carried out for the purposes of preventing, investigating, detecting and prosecuting criminal offences, and to safeguard against and prevent threats to public security, as long as they are 'laid down by law and constitute a necessary and proportionate measure in a democratic society with due regard for the legitimate interests of the natural person concerned'. Proportionality of the measure is a key concern. Laws that fail to appropriately take into account the rights of data subjects may be struck down by the Court of Justice of the European Union (CJEU).

Today, there is a clear trend towards more monitoring, collecting and sharing of personal data between state agencies in the fight against terrorism and other serious crime. In Europe, in order to ensure the availability of more personal data for law enforcement purposes, private sector entities may be under an obligation to retain and/or share personal data with these agencies. However, it is necessary to balance this need with the rights of individuals, as discussed below in relation to communications data.

15.4 Communications data

Communications surveillance may refer to traditional surveillance, such as interception of postal services and the use of human spies or surveillance devices. However, these types of surveillance are receding in favour of more modern and high-tech surveillance of telecommunications, including Internet activity, and this is the focus of this section.

Electronic communications generate two main categories of personal data:

15.4.1 The content of a communication

For example, in relation to a telephone call, this would be the conversation between the parties to the call; in relation to an SMS, the words in the message; or, in relation to an email, the email subject line, the words in the main body of the email and the attachments to the email.

15.4.2 Metadata

This is commonly referred to as 'data about data' and is information that is generated or processed as a consequence of a communication's transmission; it provides context to the communication.[3] The following are all examples of metadata:

15.4.2.1 Traffic data

This includes information about the type, format, time, duration, origin and destination, routing, protocol used, and the originating and terminating network of a communication. For instance, in relation to a telephone call, traffic data includes, amongst other information, the calling and called numbers; in relation to an email, sender and recipient email addresses and the size of attachments.

15.4.2.2 Location data

This may refer to the latitude, longitude and altitude of the user's equipment, the direction of travel, the level of accuracy of the location information, the identification of the network cell ('Cell ID') in which the user device is located at a certain time, and the time the location information was recorded.

15.4.2.3 Subscriber data

This generally constitutes the name, contact details and payment information.

A frequent contention is that the content of a communication requires greater legal protection than metadata, especially when considering the importance of the right of freedom of expression, a right recognised in the EU and many other countries, such as in the United States through the First Amendment to its Constitution.

However, metadata reveals a complete picture of a communication:

- the 'who', (i.e., the parties involved);
- the 'where' (i.e., the location of the parties);
- the 'when' (i.e., the time and duration);
- the 'what' (i.e., the type, such as email or a phone call); and
- the 'how' (i.e., the device used, such as a mobile phone or a tablet).[4]

Because metadata can be used to identify an individual, it therefore falls within the definition of personal data under the Regulation.

An EU attempt at requiring telecommunication service operators to retain call metadata for longer than could be justified from the operator's business needs is a good example of the difficulties in balancing the requirements of security and law enforcement with the rights of individuals. The EU required telecom companies and Internet service providers (ISPs) to retain communications data under the Data Retention Directive 2006/24/EC, which governed the retention of data generated or processed in connection with the provision of publicly available electronic communication services or of public communications networks. In 2014, however, a CJEU judgment rendered this Directive invalid for disproportionately infringing individuals' privacy rights as guaranteed by the Charter.[5]

This led to the rewriting of any number of member state data retention laws, many of which are still in development as of this writing.

15.5 Video surveillance

Surveillance includes video surveillance, such as CCTV. In the public's mind, the spread of CCTV cameras proves the 'surveillance society' concept more than any other type of surveillance, especially when it is overt and almost ubiquitous in city centres. The development of digital analytics tools, such as facial-recognition software, exacerbates these concerns. As a result, CCTV has attracted significant attention from privacy advocates and privacy regulators.

CCTV may capture images of people or things that may be used to identify an individual, such as a car number or licence plate. Such instances will be treated as processing personal data. Where video surveillance is considered to involve the processing of personal data, then it must comply with the requirements of the Regulation and, if applicable, the LEDP Directive.

Any time an individual's image is captured, whether it's static (e.g., a picture of a face) or moving (e.g., a video of the individual walking), the data falls within the Regulation's definition of biometric data (i.e., 'personal data resulting from specific technical processing relating to the physical, physiological or behavioural characteristics of a natural person, which allow or confirm the unique identification of that natural person, such as facial images or dactyloscopic data').[6]

15.5.1 Lawfulness of processing

It is unlikely that a data controller will be able to rely on an individual's consent as the legal basis for the use of CCTV, and so the lawfulness of processing may need to be legitimised on the basis of the legitimate interests pursued by the data controller or a third party. In that case, a balancing exercise will need to be carried out to verify that the CCTV's use does not override the rights and freedoms of the individuals whose personal data may be captured by the CCTV.

Biometric data falls within the special categories of personal data, the bases of processing for which are specified in Article 9 of the Regulation. Processing can therefore only be carried out if one of the permitted conditions applies, and it will be up to the controller to determine this prior to carrying out the video surveillance. It may be that a controller needs to rely on a provision in member state law to conduct the video surveillance in a particular context (e.g., for employers where employee consent may not meet the Article 7 conditions of consent in the Regulation), in the public interest for a public area, or in the exercise of public authority, such as for monitoring traffic.

15.5.2 Data protection impact assessments

A data protection impact assessment (DPIA) will have to be completed if:

- the video surveillance is considered to be high risk;
- it involves the systematic monitoring of a publicly accessible area on a large scale; or
- if video surveillance has been included by the relevant supervisory authority on a list of data processing operations that require a DPIA (Article 35).

The DPIA will need to describe:

- the processing to be carried out;
- the purposes of processing;
- the legitimate interests pursued by the data controller;
- an assessment of why it is necessary and proportionate in relation to the purposes;
- an assessment of the risks to the rights and freedoms of the data subjects impacted by the surveillance; and
- the measures required to address the risks, protect the personal data and demonstrate compliance with the Regulation, taking into account the rights and legitimate interests of data subjects and other persons concerned.

If the DPIA indicates that the high risks cannot be sufficiently mitigated, for example, by appropriate siting of the cameras and setting the direction they point, then the data controller must consult with the supervisory authority prior to the use of the video surveillance. Where the public interest is used as the lawful basis of processing, member states may make consultation with the supervisory authority mandatory, regardless of the mitigation (Article 36).

To assess whether the use of video surveillance is proportionate and is an adequate, relevant and not excessive solution to the problem it is intended to address, a decision to use CCTV should be made only if other, less-intrusive solutions that do not require image acquisition (e.g., improved lighting, alarms, armoured doors or access cards) have been considered and found to be clearly inapplicable or inadequate for the intended lawful purpose. The DPIA should document these investigations and inadequacies.

The requirement for the solution to be proportionate also extends to the selection of the particular system and type of technology; for example, are remote control, a zooming functionality, facial-recognition or sound-recording capabilities necessary? This process will involve considering in detail the problems that need to be addressed, the benefits to be gained from the use of CCTV, whether images of identifiable individuals are necessary or whether images not identifying individuals will suffice, and ways to minimise the intrusion on those who may be monitored.

A second element of the proportionality test entails the consideration of whether the key aspects of the use of CCTV and the processing of CCTV footage are proportionate to the purpose for which the CCTV system is used. These key aspects include:

- *Operational and monitoring arrangements.* This entails a consideration of the key operational aspects of the system, including the types of cameras (e.g., fixed or mobile); the positioning of cameras and their visual angle so that the monitoring of spaces that are not relevant can be minimised, and private areas, like washrooms and individual workspaces, potentially avoided altogether; the availability of zooming during recording or on stored images; the quality of images, which should be suitable for the purpose, otherwise, the lawfulness of the purpose may be undermined; the possibility to blur or delete irrelevant individual images; image freezing; the ability to send sound or visual alerts at the location under surveillance and the actions that may be taken on the basis of CCTV data (e.g., shutting down entrances or calling security or the police). Other considerations may be relevant depending on the purpose; for instance, when CCTV is intended to address a problem occurring at a particular time of day (i.e., normal working hours), the monitoring should not be 24/7.

- *Retention of CCTV footage.* CCTV footage should be retained only if, and only for as long as, it is strictly necessary for the purpose, such as where footage is likely to be required as evidence in subsequent investigations or legal proceedings. In practice, broadly speaking, CCTV footage should normally be retained only for short periods of time.

- The need to disclose CCTV footage to third parties, such as the police.

- Whether CCTV footage will be combined with other information, for example, to identify individuals.

- The surveillance of areas where people have high expectations of privacy, such as changing rooms or lavatories. When it is necessary to monitor such areas, cameras should be used only in the most exceptional circumstances and only where necessary to deal with very serious concerns. All reasonable effort should be made to ensure that individuals are aware that they are under surveillance.

Measures to protect the personal data and to protect the rights of individuals may include:

- *Staff training*: The authorised personnel operating the system and accessing the footage should receive adequate training and be made aware of the system operator's compliance obligations. Personnel should be familiar with the operator's relevant policies and aware of the disciplinary and legal sanctions for misuse of the CCTV system, including that it may constitute a criminal offence. Furthermore, authorised personnel should be able to handle footage securely and to deal with disclosure requests from law enforcement agencies and with subject access requests.

- *CCTV policy*: This is a written document setting out the policy governing the use of the CCTV system. It should also address important privacy issues, such as the processing purposes of the CCTV recording; whether data will be retained and, if so, the retention periods and the lawful uses of the retained data; disclosures to third parties; and responding to subject access requests.

- *Regular reviews to ensure compliance*: Proactive checks and audits should be carried out on a regular basis to ensure continuing compliance. In particular, this should include reconsidering whether the use of CCTV remains justified and renewing any notifications with regulatory authorities.

15.5.3 Data subject rights and CCTV

For overt video surveillance, the controller must comply with the transparency requirements of the Regulation to the extent that is possible in cases where the controller may not have a direct relationship with the affected data subjects, such as where the cameras cover a large, public space. Individuals will need to be provided with information to make them aware that CCTV is in operation and of the areas being monitored.

The information will need to be visible and placed within reasonable distance of the monitored area, and it may be provided in summary fashion, provided that it is effective—a prominent camera symbol with further information is a recognised approach. The information should also include the purpose of the surveillance and identify the controller with contact details. As the information that may be made available via a sign with a camera symbol is unlikely to contain all the details prescribed by Articles 13 and 14, the controller should be prepared to provide the full information necessary when a data subject makes contact.

The personal data that is captured through video surveillance will be subject to the Article 15 right of access by the data subject. Given that usually CCTV footage is only retained for short periods of time, the right of individuals to access the data held about them is normally of narrower scope compared to other contexts. Nevertheless, to the extent that data is retained, controllers must have the ability to effectively respond to subject access requests. Where CCTV footage also includes pictures of other people, measures should be taken to safeguard their privacy, for example, by blurring the images of the others.

15.6 Biometric data

Biometrics is a term that covers a variety of technologies in which unique identifiable attributes of people are used for identification and authentication.[7] Biometric data is now specifically defined in Article 4(14) of the Regulation as 'personal data resulting from specific technical processing relating to the physical, physiological or behavioural characteristics of a natural person, which allow or confirm the unique identification of that natural person, such as facial images or dactyloscopic data'. Examples include DNA, fingerprints, palms, vein patterns, retina and iris patterns, odour, voice, face, handwriting, keystroke technique and gait.

Biometric data may be in its raw form (e.g., the image of a face or a fingerprint) or in biometric template form that is a digital representation of the distinct characteristics extracted from the raw data. Fingerprint biometric data may consist of the location and direction of the minutiae, whereas iris data may include the position of the filaments around the eye centre. The template used by the biometric system must include sufficient detail to allow an individual to be identified from the population of individuals stored by the biometric system.[8]

Biometric systems may be used in the private or public sectors for a variety of purposes. The main uses of biometrics systems today are:

- *Identification: Who are you?* An example is the processing of photographs loaded up to social media and the identification of individuals through facial recognition.

- *Authentication: Are you who you claim to be?* Examples here are the use of someone's fingerprint to authenticate an individual's identity when accessing a mobile device, computer or a palm print to access a secure area of a building.

For biometric data to be included as a special category of personal data under Article 9 of the Regulation, the purpose for which the biometric data is being processed must be for uniquely identifying a natural person. If the biometric data is being used for another purpose, such as to merely permit access to a location as part of a large group of identifiers, then Article 9 will not apply, although it needs to be remembered that biometric data is, by definition, personal data. In addition, member states may implement further restrictions on the processing of biometric data, and so it will be necessary to check whether national laws impose further restrictions on the collection and use of such data.

15.7 Location data

Location-based services (LBS) utilise information about location to deliver, in various contexts, a wide array of applications and services, including social networking and gaming, entertainment, advertising and marketing, information, navigation, commerce, payment, tracking goods and people, security and emergency response services. Usually, LBS rely on the technical ability to localise a portable device, such as a mobile phone, GPS receiver, SatNav device, radio frequency identification (RFID) tag, or a chip in a credit card or a travel card.

Broadly speaking, the main types of location data used for LBS may be derived from one or more of the following technologies and services:[9]

- Satellite network-generated data, such as GPS data and, in the near future, the 'Galileo' Global Satellite Navigation System data (the European equivalent of the American GPS). Examples of LBS that use satellite-generated data include navigation services, security services and social networking services.

- Cell-based, mobile network-generated data (e.g., the Cell ID). Examples of LBS using mobile network data may include location specific information services or advertising delivered on mobile handsets; data generated from other wireless technologies, such as sensor-based systems (e.g., biometrics scanners or licence plate scanners for vehicles) and proximity, near field or personal area networks (e.g., Bluetooth, Wi-Fi, near-field communication (NFC) or RFID that can detect the presence of a device within a relatively small, local area). LBS examples include RFID applications and contactless payments using NFC-enabled smartphones.

- Chip-card-generated data (e.g., data generated from the use of payment cards or access cards, such as those used by employees to enter their workplace or members of the public using a metro system).

In its provision of services, Google identifies three broad categories of location data that it uses to deliver its services,[10] with varying levels of precision:

- *Implicit location information*: Google infers that a user is either interested in the place or that the user might be at the place. The inference could be made from a user manually typing a search query for a particular place. Implicit location information is used in a variety of ways. So, if the user types in 'Eiffel Tower', Google may infer that the user may like to see information for places around Paris and use that to provide recommendations about those local places in Paris.

- *Internet traffic information*: Information, such as an IP address, is usually assigned in country-based blocks so it can be used to at least identify the country of the user's device and so allow Google to do things such as to assume the correct language and locale for search queries.

- *Device-based location services*: Some products, such as turn-by-turn navigation in Google Maps for mobile, require more precise location information, and the user would need to enable device-based location services on their device. These are services that use information such as GPS signals, device sensors, Wi-Fi access points, and Cell IDs that can be used to derive or estimate precise locations.

15.7.1 Location data under the Regulation

Location data is referred to as an identifier in the definition of personal data, and so it is an attribute that may identify or lead to the identification of an individual. If location data can be used alone or in combination with other information to identify someone, then it should be considered to be personal data.

The security of location data has raised concerns. Location may be a major function of a mobile app, such as in dating apps or multi-user gaming, but the user's location may be employed for harmful purposes, such as stalking or harassment.[11] A user may have switched off location services on their device, but if vulnerabilities in a mobile app can be exploited, then the user of the app may unwittingly give away their location.

An app developer would need to decide whether the use of an app that makes use of location data may result in a high risk to the user of the app and so trigger the requirement to complete a DPIA (see Chapter 11).

Location data may also allow the tracking of an individual in real time through an app or from the records maintained by the mobile operators. Location history may allow certain information to be inferred about an individual—from the places an individual visits, be it the home of friends, a church or a clinic, it may be possible to make certain inferences about an individual's political opinions, religious beliefs or medical conditions. Privacy advocates raise concerns about the retention and access by public authorities to such information and push for further controls and oversight to such access to strengthen national laws that govern surveillance activities beyond the Regulation and LEDP Directive.[12]

In the employment context, a company may want to use location data to better manage its fleet of vehicles. An example would be for a delivery service where there is a requirement to maximise the route for deliveries that are to be made and to monitor progress. However, it is not just the vehicle that is being tracked, but also the driver, and so the location data could be considered to be the personal data of that driver. If the data is to be used for any purpose that relates to the employee, then the requirements of the Regulation will need to be taken into account.

15.8 Conclusion

Technological development continues apace. In the future, we will only have more ways with which to gather data about the actions of individuals, with resulting stockpiles of personal data triggering further data protection and privacy concerns. Rather than focus on the risks presented by any one particular surveillance technology, it is important to apply the basic principles of the GDPR to any data gathering activity: Are you transparent in your collection, are you minimising the data you collect, do you have legitimate reasons for processing the data, and so forth? This, above all, will keep you in good stead.

Endnotes

1 Charter of Fundamental Rights of the European Union (2000/C 364/01), *Official Journal of the European Communities,* www.europarl.europa.eu/charter/pdf/text_en.pdf.

2 Directive 2016/680 of the European Parliament and of the Council on the protection of natural persons with regard to the processing of personal data by competent authorities for the purposes of the prevention, investigation, detection or prosecution of criminal offences or the execution of criminal penalties, and on the free movement of such data, and repealing Council Framework Decision, 27 April 2016, http://eur-lex.europa.eu/legal-content/EN/TXT/?uri=CELEX:32016L0680.

3 Loideain, Nora Ni, 'EU Law and Mass Internet Metadata Surveillance in the Post-Snowden Era', *Media and Communication (ISSN: 2183-2439),* 2015, Volume 3, Issue 2, pages 53–62, http://dx.doi.org/10.17645/mac.v3i2.297.

4 Ibid.

5 Digital Rights Ireland Ltd. v. Minister for Communications, Marine and Natural Resources, Minister for Justice, Equality and Law Reform, Commissioner of the Garda Síochána, Ireland, The Attorney General, and Kärntner Landesregierung, Michael Seitlinger, Christof Tschohl and others, [2014] C293/12 and C594/12, 8 April 2014, http://curia.europa.eu/juris/document/document.jsf?text=&docid=150642&pageIndex=0&doclang=EN&mode=lst&dir=&occ=first&part=1&cid=717066.

6 'Dactyloscopy' means 'identification by comparison of fingerprints', Merriam-Webster, n.d. Web, accessed 29 June 2017, https://www.merriam-webster.com/medical/dactyloscopy.

7 Biometrics Institute, FAQ 2, accessed June 2017, www.biometricsinstitute.org/pages/faq-2.html.

8 Biometrics Institute, FAQ 13, accessed June 2017, www.biometricsinstitute.org/pages/faq-13.html.

9 See further Future of Identity in the Information Society (FIDIS), 'D11.5: The legal framework for location-based services in Europe', WP 11 Cuijpers C., Roosendaal, A., Koops, B.J. (eds), 2007, Chapter 3.

10 Google: Privacy & Terms, 'Types of location data used by Google', accessed June 2017, https://www.google.com/policies/technologies/location-data/.

11 'Dating apps found "leaking' location data", BBC News, 19 January 2015, www.bbc.co.uk/news/technology-30880534.

12 'On Locational Privacy, and How to Avoid Losing it Forever', Electronic Frontier Foundation, 3 August 2009, https://www.eff.org/wp/locational-privacy.

CHAPTER 16

Direct Marketing

Wouter Seinen, CIPP/E

16.1 Data protection and direct marketing

The application of data protection rules in the context of direct marketing is perhaps one of the most complex and technically challenging areas of data protection law. The main reason for this is that direct marketing often not only triggers data protection requirements but also all kinds of other consumer protection regulatory requirements that vary from country to country. In addition, direct marketing often involves the use of data collected through the addressee's device, such as location data from its smartphone or data collected through cookies. Finally, direct marketing messages are no longer limited to postal mail and email but are also sent via third platform messages, push messages and in-app messaging.

As a result, data controllers often find themselves struggling to navigate the bewildering array of opt-in and opt-out consent requirements that apply across the spectrum of marketing communication channels.

Failure to have a clear understanding of how data protection applies to direct marketing can be detrimental to both individuals and to business. Businesses that do not collect appropriate marketing consents may end up sending direct marketing communications to individuals who do not want to receive them, attracting both legal compliance risk and potential brand damage as a direct consequence. Conversely, a business with an overly strict application of data protection rules may impose unnecessary restrictions on its ability to send legitimate marketing communications.

In addition to data protection concerns, data controllers must be aware that other national laws, regulations and codes may also apply to their direct marketing communications.[2] These are beyond the scope of this chapter and typically concern the laws around advertising and the content of marketing communications, such as truth-in-advertising laws. Moreover, aside from data protection requirements, another layer of regulatory requirements may apply to direct marketing and govern when and how an individual's personal data may be used— sometimes imposing stricter standards than those required by data protection law alone. Examples are the regulations on unsolicited commercial messages ('anti-spam') and the use of cookies and similar technologies on web pages, emails and push notifications.

Data controllers must therefore remember to meet all national rules applicable to the direct marketing communications they send. The applicable laws may be those of the country in which the sender is located or where the recipient lives, or indeed both.

16.1.1 The concept of direct marketing

Not all communications from a business—even a marketing business—are considered direct marketing. The Article 29 Working Party (WP29) has provided guidance on the scope of the term 'direct marketing' and considers it to include any form of sales promotion, even including direct marketing by charities and political organisations (e.g., for fund-raising purposes).[3] However, the direct marketing message does not need to offer something for sale; it could be a promotion of a free offer or just promote the sender's organisation in some way—the definition of marketing is broad.

In order to fall under the scope of 'direct marketing', the communication, by whatever means of any advertising or marketing material, should be directed to particular individuals. This means that data protection laws apply to the sending of marketing messages only where individuals' personal data is processed in order to communicate the marketing message to them.

The following marketing messages are not considered direct marketing:

- *Marketing communications that are not directed at individuals* (e.g., untargeted website banner advertisements or mailings send out to companies without contact persons being mentioned): These are not subject to data protection compliance.

- *Messages that are purely service related in nature* (i.e., messages sent to individuals to inform them, for example, about the status of an order they have placed): These messages therefore do not need to comply with the specific rules applicable to direct marketing, but the associated processing of personal data will be subject to data protection compliance in general.

16.1.2 Digital and non-digital marketing

Both the Data Protection Directive ('Directive') and its successor, the General Data Protection Regulation (GDPR, or 'Regulation'), specifically address the processing of personal data to send direct marketing. In addition, when direct marketing is sent over electronic communications networks, the ePrivacy Directive (Directive 2002/58/EC) also applies. In other words:

- The Directive and Regulation, respectively, apply to all direct marketing communications—whether communicated by post, phone, fax, electronic mail or otherwise. They also apply to online advertising targeted at individuals based on their Internet browsing history (see Section 16.7 on online behavioural advertising).

- The ePrivacy Directive applies to 'digital' marketing communications—that is, direct marketing communicated over electronic communications networks, such as by phone, fax, email and SMS/MMS; it does not apply to postal marketing. The ePrivacy Directive also specifies rules that impact the use of online behavioural advertising.

16.1.3 Marketing requirements under the Regulation

Whenever processing an individual's personal data in the context of direct marketing activities, data controllers must satisfy all their compliance responsibilities under the Regulation. These include:

- Ensuring there is a lawful basis for the collection and use of the data subjects' personal data (the 'lawful processing requirement'). Normally, this is either the data subject's unambiguous consent or reliance on the 'legitimate interests' processing condition.[4]

- Providing individuals with fair processing information explaining that their personal data will be used for marketing purposes (the 'transparency requirement').

- Implementing appropriate technical and organisational measures to protect the personal data processed, including written contracts that contain appropriate data protection obligations with any service providers that send direct marketing on the data controller's behalf, such as external advertising agencies, mail house services and others.

- Not exporting personal data outside of the European Economic Area (EEA) unless adequate protection is in place on its receipt. For example, contact lists should not be sent to overseas advertising agencies to send marketing communications on the data controller's behalf without ensuring adequate protection is in place.

- Fully satisfying all other compliance duties under the Regulation.

These requirements are described in more detail in earlier chapters.

16.1.4 Right to opt out

The Directive requires that individuals must have a specific right to refuse or opt out of direct marketing sent by the data controller.[5] This requirement is already applicable in cases where the personal data is processed on the basis of the data subject's consent as any consent can be withdrawn at any time.

The Regulation makes it clear, however, that the opt-out also applies if the data collection and further processing is based on the 'legitimate interest' processing condition.

Moreover, the Regulation requires that:

- Individuals are always informed of their right to opt out. At the time of the first communication with the data subject, the right shall be explicitly brought to the attention of the data subject and shall be presented clearly and separately from any other information.

- Marketers must allow individuals to opt out across all marketing channels. Individuals must be able to opt out of all forms of direct marketing, no matter how they are sent. The right to opt out applies to direct marketing by post, phone, electronic mail or in any other way.

- Data controllers honour opt-out requests in a timely fashion and at no cost to the individual. Data controllers most promptly follow up on an individual's opt-out request and cannot unduly postpone or delay it. Moreover, they cannot impose charges or penalties on individuals who choose to exercise their opt-out rights (by, for example, requiring that individuals send a premium rate text to opt out). Minor incidental costs incurred in transmitting an opt-out request will not prevent the opt-out mechanism from being free of charge (e.g., the individual's Internet provider charges for sending an opt-out request by email).

- Personal data be deleted unless retention is strictly required. The controller must delete all personal information relating to the data subject that it has on record. There are exceptions to this rule; for example, a controller can keep personal data if retention is necessary or for the establishment, exercise or defence of legal claims. Moreover, it will be exempted from the deletion requirement if it can demonstrate that it has 'compelling legitimate grounds' for continue processing, which outweigh the controller's interest override the privacy interests of the data subject.

- Profiling data must be removed, as well. On opt-out, the controller must cease the use of any profiling data relating to the data subject, unless one of the above exemptions can be relied on.[6]

Where individuals choose to exercise their opt-out right, data controllers should suppress rather than delete their contact details. By deleting their details, data controllers run the risk that they may reacquire those individuals' details at a later date and begin marketing to them again, contrary to their expressed opt-out wish. By instead suppressing individuals' details, data controllers retain a record that those individuals must not be sent any marketing communications, unless and until they change their mind and opt back in at a later date. This may be done via a list in marketing automation software that ensures emails are not sent to certain addresses.

For this reason, data controllers should always cleanse, cross-reference and update their marketing contact lists against their internal opt-out records before initiating any direct marketing communications. Where data controllers' opt-out records indicate that intended contacts have previously opted out of direct marketing, the data controllers should not send those individuals any further direct marketing or contact them to invite them to opt back in to direct marketing.

In addition, many member states have implemented national opt-out registers (commonly referred to as a 'Robinson List' or a 'preference service') that allow individuals to submit a global opt-out from all direct marketing over a particular communication channel, regardless of the originator of the marketing (in many EU member states, separate preference services exist for mail, telephone and fax). In most instances, member states' national data protection rules require data controllers to cleanse their marketing contact lists against the applicable national opt-out registers, as well as their own internal opt-out records, before conducting direct marketing campaigns—particularly for direct marketing that is otherwise permitted on an opt-out basis. Member states may offer different categories of Robinson Lists, but the law does not in all cases require marketers to check these. For example, in the UK, there's the Mail Preference Service (MPS) for postal marketing, but there's no legal requirement to cleanse a marketing database against this. For clarity, failure to cleanse a Robinson List is generally not a breach of data protection laws but only a violation of specific national laws. Of course, if the controller has collected a valid opt-in consent from the individual, this overrides the opt-out on the Robinson List.

16.1.5 Marketing requirements under the ePrivacy Directive

As noted above, when sending digital marketing, data controllers must also comply with the specific rules set out in the ePrivacy Directive.[7] This imposes consent and information requirements to marketing by phone, fax and electronic mail, including SMS and instant messaging but also to push notifications and other messages.

The general rule is that most forms of digital marketing, other than person-to-person telephone marketing, require the prior opt-in consent of the intended recipient, although a limited exemption exists for email marketing communicated on an opt-out basis to individuals whose details the data controller collected in the context of the sale of a product or service.

The specific rules that apply to each of the different marketing communication channels are discussed in more detail below. The ePrivacy Directive also imposes particular rules that impact location-based marketing and data controllers' ability to use cookies for online behavioural advertising (OBA).

Note that the principles and provisions of the ePrivacy Directive, as opposed to the Regulation, do not have direct effect but were implemented in national laws of the EU member states. Some countries in the EU have implemented the ePrivacy Directive in their data protection laws, whereas others have chosen to implement the Directive's provisions in telecommunications laws. Similarly, the enforcement of the ePrivacy rules is in some countries left to the telecommunications regulator, where, in other countries, the data protection authority (DPA) was given this task. Internationally operating organisations should consider that there are significant differences in how the ePrivacy Directive is interpreted and how rigorously it is enforced.

16.2 Postal marketing

As postal marketing is not digital marketing, it is not subject to the requirements of the ePrivacy Directive. The processing of contact details and other personal information that goes with a direct marketing activity is, of course, regulated by data protection laws. Marketers must therefore ensure that they satisfy the general requirements under national data protection laws and the Regulation. These include ensuring lawful processing, satisfying the transparency requirement respecting opt-out requests and other data subjects' rights.

16.2.1 Consent requirements

There is no express requirement in the ePrivacy Directive to obtain individuals' consent to send direct postal marketing. However, some member states' national rules nevertheless mandate a requirement for consent (e.g., Belgium, Greece and Spain).

In the absence of a mandated national requirement to obtain consent, data controllers may instead look to rely on their legitimate interests as an alternative lawful ground to send direct postal marketing. This considers a careful balancing exercise between the interests of the data controller and the fundamental rights and freedoms of the individual. Factors to consider include:

- Whether the individual is an existing customer of the data controller, making it more likely that the individual would expect to receive marketing from the data controller.

- The nature of the products and services that the data controller wishes to market and, in particular, whether the individual would have an expectation that the data controller would send them marketing about those products and services.

- Whether the data controller has previously told the individual that it will not send any direct marketing communications. Again, in this circumstance, the individual should not be sent any marketing.

If, taking into account the above and any other relevant factors, the data controller finds itself unable to rely on legitimate interests, consent will normally be needed to legitimise the sending of direct postal marketing.

In some member states (e.g., Austria, Denmark and the Netherlands), data controllers must cleanse their contact lists against applicable national opt-out registers before sending direct postal marketing unless the controller has a valid opt-in consent from the individual. Individuals listed on national opt-out registers should not be sent direct postal marketing in this circumstance. In other member states, clearance against national opt-out registers may be necessary to comply with self-regulatory marketing standards (e.g., the Direct Marketing Association's Code of Practice in the UK) or be advisable as a matter of good practice, even if not required by law.

16.3 Telephone marketing

Telephone marketing ('telemarketing') is a form of digital marketing and is therefore subject to the requirements of the ePrivacy Directive. In addition, data controllers must ensure that they satisfy the general compliance requirements of the Regulation when processing individuals' personal data to market by telephone, including the transparency requirement and the lawful processing requirement.

16.3.1 Consent requirements

There is no express requirement in the ePrivacy Directive to obtain individuals' consent for person-to-person telephone marketing, although consent is necessary for automated calling systems (see Section 16.3.2). Instead, Article 13(3) of the ePrivacy Directive allows member states to decide under their national laws whether person-to-person telephone marketing should be conducted on an opt-in or an opt-out basis.

However, Article 13(3) does require that, at a minimum, member states ensure that individuals have a means by which to opt out free of charge from direct telephone marketing. For this reason, most member states have implemented national opt-out registers for telephone marketing. Member states that permit telephone marketing on an opt-out basis (e.g., the UK and Ireland[8]) normally require that data controllers first cleanse their call lists against the applicable national opt-out register(s).

In addition, some countries require telephone marketers to, in each call, mention the national opt-out register and offer the individual the right to be registered at once and at no charge.

Other member states have gone even further and instead mandated a requirement for prior opt-in consent before data controllers may contact an individual by telephone for direct marketing purposes (this is the case in Austria, Hungary and Slovenia, for example).

The takeaway of all this is that rules and best practices around telephone marketing vary from country to country. Opt-in is the safe option, but various countries offer options to call individuals without having their prior consent. The conditions cannot always be found in national data protection laws as they are sometimes laid down in specific laws not related to data protection. A marketer should be aware not to deploy 'one-size-fits-all' approach, unless it would choose to seek prior consent across the board.

16.3.2 Automated calling systems

Data controllers must always obtain individuals' prior opt-in consent to use automated calling systems for direct telephone marketing. These are systems that automatically dial the individual's telephone number and then play a pre-recorded message when the recipient answers the call.[9] This does not restrict the use of automatic dialling technology to call target numbers in order to facilitate live person-to-person conversations.

In addition, laws of some member states (e.g., the Poland and the UK) require that marketing communications delivered in this way provide the identity and contact details of the caller.

16.3.3 B2B versus B2C telephone marketing

The treatment and permissibility of business-to-business (B2B) direct telephone marketing varies amongst member states. Some member states do not distinguish between B2B and business-to-consumer (B2C) marketing, whilst others apply a more relaxed approach to B2B marketing.[10]

The Regulation will apply whenever an individual's personal data is processed to instigate direct telephone marketing, and this will be equally true when processing employees' contact details for B2B marketing. Data controllers must therefore have a lawful basis under the Regulation to process employees' personal data before instigating B2B telephone marketing to those employees.

The restrictions to unsolicited telephone marketing under the ePrivacy Directive apply, as from 2009, both to B2C and B2B communications. This means that there is not generic exception for B2B phone marketing.

Where national laws differentiate between B2C and B2B phone marketing and permit B2B calls on an opt-out basis, data controllers may still be required under national law to cleanse their intended phone marketing contacts against a central opt-out register. This is the case, for example, in the UK, where it is a legal requirement for marketers to cleanse their marketing contact lists against the Corporate Telephone Preference Service before making B2B direct marketing calls.[11] Data controllers must always therefore check member states' national requirements to understand the rules that apply to their marketing campaigns, regardless whether they target business contacts or private individuals.

16.4 Marketing by electronic mail, including email, SMS and MMS

Electronic mail marketing is a form of digital marketing and is therefore subject to the requirements of the ePrivacy Directive. In addition, data controllers must ensure that they satisfy the general compliance requirements of the Directive when processing individuals' personal data to send electronic mail marketing, including the transparency requirement and the lawful processing requirement.

16.4.1 Meaning of electronic mail

The ePrivacy Directive defines the term 'electronic mail' to mean 'any text, voice, sound or image message sent over a public communications network which can be stored in the network or in the recipient's terminal equipment until it is collected by the recipient'.[12] The 'technology neutral' definition of this term is wide enough to include direct marketing by email, SMS and MMS, and the rules that apply to email marketing therefore apply equally to marketing by SMS and MMS.[13]

16.4.2 Consent requirements

The ePrivacy Directive requires that, in general, data controllers must obtain prior (opt-in) consent from individuals to send them marketing by electronic mail.[14] Typically, data controllers achieve this by presenting individuals with a 'fair processing notice' at the time their data is collected that asks them to agree to direct marketing by electronic mail—for example, 'We would like to contact you by email and SMS with details of other products and services that we think may interest you. Please tick the box below if you agree to receive this'.

16.4.3 The opt-out exception

The ePrivacy Directive allows a limited exemption from this strict opt-in requirement for direct marketing by electronic mail to individuals whose details the data controller obtained 'in the context of the sale of a product or service' (sometimes known as the 'soft opt-in' rule). This allows data controllers to send electronic mail marketing on an opt-out basis provided that:

- the data controller obtained the individuals' electronic mail contact details 'in the context of the sale of a product or a service';

- the data controller sends direct marketing to those individuals about 'its own similar products or services' only; and

- the data controller clearly and distinctly gave those individuals the opportunity to opt out of marketing by electronic mail in a way that is simple and free of charge both at the time their details were initially collected and in each subsequent marketing communication.

These are some key points to note from the opt-out exception requirements:

- *Individuals' details must be collected 'in the context of the sale of a product or a service'*: Differences exist between member states as to the scope of the words 'in the context of the sale of a product or a service'. Some member states (e.g., Austria, Belgium and Denmark) apply this rule literally, requiring that individuals' contact details must have been collected during the course of a sale transaction. Other member states (e.g., the Netherlands and the UK) interpret this requirement more broadly and also apply it to contact details obtained where no sales were made (e.g., pre-sales communications, registering a website account or submitting a competition).

- *The controller must market its own similar products and services:* Subsequent marketing communications that rely on the 'soft opt-in' requirement must be sent by the data controller that collected those individuals' details—the data controller cannot share the individuals' details with third parties (e.g., affiliated group companies) for the purposes of their direct marketing. In addition, the data controller must be marketing similar products and services to those in connection with which the individual supplied its details—a data controller cannot, for example, sell an individual certain products or services and then rely on the opt-out exception to send information about different products or services when this is not within the expectations of that individual.

- *Individuals must have the ability to opt out at the time their contact details are collected:* At the point that individuals' details are collected, they must have an easy, free-of-charge way to decline marketing by electronic mail. Typically, this will be through a tick box displayed at the point of data capture with an appropriate disclosure that informs the individual that their details will be used for electronic mail marketing unless they tick the box to opt out (e.g., 'We would like to contact you by email and text message with details of other products and services we think will interest you. If you do not want to receive this, please tick the box below').

- *Individuals must be reminded of their ability to opt out in each subsequent marketing communication:* All electronic mail marketing communications sent to individuals in reliance on the opt-out exception must remind them of their right to opt out. For example, this may be done by including language at the bottom of the marketing communication that instructs users how they may opt out (e.g., 'If you do not wish to receive further marketing emails from us, please click here').

16.4.4 Information requirements

When sending direct electronic mail marketing, the ePrivacy Directive requires that data controllers provide individuals with a valid address to which they can send an opt-out request.[15] This opt-out address should be appropriate to the medium by which the marketing communication was sent—so, for email marketing, data controllers normally provide an opt-out email address or an opt-out hypertext link; for SMS or MMS marketing, data controllers normally provide a mobile short code to which individuals can send an opt-out request (e.g., 'Text STOP to 12345').

In addition to this requirement, data controllers:

- must not conceal or disguise the identity of the sender on whose behalf the communication is made;

- must ensure that the message is clearly identifiable as a commercial communication—it should not, for example, attempt to present itself as a personal communication to the recipient;

- must ensure that any promotional offers, such as discounts, premiums and gifts, are clearly identifiable as such and that the conditions to qualify for them are easily accessible and presented clearly and unambiguously; and

- must ensure that any promotional competitions or games, if permitted at all in the relevant member state, are clearly identifiable as such and that the conditions for participation are easily accessible and presented clearly and unambiguously.[16]

16.4.5 B2B versus B2C marketing by electronic mail

As with direct telephone marketing, the treatment and permissibility of B2B direct electronic mail marketing varies amongst member states.

As noted above, the Regulation will apply when processing employees' contact details for B2B marketing. Data controllers must therefore have a lawful basis under the Regulation to process employees' personal data before instigating B2B email marketing to those employees.

16.5 Fax marketing

Fax marketing is a form of digital marketing and is therefore subject to the requirements of the ePrivacy Directive. In addition, data controllers must also ensure that they satisfy the general compliance requirements of the Directive when processing individuals' personal data to send fax marketing, including the transparency requirement and the lawful processing requirement.

16.5.1 Consent requirements

The ePrivacy Directive requires that, in general, data controllers obtain prior (opt-in) consent from individuals in order to send them fax marketing.[17] As with opt-in consent for electronic mail marketing, data controllers typically achieve this by presenting the individual with a 'fair processing notice' at the time his or her personal data is collected that asks them to agree to direct fax marketing (e.g., 'We would like to contact you by fax with details of other products and services that we think may interest you. Please tick the box below if you agree to receive this').

16.5.2 B2B versus B2C fax marketing

As with direct telephone and electronic mail marketing, the treatment and permissibility of B2B direct fax marketing varies amongst member states.

As noted above, the Regulation applies when processing employees' contact details for B2B marketing. Data controllers must therefore have a lawful basis under the Regulation to process employees' personal data before instigating B2B fax marketing to those employees.

Note that where member states currently permit B2B fax marketing on an opt-out basis, data controllers may be required under national law to cleanse their intended fax marketing contacts against a central opt-out register. This is the case, for example, in the UK, where it is a legal requirement for marketers to cleanse their marketing contact lists against the Fax Preference Service before making B2B direct marketing calls.[18] Therefore, data controllers must always check member states' national requirements to understand the rules that apply to B2B marketing campaigns.

16.6 Location-based marketing

In a world of smartphones and connected cars and at the rise of the Internet of Things (IoT) era, location-based marketing is becoming an ever-more-important tool for marketers to reach their audiences. Individuals passing by their local coffee shop may receive an invitation for a free coffee, whilst those passing retail outlets may be offered a discount to enter the store and do some shopping. Location-based services have also become important in the context of social networking—individuals can find out who of their friends happen to be nearby so they can arrange to meet up.

16.6.1 Compliance with the Regulation and the ePrivacy Directive

The Regulation applies whenever the use of location data involves processing of personal data and therefore will apply in most, if not all, instances of location-based marketing. Data controllers must therefore ensure that they satisfy the general compliance requirements of this Regulation when processing individuals' personal data in the context of location-based marketing, including the transparency requirement and the lawful processing requirement.

In addition, the ePrivacy Directive mandates specific consent and opt-out provisions when individuals' location data is processed.

16.6.2 Meaning of location data

The ePrivacy Directive defines the term 'location data' to mean 'any data processed in an electronic communications network or by an electronic communications service, indicating the geographic position of the terminal equipment of a user of a publicly available electronic communications service'. This includes information about the latitude, longitude, altitude and direction of travel of the individual's terminal equipment.

The rules on location data processing under the ePrivacy Directive apply only to data revealing the geographic position of an individual's 'terminal equipment' (i.e., their smartphone or computer terminal)—not the location of the person. This can be an important distinction when, for example, a data controller wishes to process location information, but that information does not relate to the location of the individual's terminal equipment (e.g., where friends upload details of an individual's location onto a social networking site). In this instance, the location data rules of the ePrivacy Directive do not apply—although other privacy considerations still do.

16.6.3 Consent requirements

The ePrivacy Directive requires that individuals give opt-in consent to use their location data to provide a 'value-added service'.[19] This term is defined widely enough to include location-based marketing services, meaning that individuals must opt in to receiving location-based marketing.[20]

An exemption from this requirement for opt-in consent applies where the individual's location data is processed in anonymised form only. However, in the context of location-based marketing, this exemption is unlikely to apply.

16.6.4 Information requirements

To obtain valid consent from individuals to process their location data, data controllers must first inform them of:

- the types of location data that will be collected and processed;
- the purposes and duration of the processing; and

- whether the data will be transmitted to a third party for the purpose of providing the value-added service.[21]

App developers and online service providers struggle with the prior information requirement. Many apps use geo-location services and seek permission for such use by having the user of the app tick a box to allow the use of location data. Often, the use of such data for marketing data is not specifically mentioned. And, if it is, the screen would normally not allow for a detailed description of the data being processed, the purposes of processing and the opt-out process. Good practice is to include that information in the privacy policy relevant to the app.

16.6.5 Ability to withdraw consent

In addition to obtaining opt-in consent, data controllers must offer individuals the ability to withdraw their consent (or opt out) to use their location data for location-based marketing purposes. The means of opting out must be provided using means that are simple and free of charge, and must exist throughout the period during which the individuals' location data is processed. In particular, data controllers must offer:

- a right to opt out of having their location data processed for marketing purposes entirely; and

- a temporary right to opt out of having their location data processed for marketing purposes on each connection to the network or for each transmission of a communication.[22]

In addition to the above requirements, data controllers must only process location data to the extent and for the duration necessary to provide the value-added service.[23]

16.7 Online behavioural advertising

Online behavioural advertising (OBA) is website advertising that is targeted at individuals based on the observation of their behaviour over time. It enables advertisers to deliver advertising that is more relevant to individuals' likes and interests, and improves the effectiveness and click-through rates of online advertising.

16.7.1 How online behavioural advertising works

In some cases, OBA will be delivered by the website publisher itself ('first-party advertising')—a common example is where a publisher makes product recommendations to visitors based on their previous relationship with its website (e.g., an online bookstore that recommends novels to visitors based on their purchasing history).

Increasingly, however, website publishers are turning to third-party advertising networks to serve OBA on their behalf, and it is this type of relationship that often raises the most privacy issues—particularly as advertising networks may track individuals' behaviour across multiple, unaffiliated websites in order to target their advertising.

The technology powering OBA served by third-party advertising networks is very complex but, at a high level, works in the following way:

- Advertisers wishing to reach particular audiences instruct a third-party ad network to serve advertising on their behalf. The ad network has relationships with a number of partnering website publishers that allow it to serve advertising on their sites.

- When an individual visits a website that has partnered with the ad network, the ad network places a 'cookie' on the individual's computer.[24] The cookie is assigned a unique identifier, like a serial number, that is specific to that cookie.

- The ad network records the identifier assigned to that cookie in its database. It may also record other information about the individual, such as their IP address and type of browser used.

- As the individual browses the website, the ad network may record information about the content viewed, searches entered, adverts clicked on, and products and services purchased by the individual. It records this information against the unique identifier assigned to the individual's cookie and assigns a profile to that identifier (e.g., 'ABC12345: new mother' or 'DEF6789: young professional').

- When the individual later revisits the website or, alternatively, visits another website that has partnered with the ad network, the ad network examines the cookie it previously set on the individual's computer to determine its unique identifier. It then looks up the profile it recorded against that identifier to determine the individual's likely interests and delivers website advertising based on those interests.

16.7.2 OBA and the Regulation

Where there has been debate whether information collected for the purposes of OBA should qualify as 'personal data', the Regulation clearly states that this is the case. In the first place, the definition of 'personal data' specifically mentions reference to an online identifier as example of identifiable individuals. Second, the Regulation introduces the concept of 'profiling', which is defined as 'any form of automated processing of personal data consisting of the use of personal data to evaluate certain personal aspects relating to a natural person, in particular to analyse or predict aspects concerning that natural person's performance at work, economic situation, health, personal preferences, interests, reliability, behaviour, location or movements'.

During the legislative process, there were attempts to introduce significant restrictions on all profiling in the Regulation, but these have not been successful. However, Recital 72 does note that the European Data Protection Board (EDPB) may publish guidance on profiling. Until such further guidance, the data processed in the context of OBA will typically be considered 'personal data' and be subject to all requirements of the Regulation.

This is in line with the view of the WP29, as expressed in its opinion on online behavioural advertising.[25] It considered that, in many circumstances, OBA methods would entail the processing of personal data, noting that OBA 'allows the tracking of users of a specific computer even when dynamic IP addresses are used. In other words, [they] enable data subjects to be 'singled out', even if their real names are not known'.[26]

Assuming that information collected for the purposes of serving OBA is 'personal data', a related issue concerns which entity is the data controller in a third-party ad network arrangement—in other words, which entity must take responsibility for complying with the requirements of the Regulation. The WP29 considers that:

- Ad networks will often qualify as data controllers because they have complete control over the purposes and means for which website visitors' information is processed. In reaching this view, the WP29 noted that ad networks 'rent' space from publishers' websites to place adverts; they set and read cookie-related information and, in most cases, collect the IP address and possible other data that the browser may reveal. Further, the ad network providers use the information gathered on Internet users' surfing behaviour to build profiles and to select and deliver the ads to be displayed on the basis of this profile.

- A website publisher may qualify as a joint data controller with the ad network, although this will depend on the conditions of collaboration between the publisher and the ad network provider. However, by engaging ad networks to serve OBA through their websites, the WP29 considers that website publishers owe a certain degree of responsibility to their website visitors. The specific responsibilities that should fall to the website publisher will depend on the nature of its relationship with the ad network. Website publishers and ad networks should discuss and apportion their respective roles and responsibilities to visitors by, for example, agreeing contractually who will notify visitors that their personal data will be used to serve OBA and how visitors will be offered the ability to refuse OBA. Naturally, if the website publisher collects any further personal data about its visitors, such as website account registration details, then it will take on full responsibility to comply with the Regulation.

- Advertisers may qualify as an independent data controller in this scenario: An individual clicks on a targeted advert through to the advertiser's website; the advertiser then monitors the individual's subsequent browsing activity and combines it with the targeting profile relating to that individual (e.g., 'young mother', 'extreme sports fan').

The important point to note from this is that all parties to a third-party ad network relationship potentially may attract compliance responsibilities under the Regulation. The precise roles and the responsibilities that those roles will attract will depend on a case-by-case examination. Publishers, advertisers and ad networks should take care to ensure that compliance roles and responsibilities are properly considered and addressed within the service provision contracts they enter.

16.7.3 OBA and the ePrivacy Directive

The ePrivacy Directive will generally apply to OBA regardless of whether or not OBA information collected from individuals constitutes 'personal data'.

In this context, the key provision of the ePrivacy Directive is Article 5(3). This concerns the use of cookies and other devices to store or gain access to information on an individual's computer.[27] Article 5(3) was amended as part of the amendments made to the ePrivacy Directive by the Citizens' Rights Directive in November 2009.

Prior to its amendment, Article 5(3) allowed the placement of cookies provided that the individuals concerned received 'clear and comprehensive' information but not necessarily in advance about the use of cookies and were offered the right to refuse them. As a result, organisations have typically sought to achieve compliance with these requirements through privacy policy disclosures about the use of cookies and how individuals may refuse or delete cookies using their browser settings.

Following its amendment, however, Article 5(3) now states that the use of cookies to store or access information in an individual's computer is allowed only on the condition that the individual concerned has given their consent, having been provided with clear and comprehensive information.[28] In the view of the WP29, this requires the entity placing the cookie to obtain the individual's prior informed consent, meaning that:

- information about the sending and purposes of the cookie must be given to the individual; and

- the individual, having been provided with this information, has consented to receiving the cookie before it is placed or accessed.

The WP29 also stresses that, in addition to being prior and informed, an individual's consent must be a specific indication of their wishes, freely given and revocable.[29] It considers that consent should involve the active participation of the user; opt-out mechanisms, which typically involve a passive user, are generally insufficient to obtain implied consent in this context.[30]

Although the WP29's interpretation indicates that prior consent is required, Recital 66 of the Citizens' Rights Directive indicates that an individual's consent may be expressed through the use of browser or other application settings where this is 'technically possible and effective'. This is difficult to reconcile with the WP29's opinion and, indeed, the WP29 takes the view that, as most browsers do not block cookies by default and the average user is not always familiar with their browser settings, the use of browser settings is generally insufficient to obtain consent.

The amended Article 5(3) was implemented in national laws of the member states in many different flavours: Some countries, including Italy and Poland, impose a strict opt-in consent requirement in order to serve cookies. Other countries, including Germany, France and the UK, accept that consent may also be given in a more implied manner, such as the user continuing to use a website after having displayed information on the cookies served on it. In most member states, consent cannot be inferred from the user's browser settings, albeit that certain regulators would accept this, if proper information on the cookies used was displayed and the user is informed how it can change cookie consent settings.

Marketers and website publishers should be aware that most OBA solutions imply the use of third-party cookies. The website serving a third-party cookie should provide information on which cookies belongs to which third parties and where information on the processing by such third party can be found. Typically, this requirement would be satisfied by linking to the cookie statements of the third parties involved.

As there is no harmonised view on how cookie consent should be given, companies that are active in various member states should carefully consider the national regime and the available best practices to obtain consent for OBA-related cookies.

16.8 Enforcement

From the beginning, EU regulators have understood that, to be effective, the EU and member states would require means to enforce data protection.

16.8.1 Enforcement under the Regulation

Data controllers that fail to heed the compliance requirements of the Regulation and the ePrivacy Directive with regard to direct marketing, including online behavioural advertising, expose themselves to risk of enforcement, including possible:

- fines and administrative sanctions by national data protection authorities (DPAs); and

- civil and, in some instances, criminal liability.

The nature and likelihood of enforcement risk can vary significantly across member states. (See Chapter 13 for more information about enforcement risks under the Regulation.)

16.8.2 Enforcement under the ePrivacy Directive

Failure to comply with the requirements of the ePrivacy Directive will attract similar risks and liabilities to those under the Regulation. Member states are required under Article 15(2) of the ePrivacy Directive to apply the judicial remedies, liabilities and sanctions of the Regulation to infringements of the ePrivacy Directive. Again, the nature and likelihood of enforcement risk will vary amongst member states.

A specific factor to consider is that, in some EU member states, the enforcement of the regulations implementing the ePrivacy Directive is in the hands of consumer protection and telecoms regulators rather than the DPA. Such authorities may have different enforcement priorities, but they also tend to cooperate. In the Netherlands, for instance, this has resulted in a more vigorous enforcement of the rules on spam and cookie consent than of the general data protection requirements.

In addition, amendments made to the ePrivacy Directive by the Citizens' Rights Directive introduced a new right for individuals and businesses with a legitimate interest in the 'cessation or prohibition' of spam to bring a private right of action against noncompliant marketers. The expectation is that this new right will encourage a greater level of civil action against spam marketers—principally by Internet service providers (ISPs), who have deeper pockets than individuals and a clear interest in preventing flooding of their networks by spam messaging.

16.9 Conclusion

The specific mention of direct marketing and consideration for it in the Regulation are a clear indication that policymakers understand its importance to the business community. This importance, however, must be balanced by the risk to the rights and freedoms of data subjects. Further, it's important to note the distinction between the processing of personal data and the actual communication itself. They are separate things in the eyes of EU law, and careful consideration must be paid to both aspects when implementing direct marketing campaigns.

Further, it is important to look to the future. The coming ePrivacy Regulation, whenever it has finished working its way through the EU institutions, will present yet further obligations for those engaging in direct marketing campaigns.

Endnotes

1 The original version of this chapter was written by Phil Lee, it was updated by Wouter Seinen in January 2017 to address the Regulation. At the time of the update, the proposal for an ePrivacy Regulation was published, but as this regulation was not yet adopted, this chapter does not reflect any changes introduced by the future ePrivacy Regulation.

2 For example, national implementations of the Unfair Commercial Practices Directive (2005/29/EC) or industry self-regulatory rules, such as the UK Code of Non-broadcast Advertising and Direct & Promotional Marketing (CAP Code) and the Dutch Advertising Code in the Netherlands.

3 Working Party Opinion 5/2004 on unsolicited communications for marketing purposes (11601/EN: WP 90) at Paragraph 3.3.

4 General Data Protection Regulation, Article 6(1)(a) and 6(1)(f). General Data Protection Regulation, Recital 47 explicitly states that 'the processing of personal data for direct marketing purposes may be regarded as carried out for a legitimate interest'.

5 Data Protection Directive, Article 14(b).

6 'Profiling' means any form of automated processing of personal data consisting of the profiling means: use of personal data to evaluate certain personal aspects relating to a natural person, in particular to analyse or predict aspects concerning that natural person's performance at work, economic situation, health, personal preferences, interests, reliability, behaviour, location or movements (see General Data Protection Regulation, Article 4.4).

7 At the time of publication, the proposal for a ePrivacy Regulation was published, but as this is still a draft, which is subject to change, it is not discussed in this chapter.

8 Telephone Preference Service, www.tpsonline.org.uk/tps/, and Frequently asked questions about marketing calls and the National Directory Database from a subscriber's perspective, Data Protection Commissioner, www.dataprotection.ie/viewdoc.asp?DocID=279.

9 ePrivacy Directive, Article 13(1).

10 Germany, for example, permits B2B telephone marketing on the basis of implied (opt-out) consent while requiring express opt-in for B2C telephone marketing. The UK also permits B2B telephone

marketing on an opt-out basis, provided that the data controller first cleanses its call list against a centralised opt-out register for corporate subscribers maintained by the UK Direct Marketing Association.

11 Regulations 21 and 26, Privacy and Electronic Communications (EC Directive), Regulations 2003 (as amended).

12 ePrivacy Directive, Article 2(h).

13 See Working Party Opinion 5/2004 on unsolicited communications for marketing purposes (11601/EN: WP 90) at Section 3.1 for additional categories of electronic communications that fall within the definition of electronic mail.

14 ePrivacy Directive, Article 13(1); see Section 3.3.5 ante.

15 ePrivacy Directive, Article 13(4).

16 Article 6 of Directive 2000/31/EC (the e-Commerce Directive) and Article 13(4) of the ePrivacy Directive.

17 ePrivacy Directive, Article 13(1); see Section 3.3.5 ante.

18 Regulations 20 and 25, Privacy and Electronic Communications (EC Directive), Regulations 2003 (as amended).

19 See also Working Party Opinion 13/2011 on Geolocation services on smart mobile devices (881/11/EN: WP 185).

20 ePrivacy Directive, Article 9.

21 ePrivacy Directive, Article 9(1).

22 ePrivacy Directive, Article 9(2).

23 ePrivacy Directive, Article 9(3).

24 A 'cookie' is a small text file that is served by a website server onto the computers of visitors to its website. They enable the website to store certain information about those individuals on their computers, which can then be accessed and used by the website at a later time (e.g., website preferences and log-in details). Cookies are typically used to tailor website offerings and to maintain the security of individuals while they are logged in to online accounts. However, they can also be used to facilitate targeted advertising in the manner described above.

25 Article 29 Working Party Opinion on online behavioural advertising (00909/10/EN: WP 171).

26 Ibid., page 9.

27 For example, local shared objects or flash cookies.

28 Limited exemptions to this general rule apply for the use of cookies (1) for the sole purpose of carrying out or facilitating the transmission of a communication over an electronic communications network; and (2) when the use of cookies is strictly necessary to provide a service explicitly requested by the individual (e.g., to store items within an online shopping basket). These exemptions are very unlikely to apply where cookies are used for OBA, however.

29 Article 29 Working Party Opinion on online behavioural advertising (00909/10/EN: WP 171), page 13.

30 Ibid., page 16.

Internet Technology and Communications

Nick Westbrook

17.1 Introduction

The Internet has transformed our ability to collect, transmit and share data globally. Its potential has been harnessed by a plethora of new technologies, which have fundamentally altered almost every aspect of our society. But with power comes responsibility. In this chapter, we look at several categories of Internet technologies, and how EU data protection concepts and requirements apply to them.

17.2 Cloud computing

'Cloud computing' refers to the provision of information technology services over the Internet. These services may be provided by a company for its users in a 'private cloud' or by third-party suppliers. The services can include software, infrastructure (i.e., servers), hosting and platforms (i.e., operating systems). Cloud computing has numerous applications, from personal webmail to corporate data storage, and can be subdivided into different types of service models:

- Infrastructure as a service (IaaS), where the supplier simply provides remote access to and use of physical computing resources, and the user is responsible for implementing and maintaining both the operating platform and all applications.

- Platform as a service (PaaS), where the supplier provides access to and use of operating platforms, as well as the underlying hardware, but the user remains responsible for implementing and maintaining applications.

- Software as a service (SaaS), where the supplier provides the infrastructure, platform and application.

All these types of cloud service commonly have the following features:

- The service's infrastructure is shared amongst the supplier's customers and can be located in a number of countries.

- Customer data is transferred around the infrastructure according to capacity.

- The supplier determines the location, security measures and service standards applicable to the processing.

In traditional computing, an organisation's operating system, programmes and data are stored on the computer itself or on a company's own servers. Cloud services significantly change that model; those systems, programmes and/or data are now stored in a number of locations around the world, either managed privately by an organisation for its own users or through a service provider.

Although there is no specific legislative instrument regulating cloud computing, the technologically neutral General Data Protection Regulation (GDPR, or 'Regulation') is applicable in establishing a controller's obligations.

17.2.1 Applicable law

Under Article 3, the Regulation applies where either:

- the processing relates to the activities of an EU establishment of the controller; or

- the processing relates to offering goods or services to individuals in the EU, or to monitoring their behaviour, even when the controller or processor is not established in the Union.

The first of these tests is retained from the Data Protection Directive 95/46/EC ('Directive'), which the Regulation replaces. However, recent cases from the European Court of Justice (ECJ) have interpreted that test very broadly. In Weltimmo, the ECJ provided direction on what constitutes an 'establishment', stating that this was to be interpreted based on the degree of stability of the arrangements, and whether there is an effective exercise of activities.[1] Weltimmo was a Slovakian company operating a website that provided real estate brokering services in Hungary. The ECJ found that Weltimmo would have an 'establishment' in Hungary for the purposes of the Directive if it had:

- a website targeting Hungary and using the Hungarian language;

- a representative in Hungary for representation in court proceedings and for debt collection;

- a letter box in Hungary; and

- a Hungarian bank account.

This case therefore confirms that even minimal activities in a European member state can be sufficient to constitute an establishment for the purposes of European data protection law.

Recent case law also indicates that an economic link between a non-EU data controller processing personal data and an EU-based establishment is likely to mean that the activities of the data controller are subject to the Regulation (see Section 17.4.2 for a discussion of Google v. Spain).

The second limb of the Article 3 test was not contained in the Directive and represents a significant expansion in the applicability of European data protection law. Its effect is that any controller or processor whose use of personal data relates to monitoring the behaviour of or offering services to EU-based individuals will be covered by the Regulation without the need to consider whether there is an EU establishment.

Cloud service providers must consider whether either of these tests bring part or all of their processing operations under the remit of European data protection law. Even where these processing operations are not directly subject to the Regulation, if their customers are subject to the Regulation, those customers will be obliged to impose strict data processing contracts on the cloud service provider which contain many of the same controls on how personal data may be used (see Section 17.2.3).

17.2.2 Controller or processor?

As discussed in Chapter 4 of this book and defined in Article 4 of the Regulation, a controller is a 'natural or legal person, public authority, agency or any other body which, alone or jointly with others, determines the purposes and means of processing'. Key to this definition is the ability to decide how and why personal data is processed. When this decision is made jointly by different entities, those entities are joint controllers.

In contrast, a processor is a natural or legal person, public authority, agency or any other body other than an employee of the controller that processes data on behalf of a controller, acting on the instructions of the controller.

This distinction is important because controllers or joint controllers have significantly more data protection obligations than processors under the Regulation. Applying these definitions in most 'supply of services' situations results in the customer being a controller, because the customer decides on the purposes and means of processing. The supplier, acting on the instructions of the customer, is typically a processor, although in the context of cloud computing, this cannot be assumed.

The Article 29 Working Party (WP29) has stated that, although the determination of the purpose of processing would confer the status of controller, the determination of the technical and organisational means of processing (e.g., decisions on hardware) could be delegated to a processor without that processor becoming a controller. However, the determination of some 'substantial' and 'essential' elements of the means of processing, such as data retention periods, could result in the party making such decisions being considered a controller.[2] The WP29 has also noted that, where a cloud service supplier processes data for its own purposes, it will be a controller of that data.[3]

It is therefore possible for a cloud service supplier to exercise discretion regarding the technical and organisational means of processing without becoming a controller, providing it does not process customer data for its own purposes. However, where a processor determines aspects of the processing outside the controller's instructions, it will become a controller. This is increasingly relevant as cloud service providers look to make use of their customers' personal data for their own purposes (e.g., to develop or improve their services).

The extent of each party's right to determine the means of processing is likely to depend on a factual analysis of the processing and will, in part, involve an assessment of the services contract, although the contractual relationship in isolation will not be conclusive, as this could allow the parties to allocate a controller's responsibilities artificially.[4] It is therefore advisable to clearly define the scope of processing mandated by the controller and the role of the supplier. The extent to which decisions about the processing are delegated to the processor should also be addressed in the contract. Although to retain status as a processor, the supplier must operate only on the instructions of the customer (as controller); it is helpful that these instructions can be general.[5]

17.2.3 Cloud service contracts

Where a customer of a cloud service provider is subject to EU data protection law, it will be obliged to enter into a contract with its cloud service provider, which obliges the cloud provider to comply with certain data protection obligations.

The Regulation imposes significant changes to the data protection provisions that must be included in such contracts. Under the Directive, the only explicit requirements were that processors were obliged (1) to act only on instructions from the controller, and (2) to take appropriate security measures. The Regulation is far more prescriptive, setting out a detailed list of the obligations on the processor that must be included in such contracts, including:[6]

- the subject matter, duration, nature and purpose of the processing, together with the type of personal data concerned and the categories of data subject;

- that personal data is only processed on documented instructions, including with regard to international data transfers;

- that individuals authorised to process the personal data are subject to an obligation of confidentiality;

- that more prescriptive security measures are included;

- that controllers are at minimum given notice of any sub-processors and have a right of objection;

- that all sub-processors are subject to the same contractual obligations as are imposed on the processor;

- that appropriate measures are taken to ensure the data controller can meet its obligations (e.g., to allow data subjects to exercise their rights); to keep data appropriately secure, to notify in the event of data breaches, to conduct data protection impact assessments and to consult with regulators where relevant;

- that all personal data is deleted or returned once the provision of services is completed; and

- to make available all necessary information and to allow for audits to be conducted in order to monitor compliance with the contract.

In addition, the customer is likely to seek:

- assurance that the services provided will not place it in breach of its legal obligations;

- to mitigate the risks arising from mandatory disclosure requests from foreign authorities; and

- indemnification for any misuse of personal data by the supplier.

Conversely, with regard to its customers' data, the supplier will wish to ensure to the extent possible that it is not responsible for the customer's regulatory obligations.

The supplier can take operational decisions and comply with its own legal obligations without becoming a controller. Data processors should also bear in mind that they have direct responsibilities under the Regulation (e.g., with regard to security, the duty to inform controllers of data breaches, and the obligation to inform controllers if in their opinion an instruction would infringe European law).

The more specific obligations that must be imposed under the Regulation are likely to cause difficulties for cloud clients, given the tendency for cloud providers to offer their service on standard terms and conditions. Nevertheless, the WP29 has made clear that an imbalance in bargaining positions between a small cloud client and a large cloud supplier does not absolve the client data controller of any responsibility for meeting its data protection obligations.[7]

17.2.4 International data transfers

The Regulation imposes certain conditions on the transfer of personal data outside the European Economic Area (EEA). One helpful change from the Directive is that member states are unlikely to be able to continue to impose additional formalities, such as permits, for certain international transfers.

Cloud computing will almost certainly involve international data transfers. The customer, as a controller, is responsible for compliance with the Regulation regarding transfers of its personal data (see Chapter 12 for more on data transfers).

Broadly, the Regulation stipulates that controllers must be able to show evidence of safeguards for the protection of personal data transferred. Controllers in a cloud environment have a number of options to demonstrate this adequacy:

- *Geographically limiting the cloud:* By limiting a cloud to the EEA and countries or specified sectors within countries deemed to offer adequate protection, transfers of personal data would meet the requirements set by the Regulation. However, such a limitation is likely to defeat the cloud's purpose, may increase cost and may simply not be feasible.

- *Choosing Privacy Shield–certified U.S. suppliers:* From 1 August 2016, U.S. organisations have been able to sign up to the Privacy Shield scheme, administered by the U.S. Department of Commerce. Members of this scheme are deemed to adequately protect personal data, and data may be lawfully transferred to them under both the Directive and the Regulation. However, controllers should note the possibility that the scheme is subjected to a legal challenge similar to the one that invalidated its predecessor, Safe Harbor.

- *The European Commission's authorised standard contracts ('model clauses'):* In most cloud services, the 2010 controller-to-processor model clauses would need to be executed between the customer and the supplier.[8] However, model clauses may be unattractive in a cloud context as they:
  - are difficult to construct for transfers to multiple parties and locations;
  - must be updated as processing evolves; and
  - are inflexible—the substantive provisions of the clauses cannot be altered.

In addition, at the time of writing, model clauses are the subject of a legal challenge in the European courts, alleging that they offer insufficient safeguards. If successful, this challenge is likely to invalidate model clauses as a means of data transfer.

- *Tailored data transfer agreements:* As an alternative to model clauses, parties may create their own unique data transfer agreements. Such agreements afford greater flexibility than model clauses and can also include obligations that go some way to addressing the current concerns around model clauses. However, they involve greater expenditure and take longer to implement than model clauses as they involve bespoke drafting and must be approved by regulators.

- *Processor Binding Corporate Rules (BCRs):* Processor BCR have been accepted by the Article 29 Working Party as a set of binding commitments for processors that are applicable to customer personal data. Once a supplier's BCR are approved, the supplier acquires 'safe processor' status, and its customers are able to meet the Regulation's requirements for international transfers.

- *Codes of Conduct and Certification:* The Regulation introduces two new methods by which organisations in non-EEA countries may be deemed adequate: They may sign up to approved Codes of Conduct or may be designated adequate through approved certification mechanisms. At the time of writing, the Cloud Select Industry Group was working on the development of a Code of Conduct on data protection for Cloud Service Providers.[9]

- *Reliance upon a derogation under Article 49 of the Regulation:* A controller may, in theory, obtain the consent of data subjects to transfers within the cloud, for example. This is difficult in practice; for consent to be valid, it must be a clear and unambiguous indication of a data subject's wishes, specific, informed, freely given and revocable. As a result, due to the strict and multiple requirements for valid consent, consent is unlikely to be a realistic option in commercial clouds. Many European data protection authorities (DPAs) are also likely to interpret the Regulation's derogations narrowly.

17.3 Cookies, similar technologies and IP addresses

As introduced in Chapter 16, a 'cookie' is a small text file that is delivered by a website server onto the computers of visitors to its website. Cookies can then be accessed and used by the website at a later time (e.g., to identify particular devices and thereby remember a user's website preferences and log-in details). Other technologies, such as device fingerprinting, have also emerged as alternatives to cookies in recent years, in part due to the limitations of cookies when used on smartphones and other mobile devices.

An Internet protocol address ('IP address') is a numerical label assigned to devices (e.g., computers, printers) on a computer network that uses the Internet for communication.

17.3.1 Cookies and similar technologies

Cookies are typically used to tailor website offerings and to maintain the security of individuals whilst they are logged in to online accounts. However, they can also be used to facilitate targeted advertising.

When a user visits a website, a cookie is sent to the user's browser by that website or by third parties with whom the website operator has a relationship. The cookie stores information about the user's visit, which may include content viewed, language preference, time and duration of each visit and advertisements accessed.

When the website is revisited by the browser, the website can retrieve the information stored on the cookie and react accordingly (e.g., by displaying preferred language). Cookies therefore allow a website to 'remember' individual browsers and, consequently, where a browser is not shared, they remember the individual using that browser. The information collected through cookies may also be used to develop websites by identifying popular and unpopular web pages.

One practical limitation of cookies on mobile devices is that, in general, they can only be read by the app which set them. This means that organisations are unable to track users across different mobile applications (see Section 17.6.4).

Alternative technologies have emerged by organisations in order to address this perceived deficiency. One of the most visible of these is device fingerprinting, which involves collecting a large number of different technical items of information about a device (e.g., screen resolution, browser settings, operating system) in order to uniquely identify it from other devices.

17.3.2 Cookies, similar technologies and personal data

Cookies and similar technologies are often linked to information that is not personally identifiable (e.g., the time of a website visit). However, because they identify a unique computer via its browser, their data can be used to track the online movements of a computer and to form a profile of the browsing habits linked to that specific computer and, in most cases, an individual. As a result, cookies may also collect personal data and so be subject to the Regulation.

The way in which cookies are treated around Europe varies slightly, although it is common ground that, if a website operator intends to link a profile created using data obtained from cookies to a name and postal/email address, the profile will constitute personal data.

In the UK, the current guidance of the Information Commissioner's Office (ICO) states in relation to cookies that 'personal data is being processed where information is being collected and analysed with the intention of distinguishing one individual from another and to take a particular action in respect of an individual'.[10] This suggests that, where a website operator does not link a profile to further identifying information and does not seek to use the profile to take any action in relation to particular individuals, such as targeting advertising at them, the ICO may not consider the profile as personal data.

However, this guidance predates the Regulation, which makes clear that information that relates to a person who can—rather than is intended to—be identified by reference to an online identifier is personal data.[11] In addition, the Regulation introduces the concept of 'pseudonymous' data, which is a form of personal data. Pseudonymous data would include profiles that can be connected to an individual even where the controller does not, in fact, intend to make this connection.

The ICO has also previously noted that cookies are often linked to a device rather than to a specific user, and as devices can have multiple users, the information collected from cookies cannot be linked to a specific individual and so may not be personal data.

However, this argument has become also more difficult to maintain in light of the recent decision in Vidal-Hall v. Google Inc.[12] In this case, the claimants successfully argued before the English Court of Appeal that profiles of their browsing habits constituted personal data and that Google's use of these profiles to target ads to their devices was objectionable precisely because other individuals might use their device and deduce information about the claimants' browsing habits from the targeted ads which appeared.[13] The point here is that, even if Google did not know who was using the device at any particular point in time, third-party users of the device were likely to possess this information.

An additional difficulty with the 'multiple users' argument is that Internet users have increasingly moved to mobile devices, which are typically not shared between individuals.

At a European level, when an organisation uses an individual's static IP address in order to build a profile of them, the WP29 has confirmed that this profile, including the

IP address, is personal data.[14] This conclusion should also apply to profiles created using cookies or similar technologies.

Where the information collected from cookies is personal data, its collection and analysis amount to processing subject to the Regulation.

In the context of compliance with the Regulation, distinction should be drawn between first- and third-party cookies. First-party cookies are placed by the operator of the website visited and enable the operator to advertise its own products or tailor its website based on the information gathered by its own cookies. The website operator is the controller of the personal data gathered by its own first-party cookies.

Conversely, third-party cookies are sent by an entity other than the website operator. Where the third party determines the means and purposes of processing of the personal data gathered from its third-party cookies, it is a controller and must also comply with the Regulation.

17.3.3 Applicable law based on cookies

Cookies are particularly controversial because they may attract the application of EU data protection law to the operators of non-EU websites. As discussed above, the Regulation applies to any processing of personal data that relates to monitoring the behaviour of individuals within the EEA. As non-EEA websites tend to set cookies on users' devices wherever in the world those devices are located, their use to build customer profiles arguably means that the organisation setting them is subject to the Regulation in respect of the data it collects about EEA individuals.

17.3.4 Cookies and consent

As discussed in Chapter 8, Directive 2002/58/EC concerning the processing of personal data and the protection of privacy in the electronic communications sector ('ePrivacy Directive') as amended sets a number of requirements relevant to the use of cookies by website operators.[15]

Article 5(3) of the ePrivacy Directive states that the storing of information or the gaining of access to information already stored in the terminal equipment of a subscriber or a user is allowed only on the condition that the user concerned has given their consent, having been provided with clear and comprehensive information, in accordance with data protection law. There is an exemption for cookies that are strictly necessary (see Chapter 8).

In the view of the WP29, Article 5(3) imposes an obligation on the entity placing a cookie on a user's computer to obtain the prior informed consent of that user.

Practically, this means that:

- information about the sending and purposes of the cookie must be given to the user;

- the user, having been provided with this information, must consent before the cookie is placed on their computer or the information stored in their computer is retrieved; and

- the user must have a choice as to whether to give consent to the use of cookies and must provide an active indication that they do consent.[16]

Recital 66 of Directive 2009/136/EC (the Directive amending the ePrivacy Directive) states that where technically possible and effective and in accordance with the relevant provisions of data protection law, the user's consent to the processing of cookie data may be expressed by appropriate settings of a browser or other application. However, the WP29 has published an opinion on online behavioural advertising (OBA), which was formally adopted 22 June 2010, in which it expresses the view that, because browsers do not normally block cookies by default and the average user is not always familiar with browser settings or the implications of those settings, Internet users cannot be deemed to have consented by using a browser that allows cookies.[17]

Despite this, the OBA opinion states that browser settings may be relied upon to obtain the requisite consent if certain conditions apply:

- The browser settings reject third-party cookies by default.

- In conjunction with other sources, they provide Internet users with clear, comprehensive and fully visible information about the use and purpose of cookies and about any further processing that takes place in order to enable users to understand where they give consent and what they are consenting to. This will include providing information about the parties setting cookies and details about how the user can refuse them.

- They require users to take positive steps to accept both the setting of cookies and the ongoing retrieval of data from those cookies before any such cookies are set or accessed.

- It is impossible to 'bypass' the choices made by users in their browser settings. For example, mechanisms should be in place to prevent deleted cookies from being restored by technologies, such as local shared objects ('flash cookies').

The precise implementation of the revised Article 5(3) varies between member states. In the UK, the ICO has produced guidance which suggests that website operators:

- check the types of cookies used on their websites and how they are used;
- assess how intrusive the use of cookies is; and
- decide which mechanism is most suitable in order to obtain users' consent. At present, the ICO considers that most browsers are not sophisticated enough to allow website operators to assume that consent has been gained. Instead, the ICO suggests other mechanisms are used (e.g., pop-ups and website terms and conditions).

In addition to these requirements, website operators must also provide full and transparent disclosure about their use of cookies and even consider having a stand-alone cookie-use policy and keep abreast of browser developments to see whether consent expressed through browser settings could be a possibility in the future.

As another example, the cookie guidance provided by the Spanish regulator, the Agencia Española de Protección de Datos (AEPD), is very similar to the ICO's, though it makes clear that the cookie notice should contain information about how to disable or delete cookies and how to withdraw consent.[18]

17.3.5 What are IP addresses?

An IP address is a string of numbers assigned to a device that help it to identify and communicate with other devices through the Internet. An IP address may reveal an Internet service provider (ISP) and the physical location of the computer.

A device will be given either a static IP address (the device uses the same IP address each time it powers on) or a dynamic IP address (the device receives a different IP address on each start-up). Dynamic IP addresses avoid the administrative burden of assigning static addresses to each device on a network. They also allow numerous devices to share space on a network where only some are online at once.

17.3.6 IP addresses and personal data

IP addresses can be used to construct user profiles in a similar way to cookies. As discussed in Section 17.2.2, these profiles are likely to be personal data. However, in relation to IP addresses, there is an additional question as to whether the IP addresses themselves should be treated as personal data, even where they are not used to construct user profiles.

Following Scarlet Extended, it is clear that both static and dynamic IP addresses will be personal data in the hands of ISPs, because the ISP can link the IP address back to a particular customer.[19]

Where an organisation logs website visitors' IP addresses but does not link them with any further information, it has been argued that the IP addresses are not personal data. Although some regulators have previously suggested that this approach may be acceptable, there are two particular difficulties:

- The definition of personal data under both the Directive and the Regulation refers to the possibility of identifying an individual, and the possibility remains for the organisation to build a profile of the users' browsing habits, and therefore distinguish them, using their static IP address.

- Organisations can ask an ISP to identify the individual to whom an IP address relates.

The first of these arguments does not usually apply to dynamic IP addresses, because these are reset each time a device connects to the Internet and so the organisation cannot link together separate browsing sessions.[20]

However, the possibility of identifying a user by obtaining further information from an ISP is relevant to both static and dynamic IP addresses. In the recently settled Breyer v. Germany case, the ECJ considered exactly this issue in the context of dynamic IP addresses held by the German state.[21] The decision hinged on the interpretation of Recital 26 of the Directive (which is replicated by Recital 26 of the Regulation), stating that 'to determine whether a person is identifiable, account should be taken of all the means likely reasonably to be used either by the controller or by any other person to identify the said person'. Applying this principle, the ECJ ruled that dynamic IP addresses would be personal data in the hands of the German state because, 'in the event of cyber attacks', German law allowed the German state to obtain the additional identifying information from ISPs in order to determine the specific individual to whom a particular IP address related.

This decision makes clear that both static and dynamic IP addresses can constitute personal data in the hands of organisations other than ISPs. Whilst the German law referred to by the ECJ in Breyer concerned situations that involved the criminal law, there are a variety of situations in which courts will order that third parties provide information to government agencies or private parties for commercial purposes or for the purposes of a civil lawsuit. Breyer suggests that this may be enough to satisfy the Recital 26 test and bring even dynamic IP addresses within the scope of personal data in many cases.

17.4 Search engines

Search engines are services that find information on the Internet. They process large volumes of data, routinely including the following:

- *User IP addresses:* Where a search engine collects IP addresses, it can link them with searches conducted from that address. If the IP address is static, it is therefore possible for the search engine to link searches conducted from the same device.

- *Cookies:* Cookies overcome the limitations associated with dynamic IP addresses and also allow more precise user identification (e.g., identification based on a user account rather than the device associated with the IP address, for which there may be multiple users). Search engines use cookies in the ways outlined above, including to personalise and improve services.

- *User log files:* By using cookies and user IP addresses, search engines create logs of actions taken by users (e.g., requests made to a server) and provide an overview of service use. This information can be split into subcategories, including query logs (the terms searched for, their date and time, the cookie identifier, user preferences and operating system information), content (including advertisements) offered and information on the user's subsequent navigation.

- *Third-party web pages:* In order to return relevant information to the user, search engines continually scout (or 'crawl') the Internet for new content and index it in a manner that allows them to respond quickly and relevantly to search queries. The ECJ has confirmed in Google v. Spain that this involves processing the data, including any personal data, contained on those third-party web pages.[22] As previously indicated, when IP addresses and cookies are used to construct a profile of user's browsing history, the profiles, together with the IP addresses/cookies, are also likely to be personal data.

17.4.1 Search engines as controllers

It is clear that search engines determine the purposes and means of processing data about their users (e.g., user log files) and are therefore a controller of that personal data.

In Google v. Spain, the ECJ ruled that search engines are also controllers of the personal data contained in third-party web pages.[23] This finding is based in part upon the fact that a search engine 'play[s] a decisive role in the overall dissemination of [the personal data] in that it renders the latter accessible to any Internet user making a search on the basis of the data subject's name' and is therefore liable 'to affect significantly, and additionally compared with that of the publishers of websites, the fundamental rights to privacy' of individuals to whom the data relates.

17.4.2 Applicable law

If a search engine is established in the EEA, the processing activities carried out by that establishment will be subject to the Regulation by virtue of Article 3(1).

Search engines are often headquartered outside the EEA but offer their services to individuals inside the EEA. The data these organisations process about such individuals in order to offer the services will therefore be subject to the Regulation by virtue of Article 3(2)(a). User log files are also likely to be subject to the Regulation by virtue of Article 3(2)(b), as the creation of user log files about these individuals amounts to monitoring their behaviour.

Following the decision in Google v. Spain and pursuant to Article 3(1) of the Regulation, search engines outside the EEA are also likely to be subject to the Regulation in respect of their processing of personal data contained in third-party web pages if they have an EU establishment whose activities are economically linked to the search engine's core activities. In Google v. Spain, the ECJ found that Google Inc.'s processing of personal data for the purposes of operating its search engine business was subject to European data protection law because that processing was carried out in the context of the activities of Google Spain, which promoted and sold advertising space for the Google Inc. search engine. Google had argued that this should not be the case, because the processing of personal data for the purposes of operating the search engine was carried out exclusively by Google Inc. in the U.S. However, the ECJ ruled that the activities of Google Spain and Google Inc. were 'inextricably linked', because Google Spain's role of selling advertising space was necessary in order to make Google Inc.'s search engine economically viable.

17.4.3 Further data protection issues

In addition to the general requirements of the Regulation, the WP29 has identified specific issues that face search engine operators:

- *Data retention:* Data retention periods must comply with the Regulation's general principle of proportionality. In May 2010, the WP29 called on major search engines to limit their retention periods for personal data to a maximum of six months,[24] as recommended by the WP29 in 2008.[25] Once the grounds for retaining personal data no longer exist, it should be deleted or irreversibly made anonymous.

- *Correlation and further processing for different purposes:* In most cases, search engines use the personal data they collect in the provision of services to profile users and personalise search results. Where such processing occurs, its parameters must be clearly defined, and users made aware of the processing. The collection of personal data for the development of a new service, the concepts of which are not fully defined, is unlikely to be considered compliant with the Regulation. Likewise, where search engines offer a number of services, such as webmail and personalised search functions, user data is often correlated across a number of services and platforms. In these situations, the search engine must ensure that the processing is lawful under the Regulation, which, in the opinion of the WP29, means that the user's informed consent must be obtained.[26]

Where search engines link the data they collect with that from other sources, such processing may be unlawful if individuals are not provided with the necessary fair processing information when their data is collected or if their rights under the Regulation are not respected, including the right to opt out of profiling.[27] If a type of processing is not necessary for the provision of search services or if an individual's search history is retained, the WP29 also considers that the individual's consent is required.

- *Compliance with data subjects' rights:* These rights are applicable to both registered users (who have accounts with the search engine) and unregistered users (who may be identified from their IP address or via cookies or similar technologies). When data from third-party web pages is cached by a search engine operator, the WP29 considers that data subjects may exercise their rights of correction or deletion in respect of cached personal data. Following Google v. Spain, data subjects of personal data contained in third-party web pages also have a right to ask search engines to remove links to these web pages in certain situations (the 'right to be forgotten'). This right has been placed on a statutory footing under the new Regulation.[28]

17.5 Social networking services

A social networking service (SNS) is an online site designed to support social groups and build social relations amongst individuals who share interests and/or activities.

17.5.1 SNSes and others as controllers

In providing online communications platforms that enable the publication and exchange of information and in further determining the use of personal data for advertising purposes, SNS providers are data controllers; they decide the purposes and means of processing. The factors relevant to the applicability of European data protection law to SNS providers headquartered outside the EEA are similar to those described above in relation to search engines.[29]

Where the authors of applications designed to run on SNSes provide services in addition to those provided by the SNS, they too will be controllers of users' personal data.[30] The WP29 specifically addresses third-party application providers and states that SNSes should ensure these applications comply with European data protection law, in particular, concerning information provision and limiting data collection to that which is strictly necessary for the provision of the application.[31]

When SNSes users upload personal data—whether their own or that of third parties—they will be exempt from the Regulation so long as they are doing so purely for personal or household reasons (the 'household exception').[32] However, there are a number of circumstances in which the household exception will not apply:

- Where an SNS is used as a platform by an organisation and the individual using the SNS is acting on behalf of that organisation. When such SNS users add personal data relating to third parties to the SNS, they are controllers of that data and making a disclosure which is subject to the Regulation.

- The WP29 considers that the household exception does not apply where a user knowingly extends access to personal data beyond their selected contacts. In these circumstances, the individual posting personal data is a controller, and the legal framework governing their activities online is the same as when the individual uses any other channel to publish personal data on the Internet.

Where the household exception does not apply, individuals may also be able to benefit from the Regulation's exceptions that relate to the use of personal data for journalistic, artistic or literary purposes.

The Regulation's potential application to a number of parties has created an uncertain situation in which multiple individuals or entities may each be responsible as controllers of personal data held on SNSes. Where the Regulation is applicable, its provisions must be complied with (e.g., in relation to data security and retention, purpose limitation and the rights of data subjects).

17.5.2 Information provision obligations

SNS providers and entities that provide applications for SNSes which process personal data are subject to the information provisions set out in the Regulation. SNS providers should be open and transparent and, in particular, give users the following information:

- where relevant, notice that their personal data will be used for marketing purposes and the existence of the right to opt out of this;

- notice that personal data will be shared with specified third parties;

- an explanation of any profiling which is conducted;

- information about the processing of sensitive personal data;

- warnings about the risk to privacy—both to the user uploading material and any third parties about whom personal data is processed—that posting personal data to an SNS creates; and

- a warning that, if an individual uploads a third party's personal data, such as photographs, the consent of the third party should be obtained.[33]

17.5.3 Sensitive personal data

In most circumstances, unless a data subject has published the information themselves, the explicit consent of the data subject is required to make sensitive personal data available on the Internet. Therefore, where an SNS processes sensitive personal data, it must do so with the explicit consent of the data subject. Likewise, where an SNS requests information that would result in the disclosure of sensitive personal data (e.g., requesting the religious views of an individual during the creation of a profile) the SNS should make it clear that providing such information is entirely voluntary.

Although, in some instances, photographs may reveal sensitive personal data—for example, a data subject's ethnic origin (and the laws of some member states consider this information to be a special type of personal data)—unless a photograph is specifically intended to reveal such data, the WP29 generally does not consider images on the Internet as sensitive personal data.[34]

17.5.4 Third-party personal data

SNSes allow users to post information—whether through listing contacts or naming individuals in images—about third parties, including individuals who are not members of the SNS to which their personal data is added. The SNS provider must have a lawful basis for this processing under the Regulation.

Where personal data about third parties is obtained from SNS users (e.g., through the uploading of an address book linked to an email account) and aggregated to form prebuilt profiles of individuals who are not members of the SNS, the WP29 considers that this form of processing by the SNS lacks legal basis under European data protection law because the subject of the new profile is generally not in a position to learn of the existence of the processing.[35]

17.5.5 Children's data

Some SNSes are aimed specifically at children. Article 8(1) of the Regulation requires that where an individual is under 16 years of age and the data is being processed on the basis of consent, that consent must be given or authorised by a parent. Member states are free to lower this age limit to 13. In addition, Article 6(f) of the Regulation refers to situations where a data subject is a child as a particular example of where the legitimate interest ground may not be available.

The WP29 has also emphasised the requirement for controllers to have regard for the best interests of the child, as set out in the United Nations Convention on the Rights of the Child. In the context of SNSes, it encourages awareness-raising activities for children and states that the processing of minors' data should be fair and lawful. Practically, this means ensuring that sensitive personal data is not requested from minors, that default privacy-friendly settings are adopted, that minors are not targeted with direct marketing material, and that parental prior consent is obtained.[36]

17.6   Applications on mobile devices

The ubiquity of Internet-enabled mobile devices, such as smartphones and tablets, has provided organisations with a new channel of communication: mobile device applications ('apps'). Apps present several unique data protection concerns.

17.6.1 Data collection

Apps are able to collect vast amounts of information through the sensors of the mobile device they are installed on (e.g., location, audio, video, altitude, speed and user interaction). They are also able to access information stored on the mobile device, which typically includes contact details, photographs, emails and Internet browsing history. This information can be used to offer innovative services to users, but it can also be sent back to the app developer and associated with a particular device (e.g., through a unique identifier or IP address).

In comparison to desktop and laptop computers, mobile devices are less likely to be shared by multiple users. This allows a higher degree of confidence when linking this data to the owner of the mobile device, even when individuals are not logged in to a particular account.

As well as the large potential volume of data collection, this data is often of a more intimate nature. Smartphones, in particular, typically accompany their owner everywhere they go. As a result, data collected through apps on smartphones can provide a more detailed insight into more areas of their owner's lives when compared to other types of Internet-enabled device. For example, location data can allow apps to build a detailed picture over time of an individual's movements. Where an individual's movements include repeated visits to particular locations, this can be used to infer sensitive information, such as an individual's religious and political affiliations.

17.6.2 Applicable law

Where information collected through apps can be linked to a specific device, it is likely to be personal data, and the Regulation will apply. (See Section 17.3.2.)

In addition, the provisions of the ePrivacy Directive that deal with technologies similar to cookies will also be relevant.

17.6.3. Controllers and processors

Where an app collects personal data and sends it back to the app developer's servers, the app developer is likely to be a data controller of that data, as they are responsible for deciding what is collected and for how it is subsequently used.

However, where an app processes personal data only on a user's mobile device and does not send it back to the app developer's servers or elsewhere, the UK's ICO has indicated that the app owner will not be a data controller because the data remains on the user's device and under their control.[37] The WP29 is more ambiguous, stating only that the responsibilities of the app developer in this scenario will be 'considerably limited'.[38]

There are often many parties involved in the processing of personal data other than the app developer. Where these parties are acting on behalf of the app owner (e.g., hosting and analytics providers) they are likely to be data processors in relation to any personal data they process. However, some third parties, such as ad providers, may also process data for their own purposes and will therefore be data controllers in their own right. App stores, operating system and device manufacturers may also be data controllers if they process data connected to users' interactions with an app (e.g., if the app store logs the apps downloaded by a user).

17.6.4 Cookies and similar technologies

If an app uses cookies or similar technologies, it will be subject to the consent requirement in the ePrivacy Directive.

As discussed in Section 17.2.1, a limitation from the perspective of advertisers of cookies in apps as opposed to Internet browsers is that cookies can generally only be read from within the app which has set them. Because individuals increasingly use different apps to perform different online activities, whereas previously they may have performed all their online activities on the same online browser, this increasingly hinders advertisers seeking to use cookies to track individuals' actions across the Internet.

In response to the perceived need to maintain this ability, advertisers have developed new methods of tracking individuals across apps. This will often involve accessing information stored on users' devices—for example, a unique ID, such as a media access control (MAC) address, or, in the case of device fingerprinting, a large number of information points which in combination are unique to a particular user. Whenever these types of technologies access information stored in the users' device, they will also be caught by the requirement to obtain prior consent.

Similarly, where an app wishes to access contact details, photos or other media stored in a user's device, prior consent is required.

17.6.5 Notice

The requirement to adequately inform users about how their information is used requires particular attention in relation to apps on mobile devices, due to the limited screen space available on mobile devices in comparison to laptops and desktops. As a result, traditional privacy policies will not always be sufficient to discharge the obligation to adequately inform users about how their personal data is used.

The WP29 recommends that icons or other visual signifiers are useful tools for better bringing information to users' attention.[39] Given that these are specifically mentioned as a tool to be considered in the GDPR, their use can be expected to increase over coming years.[40] Layered notices, where the most important information is brought explicitly to users' attention, together with links to more complete information for users who wish to learn more, are also helpful.

In order to satisfy the requirement that information is provided by the time that personal data is processed, notice may need to be provided before an app is downloaded (e.g., through a privacy policy displayed in the app store).

17.6.6 Consent

Downloading an app onto users' devices entails storing information on their devices. This requires consent under the ePrivacy Directive. As discussed in Section 17.5.4, the use of cookies or similar technologies will also require consent.

Consent may also be required as the lawful ground on which personal data is processed. For example, in the opinion of the WP29, the intimate nature of location data collected through a user's mobile device is such that the legitimate interest ground will not generally be available, and consent will usually be required.[41]

As discussed in Chapter 7, the Regulation imposes a high standard for consent. In particular, consent for data processing which is not essential for provision of an app's functionality will generally not be valid if the user has to give such consent in order to use the app. In addition, consent has to be 'specific', which, in the WP29's opinion, means offering users the ability to consent to particular types of data processing rather than simply obtaining a single consent for all the types of data processing listed in a privacy policy.

In the context of apps, this is likely to mean asking users for granular types of consent for particular types of data processing and providing as much functionality as possible if a user does not provide a particular consent. For example, an app could ask users for permission to access their location data in order to display directions to the nearest convenience store on a map, but if this permission is denied, users are allowed to manually view the locations of convenience stores on the map in order to determine this information for themselves.

17.6.7 Data minimisation

Given the very large volume of data that can be collected by apps, app developers should note the Regulation's requirement for data minimisation. This states that personal data shall be adequate, relevant and limited to what is necessary in relation to the purposes for which they are processed.

This is also reinforced by the Regulation's 'data protection by default' requirement, which requires controllers to ensure that, by default, only personal data which is necessary for each specific processing purpose is collected and used.[42]

17.7 Internet of Things

The Internet of Things (IoT) is a broad term that refers to Internet-enabled objects which can communicate directly with other Internet-enabled objects with no human assistance. In many instances, these objects are also equipped with sensors which allow them to collect and then transmit information about their environment. Applications of such technology have already emerged in multiple industries (e.g., wearable technology, smart energy meters and other home appliances, and connected vehicles).

The sensors in such objects frequently collect information which relates to identifiable individuals. Such information constitutes personal data and is subject to the Regulation. Sometimes, this is obvious, such as wearable technology which keeps track of a user's location. Sometimes, it is less so; smart meters which monitor a home's energy consumption in two-second intervals create records which have been shown to identify the television show the occupant is watching.[43]

The IoT entails specific data protection considerations, some of the most significant of which are outlined below.

17.7.1 Controllers and processors

The considerations relevant to determining the relevant controllers and processors of data produced by Internet-enabled objects are similar to the considerations in respect of Internet-enabled mobile devices discussed in Section 17.5.3.[44]

17.7.2 Security

The requirement to appropriately secure personal data transmitted through networks connected to IoT objects is challenging, in particular, because:

- very large numbers of objects are often connected to the same network, providing a larger number of points through which malicious actors can gain access; and

- the software on Internet-enabled objects is less likely to be kept up to date with the latest security patches than on computers or other devices operated by humans.

As a result, particular attention must be paid to ensuring that such networks are designed in a secure manner. This is most likely to be accomplished if IoT networks are designed with security in mind from the beginning. Such an approach is also consistent with the 'data protection by design' approach taken in the Regulation.

17.7.3 Notice and choice

Notice and consent can pose particular challenges in the context of automatic data collection by objects that involve no human action. Consideration will need to be given to how individuals whose personal data is collected by such objects will be made aware of that fact and provided with the information required by the Regulation. The

WP29 has also noted that the potential intrusiveness of the IoT means that consent will, in most cases, be the appropriate legal ground on which to base the processing.[45] Obtaining such consent in the context of automatic data collection by objects with no human intervention creates challenges.

Solutions to these issues will be specific to the technology in question but may require innovative approaches—for example, stickers notifying individuals that their information is being collected together with information on how and where data subjects can find further information or having objects wirelessly broadcast the relevant information such that it appears on data subjects' mobile devices when they are nearby. In relation to consent, the WP29 has commented that it may be necessary for device manufacturers to build consent mechanisms into devices themselves.[46] The data protection impact assessments (DPIAs) and data protection by design obligations in the Regulation should assist organisations in devising and implementing such solutions at an appropriate stage of development.

17.8 Conclusion

In this chapter, we have attempted to introduce some of the relevant data protection considerations in respect of specific categories of Internet and communication technologies. However, the ubiquity of our subject matter means that this can only hope to be an introduction to the relevant issues.

The technicalities of routing digital communications mean that these technologies very often require the use of identifiers, whether IP addresses, MAC addresses or other. As always, organisations subject to the Regulation will need to abide by its rules whenever they collect or receive data that relates to an identified or identifiable natural person. And even where an organisation is not processing personal data, it may still be subject to the requirements of the ePrivacy Directive. We recommend that privacy and data protection practitioners develop strong relationships with the technologists in their organisations to ensure that they properly identify all instances where EU data protection laws may apply.

Endnotes

1 Weltimmo s.r.o. v. Nemzeti Adatvédelmi és Információszabadság Hatóság [2015] Case C-230/14, 1 October 2015.

2 Opinion 1/2010 on the concepts of 'controller' and 'processor' (00264/10/EN: WP 169), pages 14–15, http://ec.europa.eu/justice/policies/privacy/docs/wpdocs/2010/wp169_en.pdf.

3 Opinion 05/2012 on Cloud Computing (01037/12/EN: WP 196), page 8, http://ec.europa.eu/justice/data-protection/article-29/documentation/opinion-recommendation/files/2012/wp196_en.pdf.

4 Opinion 1/2010 on the concepts of 'controller' and 'processor' (00264/10/EN: WP 169), pages 11–12, http://ec.europa.eu/justice/policies/privacy/docs/wpdocs/2010/wp169_en.pdf.

5 A. Patrikios, 'Cloud computing: the key issues and solutions', Data Protection Law and Policy, May 2010.

6 General Data Protection Regulation, Article 28.

7 Opinion 05/2012 on Cloud Computing (01037/12/EN: WP 196), page 8, http://ec.europa.eu/justice/data-protection/article-29/documentation/opinion-recommendation/files/2012/wp196_en.pdf.

8 Commission Decision of 5 February 2010 on standard contractual clauses for the transfer of personal data to processors established in third countries under Directive 95/46/EC of the European Parliament and of the Council (notified under document C(2010) 593).

9 'Opinion of the Article 29 Data Protection Working Party on the Code of conduct on data protection for cloud service providers', European Commission, accessed June 2017, https://ec.europa.eu/digital-single-market/en/news/opinion-article-29-data-protection-working-party-code-conduct-data-protection-cloud-service.

10 'Personal Information Online Code of Practice', Information Commissioner's Office, https://ico.org.uk/media/for-organisations/documents/1591/personal_information_online_cop.pdf.

11 General Data Protection Regulation, Article 4.

12 Vidal-Hall v. Google Inc. [2015] EWCA Civ 311, 27 March 2015.

13 Ibid.

14 Opinion 4/2007 on the concept of personal data (01248/07/EN: WP 136), page 16, http://ec.europa.eu/justice/data-protection/article-29/documentation/opinion-recommendation/files/2007/wp136_en.pdf.

15 Stop press. Since the date of writing, the European Commission has published its proposal for an ePrivacy Regulation, which will ultimately replace the ePrivacy Directive. The proposal is currently being considered by the European Parliament and the European Council, who will produce their own revised drafts of the new law. A final version will then have to be agreed between all three EU bodies before passing into law. The aim is for the new rules to come into effect alongside the GDPR in May 2018, although this is widely recognised as ambitious. The Commission's proposal suggests some important changes to the current rules around the use of cookies and other tracking technologies. In particular, the standard of consent required is likely to rise to match the standard required under the GDPR; the proposal more clearly captures tracking technologies other than cookies; and there is a proposal that consent must be collected centrally through users' browser settings. As a Regulation, the new proposal would also mean greater harmonisation as compared to current national implementations of the ePrivacy Directive.

16 Working Document 02/2013 providing guidance on obtaining consent for cookies (1676/13/EN; WP 208), page 3, http://ec.europa.eu/justice/data-protection/article-29/documentation/opinion-recommendation/files/2013/wp208_en.pdf.

17 Opinion 2/2010 on online behavioural advertising (00909/10/EN: WP 171), page 13, http://ec.europa.eu/justice/policies/privacy/docs/wpdocs/2010/wp171_en.pdf.

18 Guía sobre el uso de las cookies, http://www.agpd.es/portalwebAGPD/canaldocumentacion/
    publicaciones/common/Guias/Guia_Cookies.pdf.

19 Scarlet Extended [2011] Case C-70/10, 24 November 2011.

20 Although note that if the organisation also uses or collects another form of identifier—for example, a
    cookie or unique device identifier—the device can then be identified through this alternative means.

21 Patrick Breyer v. Germany [2016] Case C-582/14, 12 May 2016.

22 Google Spain SL and Google Inc. v. Agencia Española de Protección de Datos (AEPD) and Mario
    Costeja González [2014] Case C-131/12, 13 May 2014.

23 Ibid.

24 http://ec.europa.eu/justice/data-protection/article-29/documentation/other-document/
    files/2010/2010_05_26_letter_wp_google.pdf.

25 Opinion 1/2008 on data protection issues related to search engines (00737/EN: WP 148), page 19,
    http://ec.europa.eu/justice/data-protection/article-29/documentation/opinion-recommendation/
    files/2008/wp148_en.pdf.

26 Ibid., page 21.

27 See for example the UK Information Commissioner's Office's ruling in relation to changes made to
    Google Inc.'s privacy policy in 2012: https://ico.org.uk/about-the-ico/news-and-events/news-and-
    blogs/2015/01/google-to-change-privacy-policy-after-ico-investigation/.

28 General Data Protection Regulation, Article 17.

29 Opinion 5/2009 on online social networking (01189/09/EN; WP 163), page 5, http://ec.europa.eu/
    justice/data-protection/article-29/documentation/opinion-recommendation/files/2009/wp163_
    en.pdf.

30 Ibid.

31 Ibid., page 9.

32 General Data Protection Regulation, Article 2(3); Even when the General Data Protection
    Regulation is not applicable, individuals posting personal data to an SNS may be liable under other
    national laws—for example, governing defamation or the misuse of personal information.

33 Opinion 5/2009 on online social networking (01189/09/EN: WP 163), page 7, http://ec.europa.eu/
    justice/data-protection/article-29/documentation/opinion-recommendation/files/2009/wp163_
    en.pdf.

34 Ibid, page 8.

35 Ibid.

36 Ibid, pages 11–12.

37 'Privacy in mobile apps: Guidance for app developers', Information Commissioner's Office, page 5,
    https://ico.org.uk/media/for-organisations/documents/1596/privacy-in-mobile-apps-dp-guidance
    .pdf.

38 Opinion 02/2013 on apps on smart devices (00461/13/EN: WP 202), page 10, http://ec.europa.eu/
    justice/data-protection/article-29/documentation/opinion-recommendation/files/2013/wp202_
    en.pdf.

39 Opinion 02/2013 on apps on smart devices (00461/13/EN: WP 202), page 23, http://ec.europa.eu/
    justice/data-protection/article-29/documentation/opinion-recommendation/files/2013/wp202_
    en.pdf.

40 General Data Protection Regulation, Article 12(7).

41 Opinion 13/2011 on Geolocation services on smart mobile devices (881/11/EN: WP 185), page 14, http://ec.europa.eu/justice/policies/privacy/docs/wpdocs/2011/wp185_en.pdf.

42 General Data Protection Regulation, Article 25(2).

43 'Smart meter hacking can disclose which TV shows and movies you watch', naked security by Sophos, 8 January 2012, https://nakedsecurity.sophos.com/2012/01/08/28c3-smart-meter-hacking-can-disclose-which-tv-shows-and-movies-you-watch/.

44 See Section 3.3 of the Article 29 Working Party's WP 223 for further details.

45 Opinion 8/2014 on the on Recent Developments on the Internet of Things (14/EN: WP 223), page 15, http://ec.europa.eu/justice/data-protection/article-29/documentation/opinion-recommendation/files/2014/wp223_en.pdf.

46 Ibid, page 7.

CHAPTER 18

Outsourcing

Eduardo Ustaran, CIPP/E

18.1 Introduction

As explained in Chapter 1, data protection law was created in the early 1970s in response to the increasing use of computers to process information about individuals. Although the outsourcing phenomenon had not yet begun, from the early '60s, rapid progress in the field of electronic data processing and the first appearance of mainframe computers allowed public administrations and large enterprises to set up extensive data banks and to improve and increase the collection, processing and sharing of personal data. Shortly after, a whole range of services often known as 'service bureaux' or 'computer bureaux' emerged to cater to the computing needs of organisations without their own data processing capabilities.

This emerging practice gave data protection a completely different dimension, as policymakers and legislators needed to ensure protection when the data processing operations were one step removed from the entities ultimately responsible for the processing. As described in Chapter 1, the OECD Guidelines on the Protection of Privacy and Transborder Flows of Personal Data ('Guidelines') tried to address this issue by pointing out that it was essential that under domestic law, accountability for complying with privacy protection rules and decisions should be placed on the data controller, which retains this obligation even when data processing is carried out by another party, such as a service bureaux.

This approach was then followed and elaborated on by the Data Protection Directive ('Directive'), which made controllers responsible for the actions of their processors, but the growth of outsourcing during the 1990s and 2000s has given an ever-growing importance to the delicate balance between the responsibility of data controllers for any processing carried out on their behalf and the professional duties of data processing service providers. Getting that balance right by apportioning practical responsibilities in a fair and effective manner has become one of the cornerstones of today's data protection.

The General Data Protection Regulation (GDPR, or 'Regulation') has taken this situation to a new level by establishing direct legal obligations applicable to service providers acting as 'processors' whilst giving an increased emphasis to the contractual obligations in place between customers and data processing service providers.

18.2 The roles of the parties

As in the case of the Directive, the Regulation establishes the concepts of 'controllers' and 'processors'. However, the Regulation appears to be more aware of the complexities related to the outsourcing of data processing activities. So, whilst retaining the focus on the legal obligations applicable to controllers, it includes new legal responsibilities for processors and anticipates the existence of sub-processors that do not have a direct contractual relationship with the ultimate customer.

18.2.1 Controller and processor

As has been discussed at length in earlier chapters, according to the Regulation, a controller is a natural or legal person, public authority, agency or any other body that alone or jointly with others determines the purposes and means of the processing of personal data. In contrast with the concept of controller, a processor is a person other than an employee of the controller who processes data on behalf of a controller.

This distinction is important because it is the controller rather than the processor who is primarily responsible for complying with the relevant data protection obligations under the law. As part of these obligations, it is also the controller's responsibility to ensure that a written contract governs the relationship with the processor and that the processor complies with the data protection obligations set out in that contract.

The significance of this distinction was reflected in a formal opinion of the Article 29 Working Party (WP29) adopted 16 February 2010.[1] In this opinion, the WP29 stated that it is of paramount importance that the precise meaning of these concepts and the criteria for their correct use are sufficiently clear but recognised that the concrete application of the concepts of controller and processor was becoming increasingly complex.

18.2.2 Customers as controllers and suppliers as processors

The most logical way of applying the controller and processor roles to an outsourcing relationship is to regard the customer as the controller and the supplier as the processor. This allocation of roles reflects common practice in the vast majority of outsourcing arrangements in the EU. This has two practical implications:

- *Determining the purposes and means of the processing*: The outsourcing contract may actually be silent in terms of the roles of the parties, but it should have sufficient elements to conclude that the customer exercises a dominant role in determining the purposes and means of the processing.

- *Imposing legal obligations*: The Regulation expressly states that processing carried out by a processor must be governed by a contract or legal act binding the processor to the controller and stipulating a number of detailed requirements. This is one of the areas that shows the much more prescriptive regime established by the Regulation compared to the Directive.

  Aside from the strict contractual relationship and as mentioned above, even where suppliers act purely in a processor capacity, the Regulation establishes direct legal obligations applicable to them. These obligations apply irrespective of the contractual provisions of the outsourcing contract and include the following:

  - *Article 27*: When a processor to which the Regulation applies is not established in the EU, the processor must designate a representative in the EU unless the processing it undertakes is occasional, does not include on a large scale processing of special categories of data or personal data relating to criminal convictions and offences, and is unlikely to result in a risk to the rights and freedoms of individuals.

  - *Article 28(2)*: A processor must not engage another processor without the prior specific or general written authorisation of controller. Where general written authorisation is provided, the processor must inform controller of any intended changes concerning additions or replacements of other processors, giving the controller an opportunity to object.

  - *Article 28(3)*: As mentioned above, processing conducted by a processor on behalf of a controller must be governed by a written contract or other legal act binding on the processor with regard to the controller. This contract must contain certain specific information relating to the processing.

  - *Article 28(4)*: When a processor engages a sub-processor, the same data protection obligations set out in the contract with the controller must be imposed on the sub-processor by way of contract. The initial processor remains fully liable to the controller for the performance of the sub-processor.

○ *Article 29*: A processor or a sub-processor or any person acting under their authority must not process personal data except on instructions from the controller unless required to do so by EU or member state law.

○ *Article 30(2)*: A processor or its representative must maintain a written record of all categories of personal data processing activities carried out on behalf of a controller which must include a number of details. This record must be made available by a processor to a data protection authority (DPA) upon request. This obligation does not apply, however, to processors that employ fewer than 250 employees, unless the processing conducted is high risk.

○ *Article 31*: A processor or its representative must cooperate with the data protection supervisory authority.

○ *Article 32*: A processor is required to implement appropriate technical and organisational security measures relative to the risks that arise from the processing to ensure that the personal data is protected. These measures may include, as appropriate:

- pseudonymisation and encryption;

- the ability to ensure the ongoing confidentiality, integrity, availability and resilience of systems and services;

- effective backup and disaster recovery processes; and

- regular review of the security measures applied to the processing to ensure that they remain appropriate.

○ *Article 33*: A processor must notify the controller without undue delay after becoming aware of a personal data breach.

○ *Article 37*: A processor is required to designate a data protection officer (DPO) where its core activities consist of processing operations that require regular and systematic monitoring of individuals on a large scale or the core activities involve processing of sensitive data or data on criminal convictions on a large scale. Where a DPO is appointed, the processor must publish their contact details and communicate them to the DPA.

○ *Article 38*: A processor must ensure that the DPO is involved in all issues relating to protection of personal data and must provide the necessary support to the DPO, ensure they are able to act independently, and, where a DPO has other tasks, ensure that those tasks do not result in a conflict of interest.

- *Article 44*: Processors must comply with conditions set out in the Regulation that concerns international transfers of personal data.

- *Article 49*: Where a data transfer takes place on the basis of the compelling legitimate interests of the controller, an assessment of all the circumstances and the adoption of suitable safeguards to protect the data transferred must be carried out and the processor must document the assessment.

18.2.3 Suppliers as controllers

In an outsourcing relationship, it is common for the supplier to take an active role in making certain decisions about the processing. This is a logical outcome given that suppliers normally have greater expertise in the particular processing operations than the controller. However, as indicated by the WP29 Opinion WP 169 and expressly stated in Article 28(10) of the Regulation, a processor that goes beyond its mandate and acquires a relevant role in determining the purposes or the essential means of processing is a controller rather than a processor.

Whilst there is a risk that a supplier may become a controller in its own right, the WP29 also points out that delegation may still imply a certain degree of discretion about how to best serve the controller's interests, allowing the processor to choose the most suitable technical and organisational means.

On balance, despite the increasing decision-making power of suppliers in an outsourcing relationship, it is more likely than not that a supplier will still remain a processor unless it is obvious that any decisions made by that party exceed the scope of what was envisaged by the contract.

18.2.4 Chains of processors and sub-processors

Modern outsourcing is hardly ever limited to a relationship between two parties. Frequently, outsourcing arrangements follow this model:

- Within a corporate group, operating companies established in different jurisdictions rely on a procurement entity within that group of companies to procure data processing services.

- The procurement entity appoints a particular supplier as a prime contractor for the relevant data processing services.

- The supplier then subcontracts some of those services to other entities within its group of companies or externally to third parties.

These arrangements have important data protection implications and normally result in a chain of agreements where the different parties are required to flow obligations down the chain. In this situation, whilst it is not necessary that the controller define and agree on all the details of the means used, the WP29 made it clear that the customer should be informed of at least the main elements of the processing structure so that it remains in control. The Regulation is again more prescriptive than the Directive was in this regard and includes specific provisions that regulate sub-processing as explained below.

18.3 Data protection obligations in an outsourcing contract

For both legal and practical reasons, the data protection provisions are critical to the effectiveness of an outsourcing contract. As with any other contractual clause, the precise content of the data protection obligations will often depend on the strength of the bargaining position of the parties, but from the controller's point of view, it is particularly important that such obligations are as explicit as possible. This has become even more obvious under the Regulation, which, in Article 28(3), sets out the specific issues that should be stipulated by the contract.

18.3.1 Acting under the controller's documented instructions

To maintain a clear distinction between the role of the controller (i.e., the customer) and the processor (i.e., the supplier), it is essential that any outsourcing contract that involves the processing of personal data establishes who is in control. This is a requirement of the Regulation itself and, accordingly, the contract should include a provision that states the supplier will process the relevant personal data only on documented instructions from the customer. These instructions may be generic, but the more specific they are, the easier it will be for the customer to demonstrate its role as a controller.

The Regulation goes even further in saying that such a requirement also applies with regard to international transfers of personal data, unless EU or member state law to which the processor is subject requires otherwise, in which case, the processor must inform the controller of that legal requirement before processing unless prohibited from doing so by that law.

18.3.2 Implementing appropriate technical and organisational measures

This is another essential obligation stated in the Regulation; it is discussed in detail in Chapter 10. Given the current level of attention given to data security breaches, it may be wise for controllers to rely on the supplier's expertise to decide the precise security measures to be adopted and to require the supplier to acknowledge:

- that the customer is relying upon the supplier's skill and knowledge to assess what is 'appropriate' to protect the personal data against unauthorised or unlawful processing and against accidental loss, destruction, damage, alteration or disclosure; and

- that the technical and organisational measures must be appropriate to the harm that might result from any unauthorised or unlawful processing and accidental loss, destruction or damage to the personal data and also appropriate to the nature of the personal data that is to be protected.

In addition, when implementing technical and organisational security measures, the supplier may often be asked to consider:

- the sensitive nature of the personal data and the substantial harm that would result from unauthorised or unlawful processing or accidental loss or destruction of or damage to such personal data; and

- the state of technological development and the cost of implementing such measures.

18.3.3 Employee vetting

Linked to the organisational security measures is the task of vetting employees. It has become increasingly common to place specific obligations on the supplier relating to the reliability of its employees and subcontractors. These obligations may require the supplier to ensure:

- the reliability of any employees and subcontractor personnel who have access to the customer personal data;

- that all employees and subcontractor personnel involved in the processing of personal data have undergone adequate training in the care, protection and handling of it; and

- that all employees and subcontractor personnel perform their duties strictly in compliance with the applicable confidentiality provisions under the contract by treating such customer personal data as confidential information.

18.3.4 Other data protection obligations

In addition to the basic obligations set out above, under the Regulation, the outsourcing contract must include provisions that require the supplier:

- complies with the obligations imposed on the processor under the Regulation regarding the appointment of other processors;

- assists the controller by implementing appropriate technical and organisational measures, insofar as this is possible, to enable the controller to respond to individuals who wish to exercise their rights under the Regulation;

- assists the controller in ensuring compliance with the obligations set out in Articles 32 to 36 (relating to data security, breach notification, impact assessments and prior consultation with DPAs), taking into account the nature of processing and the information available to the processor;

- at the choice of the controller, deletes or returns all the personal data to the controller after the end of the provision of services, and deletes existing copies unless EU or member state law requires storage of the personal data;

- makes available to the controller all information necessary to demonstrate compliance with Article 28 of the Regulation; and

- allows for and contributes to audits by the controller or an auditor appointed by the controller.

18.3.5 Subcontracting

Where the outsourcing relationship is likely to involve a chain of processors and sub-processors, as mentioned above, according to Articles 28(2) and (4) of the Regulation, the contract between the controller or the entity within the corporate group of the controller entering into the outsourcing contract and the main supplier should take place subject to the following conditions:

- The customer must provide prior specific or general written authorisation to the supplier regarding the engagement of a sub-processor.

- In the case of general written authorisation, the processor must inform the controller of any intended changes that concern the addition or replacement of other sub-processors, giving the controller the opportunity to object to such changes.

- The processor has an obligation to impose the same contractual obligations applicable to it onto any sub-processors.

- The main supplier must remain liable to the customer for any breach of the sub-processor.

18.4 The German case

Germany has experienced a number of serious data protection breaches in the past few years. For example, Deutsche Telekom lost personal data for about 17 million T-Mobile German customers when a storage device that contained personal data was stolen.[2] The device contained names, addresses, cell phone numbers, birth dates and email addresses, including some for high-profile German citizens.

In response, to this case and others, in July 2009, the German federal legislature amended its data protection legislation. The German data protection law, Bundesdatenschutzgesetz (BDSG), is unique in the sense that it includes very specific requirements that affect data services outsourcing agreements and follows the expectations that had already been set out by the DPAs and the courts.[3] Until 2009, there was a generic obligation to enter into a written agreement, but there were no clear legal criteria in terms of the issues that had to be addressed in such a contract. The legislature reacted to this and established 10 specific requirements. These are set out in Section 11 of the legislation.

18.4.1 Specific requirements

The general requirement under Section 11 BDSG to enter into a written data processing agreement remains unchanged. Moreover, the following items must be specifically addressed in the contract:

1. The subject and duration of the work to be carried out

2. The extent, type and purpose of the intended collection, processing or use of data, the type of data and category of data subjects

3. The technical and organisational measures to be taken under Section 9

4. The rectification, erasure and blocking of data

5. The processor's obligations under Subsection 4, in particular monitoring

6. Any right to issue subcontracts

7. The controller's rights to monitor and the processor's corresponding obligations to cooperate with the controller

8. Violations by the processor or its employees of provisions to protect personal data or of the terms specified by the controller that are subject to the obligation to notify

9. The extent of the controller's authority to issue instructions to the processor

10. The return of data storage media and the erasure of data recorded by the processor after the work has been carried out

In addition, the data controller has to verify and be satisfied with the technical and organisational processes implemented by the data processor before the data processing begins, and that verification must be repeated periodically afterwards. The result of such verification must be documented.

A breach of Section 11 BDSG is regarded as a regulatory offence that may lead to administrative fines of up to 50,000 euros, plus a potential deduction of profits that a party may have had as a result of the breach. The administrative fines may be issued to anyone who (1) does not enter into a controller/processor agreement correctly, completely or in the prescribed way; or (2) does not verify that the data processor's technical and organisational processes are in place before the data processing begins.

In practice, it could be argued that these requirements do not lead to substantial new obligations for the data processor but simply identify the issues that should have been addressed in a controller/processor agreement. However, to ensure a greater degree of legal certainty, organisations that rely on data processors for their core data processing activities are advised to enter into comprehensive agreements with their data processors. The BDSG does not include any transitional provisions that deal with situations where data processing agreements were entered into by the parties prior to these legislative changes. Accordingly, even existing agreements pre-2009 should be revised in line with the new requirements.

18.4.2 Effect of data processors' location

The requirements set out above are applicable to any data processor located in Germany or within the EU that is processing personal data on behalf of a German data controller.

However, it remains unclear whether the requirements set out in Section 11 BDSG must be applied in cases where the data processor is based outside the EU or the European Economic Area (EEA) and is subject to the obligations of the standard model clauses approved by the EU Commission ('Commission') for overseas transfers of personal data.

According to the Bavarian data protection regulator ('Ansbach regional DPA'), Section 11 BDSG requirements should be included as an attachment to the standard model clauses. However, the German Federal Commissioner for Data Protection and Freedom of Information is of the opinion that the standard model clauses may be used as a sole agreement and that Section 11 BDSG may be ignored for the purposes of transfers to data processors located outside the EEA.

On a practical level, at least in those states ('Länder') in Germany, which have stated that a regulator does not have to confirm the adequate level of protection in the event of a transfer to a data processor outside the EU (where the standard model clauses for the controller/processor agreements are used), it is unlikely to be necessary to include the Section 11 BDSG requirements as an attachment. Only those authorities that have expressed that they wish to review the transfer contracts even if the standard model clauses are used without amendments are likely to require the additional data protection measures set out in Section 11 BDSG.

18.5 Offshoring and international data transfers

As mentioned in Chapter 12, Article 44 of the Regulation limits the transfer of personal data to any country outside the EEA unless that third country ensures an adequate level of data protection. Given the development of offshoring and, more particularly, cloud computing, how to overcome this restriction has become the single most difficult data protection compliance aspect for EU-based customers wishing to engage a supplier or chain of suppliers that is based overseas.

However, the restriction set out in the Regulation is not an absolute prohibition. Chapter 5 of the Regulation sets out the conditions that must be complied with to allow such transfers to take place. In practical terms, the Regulation provides various possible routes to legitimise the data transfers in the context of an offshoring relationship.

18.5.1 Privacy Shield

Following the demise of Safe Harbor in 2015, reliance on the Privacy Shield has progressively increased since it became operational in August 2016.[4] The use of the Privacy Shield—and previously Safe Harbor—by U.S.-based data processing service providers is a common approach to legitimising data transfers despite the uncertainties that affect this framework. The fact that so many leading technology companies are either headquartered in the U.S. or reliant on infrastructure and means (e.g., servers and data centres) located in the U.S. has made the Privacy Shield a much sought-after mechanism.

Since the Privacy Shield Framework is subject to an adequacy decision by the Commission, unless and until this decision becomes invalid, transfers of personal data by EU customers to Privacy Shield signatories providing data processing services are in principle regarded as lawful and in accordance with Article 45 of the Regulation. However, it is important to note that for such EU controllers to be able to rely on this mechanism, the U.S.-based data importers must have included the data processing activities carried out on behalf of customers within the scope of their Privacy Shield certification. Accordingly, EU controllers should seek to include an express obligation in the data processing agreement that requires the U.S. processor to maintain a valid and relevant Privacy Shield certification and comply at all times with the principles set out in the framework.

18.5.2 Standard contractual clauses

Over the years, a mechanism that has frequently been relied on in this context is the use of standard data protection clauses adopted by the Commission. This mechanism is present in the Regulation as a way of deploying appropriate safeguards to overcome the restriction on international data transfers from an EU-based customer to an overseas supplier under Article 46.

This route was already available under the Directive, so on 27 December 2001, the Commission adopted a decision that set out standard contractual clauses for the transfer of personal data from controllers to processors established in non-EEA countries that were not recognised as offering an adequate level of data protection (the 'original controller-to-processor clauses').[5] However, the inflexible nature of the original controller-to-processor clauses led to the drafting of an alternative version, and on 5 February 2010, the Commission issued its decision to update and replace the original controller-to-processor standard clauses with a new set of model clauses (the 'updated controller-to-processor clauses').[6]

Accordingly, the parties in an outsourcing relationship that involves data transfers outside the EEA may provide appropriate safeguards to legitimise such transfers by entering into an agreement that contains the updated controller-to-processor clauses. However, the updated clauses retain the onerous obligations imposed on the exporter and the importer by the original controller-to-processor clauses and set out very strict rules concerning the processor's ability to subcontract its services. In reality, the step-by-step subcontracting process is so cumbersome that it hardly solves the problem that it was meant to address.

As stated in Chapter 12, this approach is not likely to be accepted straightaway by the majority of global outsourcing service providers. In the context of complex data processing arrangements involving chains of service providers, the step-by-step process is entirely at odds with the ability to engage different providers for different aspects of the service without direct involvement of the customer. Sophisticated organisations are therefore likely to move away from the standard contractual clauses and explore other more suitable solutions as explained below.

18.5.3 Alternative contractual mechanisms

One route that is increasingly being followed in response to the cumbersome nature of the updated controller-to-processor clauses is the tailored or ad hoc data processing and transfer agreement. Under this approach, the parties negotiate the data protection provisions of their international data processing agreement and rely on their own judgment to procure an adequate level of protection. This route has been acknowledged by the Regulation, which refers in Article 46(3) to the possibility of providing appropriate safeguards through contractual clauses approved by a competent data protection supervisory authority.

Crucially, the Regulation refers to the fact that these ad hoc contractual clauses may be entered into by an exporting controller or processor and the recipient of the personal data in the third country. This suggests that, unlike with the current standard contractual clauses adopted by the Commission referred to above, the alternative contractual mechanisms envisaged by Article 46(3) can be suitable for processor-to-processor data transfers (where, for example, an EU-based controller engages an EU-based processor, which then transfers the data to a non-EU sub-processor).

The future success of this approach will largely depend on the willingness of DPAs to approve different versions of these types of alternative contractual mechanisms, but logic suggests that the authorities are unlikely to approve clauses that substantially depart from the standard versions adopted by the Commission.

18.5.4 Binding Corporate Rules for processors

In recent years, the EU DPAs have encouraged multinationals to adopt internal Binding Corporate Rules (BCRs) based on European standards as a more flexible way of legitimising their global data processing operations. However, the original BCR model had only been applied to cases where companies are controllers of the personal data they process and not to cases where they are processors.

Before the adoption of the Regulation, the WP29 started the process of extending the BCR concept to processors by approving legally binding internal data protection rules that apply to clients' data processed by service providers. This was explicitly recognised by the Regulation, which defined BCR as personal data protection policies which could be adhered to by a controller or processor. Unlike the standard contractual clauses approved by the Commission, the Processor BCR ('Binding Safe Processor Rules', or BSPR) can be tailored to the data protection practices of the service provider, and, as long as they include the appropriate adequacy standards, they can become a very useful tool for the benefit of international data protection and the outsourcing industry alike.

In terms of content, the standards required under Processor BCR mirror the accepted standards applicable in relation to BCR but from the point of view of the processor. In other words, under the Processor BCR, a corporate group with entities or means of processing based outside the EEA will undertake to abide by certain data protection standards in accordance with the same criteria established for BCR but adapted to their role as data processors. Those service providers would then be regarded as 'safe processors', irrespective of their geographical location and, when using a safe processor to transfer data, their customers would be able to overcome the restriction that affects global data transfers under EU data protection law.

From the point of view of individual data subjects, this mechanism provides an additional layer of protection over and above that provided by the standard contractual clauses, as the Processor BCR will include a direct redress route to the data processor for any breaches of the safeguards provided by the Processor BCR.

18.6 Conclusion

One of the most significant changes brought about by the Regulation is the recalibration of responsibilities between controllers and processors. Whilst controllers continue to be primarily accountable for the handling of personal data, the status of processors has been elevated to a much higher level of responsibility than under the previous data protection framework. However, the obligation on both parties of an outsourcing relationship to enter into a written contract setting out very specific commitments in relation to the processing of personal data remains the cornerstone of this complex balance.

Endnotes

1 Opinion 1/2010 on the concepts of 'controller' and 'processor' (00264/10/EN: WP 169), http://ec.europa.eu/justice/policies/privacy/docs/wpdocs/2010/wp169_en.pdf.

2 Sayer, Peter, 'T-Mobile Lost Control of Data on 17 Million Customers', CIO from IDG, 6 October 2008, www.cio.com/article/2433190/infrastructure/t-mobile-lost-control-of-data-on-17-million-customers.html.

3 Bundesdatenschutzgesetz (BDSG), Bundesdatenschutzgesetz der Justiz und fü Verbraucherschutz, https://www.gesetze-im-internet.de/bdsg_1990/index.html.

4 Maximillian Schrems v. Data Protection Commissioner [2015] Case C-362/14, 6 October 2015; EU-U.S. Privacy Shield, Department of Commerce, 2 February 2016, www.commerce.gov/news/fact-sheets/2016/02/eu-us-privacy-shield.

5 Commission Decision on standard contractual clauses for the transfer of personal data to processors established in third countries, under Directive 95/46/EC (notified under document number C(2001) 4540), 27 December 2001, http://eur-lex.europa.eu/legal-content/en/ALL/?uri=CELEX:32002D0016.

6 Commission Decision on standard contractual clauses for the transfer of personal data to processors established in third countries under Directive 95/46/EC of the European Parliament and of the Council (notified under document C(2010) 593), 5 February 2010, http://eur-lex.europa.eu/legal-content/EN/TXT/?uri=celex%3A32010D0087.

About the Contributors

Executive Editor

Eduardo Ustaran, CIPP/E
Partner, Hogan Lovells
Eduardo Ustaran is an internationally recognised expert in privacy and data protection law and a partner in the global privacy and cybersecurity practice of Hogan Lovells. He is a dually qualified English solicitor and Spanish abogado based in London.

Ustaran is also the author of *The Future of Privacy* (DataGuidance, 2013), a ground-breaking book in which he anticipates the key elements that organisations and privacy professionals will need to tackle in order to comply with the regulatory framework of the future.

Ustaran advises some of the world's leading companies on the adoption of global privacy strategies and is closely involved in the development of the new EU data protection framework. He has been named by *Revolution* magazine as one of the 40 most influential people in the growth of the digital sector in the UK and is ranked as a leading privacy and Internet lawyer by prestigious international directories.

Ustaran is co-founder and editor of *Data Protection Leader*, a member of the panel of experts of DataGuidance and a former member of the Board of Directors of the International Association of Privacy Professionals. Ustaran is executive editor of *European Data Protection: Law and Practice* (IAPP, 2018) and co-author of *Beyond Data Protection* (Springer, 2013), *E-Privacy and Online Data Protection* (Tottel Publishing, 2007) and *The Law Society's Data Protection Handbook* (2004). He has lectured at the University of Cambridge on data protection as part of its masters of bioscience enterprise and regularly speaks at international conferences.

Contributors

Ruth Boardman
Co-Head, International Data Protection Practice, Bird & Bird
Ruth Boardman jointly heads Bird & Bird's International Privacy and Data Protection Group based in London. Boardman's extensive experience includes advising a broad range of public- and private-sector organisations on information law matters, including representing them in their dealings with data protection authorities.

Boardman has particular expertise helping organisations in the life sciences, ad-tech and online and financial services sectors and has also worked with a number of professional and sporting bodies on data protection requirements. Boardman has run a large number of international compliance programmes.

Boardman co-wrote *Data Protection Strategy* (Sweet & Maxwell, 2012), has edited the *Encyclopaedia of Data Protection* (Sweet & Maxwell, 2012), is on the editorial board of the journal *Data Protection Leader* and is a contributor to leading online data compliance tool DataGuidance. She has also served on boards of the International Association of Privacy Professionals.

Boardman assists the Global Alliance on Responsible Genome and Clinical Data Sharing, where she is a member of the Security Expert Working Group.

Mariel Filippidis, CIPP/E, CIPM, FIP
Global Privacy Director, adidas Group
Mariel Filippidis is the global privacy director of the adidas Group on consumer data. She is a Spanish-qualified attorney with LLM at McGill University, currently based in Amsterdam. Filippidis assists on the development of the global privacy strategy, privacy compliance program and the data governance structure of the group. She leads a team of privacy experts, performs privacy assessments and provides legal advice on global projects in relation to products and services of the different brands of the adidas Group. Previously, she lived in several countries while collaborating as attorney in a leading law firm and several multinationals, acquiring extensive international experience and deep knowledge on privacy and data protections laws and matters. Filippidis holds certifications in CIPP/E, CIPM and FIP from the International Association of Privacy Professionals.

Victoria Hordern, CIPP/E, CIPT
Counsel, Hogan Lovells

Victoria Hordern is a counsel in the global privacy and cybersecurity practice at Hogan Lovells, based in London, and advises on data protection, privacy and information law. She studied at Oxford University and subsequently trained and qualified as a solicitor at London-based law firm Field Fisher Waterhouse. Hordern regularly assists organisations with multi-jurisdictional data protection compliance projects, as well as advising on all matters connected with data protection and privacy, including the General Data Protection Regulation, international data transfers, whistle-blowing, outsourcing, cookie compliance, data security and monitoring. She was part of the team that advised the Government of Bermuda on the development of their Personal Information Protection Act 2016 and contributed to the management of the public consultation process for the new law. Hordern wrote the chapters on employment relationships and legitimate processing criteria in the International Association of Privacy Professionals' *European Privacy: Law and Practice for Data Protection Professionals* (2012).

Hannah Jackson, CIPP/E
Senior Associate, Hogan Lovells

Hannah Jackson has experience advising clients on all aspects of data protection law and has assisted organisations in both the public and private sectors on matters that range from international data transfer projects (including the adoption of Binding Corporate Rules for controllers and processors) to data-sharing arrangements, data protection compliance audits, and the adoption of employee monitoring and whistle-blowing schemes.

Jackson has worked with clients in all stages of development, from helping start-up ventures to understand their obligations under data protection law to advising established organisations and sophisticated in-house teams on strategies for better compliance. Jackson was a contributor to *European Privacy: Law and Practice for Data Protection Professionals* (IAPP, 2012) and holds a CIPP/E certification.

Mac Macmillan
Counsel

Mac Macmillan worked as a software developer before becoming a solicitor. She now concentrates on all aspects of IT law with a particular focus on data protection and the provision of IT-related services. In addition to UK-focused data protection advice on day-to-day compliance issues, such as customer-facing privacy policies, managing data breaches and cross-border data transfers, she has extensive experience managing multi-jurisdictional compliance projects and negotiating large services contracts.

Katie McMullan
Senior Associate, Hogan Lovells
Katie McMullan focuses her practice at Hogan Lovells on data privacy issues. She has extensive experience in advising top technology businesses on strategies for dealing with ePrivacy matters, including digital marketing, data analytics and cross-device tracking.

McMullan regularly advises on global compliance programmes, cloud-based services, outsourcing arrangements and data transfer solutions (including Binding Corporate Rules and Binding Corporate Rules for processors). She is also involved in public policy matters, advising EU-based and international businesses on the implications of the forthcoming EU data protection legislative reform.

Prior to returning to private practice in 2011, McMullan worked in-house as a data protection and freedom of information specialist for the BBC and regularly undertakes client secondments. As a result, she understands business, as well as law, and uses this first-hand, practical experience to provide real-world, commercial advice to clients.

Mary Pothos
Head of Privacy (EMEA), Marsh & McLennan Companies (MMC)
Mary Pothos is responsible for leading and coordinating MMC's efforts in the EMEA regions, establishing a shared vision and approach to compliance with regulatory and other legal and contractual requirements, with the aim of protecting the personal data entrusted to MMC and its operating companies by clients and colleagues. She is currently leading on the work to develop and implement a company-wide Binding Corporate Rules framework and is the Europe project leader for the implementation of the General Data Protection Regulation.

Prior to joining MMC, Pothos worked as senior in-house counsel for Santander UK and for Visa Europe Inc. Pothos began her career in the UK with the London law firm Freshfields Bruckhaus Deringer.

Pothos has a keen interest in the future development of privacy policy and regulation and how it will evolve to operate and respond more effectively in a fast-moving, technology-dependent world, where the use and exploitation of data, generated at an ever-increasing rate, brings about new challenges on how to compete and, at the same time, remain compliant.

Pothos is a dual-qualified lawyer in Australia and England/Wales and holds two degrees: a bachelor of laws (LLB) and a bachelor of arts (BA) from the University of Adelaide.

Stewart Room, CIPP/E
Partner, PwC LLP

Stewart Room is a partner at PwC LLP. He is the global leader of the cybersecurity and data protection legal services practice, the joint global leader of the multidisciplinary data protection practice and the UK data protection practice leader. He has more than 25 years of experience as a barrister and solicitor, focusing for the majority of this time on data, technology and communications.

Room specialises in the field of data protection, information management and cybersecurity, including programme design and delivery, the commercial exploitation of data, the security of data, regulatory investigations and litigation arising from the misuse of data. He is rated as a leading individual in data protection by legal directory Chambers UK, who says he 'is the kind of lawyer who inspires confidence' and 'he is an excellent, first-rate, tactical lawyer'.

He is one of the founding directors of Cyber Security Challenge UK (which forms part of the UK National Strategy for Cyber Security), the president of the National Association of Data Protection Officers and the editor of the *Cyber Security Practitioner* journal. Room has written a number of textbooks on information law and is regularly quoted in the press. He is a past winner of the *Financial Times* 'Innovative Lawyer of the Year' award.

Sian Rudgard, CIPP/E
Counsel, Hogan Lovells

Sian Rudgard advises on all aspects of data protection law and spent several years working as a solicitor for the information commissioner before returning to private practice. Rudgard has extensive experience in managing international data transfer projects and, specifically, has an unrivalled level of knowledge of BCRs and BCR for processors as a means of legitimising international data transfers.

Dr. Jyn Schultze-Melling
Associate Partner, EY Law

Jyn Schultze-Melling is an internationally recognised privacy expert. He joined EY Law in Berlin as an associated partner to return to his advisory roots, counselling his clients as a DPO coach and GDPR implementation strategy consultant. Until recently, he was Facebook's director for privacy policy for Europe and worked at the social network's headquarters office in Dublin, steering the company's policy efforts in data protection and privacy all over Europe. Before Facebook, he served as the chief privacy officer (CPO) of the Allianz group, the German multinational financial services company headquartered in Munich, Germany, and, before that, as head of the employee privacy division of Deutsche Bahn AG, a major multinational transportation and logistics group with nearly 300,000 employees worldwide. He studied law and earned his PhD at the University of Freiburg and completed an additional master's degree in IT and telecommunications law at the Strathclyde University of Glasgow, UK

Over the course of his career as a technology attorney and privacy professional, Schultze-Melling gained considerable knowledge and experience in all fields of IT compliance, including information governance, data protection, privacy and information security. Having studied and worked internationally—amongst others, as a visiting attorney at Morrison Foerster's New York office—he is proud to be part of the small group of internationally recognised experts in privacy, privacy compliance and information governance issues.

Amongst other engagements, Schultze-Melling is a university lecturer on privacy law; an active participant to the global community of privacy professionals; a regular speaker, writer and editor of books and articles on the subject; a member of the scientific advisory board of the ZD, the leading German professional journal on data protection law; and a member of the European advisory board of the International Association of Privacy Professionals.

Wouter Seinen, CIPP/E
Partner, Baker & McKenzie
Wouter Seinen is partner of the IP/IT and commercial practice of Baker & McKenzie in Amsterdam. Seinen's practice focuses on data protection law and associated compliance matters, such as data security and data breaches. Seinen regularly assists national and international clients on issues that relate to the protection, compliant use and exploitation of data and digital assets. Internet-related businesses, such as social media operators, regularly seek his advice on compliance aspects of new services or business models before their commercial launch in the Netherlands.

Seinen has worked for IT, data-driven and Internet companies for the past 18 years. He has a thorough knowledge of data protection law and is often involved in research that touches on both the compliance side of the law and the fundamental rights that are the foundation of data protection laws and play a fundamental role in online legal issues, including right to be forgotten, intermediary liability and IP infringement in online settings.

Aside from advising clients, Seinen also teaches specialisation courses at private institutions and has contributed to tech law programmes of various universities. Moreover, Seinen works regularly on pro bono projects and projects for the legal community. Examples include the Citizen Lab study on reverse engineering and data protection advice for several med-tech start-up companies. Seinen is also one of the founders and editors in chief of the leading tech law blog ITenRecht.nl and the chairperson of the VIRA, the Dutch Computer Law Association.

Robert Streeter, CIPP/E, CIPP/US
Data Protection and Privacy Officer, News UK

Robert Streeter is a data protection practitioner experienced in operationalising data protection within an organisation. He joined News UK in 2013 after previous data protection roles at Betfair, British Gas, Sky and Cancer Research UK.

Streeter entered the field in 2009, having previously worked with technology and information security companies—mainly venture-capital-backed start-ups from the U.S.—moving through technical, marketing, sales, business development and general management roles. This broad background allows him to more readily align and integrate privacy and information governance goals with those of the organisation.

His current areas of focus include contentious and noncontentious data protection and privacy advice, compliance management, privacy risk assessment, policy development, information governance and breach management.

Streeter graduated from Imperial College of Science and Technology, London, with a BSc in physics, and from Royal Holloway, University of London with an MSc in information security.

Lilly Taranto, CIPP/E
Senior Associate, Hogan Lovells

As a senior associate in the global privacy and information management practice of Hogan Lovells, Lilly Taranto has in-depth knowledge in advising major international and domestic companies on cross-border data transfers, including Binding Corporate Rules, employee monitoring, e-marketing, data security breaches, online privacy and general data protection compliance issues. Taranto focuses on running large, multi-jurisdictional data privacy projects, involving more than 80 countries, in the sectors of travel, entertainment, technology, telecom, pharmaceutical, finance and retail.

As a member of the International Association of Privacy Professionals with CIPP/E status, Taranto has written many articles and is also one of the authors of the IAPP's *European Privacy: Law and Practice for Data Protection Professionals.*

Taranto is bilingual (English and Italian), and Italian is her mother language.

Nick Westbrook
Associate, Hogan Lovells
As an associate in the global privacy and cybersecurity practice at Hogan Lovells, Nick Westbrook advises on all aspects of data protection and cybersecurity law. He has worked on a wide range of matters, including General Data Protection compliance projects, contract negotiations, Binding Corporate Rules applications, strategic advice relating to the draft ePrivacy Regulation and cybersecurity governance programs. Westbrook has particular experience advising clients in the online behavioural advertising and automotive sectors.

Index

Biometric data, 282, 286, 290–291
Boardman, Ruth, 85, 362
Bouchacourt v. France (2009), 38
Breaches of data security. *See* Data breaches
Breyer v. Germany, 329
Bring your own device (BYOD) strategies, 182, 278
Brussels I Regulation, 90–91
B2B v. B2C marketing, 303, 306–307
Bundesamt für Sicherheit in der Informationstechnik (BSI, German Federal Office for Information Security), 207
Bundesdatenschutzgesetz (BDSG, German data protection law), 353–355
BYOD (bring your own device) strategies, 182, 278

C

Cavoukian, Ann, 202
CBEST framework, 183
CCTV (closed-circuit television)
  information collected by, 154
  surveillance by, 282, 286–290
Certification
  in cloud computing service contracts, 323
  as data protection adequacy mechanism, 225, 235–236, 242
Charter of Fundamental Rights of the European Union of 2000, 14–15, 20, 26, 269, 283
Children
  minimum age of consent and, 117–118
  personal data of, 103
  social networking services information on, 335
Chip-card generated data, 291
Citizens' Rights Directive, 313–314
Civil Society Organisations (CSOs), 237
Closed-circuit television (CCTV)
  information collected by, 154
  surveillance by, 282, 286–290
Cloud computing
  as controller or processor, 319–320

international data transfers by, 322–323
law applicable to, 318–319
overview, 317–318
personal data security issues in, 182
service contracts for, 320–322
Cloud Security Alliance, 183
Codes of conduct
  in cloud computing service contracts, 323
  as data protection adequacy mechanism, 225, 235–236, 242
Collection limitation principle, of OECD guidelines, 8
Collective bargaining agreements, 269–270
Commission Nationale de l'Informatique et des Libertés (CNIL, French data protection authority), 196, 240
Commission v. Germany, 241
Communications, 284–285. *See also* Internet technology and communications
Confidentiality, 109, 175
Consent
  for automated calling systems, 301–302
  for cookies and similar technologies, 148–149, 326–328
  of data subject for processing personal data, 114–118
  data subject incapable of giving, 126
  for electronic mail marketing, 305
  in employment relationships, 262–263
  for fax marketing, 306–307
  for international data transfer, 227–228
  as legal grounds for data processing, 100
  for location-based marketing, 308–309
Consistency mechanism, 248–249
Contract performance
  in cloud computing, 320–322
  in employment relationships, 263
  for international data transfers, 224–225, 228, 243, 356–357
  as legal grounds for data processing, 100
  personal data processed to meet, 118
Controllers
  accountability of, 196–201, 234–235

accuracy principles and, 107-108
acting alone or jointly with others, 76–77
cloud computing as, 319–320
concept of, 74–75
consent documentation requirements of, 114
data minimisation and, 106
data subject rights to regulate, 237–238
definition of, 75
to determine the purposes and means of
  processing personal data, 77
General Data Protection Regulation
  (GDPR) impact on, 85–89
Internet of Things and, 339
of mobile apps, 336
as 'natural person, legal person or any other
  body', 75
opting out rights and, 298–299
in outsourcing situations, 346–350
personal data of legitimate interest to,
  120–121
processor role *v.*, 81–82
processors' relationship with, 175–176
purpose limitation in data processing and,
  104–105
regulating competence of, 245–246
search engines as, 330–331
social networking services as, 333
source of control as, 77–78
storage limitation and, 108–109
transparency principle and, 142
verifying data subject identities, 159
Controls and processes for data security,
  185–188
Convention 108 (Convention for the Protection
  of Individuals with regard to Automatic
  Processing of Personal Data)
  in data protection law evolution, 20
  highlights of, 41–42
  OECD guidelines similar to, 7–8
  overview, 10–13
Cookies and similar technologies
  consent and, 56–59, 148–149, 326–328
  law applicable to, 326

for online behavioural advertising (OBA),
  300, 312–313
overview, 323–324
personal data and, 324–326
search engines to process, 330
Copland v. United Kingdom (2007), 38, 189
Corporate Telephone Preference Service (UK),
  303
Council Framework Decision 2008/977/JHA of
  27 November 2008, 21
Council of Europe
  Convention for Protection of Individuals
    with regard to Automatic Processing of
    Personal Data, 7–8, 10, 20
  European Convention on Human Rights
    (ECHR) of 1950, 5–6
  Recommendation 509 on human rights
    and modern scientific and technological
    developments of 1968, 7
Court of Justice of the European Union (CJEU)
  on Charter of Fundamental Rights, 269
  data protection role of, 14, 35–36
  establishment concept in case law of, 86–87
  on EU-U.S. Privacy Shield Framework,
    222–223
  practice of, 35
  private and family life interpretation by, 69
  rationale and functions, 34
  on Safe Harbor Framework, 220–221
  on surveillance regulation, 284
  VKI v. Amazon.pdf, 89
Criminal conviction data, processing criteria
  for, 131
Cross-border processing, 246. *See also*
  International data transfers
CSOs (Civil Society Organisations), 237
Culture, organizational, personal data security
  and, 184–185
Customers, as controllers in outsourcing,
  346–351
Cybercrime Directive, 182
Cybersecurity. *See* Personal data, security of

D

Dashboards, fair processing notices linked to, 154

Data Act of 1973 (Sweden), 19

Data breaches
notification of, 176–180
reporting requirements for, 200
self-regulatory role in notification of, 234–235

Data controllers. *See* Controllers

Data loss prevention (DLP), 266

Data minimisation
as data processing principle, 106–107, 269–270
mobile app requirements for, 338

Data mining, 282

Data processing principles, 99–112. *See also* Controllers; International data transfers; Processors
accuracy, 107–108
data minimisation, 106–107, 269–270
fairness, 101–102
in General Data Protection Regulation (GDPR), 99
integrity and confidentiality as, 109
international scale of, 3
lawfulness, 100–101
purpose limitation, 104–105
by search engines, 332
storage limitation, 108–109
transparency, 102–103

Data protection, 67–84
controller
'alone or jointly with others', 76–77
concept of, 74–75
definition of, 75
'determines the purposes and means of processing personal data', 77
as 'natural person, legal person or any other body', 75
processor role *v.*, 81–82
source of, 77–78
data subject, 82–83

by design and default, 202–204, 340
direct marketing and, 295–300
introduction to, 67
in outsourcing, 350–353
personal data, 67–72
processing, 82
processor
concept of, 79
controller role *v.*, 81–82
definition of, 79–81
determining purposes and means of, 78–79
sensitive personal data, 73

Data Protection Authorities (DPAs)
on Binding Corporation Rules, 226
data controller in enforcement actions of, 74
Data Protection Directive mandate for, 46
notification of breaches to, 176
overview, 14
privacy by design principles advocated by, 202
on Safe Harbor Framework, 219–220
tasks of, 241–243

Data Protection Directive (Directive 95/46/EC). *See also* Data processing principles
background on, 43–44
consent documentation requirements of, 114
content of, 44–45
European Commission suits against member states in relation to, 61–62
in evolution of data protection law, 20
key principles of, 45–46
overview, 14
in reform of EU data protection framework, 46–48
transparency principle in, 135

Data protection impact assessments (DPIAs)
complying with, 208–209
controllers to perform, 235
Data Protection Authorities and, 242
in enforcement, 267–268
Internet of Things and, 340
for location information collection, 292

Security (Bundesamt für Sicherheit in der
Informationstechnik, BSI), 207
German Works Council Act, 274
Global positioning system (GPS), 282
Google, Inc., 225, 292
Google Spain v. AEPD, 36, 87, 330–332

H

Halford v. United Kingdom, 189
Haralambie v. Romania (2009), 38
Healthcare, sensitive data on, 128–129
Hordern, Victoria, 113, 261, 363
Household exemptions, 92–93, 333
Human rights law, 4–6

I

IaaS (infrastructure as a service), 317
ICC (International Chamber of Commerce), 224
Implicit location information, 292
In-app messaging, 295
Incident response, 178, 190–194
Individual participation principle, of OECD
guidelines, 9
Information and Privacy Commission, Ontario,
Canada, 202
Information Commissioner's Office (ICO, UK)
on cookies, 325, 328
on DPIA as best practice tool, 207
enforcement powers of, 240
on information given to data subjects,
139–140
on privacy by design, 202
on record keeping of correcting errors, 108
Information provision obligations, 135–158
in ePrivacy Directive, 148–149
exemptions to, 144–148
fair processing notices
effective, 151–155
practical considerations for, 149–151
transparency principle
areas for further information provision
requirements, 144

information not obtained from data
subjects, 140
information obtained from data subjects,
137–139
method of providing information to data
subjects, 143–144
overview, 135–136
requirements for additional information,
140–142
timing of providing information to data
subjects, 142–143
Information Security Forum, 183
Informed consent, 114, 116
Infrastructure as a service (IaaS), 317
Integrity, as data processing principle, 109
International Chamber of Commerce (ICC), 224
International data transfers, 215–231
'adequate level of protection' in, 217–218
adequate safeguards for, 223–224
by cloud computing, 322–323
contractual route for, 224–225
derogations for, 227–229
designating countries with 'adequate level of
protection', 218–219
futures of restrictions on, 229–230
limitations on, 215–216
in multinational corporate groups, 225–227
outsourcing, 355–358
scope of, 216–217
transparency in, 141–142
to United States, 219–223
Internet of Things (IoT), 282, 338–340
Internet technology and communications,
317–343
cloud computing
as controller or processor, 319–320
international data transfers by, 322–323
law applicable to, 318–319
overview, 317–318
service contracts for, 320–322
cookies and similar technologies, 323–328
Internet of Things (IoT), 338–340
IP addresses, 328–329

M.M. v. United Kingdom (2012), 38

Mobile devices, 282, 335–338

Multinational corporate groups, international data transfers in, 225–227

N

NAI (Network Advertising Initiative) Code of Conduct, 236

National Cyber Security Centre (UK), 182

Near-field communication (NFC), 291

Necessity
  as data minimisation factor, 106
  personal data processed to meet requirements of, 118
  in workplace monitoring, 267–268

Network Advertising Initiative (NAI) Code of Conduct, 236

NFC (near-field communication), 291

NIST framework (US), 183

Non-digital marketing, 296–297

Non-EU 'established' organisations, 89–91

Non-identifiable data, processing criteria for, 131–132

Not-for-profit bodies, sensitive data processed by, 126–127

O

OBA (online behavioural advertising). *See* Online behavioural advertising (OBA)

Offences, processing criteria for, 131

Offshoring, 355–358

Online behavioural advertising (OBA)
  cookies for, 300
  ePrivacy Directive on, 297, 312–313
  operation of, 309–310
  regulation of, 310–312
  technology for, 282

Opt-in consent requirements, for digital marketing, 55

Opting out, right of, 298, 305–306, 309

Organizational culture of personal data security, 184–185

Organisation for Economic Co-operation and Development (OECD)
  accountability requirements of, 195
  data protection guidelines of, 7–10, 20

Outsourcing, 345–359
  controllers and processors in
    chains of processors and sub-processors, 349–350
    customers as controllers, 346–349
    overview, 346
    role differences, 81–82
    suppliers as controllers, 349
    suppliers as processors, 346–349
  data protection obligations in, 350–353
  German data protection law on, 353–355
  offshoring and international data transfers, 355–358
  overview, 345–346

P

PaaS (platform as a service), 317

Patrick Breyer v. Bundesrepublik Deutschland, 71

Payment Card Industry Data Security Standard, 183

Payment cards, 282

Payment Services Directive No. 2, 182

Personal data
  automated storage of, 3
  consent given by data subject to process, 114–118
  content of, 69
  contract performance requirements and, 118
  cookies and similar technologies and, 324–326
  data subject rights on collection and processing of, 161
  format of, 69
  as identifiable information, 70–72
  IP addresses and, 328–329
  in legal obligation compliance, 118–119
  legal obligations, 121–122

Processors
  Binding Corporate Rules (BCRs) for, 358
  cloud computing as, 319–320
  concept of, 79
  controller role v., 81–82
  controllers' relationship with, 175–176
  definition of, 79–81
  determining purposes and means of, 78–79
  General Data Protection Regulation
    (GDPR) impact on, 85–89
  Internet of Things and, 339
  of mobile apps, 336
  in outsourcing situations, 346–350
  regulating competence of, 245–246
Proportionality
  as data minimisation factor, 106–107
  in workplace monitoring, 269–270
Protection of Individuals with regard to
  Automatic Processing of Personal Data,
  Convention for (Convention 108, Council of
  Europe)
    in data protection law evolution, 20
    highlights of, 41–42
    OECD guidelines similarity to, 7–8
    overview, 10–13
Protection of Privacy and Transborder Flows of
  Personal Data, Guidelines on (OECD, 1980),
  7–8, 195
Pseudonymisation, 72
Public health, sensitive data for, 129–130
Public interest
  as grounds for data processing, 100
  for international data transfers, 228
  personal data and, 119, 121–122
  sensitive data of substantial, 127–128
Public international law, 92
Purpose limitation, as data processing principle,
  104–105
Purpose specification principle, of OECD
  guidelines, 9
Push messaging, 295

R

Radio-frequency identification (RFID)
  applications, 207, 291
Recommendation 509 on human rights
  and modern scientific and technological
  developments of 1968 (Council of Europe), 7
Recruitment, in employment, 183–184
Rectification, right of, 162
Reding, Viviane, 220
Regulation (EU) 2016/679 of the European
  Parliament and of the Council of 27 April
  2016 on personal data processing and free
  movement of that data, 22
Regulation on Privacy and Electronic
  Communications (in review), 18
Regulators, accountability to, 204–207
Research, sensitive data processed for, 130–131
Resolutions 73/22 and 74/29 to protect
  personal data in automated databanks, 7, 19
Right to be forgotten (RTBF), 162–164
Risk management
  assessment in, 181–182
  compliance with enforcement requirements
    through, 234–235
  for personal data security, 183–184
  as personal data security approach, 172–176
  for processors, suppliers, and vendors,
    189–190
'Robinson List' (opt-out register), 299
Room, Stewart, 169, 233, 365
RTBF (right to be forgotten), 162–164
Rudgard, Sian, 3, 365

S

SaaS (software as a service), 317
Safe Harbor Framework, 169–170, 219–221,
  240
Sarbanes-Oxley Act of 2002 (US), 275
Satellite imaging, 282
Schrems, Maximillian, 220, 222, 240
Schrems case (2015) on international data
  transfers, 36